Biology Foundations
Reading and Study Guide Workbook

Miller & Levine
Biology

Savvas Learning Company LLC, 15 East Midland Avenue, Paramus, NJ 07652

Photo Credits: Front cover: ftotti1984/Fotolia   Back cover, Spine: Daniel Prudek/Shutterstock

Savvas™ and **Savvas Learning Company™** are the exclusive trademarks of Savvas Learning Company LLC in the U.S. and other countries.

Savvas Learning Company publishes through its famous imprints **Prentice Hall®** and **Scott Foresman®** which are exclusive registered trademarks owned by Savvas Learning Company LLC in the U.S. and/or other countries.

Savvas Realize™ is the exclusive trademark of Savvas Learning Company LLC in the U.S. and/or other countries.

Unless otherwise indicated herein, any third party trademarks that may appear in this work are the property of their respective owners, and any references to third party trademarks, logos, or other trade dress are for demonstrative or descriptive purposes only. Such references are not intended to imply any sponsorship, endorsement, authorization, or promotion of Savvas Learning Company products by the owners of such marks, or any relationship between the owner and Savvas Learning Company LLC or its authors, licensees, or distributors.

ISBN-13: 9780328936557
ISBN-10:   0328936553

10 20

Contents

iii

READING TOOL **Sequence of Events** List in order the parts of a typical experiment that uses scientific methodology. Use the headings in your text as a guide. Give a brief explanation or example of each. The first one is filled in for you.

	Scientific Methodology	Explanation or Example
1	observing and asking questions	Scientists observe and ask questions.
2	_____	_____
3	_____	_____
4	_____	_____
5	_____	_____

Lesson Summary

What Science Is and Is Not

⚲ **KEY QUESTION** *What are the goals of science?*

Biologists try to understand life and nature. Scientific knowledge is always changing, so scientists have to constantly test, debate, and revise explanations of the natural world.

The Nature of Science Science is a process of explaining natural events. Scientists observe and ask questions about the natural world, then use their observations to make explanations that can be tested in experiments. Scientists gather and analyze data to support or reject their explanations.

The word *science* also refers to the accumulated knowledge about the natural world. Scientific explanations are based on evidence and understanding, not just beliefs, therefore, they are not concerned with supernatural explanations or events.

⚲ As you read, circle the answers to each Key Question. Underline any words you do not understand.

The Goals of Science A goal of science is to provide natural and testable explanations for natural events. Science also uses explanations that are supported by data to understand patterns in nature. Scientific explanations can be used to make useful predictions about natural events.

Science, Change, and Uncertainty Scientists have learned many things about the natural world. However, there is much about the natural world that is not yet understood. New scientific discoveries often lead to surprises and new questions. Changes in scientific knowledge are not a failure of science, but show that science continues to move forward. Studying science also means understanding what is not known. Uncertainty is part of science. Understanding science is also about learning how scientists work and think and where scientific ideas come from.

Scientific Methodology

🔍 **KEY QUESTION** *What procedures are at the core of scientific methodology?*

People other than scientists use scientific methods to solve everyday problems. There is not just one scientific method, but there is a common style of investigation. Scientific methodology involves observing and asking questions, forming hypotheses, conducting controlled experiments, collecting and analyzing data, and drawing conclusions.

Observing and Asking Questions Scientific investigations begin with observation. Observation is the act of noticing and describing events and processes. Observation leads to the asking of new questions that have not been answered.

Inferring and Forming a Hypothesis After asking questions, scientists use further observation to make inferences. An inference is a logical interpretation of an event. Inference and imagination can lead to a hypothesis. A hypothesis is a possible scientific explanation that can be tested by further observation or by experimentation. Testing gathers data that can support or reject the hypothesis.

Designing Controlled Experiments Testing a hypothesis involves designing experiments to measure changes in factors. Factors that can change are called variables. An experiment ideally changes only one variable. This is called a controlled experiment.

Controlling Variables Variables must be controlled because if several variables are changed, scientists will not know which variable causes an effect. The variable that is deliberately changed in an experiment is called the independent variable. The variable that is observed and changes in response to the independent variable is called the dependent variable.

Control and Experimental Groups Experiments are ideally divided into control and experimental groups. In the experimental group, the independent variable is changed. In the **control group**, the independent variable is not changed.

Collecting and Analyzing Data Scientists collect two main types of information, or **data**, from observations and experiments. *Quantitative data* are numbers obtained from counting or measuring. *Qualitative data* are descriptions of events that cannot be measured.

Selecting Equipment and Technology Scientists collect data using simple tools such as a measuring stick, or complex tools such as instruments that measure the chemical composition of a substance. Data is collected and analyzed on computers. Statistics are used to determine if a significant difference exists between an experimental group and a control group.

Sources of Error Scientists must avoid errors in data. Tools for measurement have limits to their accuracy. Data analysis must take into account the sample size. Larger sample sizes allow scientists to more confidently identify differences between experimental groups and control groups.

Interpreting Data and Drawing Conclusions Analyzing data may lead to conclusions that support or reject the hypothesis that is being tested by the experiment. Data may show that a hypothesis is partly correct but must be adjusted. Data can sometimes lead to new questions and hypotheses.

When Experiments Aren't Possible Not all hypotheses can be tested in experiments. Some hypotheses about animals must be tested by observation of natural behavior. Scientists cannot carry out experiments that they know will harm humans.

Scientific Theories

⚲ **KEY QUESTION** *What is a scientific theory?*

In science, a **theory** is a scientific explanation of events in the natural world that has been tested and is reliable. A scientific theory comes from many repeated observations and includes several well-supported hypotheses. Scientific theories can be used to make accurate predictions. In everyday language, *theory* is sometimes used to mean a guess. In science, *hypothesis* is used to mean a guess. Charles Darwin developed his theory of evolution from many hypotheses. Today, evolutionary theory is one of the central organizing principles of biology. Theories can be revised or replaced by better theories if they are supported by new data.

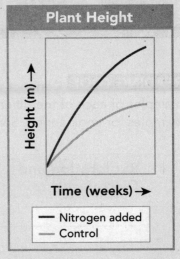

Visual Reading Tool: Analyzing Data

Plant Height

— Nitrogen added
— Control

1. Identify the independent variable.

_____

2. Identify the dependent variable.

_____

3. Which plants grew taller: those in the experimental group or those in the control group?

_____

4. Describe why this is a controlled experiment.

_____
_____
_____
_____
_____
_____

LESSON 2 Science in Context

Connect to Visuals Before you read, study Figure 1-4. As you read, list examples of each of the different aspects of science in the table below. Then use Figure 1-9 to add examples for engineering. Some answers may be the same for both science and engineering.

	Exploration and Discovery	Community Analysis and Feedback	Benefits and Outcomes
SCIENCE	_____ _____ _____ _____ _____ _____	_____ _____ _____ _____ _____ _____	_____ _____ _____ _____ _____ _____
ENGINEERING	_____ _____ _____ _____ _____ _____	_____ _____ _____ _____ _____ _____	_____ _____ _____ _____ _____ _____

Lesson Summary

The process of science includes exploration and discovery, community analysis and feedback, and benefits and outcomes.

Exploration and Discovery

🔍 As you read, circle the answers to each Key Question. Underline any words you do not understand.

🔍 **KEY QUESTION** *What attitudes and experiences generate new ideas?*

Scientific Attitudes Scientific attitudes like curiosity, skepticism, open-mindedness, and creativity help scientists and engineers ask new questions and define new problems.

Curiosity A scientist will make an observation and then ask questions about it. An engineer will see a problem and ask how to solve it.

Skepticism Scientists and engineers should be skeptical, question hypotheses, and demand evidence before accepting explanations.

Open-Mindedness Scientists and engineers should be willing to accept data that disagree with their hypotheses, or to consider hypotheses that disagree with their own.

Creativity Scientists and engineers must be creative and apply critical thinking when asking questions, proposing hypotheses, and designing experiments.

Practical Problems Many scientific investigations come from attempts to solve problems involving humans, health, or environmental issues.

New Technology New technology provides scientists and engineers with new and better ways to make observations and collect data.

Community Analysis and Feedback

🔍 **KEY QUESTION** *Why is peer review important?*

Scientists usually work in groups and collaborate and communicate with other groups. Research must be shared with the scientific community in order to be accepted. Scientists also communicate with the general public.

Peer Review Scientists share their research and ideas with other scientists by publishing their hypotheses, experimental methods, results, data analysis, and conclusions. Scientific papers are reviewed by other scientists before publication. Reviewers look for mistakes and fraud in methods and analysis. This process allows other scientists to evaluate and test the data and analysis. Peer review does not guarantee that research is correct, but that it meets certain standards.

Sharing Knowledge and New Ideas After research is published, scientists who read it will come up with new questions. New questions lead to new hypotheses that must be supported or rejected by experiments.

READING TOOL

Connecting to Visuals

View Figure 1-4 in your textbook. It outlines the three different processes that define science.

☑ **Is this process a rigid order of events, or is it a flexible process?**

READING TOOL

Academic Words

Peer Someone who belongs to the same group in society and is equal in rank or level. Scientists have their research reviewed by their peers, who are other scientists. As a student, you have your work reviewed by your teachers and parents, but they are not your peers. ☑ **Who are your peers?**

Benefits and Outcomes

KEY QUESTION *What is the relationship between science and society?*

Science interacts with society, laws, and moral principles. Science also has a big impact on health, medical issues, and environmental issues such as energy and waste disposal.

Science, Ethics, and Morality Science and engineering usually only tell us what is possible or what we *could* do. They do not tell us what we *should* or *should not* do. Applying scientific information involves understanding the role of science in society and its limitations. Science by itself does not include ethical or moral viewpoints.

Avoiding Bias Scientists should be objective, but like everyone else, they have likes, dislikes, and biases. A **bias** is a personal, rather than scientific, view for or against something. Scientists with different personal biases may interpret data in different ways. Bias affects what actions scientists recommend.

Science and Engineering Practices

KEY QUESTION *What practices are shared by science and engineering?*

Although some of the specifics vary, the steps in scientific inquiry and engineering design are basically the same.

Developing and Using Models Scientists and engineers both use models. Models include diagrams and three-dimensional models, but also include mathematical models and computer simulations. Models help people to visualize and summarize ideas.

Using Mathematics and Computational Thinking Mathematics is important to science and engineering. Ratios, rates, percentages, and unit conversions are some basic ways to analyze data. A mathematical representation can model data and support explanations.

Constructing Explanations and Designing Solutions Scientists attempt to answer questions about the natural world. Scientists then construct explanations that are supported by evidence. Engineers design solutions to problems.

Engaging in Argument From Evidence In science, an argument is a set of reasons that explain why an idea is right or wrong. Scientists must respond thoughtfully to criticisms. Engineers must argue that their design solutions will work and compare them to competing design solutions.

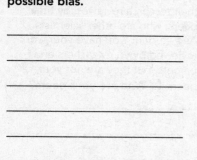

BUILD Vocabulary

bias a particular preference or point of view that is personal, rather than scientific

Word Origins *Bias* comes from the French word *biais*, meaning "slant" or "slope." Therefore, when someone has a bias, his or her point of view is "slanted" in one direction.

☑ **A scientist who works for a company that makes products from plants publishes a paper on energy efficiency. They claim that converting corn to ethanol is more efficient than solar power. Describe their possible bias.**

_____

_____

_____

_____

_____

_____

LESSON 3 Patterns of Life

READING TOOL **Main Idea and Details** Complete the chart. Write the main ideas in the left column and the details or examples that explain the main idea in the right column. Part of the table is filled out for you.

Characteristics of Living Things	
Main Idea	Details
Made up of cells	Cells are the smallest units of living things.

Lesson Summary

Characteristics of Living Things

🔑 **KEY QUESTION** *What characteristics do all living things share?*

Biology is the science of living things. Living things are made up of basic units called cells, reproduce, are based on a universal genetic code, grow and develop, obtain and use materials and energy, respond to their environment, maintain a stable internal environment, and change over time.

🔑 As you read, circle the answers to each Key Question. Underline any words you do not understand.

Made Up of Cells All living things, or organisms, are made up of cells. Cells are the smallest living units of an organism.

Reproduction All organisms produce new organisms through a process called reproduction. There are two basic kinds of reproduction: sexual and asexual. In **sexual reproduction**, cells from two different parents come together to produce the first cell of the new organism. In **asexual reproduction**, the new organism has a single parent.

Based on a Universal Genetic Code New organisms usually resemble their parents because of inherited characteristics called traits. Traits are passed from parents to offspring by a molecule called **DNA**. DNA contains information in a genetic code. The genetic code, with a few small variations, is the same for every organism on Earth.

Growth and Development All organisms grow during part of their lives. Single-celled organisms simply increase in size. Multicellular organisms begin as a single cell. During a process called development, the single cell divides repeatedly. As the cells divide, they change in order to perform different functions. This process is called differentiation.

Need for Materials and Energy Organisms need energy and a constant supply of materials to grow, develop, reproduce, and to stay alive. The combination of chemical reactions a cell carries out is called **metabolism**.

Response to the Environment Organisms detect and respond to stimuli. A **stimulus** is a signal that leads to a response. External stimuli come from the environment outside an organism. Internal stimuli come from within the organism.

Maintaining Internal Balance Environmental conditions may vary widely, but most organisms must keep their internal conditions, such as temperature and water content, fairly constant. The process of maintaining internal conditions is called **homeostasis**. Internal stimuli, such as thirst, are important in maintaining homeostasis.

Evolution The traits an organism inherits from its parent usually do not change during its life. As a group, however, organisms **evolve**, or change over time. The ability of groups of organisms to change gradually is necessary for survival in a changing world.

What About Viruses? Viruses exist at the border between living and nonliving things. Viruses are parasites that cannot carry out the functions of life on their own. Viruses can only reproduce after infecting living organisms.

BUILD Vocabulary

biology scientific study of life

sexual reproduction type of reproduction in which cells from two parents unite to form the first cell of a new organism

asexual reproduction process of reproduction involving a single parent that results in offspring that are genetically identical to the parent

DNA deoxyribonucleic acid; genetic material that organisms inherit from their parents

metabolism the combination of chemical reactions through which an organism builds up or breaks down materials

stimulus signal to which an organism responds

homeostasis relatively constant internal, physical, and chemical conditions that organisms maintain

evolve change over time

Word Origins *Homeostasis* comes from the Greek words *homio-*, meaning "like" or "similar to," and *stasis*, meaning "standing still." ☑ **Diseases can alter an organism's homeostasis. When you get sick and have a fever, what internal condition has changed?**

Crosscutting Concepts in Biology

🔑 KEY QUESTION *What are the crosscutting concepts of biology?*

All of the biological sciences are linked together by shared themes and methods of study. The study of biology revolves around several crosscutting concepts: cause and effect; systems and system models; stability and change; patterns; <u>scale</u>, <u>proportion</u>, and quantity; energy and matter; and structure and function.

Cause and Effect: Mechanism and Explanation

Science uses observations, questions, and experiments to explain the world in terms of natural forces and events, or cause and effect. Science reveals rules and patterns that can explain and predict events in nature.

Systems and System Models
All living things on Earth form a system called the biosphere. The parts of this system interact and work together. Within an organism, different systems interact to maintain the organism.

Stability and Change
Organisms must maintain a stable internal environment, a process called homeostasis.

Patterns
Similar patterns occur throughout nature. Patterns can be linear, such as the increasing complexity of similar organs from fish to mammals. Patterns can also be cyclical, or repeating, such as seasonal changes in the behavior of living things.

Scale, Proportion, and Quantity
Organisms can be described and studied at different scales. Studies at a very small, or molecular, scale might examine the proteins in an organism. Studies at a very large, or global, scale might examine the effects of humans on the atmosphere.

Energy and Matter: Flows, Cycles, and Conservation
Organisms require material as nutrients to build body structures and provide energy. The need for matter and energy link all organisms on Earth in a web of interdependent relationships.

Structure and Function
Each major group of organisms has evolved a particular collection of body parts, or structures, for carrying out particular functions. These structures have evolved as organisms have adapted to life in different environments.

READING TOOLS

Academic Words

scale the size of something, especially in comparison to something else

proportion the relation of the size of a part to the size of the whole

☑ Place the following biological processes in order from smaller to larger according to the scale at which they would be studied.

1. A cell reproduces by dividing.

2. A multicellular animal obtains nutrients.

3. The genetic code of a piece of DNA.

4. The effects on the atmosphere of burning fossil fuels.

5. The response of all the plants in a region to a change in climate.

_____

Fields of Biology

⚲ KEY QUESTION *How do fields of biology differ in their approaches?*

Biology includes many overlapping fields that use different tools to study life from the molecular level to the planetary level.

Global Ecology Life is shaped by weather and processes in the atmosphere. The activities of organisms, including humans, can affect the atmosphere and climate. Humans move more matter and use more energy than any other species on Earth. Global ecological studies help us to learn about human impacts on life on Earth.

Biotechnology Biotechnology is based on the ability to change genetic information to make changes in the living world. Scientists are working to change genes to cure diseases and to clean up the environment. Biotechnology involves ethical, legal and social issues because of the ability to change the genetic information that makes us human.

Building the Tree of Life Biologists have discovered about 1.8 million different organisms. However, there are still many organisms that have not yet been identified. Biologists wish to identify and catalogue all forms of life. Biologists also want to use genetic information to organize all organisms into a single "Tree of All Life."

Ecology and Evolution of Infectious Diseases New disease-causing organisms often appear. The relationships between organisms and pathogens that cause disease constantly change. Pathogens evolve in response to new medicines and changes in how humans interact with the environment. Understanding interactions between humans and pathogens is important to our health.

Genomics and Molecular Biology These fields focus on DNA and other molecules inside the cell. The entire DNA content of organisms can now be studied. This information is helping scientists to understand growth, development, aging, disease, cancer, and the history of life.

Performing Biological Investigations

KEY QUESTION *How is the metric system important to science?*

Biologists, like all scientists, rely on a common system of measurement and safety practices while carrying out research. You will learn about scientific measurement and safety as you begin to carry out experiments.

Scientific Measurement Scientists use a common system of measurement to understand and replicate each other's experiments. Scientists use the metric system when collecting data and performing experiments. The metric system is a decimal system, meaning that the units are scaled on multiples of 10. The basic units of length (meter), volume (liter), and mass (gram) can be multiplied or divided by multiples of 10 to measure amounts much larger or smaller than the basic unit.

Safety Laboratory work may involve flames, heat, electricity, chemicals, sharp instruments, or things that can break. Therefore, it is important to follow safe practices and to protect yourself with glasses and gloves. You must also wash your hands after every laboratory activity. The most important safety rule is to follow your teacher's instructions and the directions in the textbook. If you do not understand something, ask your teacher for an explanation. You are responsible for your own safety and the safety of your classmates and teacher. If you are using live animals, you are also responsible for their safety.

Visual Reading Tool: The Metric System

1. Using the ruler above, draw a centipede that is 6 centimeters long.

2. The centipede is about _____ millimeters long.

3. The bottle holds 1 _____ of water, which weighs 1 kilogram.

4. Samir drinks half of the bottle of water. It now has _____ milliliters of water, which weighs about 500 _____.

Review Vocabulary

Choose the letter of the best answer.

1. A possible explanation for a set of observations that must be tested is called a
   - A. theory.
   - B. law.
   - C. fact.
   - D. hypothesis.

2. A well-tested explanation for a broad range of natural events is called a
   - A. theory.
   - B. law.
   - C. fact.
   - D. hypothesis.

Match the vocabulary term to its definition.

3. _____ In an experiment, its variables are changed.

   a. bias

4. _____ All of the chemical reactions that an organism carries out to stay alive.

   b. control group

5. _____ A personal preference that is not scientific.

   c. metabolism

Review Key Questions

Provide evidence and details to support your answers.

6. A scientist grows tomatoes in greenhouses that differ only in the amount of carbon dioxide in the air. He determines the weight of tomatoes produced by plants in each greenhouse, and compares them to each other and to tomatoes grown in air with a natural, unaltered amount of carbon dioxide. Is this a controlled experiment? Why or why not?

   _____

   _____

7. A group of scientists decide to post their research results on the Internet instead of publishing in a scientific journal. What part of the scientific process have they skipped and why does it matter?

   _____

   _____

8. Why is a virus not considered a living organism?

   _____

   _____

READING TOOL **Use Structure** As you read your textbook, outline the headings and sub-headings throughout this lesson. Fill in the table below with the key points from each section. One has been filled in for you.

Heading	Sub-Heading	Key Points
Atoms	Protons and Neutrons	
	Electrons	Electrons are negatively charged and surround the nucleus.
Elements and Isotopes	Isotopes	
	Radioactive Isotopes	
Chemical Compounds		
Chemical Bonds	Ionic Bonds	
	Covalent Bonds	
	Weak Interactions	

2.1 The Nature of Matter **13**

Lesson Summary

Atoms

⚲ As you read, circle the answers to each Key Question. Underline any words you do not understand.

⚲ **KEY QUESTION** *What three subatomic particles make up atoms?*

All living things are made from chemical compounds. Chemical compounds are made up of the basic unit of matter, the **atom**. The particles that make up atoms are protons, neutrons, and electrons.

Protons and Neutrons Protons and neutrons are particles that are bound together by strong atomic forces. They form the center of the atom, called the **nucleus**. Protons have a positive charge, and neutrons carry no charge at all. Protons and neutrons have about the same mass.

Electrons The **electron** is the negatively charged particle in an atom. It is only 1/1840 of the mass of a proton. Electrons are in constant motion around the nucleus of the atom. They are arranged in a series of orbits called shells, that can only hold a certain number of electrons. The first shell can hold two, and the second can hold up to eight. Atoms have an equal number of protons and electrons. All atoms are electrically neutral because the positive charge of the protons and the negative charge of the electrons cancel out.

BUILD Vocabulary

atom the basic unit of matter

nucleus the center of an atom, which contains the protons and neutrons

electron negatively charged particle; constantly moving around the nucleus

element pure substance that consists entirely of one type of atom

isotope one of several forms of a single element, which contains the same number of protons but different numbers of neutrons

compound substance formed by the chemical combination of two or more elements in definite proportions

Word Origins The word *compound* is from the Latin word *componere* which means "to put together." ☑ **In a chemical compound, what things are being put together?**

_____

_____

Elements and Isotopes

⚲ **KEY QUESTION** *How are all of the isotopes of an element similar?*

A chemical **element** is a pure substance made up entirely of one type of atom. Elements are represented by one- or two-letter symbols and organized by atomic number, which is how many protons they have. About 99 percent of the mass of living things is made up of six elements. They are calcium (Ca), carbon (C), hydrogen (H), oxygen (O), nitrogen (N), and phosphorous (P).

When two atoms interact, their electron shells overlap. The number of electrons in the outer electron shell determines some of the properties of an element. The electron shell affects how an atom may participate in chemical reactions.

Isotopes Atoms of the same element that contain different numbers of neutrons are called **isotopes**. The total number of protons and neutrons in the nucleus of an atom is called its mass number. Since isotopes have a different number of neutrons, their masses differ and they are identified by their mass numbers. Isotopes have different masses, but their chemical properties are the same.

Radioactive Isotopes Some isotopes have nuclei that are unstable and break down at a constant rate over time. These are radioactive isotopes. The radiation can be dangerous, but there are important uses for radioactive isotopes. They can be used to date rocks and fossils. They can be used to treat cancer and to kill bacteria. They can be used as "tracers" to follow the movements of substances within organisms.

Chemical Compounds

🔍 **KEY QUESTION** *In what ways does a compound differ from its component elements?*

A chemical **compound** is formed by the chemical combination of two or more elements in definite proportions. The composition of a compound is written in a chemical formula. Water is a compound with two atoms of hydrogen (H) for each element of oxygen (O). The formula for water is H_2O.

The physical and chemical properties of a compound are usually very different from those of the elements from which it is formed. Water is a liquid formed from two gases, hydrogen and oxygen. The element chlorine is a poisonous gas. However chlorine is part of the compound sodium chloride, or table salt. Sodium chloride is essential for living things.

READING TOOL

Make Connections
As you read, think about how each of vocabulary terms are related to each other.

☑ **Order the following components of matter from smallest to largest:** *compounds, electrons, elements, protons, and neutrons.*

_____

_____

_____

Visual Reading Tool: Isotopes

1. How many electrons does an atom of Carbon have? _____

2. Draw in the electrons that circle around Carbon's Nucleus on the images of Carbon-12 and Carbon-14 below.

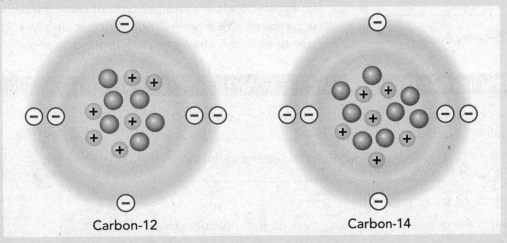

Carbon-12   Carbon-14

3. Complete the Carbon Isotope chart below based upon what you know about the number of protons, neutrons, and electrons in an isotope.

Isotopes of Carbon			
Isotopes	**Number of Protons**	**Number of Electrons**	**Number of Neutrons**
Carbon-12 (nonradioactive)		6	6
Carbon-14 (radioactive)	6		

Chemical Bonds

The atoms in compounds are held together by chemical bonds. Bonds are formed by the electrons in the outer shell, which are called valence electrons. The main types of chemical bonds are ionic bonds and covalent bonds.

Ionic Bonds Ionic bonds are formed when one or more electrons are transferred from one atom to another. This transfer causes the atom losing the electrons to become positively charged. The atom gaining the electrons becomes negatively charged. The positively and negatively charged atoms become ions. The oppositely charged ions are attracted to each other and form an ionic bond.

Covalent Bonds Sometimes atoms share electrons rather than transferring them. These shared electrons move around the nuclei of both atoms. The bond formed by sharing electrons is called a covalent bond. Atoms can share between two and six electrons. The structure that results is known as a molecule. A molecule is the smallest unit of most compounds.

Weak Interactions The strongest chemical bonds are ionic or covalent. Weak interactions between atoms are also important. Within living organisms, many molecules interact only briefly. Van der Waals forces are one type of weak interaction between molecules. They occur when molecules are very close together.

Hydrogen bonds are another type of weak interaction. They occur between a hydrogen atom of one molecule and an oxygen or nitrogen atom of a neighboring molecule.

BUILD Vocabulary

ionic bond chemical bond formed when one or more electrons are transferred from one atom to another

ion atom that has a positive or negative charge

covalent bond type of bond between atoms in which the electrons are shared

molecule smallest unit of most compounds that displays all the properties of that compound

van der Waals forces weak attraction that develops between oppositely charged regions of nearby molecules

Prefixes The prefixes *com-* and *co-* mean "together." A compound is made up of elements joined together, and a covalent bond contains atoms that share electrons together. ☑ **How are covalent bonds different from ionic bonds?**

_____

_____

_____

_____

_____

Visual Reading Tool: Chemical Bonds

1. What kind of chemical bond holds the water molecule together? _____

2. What particles are shared between the atoms in the molecule? _____

3. What is the other main type of chemical bond? _____

4. What is the difference between covalent and ionic bonds?

_____

_____

_____

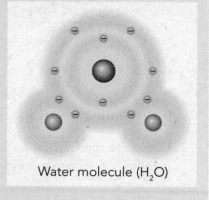

Water molecule (H_2O)

LESSON 2

Properties of Water

READING TOOL **Cause and Effect** As you read the part of the lesson under "The Water Molecule," use the table below to list the causes and effects of the properties of water. Many of the causes may be the same, but each characteristic will have a different effect. Part of the table is completed for you.

Characteristic of Water	Cause	Effect
Hydrogen Bonding		The slightly negative end of a water molecule is attracted to the slightly positive end of another water molecule.
Expands Upon Freezing		
Dissolves Many Substances	Water forms hydrogen bonds.	
Cohesion		
Adhesion		
Heat Capacity		

Lesson Summary

The Water Molecule

🔍 As you read, circle the answers to each Key Question. Underline any words you do not understand.

🔍 **KEY QUESTION** *How does the structure of water contribute to its unique properties?*

Water covers nearly three-fourths of Earth's surface. Water is one of the few compounds found in a liquid state on Earth.

Polarity Water is made up of one oxygen atom and two hydrogen atoms. The oxygen atom has eight protons that pull the shared electrons slightly towards it, because it is stronger than the two protons that the hydrogens have. This causes a slight positive charge on the hydrogen end of the molecule and a slight negative charge on the oxygen end. Overall the charge remains neutral. A molecule in which the charge is unevenly distributed is said to be polar, because the molecule is like a magnet with two poles. Because of this polarity, water molecules are attracted to each other. The attraction between a hydrogen atom with a partial positive charge and an atom with a partial negative charge in another molecule creates a **hydrogen bond**.

Special Properties of Water Hydrogen bonds are not as strong as covalent or ionic bonds, but hydrogen bonds give water many of its unique characteristics. Because water is a polar molecule, it is able to form multiple hydrogen bonds that account for many of water's special properties. One of these properties is that water expands upon freezing, making ice less dense than water. Water can also dissolve many substances, which is why it is the basis for many living things. All of the properties of water listed below are caused by hydrogen bonds.

Cohesion The attraction of molecules of the same substance is called **cohesion**. This is why drops of water form beads on surfaces. Cohesion also causes surface tension, which explains why some bugs can walk on water.

Adhesion The attraction between molecules of different substances is called **adhesion**. The adhesion of water to the sides of a cylinder causes it to dip slightly in the center. Capillary action describes how water moves up a narrow tube. This phenomena is caused by both adhesion and cohesion.

Heat Capacity The amount of energy needed to raise the temperature of a substance is its heat capacity. Water has a high heat capacity, which means that bodies of water can absorb a lot of heat from sunlight with only a small change in temperature.

BUILD Vocabulary

hydrogen bond weak attraction between a slightly positive hydrogen atom and another atom that is slightly negative

cohesion attraction between molecules of the same substance

adhesion force of attraction between different kinds of molecules

Prefixes *Cohesion* and *adhesion* share a root based on the Latin word *haerēre*, meaning "to cling." The prefix *co-* means "together," and the prefix *ad-* means "toward."

☑ **Some bugs can walk on the surface of water because the attraction between water molecules is strong enough to hold up the bug. What do we call this attraction?** adhesion/cohesion.

Water in Living Things Living things are mostly water. Water is 60 percent of the mass of the human body. Many chemical reactions in living things take place in water, which is why all living things need water.

Solutions and Suspensions

🔍 KEY QUESTION *How does water's polarity influence its properties as a solvent?*

Water is often part of a mixture. A **mixture** is two or more elements or compounds physically mixed together, but not chemically combined. There are two types of mixtures with water: solutions and suspensions.

Solutions A **solution** is a mixture with the components evenly distributed throughout the solution. In a solution of saltwater, table salt is the substance dissolved, called the **solute**, and water is the **solvent**, the substance in which the solute is dissolved. Water's polarity gives it the ability to dissolve both ionic compounds and other polar molecules. When a given amount of water has dissolved all of the solute that it can, the solution is said to be saturated.

Suspensions Some materials do not dissolve when placed in water. They separate into pieces so small that they are suspended in the water. Mixtures of water and nondissolved material are called **suspensions**.

Acids, Bases, and pH

🔍 KEY QUESTION *Why is it important for cells to buffer solutions against rapid changes in pH?*

A small number of water molecules will split apart to form ions. One water molecule can split apart to form one positive hydrogen ion, H^+, and one negative hydroxide ion, OH^-.

The pH Scale The **pH scale** indicates the concentration of H^+ ions in solution. The scale ranges from 0 to 14. Solutions below seven are considered acidic, and have more H^+ ions than OH^- ions. Solutions above seven are considered basic, and have more OH^- ions than H^+ ions. Pure water has a pH of 7, and the concentration of H^+ and OH^- ions is equal. Each step of the pH scale is a ten-fold difference in H^+ ion concentration. A liter of a solution with a pH of 4 has 10 times as many H^+ ions as a liter of solution with a pH of 5.

BUILD Vocabulary

mixture material composed of two or more elements or compounds that are physically mixed together but not chemically combined

solution type of mixture in which all the components are evenly distributed

solute substance that is dissolved in a solution

solvent dissolving substance in a solution

suspension mixture of water and nondissolved material

pH scale scale with values from 0 to 14, used to measure the concentration of H^+ ions in a solution

Multiple Meanings A solution can be a mixture within a solvent where the solute is evenly dissolved, or a solution can mean an answer to a problem. ☑ **What type of molecules will create a solution when mixed with water?**

_____

_____

Acids An **acid** is any compound that releases H⁺ ions when in a solution. Acidic solutions have higher concentrations of H⁺ ions than pure water and have pH values below 7. Strong acids generally have pH values ranging from 1.5 to 3.0.

Bases A **base** is any compound that releases OH⁻ ions when in a solution. Basic, or alkaline, solutions have lower concentrations of H⁺ ions than pure water and have pH values above 7. Strong bases generally have pH values ranging from 11 to 14.

Buffers The internal pH of most cells in the human body must generally be kept between 6.5 and 7.5. If the pH is lower or higher, it will affect the chemical reactions that take place within the cells. Thus, controlling pH is important for maintaining homeostasis. One of the ways that organisms control pH is through dissolved compounds called **buffers**. Buffers are weak acids or bases that can react with strong acids or bases to prevent sharp, sudden changes in pH. Blood, for example, has a normal pH of 7.4. Sudden changes in blood pH are usually prevented by a number of chemical buffers, such as bicarbonate and phosphate ions. Buffers in living things play an important role in maintaining homeostasis.

Visual Reading Tool: Buffers

The figure below shows what happens to the pH of two solutions when an acid is added. Use the key above the image to answer the questions about the image.

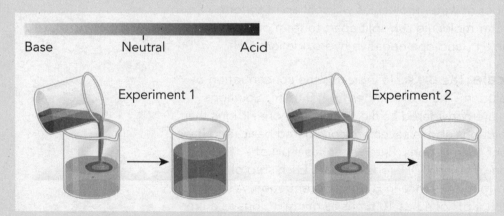

1. In Experiment 1, does adding an acid to a basic solution result in an acid or a base? _____

2. In Experiment 2, does adding an acid to a basic solution result in an acid or a base? _____

3. In which experiment is the acid added to a buffered base? How can you tell?

_____

_____

LESSON 3 Carbon Compounds

READING TOOL **Compare and Contrast** As you read, identify the similarities and differences between the different groups of macromolecules. Take notes in the table below. Circle elements that all of the compounds have in common. Some boxes have been filled in for you.

	Macromolecules			
	Carbohydrates	Lipids	Nucleic Acids	Proteins
Examples	glucose fructose galactose			
Single Units		fatty acids glycerol		
Elements			carbon hydrogen oxygen nitrogen phosphorus	
Functions				structure control reactions regulation fight disease receptors

Lesson Summary

The Chemistry of Carbon

KEY QUESTION *What elements does carbon bond with to make up life's molecules?*

Carbon is essential to life as we know it. Organic chemistry is the branch of chemistry that studies compounds that contain carbon. Carbon atoms have four valence electrons, allowing them to form covalent bonds with many elements such as hydrogen, oxygen, phosphorus, sulfur, and nitrogen. These carbon compounds have many different chemical properties that living things depend on. Carbon atoms can also bond to one another. This makes it possible for carbon to form long chains, or even rings. No other element can build molecules as large as carbon can build, which makes it the building block for life on our planet.

As you read, circle the answers to each Key Question. Underline any words you do not understand.

Macromolecules

BUILD Vocabulary

monomer small chemical unit that makes up a polymer

polymer molecules composed of many monomers; makes up macromolecules

carbohydrate compound made up of carbon, hydrogen, and oxygen atoms; type of nutrient that is the major source of energy for the body

Prefixes *Mono-* means "one." *Poly-* means "many." Macromolecules built through polymerization use single units (monomers) to form a larger compound of many units (polymers). ☑ **What are three examples of carbohydrate polymers?**

KEY QUESTION *What are the functions of each of the four groups of macromolecules?*

Macromolecules are "giant molecules" because they are very large. Most macromolecules form through polymerization, a process in which larger and larger compounds are built by joining smaller compounds together. The smaller compounds are called **monomers**. They join together to form **polymers**. The monomers in a polymer can be identical. The monomers can also differ. The four major groups of macromolecules found in living things are carbohydrates, lipids, nucleic acids, and proteins.

Carbohydrates Sugar, starch, and cellulose are different types of carbohydrates. **Carbohydrates** have carbon, hydrogen, and oxygen atoms, usually in a 1:2:1 ratio—that is, one carbon to two hydrogen and one oxygen atom. Organisms use carbohydrates to store and release energy as well as for structural support and protection. The breakdown of sugars such as glucose supplies energy to cells. Extra sugar is stored in complex carbohydrates.

Simple Sugars Single sugar molecules called monosaccharides (mahn oh SAK uh rydz) include glucose, galactose, and fructose. Galactose is found in milk; fructose is found in fruits.

Complex Carbohydrates Complex carbohydrates are polysaccharides formed by joining together many monosaccharides. Many animals store excess sugar as a polysaccharide called glycogen. Glycogen is broken down into glucose when glucose levels are low or when needed for muscle contraction.

Starches and Cellulose Plants store excess sugar in a polysaccharide called starch. They also make another polysaccharide called cellulose. Cellulose gives plants rigidity. Wood is mostly cellulose.

Lipids Lipids are macromolecules that are usually not soluble in water. Lipids are mostly carbon and hydrogen. Lipids include the compounds called fats, oils, and waxes. Lipids can be used to store energy, and they form important parts of biological membranes and waterproof coverings. Many lipids are formed by combining a glycerol molecule with fatty acids. If the carbon atoms in a fatty acid are all joined by single bonds, the fatty acid is said to be saturated. If there is at least one carbon-carbon double bond, the fatty acid is unsaturated. Lipids with fatty acids containing more than one double bond are polyunsaturated. The terms *saturated*, *unsaturated*, and *polyunsaturated*, appear on food labels.

Nucleic Acids Nucleotides are monomers that consist of three components: a 5-carbon sugar, a phosphate group, and a nitrogenous base. Nucleic acids are polymers made from nucleotide monomers. Nucleotides such as ATP are important for capturing and transferring energy. Two types of nucleic acids are ribonucleic acid, or RNA, and deoxyribonucleic acid, or DNA. Nucleic acids function to store and transmit heredity, or genetic information.

Proteins Proteins are macromolecules that have nitrogen, carbon, hydrogen, and oxygen atoms. Proteins are polymers of molecules known as amino acids. Amino acids are compounds with an amino group ($-NH_2$) and a carboxyl group (-COOH). In addition to forming proteins, amino acids have other functions.

Peptide Bonding Amino acids are linked by covalent peptide bonds to form polypeptides or proteins. The peptide bond is formed between the amino group of one amino acid and the carboxyl group of another amino acid.

Function Some proteins function to control the rate of reactions and regulate cell processes. Others form important cellular structures, while still others transport substances into or out of cells or help to fight disease.

Structure There are more than 20 different amino acids found in nature. All amino acids have the amino and carboxyl groups needed to join them together by covalent peptide bonds.

Amino acids differ from each other because they have different side chains called the R-group. These R-groups have different chemical properties.

BUILD Vocabulary

lipid macromolecule made mostly from carbon and hydrogen atoms; includes fats, oils, and waxes

nucleotide subunit of which nucleic acids are composed; made up of a 5-carbon sugar, a phosphate group, and a nitrogenous base

nucleic acid macromolecules containing hydrogen, oxygen, nitrogen, carbon, and phosphorus

protein macromolecule that contains carbon, hydrogen, oxygen, and nitrogen; needed by the body for growth and repair

amino acid compound with an amino group on one end and a carboxyl group on the other end

Related Words A polypeptide is a chain of amino acids joined by peptide bonds. A protein is made up of one or more polypeptides. Not all polypeptides are proteins.
☑ **How many levels of structure are there in a protein with only one polypeptide chain?**

Levels of Organization Amino acids form polypeptide chains. They form them according to the instructions in the DNA. Polypeptides are not straight chains. They bend and twist to form three-dimensional shapes.

Scientists describe four levels of structure in proteins:

➤ Primary structure: the sequence of the amino acids

➤ Secondary structure: folding or coiling of the polypeptide chain

➤ Tertiary structure: the complete three-dimensional arrangement of the polypeptide chain

➤ Fourth level structure: If the protein has more than one polypeptide chain, the fourth level is the way the polypeptides are arranged in relation to each other.

Proteins retain their shape because of forces that include ionic and covalent bonds, van der Waals forces, and hydrogen bonds.

Visual Reading Tool: Macromolecules

The four major groups of macromolecules are carbohydrates, lipids, nucleic acids, and proteins. Identify each type of macromolecule from its monomer.

1.

Glucose

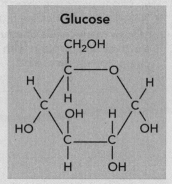

_____

2.

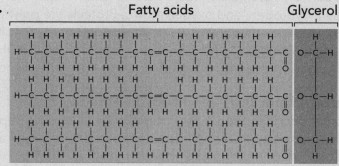

Fatty acids   Glycerol

_____

3. Nitrogenous base

Phosphate group

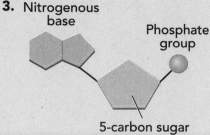

5-carbon sugar

_____

4.

```
   H      H      O
    \     |     ⫽
     N ─ C ─ C
    /     |     \
   H      R      OH
```

Amino group   Carboxyl group

_____

Chemical Reactions and Enzymes

READING TOOL **Make Connections** The concept map below shows the relationship between vocabulary terms in this lesson. As you read the lesson, complete the concept map below. Each word will only be used once and some words have already been entered for you.

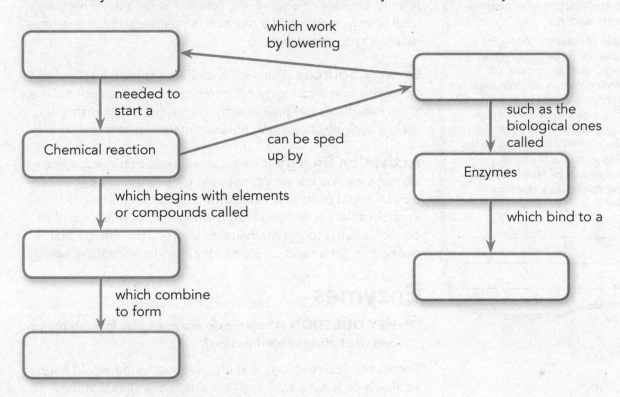

Lesson Summary

Chemical Reactions

🔑 **KEY QUESTION** *What happens to chemical bonds during chemical reactions?*

A **chemical reaction** is a process that changes, or transforms, one set of compounds into another. An important scientific principle is that mass and energy are conserved during chemical transformations. This is also true for chemical reactions that occur in living organisms. Some chemical reactions occur slowly, such as the combination of iron and oxygen to form an iron oxide called rust. Other reactions occur quickly. The elements or compounds that engage in a chemical reaction are known as **reactants**. The elements or compounds produced by a chemical reaction are known as **products**. Chemical reactions involve changes in the chemical bonds that join atoms in compounds.

🔑 As you read, circle the answers to each Key Question. Underline any words you do not understand.

BUILD Vocabulary

chemical reaction process that changes, or transforms, one set of chemicals into another set of chemicals

reactant elements or compounds that enter into a chemical reaction

product elements or compounds produced by a chemical reaction

Energy in Reactions

🔑 KEY QUESTION *How do energy changes affect whether a chemical reaction will occur?*

Whenever chemical bonds are formed or broken, energy is released or absorbed. Chemical reactions that release energy often occur on their own, or spontaneously. Chemical reactions that absorb energy require a source of energy. In the first case, the energy is released as heat, light or sound. When reactions require a source of energy, the reaction is unlikely to happen until energy is added. If a reaction releases energy, the reverse reaction requires energy.

Energy Sources Every form of life must have a source of energy so that it can carry out chemical reactions. Without this, it will die. Plants get their energy from sunlight. Animals get their energy by consuming other animals or plants.

Activation Energy Chemical reactions that release energy do not always occur spontaneously. Otherwise, the pages of a book might burst into flames without warning. The cellulose in paper burns only if you light it with a flame, which supplies enough energy to get the reaction started. The energy that is needed to get a reaction started is called its **activation energy**.

Enzymes

🔑 KEY QUESTION *What role do enzymes play in living things, and what affects their function?*

Some chemical reactions that are essential to life would happen so slowly or require such high activation energies that they could never take place on their own. These chemical reactions are made possible by **catalysts**. A catalyst is a substance that speeds up the rate of a chemical reaction by lowering the activation energy.

Nature's Catalysts Enzymes are biological catalysts, and most enzymes are proteins. The role of enzymes is to speed up chemical reactions that take place in cells. Enzymes lower the activation energy of the reaction. Lowering the activation energy has a dramatic effect on how quickly the reaction is completed. Enzymes are very specific and usually only catalyze one kind of chemical reaction. The name of an enzyme is usually related to the reaction it catalyzes.

The Enzyme-Substrate Complex For a chemical reaction to occur, the reactants must collide with sufficient energy to break existing bonds and form new bonds. If the reactants do not have enough energy, they will be unchanged after the collison. Enzymes reduce the energy needed by providing sites where reactants can be brought together. The reactants in an enzyme-catalyzed reaction are called **substrates**. The substrates bind to a part of the enzyme called the active site. They have complementary shapes, which fit together like a lock and key. The substrates and the active site may be kept together by weak interactions such as hydrogen bonds and van der Waals forces.

Regulation of Enzyme Activity Enzymes play an <u>essential</u> role in chemical reactions. Anything that changes the structure of the protein can change the shape of the active site. High temperature and very high or low pH can change the active site and cause the enzyme to not work well. Enzymes produced by human cells generally work best at temperartures close to 37°C, the normal temperature of the human body. Enzymes activity can be changed or turned on and off by molecules that carry chemical signals.

READING TOOL

Academic Words
The word *essential* refers to something that is of the utmost importance. It is essential that enzymes are kept within a certain temperature and pH range, or else they will change shape and no longer be able to catalyze their specific chemical reaction.

☑ **What temperature do most of the enzymes in the human body function at?**

_____

Visual Reading Tool: Effect of Enzymes

Use the chart to answer the following questions about the effect of enzymes on a chemical reaction.

1. Which curve shows the reaction pathway with the enzyme? _____

2. Which reaction has the higher activation energy? _____

3. Which arrow shows the activation energy with the enzyme? A or B? _____

4. Does this reaction absorb or release energy? How do you know?

_____

_____

_____

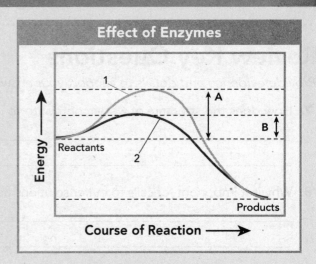

Effect of Enzymes

Energy (vertical axis), *Course of Reaction* (horizontal axis), Reactants, Products, 1, 2, A, B

Review Vocabulary

Choose the letter of the best answer.

1. Which is NOT one of the three subatomic particles that make up atoms?

   A. electron

   B. neutron

   C. boson

   D. proton

2. Which is a weak interaction between molecules?

   A. van der Waals

   B. bionic

   C. covalent

   D. ionic

Match each vocabulary word with its meaning.

3. _____ Element with 4 valence electrons that can covalently bond to many other elements.

   a. cohesion

4. _____ Attraction between molecules of the same substance.

   b. nucleic acid

5. _____ A macromolecule that contains phosphorus.

   c. catalyst

6. _____ Increases speed of chemical reactions without itself changing.

   d. carbon

Review Key Questions

Provide evidence and details to support your answers.

7. How does the structure of water contribute to its unique properties?

_____

_____

8. Why is it important for cells to buffer solutions against rapid changes in pH? What does a buffer do?

_____

_____

9. How do enzymes play a role in living things, and what affects their function?

_____

_____

_____

Introduction to Global Systems

READING TOOL **Make Connections** The chart below shows key terms from the lesson with their definitions. As you read, complete the chart by writing a strategy to help you remember the meaning of each term. Two examples have been filled in for you.

Term	Definition	How I'm Going to Remember the Meaning
Biosphere	consists of all life on Earth and all parts of Earth in which life exists	
Ecology	the scientific study of the interactions between organisms and between organisms and their surroundings	
Species	group of organisms that breed and produce offspring	
Population	a group of individuals that belong to the same species and live in the same area	
Community	a group of different populations that live together in a defined area	
Ecosystem	all of the organisms that live in a place, together with their physical environment	an ecosystem includes the organisms exchanging energy in an environment
Biotic factor	any living part of the environment	
Abiotic factor	any nonliving part of the environment	the prefix a- means "without," and bio- means "life": *abiotic* = nonliving
Atmosphere	a layer of all the gases that surround Earth	
Hydrosphere	all the water of the Earth's surface as well as the water vapor and rain in the atmosphere and water underground	
Geosphere	solid earth which consists of rocks, continents, and the ocean floor	

Lesson Summary

⚲ As you read, circle the answers to each Key Question. Underline any words you do not understand.

BUILD Vocabulary

biosphere part of Earth in which life exists including land, water, and air or atmosphere

ecology scientific study of interactions among organisms and between organisms and their environment

species a group of similar organisms that can breed and produce fertile offspring

population group of individuals of the same species that live in the same area

community assemblage of different populations that live together in a defined area

ecosystem all the organisms that live in a place, together with their nonliving environment

Understand Prefixes The prefix *bio-* means "life." ☑ **Which vocabulary words in this lesson contain this prefix and what are their meanings?**

_____

_____

_____

_____

_____

_____

Ecology: Studying Our Living Planet

⚲ **KEY QUESTION** *Why is ecology important?*

The **biosphere** includes all parts of Earth in which life exists, underground, on land, and in the water and air. The biosphere therefore includes humans and all other living things.

The Science of Ecology All forms of life interact with each other and with their environments. **Ecology** is the scientific study of interactions among organisms, populations, and communities and their interactions with their environment.

Why Study Ecology? When human populations were small and scattered, humans only had local effects on the environment. As human populations have grown and the power of technology has increased, human impact on the environment has increased. Humans depend on healthy ecological systems for clean water and good soil for growing food. We need to understand ecology so that human activity does not continue to damage the environment.

Levels of Ecological Organization Ecologists study organisms and their environment at different levels. A **species** is a group of similar organisms that produce offspring together. A **population** is a group of individuals that belong to the same species and live in the same area. Different populations that live in the same area form a **community**. A community and its physical environment form an **ecosystem**. Similar ecosystems around the world form a biome. The biosphere is all living things on Earth.

Gathering Ecological Data

⚲ **KEY QUESTION** *What methods are used in ecological studies?*

Ecologists generally rely on three main approaches, all of which are part of scientific methodology: observation, experimentation, and modeling. Many studies involve all three approaches. Ecologists may use tools ranging from DNA analysis to data gathered from satellites.

Observation Observation is often the first step in asking ecological questions. Questions can lead to new scientific hypotheses that can be tested during experimentation.

Experimentation Experiments are designed to test hypotheses. Experiments gather data that support or reject hypotheses. In some experiments, ecologists may carefully alter conditions in parts of natural environments. Or ecologists may design artificial environments. In these experiments, ecologists examine how organisms react to changes in the environment.

Modeling Many ecological models consist of mathematical formulas. These formulas are based on data that have been collected through observation and experimentation. Useful models can lead to new hypotheses and new experiments to test them.

Biotic and Abiotic Factors

🔍 **KEY QUESTION** *What are biotic and abiotic factors?*

An organism's environment consists of all the conditions, or factors, around the organism that affect it in any way. These factors are divided into biotic factors and abiotic factors.

Biotic Factors Living things affect one another. A biotic factor is any other living thing with which an organism might interact. Biotic factors include animals, plants, mushrooms, and bacteria.

Abiotic Factors Physical factors also affect living organisms. An abiotic factor is any nonliving part of the environment, such as sunlight, heat, precipitation, humidity, wind or water currents, and soil type.

Biotic and Abiotic Factors Together Biotic factors can influence abiotic factors. For example, soils contain decomposing plant and animal material. Decomposing plant matter can make soil more or less acidic. Plants can affect how much sunlight reaches the ground.

Modeling Global Systems

🔍 **KEY QUESTION** *How can we model global systems?*

One way to understand global systems is to develop a model that shows those systems, the processes that operate within each system, and the ways those systems and processes interact. One model, that is shown in Figure 3-4 of your textbook, begins with the four major global systems. The biosphere includes all living organisms and the environments they live in. The atmosphere includes all the gases that surround Earth. The hydrosphere consists of all Earth's fresh and salt water, including the water vapor and rain in the atmosphere and the water underground. The geosphere includes the rocks, continents, ocean floor, and the interior of the planet.

BUILD Vocabulary

biotic factor any living part of the environment with which an organism might interact

abiotic factor physical, or nonliving, factor that shapes an ecosystem

---

READING TOOL

Connect to Visuals
Study Figure 3-3 in your textbook. Think about the biotic factors, the abiotic factors, and the factors that are both biotic and abiotic in the pond ecosystem shown. ☑ **What factors can be both abiotic and biotic? How so?**

_____

_____

_____

_____

_____

BUILD Vocabulary

atmosphere relatively thin layer of gases that form Earth's outermost layer

hydrosphere portion of Earth that consists of water in any of its forms, including oceans, glaciers, rivers, lakes, groundwater, and water vapor

geosphere the densest parts of Earth, which includes the crust, mantle, and core

Related Words Think of other words that start with *geo-*. such as *geography*. This prefix comes from the Greek word meaning "earth." ☑ **What field of science studies the rocks and solid materials that make up our planet?**

_____

Global Systems and Change Our model of Earth systems has three main parts, or rings. Each ring represents an ecological category.

The outer ring, "Causes of Global Change," represents human and non-human causes of change in global systems.

The middle ring, "How the Earth System Works," represents processes within each of the four global systems. It includes the global climate system, cycles of matter, energy flow, and interactions of organisms.

The inner ring, "Measurable Changes in the Earth System," represents changes in global systems that can scientists can measure.

Building and Using the Model You will learn about many events, processes, and interactions in this unit. Alone, these facts are like pieces in a jigsaw puzzle. The Understanding Global Change model organizes this information so that you can see how the pieces fit together. You will be able to use the model to explore connections among causes and effects in global change.

Visual Reading Tool: Modeling Global Systems

Adapted from the *Understanding Global Change Infographic*,
© University of California Museum of Paleontology, Berkeley.

1. Label Earth's four spheres on the model above and color in each with a different color. Use the same colors to highlight the definitions of these spheres on the previous page.

2. How do processes in the hydrosphere and atmosphere interact to affect climate and ecosystems? Provide at least one example.

_____

_____

_____

3. How do processes in the atmosphere affect the biosphere?

_____

_____

_____

Climate, Weather, and Life

READING TOOL **Cause and Effect** As you read your textbook, identify the cause-and-effect relationships that the text describes. Record your work in the table.

Cause →	Effect
Sunlight, carbon dioxide, water vapor, methane	
Earth's curvature and tilt	
Uneven heat distribution	
Winds, surface current	
Slow climate change	
Giant meteorite hits Earth	
Rapid climate change	

Lesson Summary

Climate and Weather

KEY QUESTION *What is the difference between weather and climate?*

Climate is defined by patterns and averages of temperature, precipitation, clouds, and wind over many years. It also includes the frequency of extreme weather events such as heat waves, droughts, and floods. **Weather** consists of short-term changes in temperature, precipitation, clouds, and wind from day to day, or minute to minute. Weather can change rapidly and can be difficult to predict. Climate is usually more predictable. Short-term changes in weather and long-term changes in climate determine whether food crops succeed or fail. Weather and climate also shape natural populations, communities, and ecosystems.

As you read, circle the answers to each Key Question. Underline any words you do not understand.

BUILD Vocabulary

climate average year-to-year conditions of temperature and precipitation in an area over a long period of time

weather day-to-day conditions of the atmosphere, including temperature, precipitation, and other factors

The Global Climate System

🔍 **KEY QUESTION** *How is Earth's climate and average temperature determined?*

The global climate system is powered and shaped by the total amount of solar energy retained in the biosphere as heat. The global climate system is also shaped by the unequal distribution of that heat between the equator and the poles.

Solar Energy and the Greenhouse Effect Some of the sunlight that strikes Earth is reflected into space, and some is converted to heat. Some of this heat is trapped in the atmosphere. Earth's average temperature is determined by the balance between the amount of heat that stays in the atmosphere and the amount of heat that is lost to space. The amount of heat trapped in the atmosphere is mostly determined by three gases in the atmosphere: carbon dioxide, methane, and water vapor. These gases are called greenhouse gases, because they act like glass in a greenhouse. The greenhouse gases allow light to enter the atmosphere but trap heat. This is called the **greenhouse effect**. Both natural and human-related processes affect the amount of greenhouse gases in the atmosphere.

Latitude and Solar Energy The curvature and the tilt of Earth on its axis affect the angle that sunlight strikes the surface. There is more solar energy and therefore more heat near the equator, where the sun is directly overhead, than at the poles. This distribution of heat creates three main climate zones: tropical, temperate, and polar. The tropical zone, near the equator, has warm or hot temperatures all year. The temperate zone, further from the equator, has hot summers and cold winters. The polar zones have very cold winters and summers that are barely warm.

Differential Heating and Global Winds The unequal distribution of heat between the equator and the poles creates winds and ocean currents. Earth has winds because warm air rises and cool air sinks. Between the places where air sinks and the places where it rises, air travels over Earth's surface, creating winds. Earth's rotation causes winds to blow from west to east over the temperate zones, and from east to west over the tropics and poles.

Ocean Currents

🔍 **KEY QUESTION** *What causes ocean currents?*

Ocean currents are driven and shaped by patterns of warming and cooling, by winds, and by the location of continents.

Winds and Surface Currents Winds blowing over the ocean create surface ocean currents. Currents flowing from the tropics to the temperate zones have a warming effect on nearby coastal areas. Currents flowing from cool regions toward the tropics have a cooling effect. These interactions between atmosphere and hydrosphere affect weather and climate in coastal areas.

Deep Ocean Currents Cold water near the poles sinks but can rise to the surface in places where winds push surface water away from a continent. One such upwelling occurs off the coast of Peru, creating the weather phenomenon called El Niño.

READING TOOL

Connect to Visuals Examine Figure 3-9, Climate Zones, in your textbook. Identify the locations of the three main climate zones on Earth. ☑ **How does the angle of sunlight affect the climate of each of the climate zones?**

_____

_____

_____

_____

Regional Climate

🔍 **KEY QUESTION** *What factors shape regional climate?*

Regional climates are shaped by latitude, the transport of heat and moisture by winds and ocean currents, and by geographic features such as mountain ranges, large bodies of water, and ocean currents. Temperature and precipitation can be very different on different sides of a mountain range.

Changes in Climate

🔍 **KEY QUESTION** *What does climate change involve?*

Earth's climate has remained relatively stable during recorded human history. But global climate has changed dramatically over the much longer history of life. Climate change involves changes in temperature, clouds, winds, patterns and amounts of precipitation, and the frequency and severity of extreme weather events.

Non-Human Causes of Climate Change Several factors cause long-term changes in global climate. These factors include changes in solar energy and variations in Earth's orbit. Sudden events such as collisions with meteorites have had major effects on climate. The positions of Earth's continents change over millions of years because of plate tectonics, affecting winds and currents. Volcanic activity can change the amount of greenhouse gases in the atmosphere.

Results of Past Changes in Global Climate Non-human causes have produced both warm and cold periods over long periods of time. The most recent cold cycle caused the last major glacial period, which ended about 10,000 years ago. Changes in global climate can occur slowly enough that life on Earth can adapt and survive. At least five times in Earth's history, climate changes happened too fast for organisms to adapt, so many died. These episodes are known as mass extinctions.

LESSON 3

Biomes and Aquatic Ecosystems

READING TOOL **Organize Information** As you read your textbook, note the similarities and differences between the different land biomes and aquatic ecosystems. There will be more than 1 biome that fits into each feature, and each biome can be used more than once. Record your work in the table.

Feature	Biome	Feature	Biome
Year-round precipitation		Warm year-round	
Seasonal precipitation		Warm summers, cool winters	
Low precipitation		Cold year-round	
Nutrient-rich soil		Nutrient-poor soil	

Lesson Summary

Life on Land: Natural Biomes

🔍 As you read, circle the answers to each Key Question. Underline any words you do not understand.

🔍 **KEY QUESTION** *What abiotic and biotic factors characterize a biome?*

Biomes are regional climate communities on land. Biomes are described in terms of abiotic factors and biotic factors. A graph called a climate diagram summarizes the seasonal pattern of temperature and precipitation in a biome. The organisms living in a biome can vary, due to differing conditions such as elevation or soil.

Ecologists classify climate communities into roughly ten different biomes.

Tropical Rain Forest Tropical rain forests have more species than all other biomes combined. Tall trees form a dense leafy covering called a **canopy** high above the forest floor. In the shade below, shorter plants form a layer called the **understory**. Organic matter on the forest floor is reused so quickly that the soil is not very rich in nutrients.

Tropical Dry Forest Tropical dry forests grow where there are long periods without rain. Plants and animals are adapted to store water or to use less water.

Tropical Grassland/Savanna/Shrubland This biome receives less rain that a tropical dry forest but more than a desert. Grass is interspersed with small groves of trees and shrubs. Organisms are adapted as in a tropical dry forest.

Desert Deserts receive very little rain and often have extreme temperature changes between day and night. Animals get water from their food and are inactive during the hot daytime.

Temperate Grassland This biome includes plains and prairies dominated by grasses, and has fertile soils. Large animals graze on the grasses and small animals depend on camouflage and burrowing for protection from predators.

Temperate Woodland and Shrubland In this biome large areas of grasses are interspersed with trees, and includes shrubland called chaparral. Woody plants resist water loss and may be fire resistant. Animals use camouflage.

Temperate Forest Temperate forests have cold winters and warm summers. The fertile soil is rich in **humus** formed from decaying leaves and other organic matter. Animals may hibernate or migrate in winter.

Northwestern Coniferous Forest This biome has mild temperatures and abundant rain. Tall conifers such as giant redwoods grow here.

Boreal Forest/Taiga Dense forests of evergreen conifers at the northern edge of the temperate zone are called boreal forests or **taiga**. Winters are very cold, but summers are mild. Animals have extra insulation or migrate in winter.

Tundra The tundra is characterized by **permafrost**, a layer of permanently frozen subsoil. Tundra plants are small because it is hard for them to take root in the permafrost. Animals are adapted to limit heat loss or to migrate to avoid winters.

Polar Regions The polar regions are not one of the biomes, but they border the tundra and are cold all year. Plants are few. Animals include insects and marine mammals that have insulation to survive in the cold waters.

BUILD Vocabulary

biome a group of ecosystems that share similar climates and typical organisms

canopy dense covering formed by the leafy tops of tall rain forest trees

understory layer in a rain forest found underneath the canopy formed by shorter trees and vines

humus material formed from decaying leaves and other organic matter

taiga biome with long cold winters and a few months of warm weather; dominated by coniferous evergreens; also called boreal forest

permafrost layer of permanently frozen subsoil found in the tundra

Root Words Break words into component parts to understand their meanings. For example, *permafrost* combines "permanent" and "frost" to indicate the word's meaning. ☑ **What effect does the permafrost have on plants in the tundra?**

_____

_____

_____

Biomes Today Biomes are useful for describing large regions with similar climate and types of organisms. However, there are not many natural communities left today. Humans have altered nearly 75 percent of all land outside the steepest mountains, the polar regions, and the deserts.

Marine Ecosystems

🔍 **KEY QUESTION** *What factors shape aquatic ecosystems?*

Aquatic ecosystems are described primarily by salinity, depth, temperature, flow rate, and concentrations of dissolved nutrients. There are three main groups of aquatic ecosystems: marine ecosystems, freshwater ecosystems, and estuaries. Ecologists divide the ocean into zones based on depth and distance from shore. Water depth influences life because sunlight doesn't penetrate the water very far. Photosynthesis can occur in the sunlit region near the surface called the **photic zone**. Below the photic zone is the dark **aphotic zone**, where photosynthesis cannot occur. Aquatic food chains are based on **plankton**, which includes floating algae, or phytoplankton, and small animals called zooplankton. Phytoplankton require sunlight and only grow in the photic zone. Zooplankton may swim in or out of the photic zone.

Intertidal Zone Organisms in the intertidal zone are submerged in seawater at high tide and exposed to air and sunlight at low tide. Organisms experience extreme changes in temperature.

Coastal Ocean The coastal ocean extends from the low-tide mark to the outer edge of the continental shelf. The continental shelf is a relatively shallow part of the ocean surrounding the continents. Water here is lit by sunlight and often fed by nutrients in freshwater runoff from land. Kelp forests and coastal reefs flourish here.

Open Ocean More than 90% of the world's ocean lies past the edge of the continental shelf. Depths range from 500 meters along the continental slopes to more than 10,000 meters in deep ocean trenches. The open ocean is divided into photic and aphotic zones.

Open Ocean Photic Zone The sunlit top 100 meters of the open ocean supports small species of phytoplankton. Most photosynthesis on Earth occurs here, not in forests.

Open Ocean Aphotic Zone The permanently dark aphotic zone includes the deepest parts of the ocean. Deep ocean organisms are exposed to high pressure, cold temperatures, and total darkness. Deep-sea vents, where hot water boils from cracks in the ocean floor, support entire ecosystems based on chemical energy.

Freshwater Ecosystems

🔍 KEY QUESTION *What are the major categories of freshwater ecosystems?*

Only three percent of Earth's surface water is fresh water, but that small percentage provides organisms with drinking water, food, and transportation. Freshwater ecosystems can be divided into three main categories: rivers and streams, lakes and ponds, and freshwater wetlands.

Rivers and Streams Rivers, streams, creeks, and brooks often originate from underground water sources. A chain of rivers and streams may flow through several biomes.

Lakes and Ponds Most life in lakes and ponds depends on plankton, algae, and plants. Water typically enters and leaves lakes and ponds through rivers and streams.

Freshwater Wetlands A wetland is an ecosystem in which water either covers the soil or is present at or near the surface for at least part of a year. Freshwater wetlands include freshwater bogs, marshes, and swamps.

Estuaries

🔍 KEY QUESTION *Why are estuaries so important?*

An estuary (ES tyoo ere e) is a wetland formed where a river meets the sea. Fresh water and salt water often mix here. Estuaries serve as spawning and nursery grounds for many ecologically and commercially important fish and shellfish. Salt marshes are temperate estuaries, and mangrove swamps are tropical estuaries.

Visual Reading Tool: Climate Diagram

Use the climate diagram to answer the questions. The bar graph data shows the amount of precipitation, and the line graph shows the average temperature.

1: Describe the pattern of precipitation in this place. Is it seasonal or year-round?

_____

_____

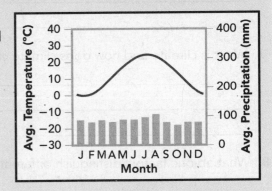

2. Describe the annual temperature pattern in this place.

_____

3. What makes this chart a climate representation, and not one that shows the weather?

_____

Review Vocabulary

Choose the letter of the best answer.

1. The gases in the atmosphere that trap heat produce
   A. radiation.
   B. solar energy.
   C. the greenhouse effect.
   D. the hydrosphere.

2. Nonliving factors of an environment are called
   A. biotic.
   B. bacteria.
   C. abiotic.
   D. plankton.

Match the vocabulary term to its definition.

3. _____ dense forests of coniferous boreal forests along the northern edge of the temperate zone   a. estuary

4. _____ a wetland formed where a river meets the sea   b. canopy

5. _____ a dense, leafy covering at the tops of tall trees in a rainforest   c. taiga

Review Key Questions

Provide evidence and details to support your answers.

6. How do models help ecologists understand global systems?

   _____

   _____

7. What is climate and how does climate change affect ecosystems?

   _____

   _____

   _____

8. What abiotic factors distinguish different biomes?

   _____

   _____

9. What factors describe aquatic ecosystems?

   _____

   _____

READING TOOL **Make Connections** The concept map below shows the relationships between different organisms in this lesson. As you read, complete the concept map using vocabulary terms and other key terms from the lesson. After you have completed the concept map, use a colored pencil to shade all the producers. Then use a different colored pencil to shade all the consumers.

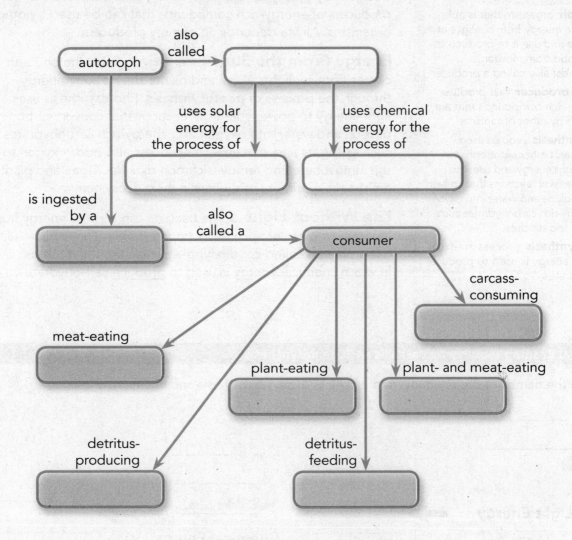

Lesson Summary

🔍 As you read, circle the answers to each Key Question. Underline any words you do not understand.

Primary Producers

🔍 **KEY QUESTION** *What are primary producers?*

All living things need energy, but no living thing can create energy. Organisms called **autotrophs** capture energy from nonliving sources. Autotrophs store this energy in forms that make it available to other organisms, which is why they are also called **primary producers**. Primary producers are the first producers of energy-rich compounds that can be used by other organisms. All life depends on primary producers.

Energy From the Sun The energy for most life on Earth comes from sunlight. Algae and plants absorb solar energy through the process of **photosynthesis**. Photosynthesis uses light energy to power chemical reactions that convert carbon dioxide and water into oxygen and energy-rich carbohydrates such as sugars and starches. This process also adds oxygen to the atmosphere and removes carbon dioxide. Algae and plants are the main primary producers in most ecosystems.

Life Without Light Some bacteria can capture energy from inorganic molecules such as hydrogen sulfide. These bacteria use a process called **chemosynthesis** (kee moh SIN thuh sis), in which chemical energy is used to <u>produce</u> carbohydrates.

BUILD Vocabulary

autotroph organism that is able to capture energy from sunlight or chemicals and use it to produce its own food from inorganic compounds; also called a producer

primary producer first producer of energy-rich compounds that are later used by other organisms

photosynthesis process used by plants and other autotrophs to capture light energy and use it to power chemical reactions that convert carbon dioxide and water into oxygen and energy-rich carbohydrates such as sugars and starches

chemosynthesis process in which chemical energy is used to produce carbohydrates

Visual Reading Tool: Photosynthesis and Chemosynthesis

Write the names of the reactants and products of photosynthesis and chemosynthesis.

_____ + _____

_____ + _____

Light Energy ➡ _____ + _____

_____ + _____ + _____

Chemical Energy ➡ _____ + _____

1. Describe how photosynthesis and chemosynthesis differ in terms of how energy is converted.

_____

_____

_____

2. What important product do both photosynthesis and chemosynthesis have in common?

_____

Chemosynthetic bacteria thrive in places of total darkness and high temperature, such as Earth's crust and volcanic vents in the ocean floor. They are also found in underground streams, caves, and the mud of tidal flats.

Consumers

🔑 **KEY QUESTION** *How do consumers obtain energy and nutrients?*

Animals, fungi, and many bacteria cannot capture energy directly from sunlight or inorganic sources. These organisms, called **heterotrophs** (HET uh roh trohfs), acquire energy from other organisms, usually by eating them. Heterotrophs are also called **consumers**. Consumers are organisms that rely on other organisms for energy and nutrients.

Types of Consumers Consumers are classified by the way they acquire energy and nutrients.
- ➤ Carnivores eat other animals.
- ➤ Herbivores eat plant leaves, roots, seeds, and fruits.
- ➤ Omnivores, such as humans, eat both plants and animals.
- ➤ Scavengers eat carcasses of dead animals.
- ➤ Decomposers "feed" by chemically breaking down organic matter. This produces **detritus**, small pieces of dead and decaying plant and animal remains.
- ➤ Detritivores (dee TRYT uh vawrz) chew or grind detritus into smaller pieces, often digesting the decomposers that live on detritus.

Beyond Consumer Categories Many organisms do not fit neatly into one category. For example, some carnivores, such as hyenas, will scavenge. Many aquatic animals eat a mixture of algae, animal carcasses, and other organic matter.

Consumers in one category may differ from one another in subtle ways. Herbivores may eat different parts of plants. Different plant parts often contain different amounts of available energy. Fruits and seeds are easy to digest and contain a lot of energy and nutrients. Leaves are plentiful but hard to digest and poor in nutrients. No multicellular organism by itself can break down the cellulose molecules found in leaves. Animals that eat leaves have cellulose-digesting microorganisms inside their guts!

Some grazing animals, such as cattle, spend a long time chewing their food into pulp. When they swallow the pulp, it goes into a part of their digestive tract that has microorganisms that can break down cellulose. Many grazers regurgitate the mixture of food and bacteria, called cud. They chew the cud and swallow it again. With all this extra work, grazers extract only a small amount of energy from the plants they eat. They must spend a lot of time eating.

BUILD Vocabulary

heterotroph organism that obtains food by consuming other living things; also called a consumer

consumer organism that relies on other organisms for its energy and food supply; also called a heterotroph

detritus small pieces of dead or decaying plant or animal remains

Word Origins The word element *-troph* comes from the Greek word *trophos*, which means "feeder." The word elements *auto-* and *hetero-* are also of Greek origin. *Autos* means "self," while *heteros* means "other."

☑ **Using the word elements, explain the difference between an autotroph and an heterotroph.**

_____

_____

_____

_____

READING TOOL

Academic Words

produce create or form something as part of a physical, chemical, or biological process

acquire to gain an object or asset for oneself

☑ **Look at the photosynthesis diagram on the prior page. If there were suddenly no sunlight reaching Earth, how would this affect the ability of plants to produce carbohydrates?**

_____

_____

_____

_____

Energy Flow in Ecosystems

READING TOOL **Main Idea and Details** As you read your textbook, identify the main ideas and details or evidence that support the main ideas. Use the lesson headings to organize the main ideas and details. Record your work in the table. Two examples are entered for you.

Heading	Main Idea	Details/Evidence
Food Chains and Food Webs		
Food Chains	A food chain shows how energy transfers through feeding relationships.	
Food Webs • Food Chains Within Food Webs • Decomposers and Detritivores in Food Webs		
Food Webs and Disturbance		
Ecological Pyramids		
Pyramids of Energy		On average, about 10% of the energy is transferred from one trophic level to the next.
Pyramids of Biomass Numbers		

Food Chains and Food Webs

🔍 KEY QUESTION *How does energy flow through ecosystems?*

When one organism eats another, energy moves from the "eaten" to the "eater." In every ecosystem, primary producers and consumers are linked through feeding relationships. These relationships vary, but energy in an ecosystem always flows in one direction: from primary producers through various consumers.

Food Chains The simplest way to think of energy moving through an ecosystem is to imagine it flowing along a food chain. A **food chain** is a series of organisms in which energy is transferred from one organism to another. Food chains vary in length, with some food chains having just one or two steps from a primary producer. For example, in a short food chain, a plant is eaten by a herbivore, which is eaten by a carnivore. Other food chains can be much longer. For example, food chains in the ocean may have four or five steps from primary producers to the largest fish. In the ocean, primary producers are usually tiny floating algae called **phytoplankton**. Phytoplankton are eaten by small animal plankton. The animal plankton are eaten by a series of larger consumers.

Food Webs Many animals eat more than one kind of food. This means that the movement of energy and matter is not a simple chain, but can be much more complicated. A network of feeding interactions, through which both energy and matter move, is called a **food web**.

Food Chains Within Food Webs Within a food web, there are many food chains connecting a primary producer to different consumers. A food web, therefore, is a network that includes all the food chains in an ecosystem. Food webs can be very complicated because of the large number of producers and consumers found within some ecosystems.

Decomposers and Detritivores in Food Webs
Decomposers and detritivores have vital roles in the movement of energy and matter through food webs. Many producers and consumers die without being eaten. Decomposers convert dead material to detritus, which is eaten by detritivores. Decomposition also releases matter in the form of nutrients that can be used by primary producers. Without decomposers, nutrients would remain locked within dead organisms.

🔍 As you read, circle the answers to each Key Question. Underline any words you do not understand.

BUILD Vocabulary

food chain a series of in an ecosystem steps in which organisms transfer energy by eating and being eaten

phytoplankton photosynthetic algae found near the surface of the ocean

food web network of complex interactions formed by the feeding relationships among the various organisms in an ecosystem

Use Prior Knowledge A chain could be made of beads on a string, or loops of paper or metal. Many chains could join together to make a model of a spider web. Food chains join together to form a food web.
☑ Draw a model of a spider web. Then describe how a spider web is similar to a food web.

_____

_____

_____

_____

_____

_____

1. Find a food chain that connects algae to the alligator. Then find another food chain from the saltmeadow grass to the alligator. Use two pencils of different colors to highlight the two food chains.

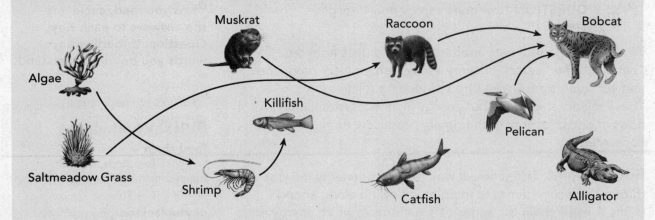

2. How are primary producers important to the alligator's energy supply?

_____

_____

_____

3. How could decomposers be added to the diagram? Which parts of the food web do they affect?

_____

_____

_____

Food Webs and Disturbance Changes to a food web can cause a variety of effects. These effects are hard to predict because food webs are complex. Sometimes the effects of changes are minor. Some animals can <u>adjust</u> well to changes in food webs, for example, if they eat a variety of foods. Other times a change can have dramatic effects throughout a food web.

READING TOOL

Academic Words

adjust To adjust is to change slightly, often to meet a need. Some animals adjust their diets when food sources change.

☑ **Look at the food web above. Suppose that the population of pelicans declined. Bobcats may adjust and eat more _____**

_____

Ecological Pyramids

🔍 **KEY QUESTION** *How do ecological pyramids help analyze energy flow through trophic levels?*

Each step in a food chain or food web is called a **trophic level**. Primary producers make up the first trophic level. Consumers occupy the other levels. **Ecological pyramids** are models of trophic levels in a food chain or food web. The shape of the pyramid shows the relative amount of energy or matter in each level.

Pyramids of Energy

Only a small amount of the energy in any trophic level is available to organisms at the next trophic level. This is because organisms use much of the energy they consume on processes to stay alive. Energy is also released as heat. Pyramids of energy show the relative amount of energy available at each trophic level of a food chain or food web. The pyramid is widest at the bottom. The shape of the pyramid shows the efficiency of energy transfer between levels. On average, about 10 percent of the energy in one trophic level is transferred up to the next trophic level.

Pyramids of Biomass and Pyramids of Numbers

The amount of living tissue in a trophic level is called its **biomass**. The amount of biomass in a trophic level is determined by the amount of energy in that level. A pyramid of biomass is a model that shows the relative amount of living organic matter in each trophic level of an ecosystem.

A pyramid of numbers is a model that shows the relative number of individual organisms at each trophic level in an ecosystem. The pyramid of numbers for an ecosystem is usually similar in shape to the pyramid of biomass. The number of organisms on each level decreases from the level below it. Sometimes consumers are much smaller than the organisms they feed upon. For example, thousands of insects may eat from a single tree. In such cases, the pyramid of numbers may be upside down, but the pyramid of biomass will still be smaller at the top than at the bottom.

BUILD Vocabulary

trophic (TROH fick) **level** each step in a food chain or food web

ecological (ee coh lah gi kal) **pyramid** illustration of the relative amounts of energy or matter contained within each trophic level in a food chain or food web

biomass the total mass of living tissue within a trophic level

Word Origins The word *trophic* comes from a Greek word that means "food or feeding." ☑ What other terms did you study in this chapter that contain the root word *troph*?

_____

Visual Reading Tool: Ecological Pyramids

Bear 0.1%
Bluebird 1%
Beetles 10%
Tree 100%

Write the name of the pyramid on the line above each pyramid. Then, below, explain the relationships among trophic levels that are shown by the pyramids.

_____

_____

_____

LESSON 3 Cycles of Matter

Compare and Contrast Before you read, preview the cycle diagrams in your textbook. Note the similarities and differences of the cycles in the graphic organizer.

Water Cycle	Carbon Cycle	Nitrogen Cycle
_____	_____	_____
_____	_____	_____
_____	_____	_____
_____	_____	_____
_____		_____

↓ ↓ ↓

All Three Cycles

_____
_____
_____

Lesson Summary

🔑 As you read, circle the answers to each Key Question. Underline any words you do not understand.

Recycling in Nature

🔑 **KEY QUESTION** *How does matter flow between trophic levels and among ecosystems?*

All organisms contain the compounds water, carbohydrates, lipids, nucleic acids, and proteins. These compounds are mainly made of the elements oxygen, hydrogen, carbon, nitrogen, phosphorus, and potassium. Organisms cannot make these elements. These elements, like all matter, can never be created or destroyed. Matter flows from one trophic level to another. Matter also moves by being recycled within and among ecosystems. These cycles of elements and compounds are called **biogeochemical cycles**.

The processes that occur in biogeochemical cycles are:
➤ Biological processes occur in the biosphere and are any activities done by organisms, such as photosynthesis.
➤ Geological processes occur in the geosphere and include volcanoes, earthquakes, and formation of rock.

- Chemical and physical processes mostly occur in the hydrosphere or atmosphere and include the formation of precipitation, the flow of water, and lightning.
- Human activities that affect cycles of matter on a global scale include the burning of fossil fuels and forests.

The Water Cycle

🔍 **KEY QUESTION** *How does water cycle globally?*

Water cycles among the hydrosphere, atmosphere, and geosphere—sometimes outside the biosphere and sometimes in it. Water enters the atmosphere as water vapor when it evaporates from bodies of water. Water evaporates from leaves through transpiration (tran spuh RAY shun).

Water vapor condenses into droplets that form clouds. Droplets fall as rain, snow, sleet, or hail. On land, precipitation flows along the surface as runoff. Runoff enters streams and rivers and flows into oceans or lakes. Water enters the soil as groundwater and then enters plants through their roots. Water then reenters the atmosphere through evaporation and transpiration. Human activity, such as the cutting of forests, affects the water cycle in an ecosystem.

Nutrient Cycles

🔍 **KEY QUESTION** *What is the importance of the main nutrient cycles?*

Nutrients are elements that an organism needs to sustain life. Every organism needs nutrients to build tissues and carry out life functions. Like water, nutrients pass through organisms and the environment through biogeochemical cycles. The cycles that carry carbon, nitrogen, and phosphorus through the biosphere are vital for life. Oxygen participates in the carbon, nitrogen, and phosphorus cycles by combining with these elements. Photosynthesis releases oxygen gas. Oxygen is also used in cellular respiration.

The Carbon Cycle Carbon is a major component of organic compounds, including carbohydrates, lipids, proteins, and nucleic acids. Fossil fuels are made of carbon. Animal skeletons contain carbon as calcium carbonate. Carbon dioxide (CO_2) is an important gas in the atmosphere.

Biological Processes Photosynthesis removes carbon dioxide from the atmosphere. Respiration returns carbon dioxide to the atmosphere. Producers use carbon dioxide to make organic compounds that are consumed by heterotrophs. Decomposers break down organic compounds, releasing carbon (and other nutrients) to the environment. Not all carbon is released by decomposition. Remains of primary producers buried millions of years ago were transformed into fossil fuels.

READING TOOL

Use Headings The headings that organize the text can to help you understand what you are reading.
☑ On this page, how do the headings show changes in the topic of the text?

_____

_____

_____

_____

_____

BUILD Vocabulary

biogeochemical cycle process in which elements, chemical compounds, and other forms of matter are passed from one organism to another and from one part of the biosphere to another

nutrient chemical substance that an organism needs to sustain life

Root Words The Latin word *nutrire* means "to feed or nourish."
☑ What is an example of a nutrient discussed in this lesson? Describe how it helps to nourish an organism.

_____

_____

_____

_____

_____

_____

1. Use colored pencils to color the arrows in the diagram according to the processes listed in the key. Color the biological processes blue; the human processes orange; the geological processes green; and the physical and chemical processes red.

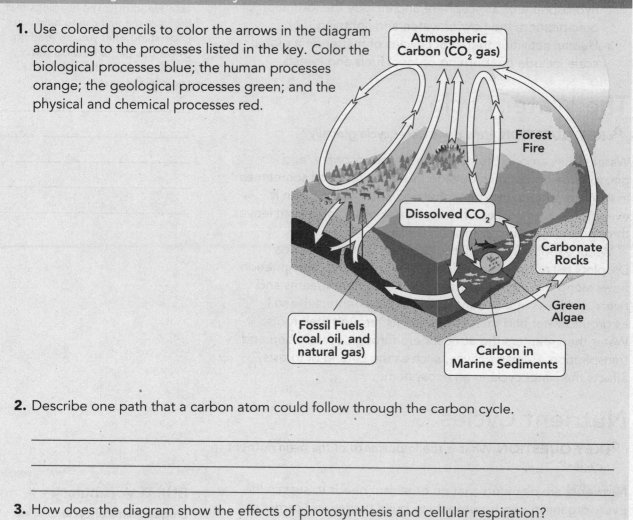

2. Describe one path that a carbon atom could follow through the carbon cycle.

_____

_____

_____

3. How does the diagram show the effects of photosynthesis and cellular respiration?

_____

_____

_____

Geological Processes Dissolved carbon dioxide in the ocean can form carbonates that combine with skeletons of marine organisms to form rocks. These rocks are driven deep underground by geological activity. Heat and volcanic eruptions release this carbon dioxide into the atmosphere.

Chemical and Physical Processes Carbon dioxide is exchanged between the atmosphere and oceans through chemical and physical processes. Carbon dioxide in the atmosphere can dissolve in rainwater, forming a weak acid.

Human Activity When humans burn coal, oil, natural gas, or even forests, we return carbon stored over millions of years to the atmosphere in a very short time. Such human activity has a large impact on the carbon cycle. More carbon dioxide in the atmosphere adds to the greenhouse effect.

The Nitrogen Cycle All organisms require nitrogen to make amino acids and nucleic acids. Most nitrogen is in the form of nitrogen gas in the atmosphere. Nitrogen-containing compounds, such as ammonia, nitrite, and nitrate, are in the biosphere, geosphere, and hydrosphere.

Natural Processes Nitrogen gas is abundant, but most organisms can't use it. Only certain types of bacteria can convert nitrogen gas into ammonia through a process called **nitrogen fixation**. Nitrogen-fixing bacteria live in soil and on the roots of certain plants. Other bacteria convert ammonia into nitrite and nitrate, which can be used by primary producers. When consumers eat producers, those nitrogen compounds are reused. Decomposers release nitrogen compounds from animal wastes and dead organisms. Some bacteria obtain energy by converting nitrates into nitrogen gas, which is released into the atmosphere in a process called **denitrification**.

Human Activities Human involvement in the nitrogen cycle increased greatly when chemists discovered a process to use nitrogen gas from the atmosphere to make chemicals that are used in fertilizer. Humans now use this process to fix more nitrogen than all natural processes combined.

The Phosphorus Cycle Phosphorus is necessary for molecules such as nucleic acids. Phosphorus does not cycle through the atmosphere. Phosphorus is found as phosphates in the geosphere, and dissolved in water in the hydrosphere.

Nutrient Limitation

🔑 **KEY QUESTION** *How does nutrient availability affect primary productivity?*

If ample sunlight and water are available, the primary productivity of an ecosystem may be limited by the availability of nutrients. Any nutrient whose supply limits productivity is called a **limiting nutrient**.

Nutrient Limitation in Soil Plant growth can be limited by the supply of one or more nutrients. Nutrient limitation is why farmers use fertilizers. Most fertilizers contain nitrogen, phosphorus, and potassium. Micronutrients such as calcium, magnesium, sulfur, iron, and manganese are sometimes included in small amounts.

Nutrient Limitation in Aquatic Ecosystems
Nitrogen is often the limiting nutrient in the ocean. In freshwater, phosphorus is often the limiting nutrient. Runoff from rain may contain fertilizer from farms. This delivers a large amount of limiting nutrients into bodies of water. This stimulates producers such as algae to grow more than normal, causing what is called an algal bloom. Severe algal blooms can disrupt the functioning of ecosystems.

BUILD Vocabulary

nitrogen fixation process of converting nitrogen gas into nitrogen compounds that plants can absorb and use

denitrification process by which soil bacteria convert nitrates into nitrogen gas

limiting nutrient single essential nutrient that limits productivity in an ecosystem

Use Prior Knowledge To fix something is to repair it or make it useful. Nitrogen fixation changes nitrogen into a form that is useful to living things. ☑ **Which type of living things perform nitrogen fixation?**

_____

_____

Review Vocabulary

Choose the letter of the best answer.

1. The conversion of nitrogen gas (N_2) to ammonia is called

    A. denitrification

    B. nitrogen cycle

    C. nitrogen fixation

    D. nitrogen limitation

2. Which rely on other organisms for their energy and food supply?

    A. primary producers

    B. biomass

    C. autotrophs

    D. consumers

Match the vocabulary term to its definition.

3. _____ The total amount of living tissue

    a. biomass

4. _____ Small pieces of dead or decaying plant or animal remains

    b. denitrification

5. _____ A model of feeding levels in a food chain or food web

    c. energy pyramid

6. _____ Changing nitrogen compounds to nitrogen gas

    d. detritus

Review Key Questions

Provide evidence and details to support your answers.

7. How does energy flow through ecosystems?

_____

8. Describe two ways that primary producers produce high-energy compounds.

_____

_____

9. How does nutrient availability relate to productivity and species survival?

_____

_____

_____

How Populations Grow

READING TOOL **Cause and Effect** As you read this lesson, use the grapic organizer to take notes on how both types of population growth occur. Make sure to include notes on birth rates, death rates, and growth rates.

Type of Population Growth		Cause	Effect
Exponential Growth		A species is introduced into a new region with plentiful resources and few predators.	
Logistic Growth	Phase 1	A species is introduced into a new region with plentiful resources and few predators.	
	Phase 2	Resources become limited.	
	Phase 3	The carrying capacity of the environment is reached.	

Lesson Summary

Describing Populations

⚲ **KEY QUESTION** *How do ecologists study populations?*

Ecologists study populations by examining their geographic range, growth rate, density and distribution, and age structure.

Geographic Range The places a population lives make up its geographic range. A population range can vary enormously in size. For example, the population of bacteria in a single rotting vegetable is in a small area. The part of an ocean inhabited by a population of fish can be a very large area. Geographic ranges can grow or shrink over time.

Growth Rate The number of individuals in a population can change over time, or it can stay the same. Population numbers can grow rapidly when moving into a new area, or they can shrink over time due to activities such as hunting.

⚲ As you read, circle the answers to each Key Question. Underline any words you do not understand.

Individuals in a population can be spaced out randomly, uniformly, or in clumps.
Into each box, draw how 16 individuals would be spaced for each type of distribution
pattern. Draw each individual as a small circle.

Random	Uniform	Clumped

Density and Distribution The number of individuals that can be found per unit area is called the **population density**. In a given environment, one species may have very few individuals, or a low density, while another species has a much higher density, with many individuals. **Population distribution** is a description of the way individuals are spaced out across the population's range. There are three distribution patterns: random, uniform, and clumped. In a clumped population, individuals are packed closely together. This may, for example, help protect individuals from predators. In a uniform population, individuals are spaced evenly. This occurs when individuals compete for resources. In a random distribution, individuals are spaced unevenly. This occurs when the location of an individual has little effect on another individual.

Age Structure To understand a population, ecologists need to know the age of individuals, and how many are male and how many are female. This information describes the **age structure** of the population, which is important because most plants and animals must reach a certain age to reproduce. For animals, only females can produce offspring.

Population Growth

🔍 **KEY QUESTION** *What factors affect population growth?*

A population will increase or decrease in size depending on how many individuals are added to it or removed from it. Birthrate, death rate, and the rate at which individuals enter or leave a population all affect population growth.

Birthrate and Death Rate Populations can increase if more individuals are born in a period of time than die during the same period. In other words, a population can increase when its birthrate is higher than its death rate. If the birthrate equals the death rate, the population may stay the same size. If the death rate is greater than the birthrate, the population will decrease.

Immigration and Emigration A population may increase if individuals move into its range from elsewhere. This is called **immigration**. A surplus of food can cause immigration. A population may decrease if individuals move out of the population's range. This is called **emigration**, which can be caused by a shortage of food or other resources. Immigration and emigration depend in part on how far and how fast individuals can travel, or whether human activity moves them around.

Exponential Growth

🔍 **KEY QUESTION** *What happens during exponential growth?*

If a population has all of the food and space it needs and protection from predators and disease, the population can increase. The rate of population growth increases because each generation contains more individuals than the generation before it. More and more offspring are produced in a situation called **exponential growth**. Under ideal conditions with unlimited resources, a population will increase exponentially. This means that the larger the population gets, the faster it grows.

Organisms That Reproduce Rapidly Bacteria can grow very rapidly. If a single bacterium in ideal conditions can divide every 20 minutes, then after 20 minutes there are two bacteria, after another 20 minutes there are four bacteria, and at the end of the first hour, there are eight bacteria cells. After three 20-minute periods, there are $2 \times 2 \times 2$, or $2^3 = 8$ cells. In two hours there are $2^6 = 64$ cells. After one day, there are 4720 quintillion cells. If you plot the bacterial population on a graph, you get a curve shaped like the letter *J* that rises slowly at first and then rises faster and faster. If nothing interfered with this growth, the population would become infinitely large.

Organisms That Reproduce Slowly Most organisms reproduce much more slowly than bacteria. But if exponential growth continued indefinitely, the result would still be an impossible number of individuals.

Organisms in New Environments Sometimes when an organism migrates or is moved to a new location, its population grows exponentially for a time.

BUILD Vocabulary

immigration movement of individuals into an area occupied by an existing population

emigration movement of individuals out of an area

exponential growth growth pattern in which the individuals in a population reproduce at an increasing rate

Prefixes *Immigration* and *emigration* both have the root word *migration*. The prefix *im-* means "into," and the prefix *e-* means "out of." For some uses, the prefix *ex-* is used instead of *e-*. ☑ **Which word listed below means bringing products into a country from another country? Circle your answer.**

Import

Export

Logistic Growth

⚲ KEY QUESTION *What happens during logistic growth?*

Phases of Growth Natural populations do not grow exponentially for very long. Sooner or later things happen that stop exponential growth. After a few individuals are introduced into a real-world environment, growth follows the following steps, or phases.

Phase 1: Population Grows Rapidly After a short time, the population begins to grow exponentially. During this phase, resources are unlimited. Individuals grow and reproduce rapidly and few individuals die, and many offspring are produced. The population size and rate of growth increase more and more rapidly.

Phase 2: Growth Slows Down In real-world populations, exponential growth begins to slow down. This slowing down of growth is due to limiting factors such as competition for resources. This does not mean that the population size decreases. The population still increases, but not as rapidly as before.

Phase 3: Growth Stops At some point the rate of population growth decreases to zero. The size of the population levels off and may remain about the same size for a long time.

The Logistic Growth Curve The logistic growth curve is shaped like the letter *S*. **Logistic growth** occurs when a population's growth slows and then stops, following a period of exponential growth.

Many plant and animal populations follow a logistic growth curve. Growth may slow if the birthrate decreases or if the death rate increases. Changing rates of immigration and emigration also affect population growth.

Carrying Capacity A population stops growing when its birthrate and death rate are the same, and when immigration equals emigration. The population size may rise and fall somewhat, but the changes average out around a certain population size.

The **carrying capacity** is the maximum number of individuals of a particular species that a particular environment can support. Once a population reaches the carrying capacity of its environment, various factors affect the population and help stabilize its size.

LESSON 2 Limits to Growth

Compare and Contrast As you read your textbook, complete the Venn diagram to compare and contrast density-dependent limiting factors and density-independent limiting factors.

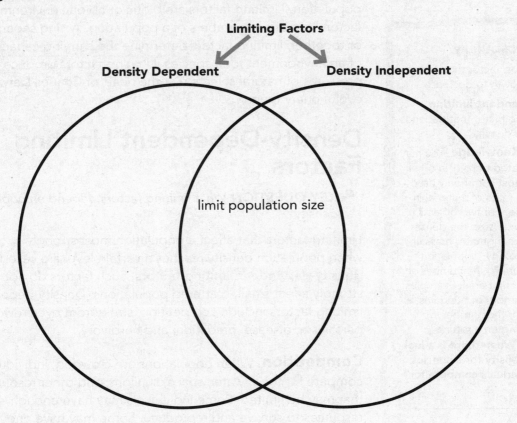

Limiting Factors

Density Dependent   **Density Independent**

limit population size

Once you have finished the venn diagram, categorize the following scenarios as density-dependent and density-independent limiting factors.

Scenario A: A flood wipes out all the plant species that live on a riverbed.

Scenario B: A pack of wolves migrates to a new valley and eats all the deer that inhabit that space.

Scenario C: A large population of zebras are killed due to a very contagious virus.

Scenario D: A drought kills many of the deer that live in a valley.

Limiting Factor	Density-Dependent	Density-Independent
Scenario(s)		

Limiting Factors

🔎 **As you read, circle the answers to each Key Question. Underline any words you do not understand.**

🔎 **KEY QUESTION** *What factors determine carrying capacity?*

The growth of primary producers can be controlled by a limiting nutrient. A limiting nutrient is one example of a limiting factor. A **limiting factor** is any factor that controls the growth of a population. Limiting factors are biotic or abiotic environmental factors that affect members of a population. Acting separately or together, limiting factors determine the carrying capacity of an environment for a species. Limiting factors produce the pressures of natural selection at the heart of Charles Darwin's evolutionary theory.

BUILD Vocabulary

limiting factor factor that causes population growth to decrease

density-dependent limiting factor limiting factor that depends on population density

Using Prior Knowledge You may have encountered *density* in other classes. It is most commonly used to refer to the mass of material in a given volume. For two objects that are the same size, the denser object will have a greater mass. In population ecology, *population density* can refer to the number of individuals per unit area. Examples include the number of penguins on an island, or the number of bacteria living on a rotting vegetable. ☑ **When there is a high population density for a species, what do individuals compete for?**

_____

_____

Density-Dependent Limiting Factors

🔎 **KEY QUESTION** *What limiting factors depend on population density?*

Limiting factors that affect a population most strongly when population density reaches a certain level are called **density-dependent limiting factors**. Such factors do not strongly affect small, scattered populations. Density-dependent limiting factors include competition, stress from overcrowding, parasitism, disease, predation, and herbivory.

Competition When populations are crowded, individuals compete for food, water, space, sunlight, and other resources that may be limited. Some individuals may have enough resources to survive and reproduce. Some may have enough to survive, but not to reproduce. Others may die from lack of resources. Competition for resources can decrease birthrates, increase death rates, or both. Competition is density dependent because resources can be used up when there are more individuals. Competition can be between members of the same species, or between species.

Parasitism and Disease Parasites and disease-causing organisms weaken their hosts and can cause death. Parasitism and disease are density-dependent factors because they spread from one host to another more easily when populations are dense.

Stress From Overcrowding Some organisms fight each other if they are overcrowded. Individuals can be weakened and may die. In some species, overcrowding stress can cause animals to neglect or kill their own offspring. Overcrowding stress can lower birthrates, raise death rates, or increase emigration.

Predation and Herbivory The effects of predators on prey or herbivores on plants are density dependent.

Predator-Prey Relationships Populations of predators and prey may rise and fall. When there is plenty of prey, the predator has plenty to eat and may increase in number. This causes the prey death rate to rise higher than its birthrate, so the prey population decreases. As the prey decreases, the predators begin to starve, so the predator population falls. This allows the prey population to start rising again.

Herbivore Effects An herbivore is a predator of a plant. Populations of herbivores and plants cycle up and down, just like populations of predator and prey.

Humans as Predators Human activity may limit populations of other organisms. Hunting is one way that humans can cause large decreases in animal populations.

Density-Independent Limiting Factors

🔍 **KEY QUESTION** *What limiting factors do not typically depend on population density?*

Density-independent limiting factors affect populations regardless of population size and density. Environmental extremes—including weather extremes such as hurricanes, droughts, or floods, and natural disasters such as wildfires—can act as density-independent limiting factors. Such factors may cause a population to "crash," or reach very small sizes. After a crash, a population may increase again or stay low for a long time. Extreme hot and cold weather and severe drought along with human-caused environmental damage can affect populations of plants and animals.

True Density Independence? Bad weather can affect dense populations more than it would affect less dense populations by, for example, making food less available. It is sometimes difficult to say that a limiting factor acts only in a density-independent way.

BUILD Vocabulary
density-independent limiting factor limiting factor that affects all populations in similar ways, regardless of the population density

READING TOOL

Connect to Visuals The graph shows the rabbit population in South Australia before and after a virus, myxomatosis, was introduced to reduce the rabbit population. Use the graph and the information presented in this lesson to answer the questions.

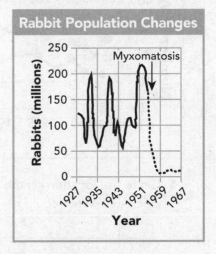

Rabbit Population Changes

☑ Was the virus a density-dependent or a density-independent limiting factor?

_____

Controlling Introduced Species The number of individuals of a species can increase rapidly when introduced into a new environment. Hunting is not always an effective way to control introduced species. A predator or a pathogen can be introduced to control a population, but if this works, the effect may be only temporary.

Limiting Factors and Extinction

⚲ KEY QUESTION *What is the relationship between limiting factors and extinction?*

Limiting factors such as temperature and rainfall can change over time. Human activity can divide natural environments into smaller pieces, reducing available space and carrying capacity. If carrying capacity falls low enough, populations can be wiped out, leading to species extinction. An extinct species has no members remaining.

Visual Reading Tool: Analyzing Changes in Wolf and Moose Populations

Figure 5-9 shows the populations of wolves and moose on Isle Royale from 1955–2005. Use the data to answer the questions below.

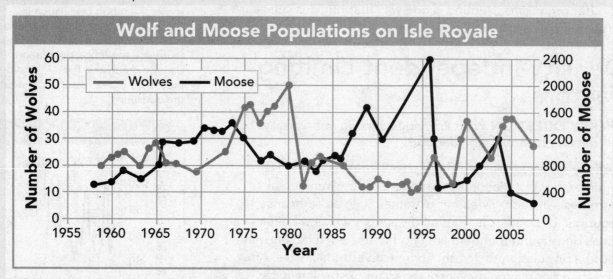

1. Circle the location on the graph where the wolves experienced a steep population decrease. What could have caused this?

_____

_____

_____

2. Why is there a steep increase in Moose from 1985–1995?

_____

_____

_____

Human Population Growth

Sequence of Events

As you read this lesson, use your workbook to explain the three stages of The Demographic Transition. Look for words like "next" and "lastly" in the text, and use Figure 5-14 to help you enter the correct words to finish each sentence in the graphic organizer.

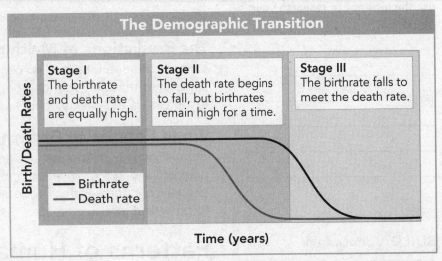

The Demographic Transition

Stage I
The birthrate and death rate are equally high.

Stage II
The death rate begins to fall, but birthrates remain high for a time.

Stage III
The birthrate falls to meet the death rate.

Birth/Death Rates

— Birthrate
— Death rate

Time (years)

| STAGE 1 | STAGE 2 | STAGE 3 |

STAGE 1
- Death rates and birth-rates are both _____ _____.
- For most of human history, not all children that were born made it to adulthood.

STAGE 2
- Advances in _____, _____, _____, lower death rates .
- Birth rates are _____.

STAGE 3
- Living standards rise and birthrates _____.
- This makes birthrates and death rates _____.

Lesson Summary

Historical Overview

🔑 **KEY QUESTION** *How has human population size changed over time?*

Human populations can increase, remain the same, or decrease, due to the same factors that affect the population growth of other species. Human populations, like other populations, tend to increase, and the rate of those increases has changed over time. In some countries, population growth is more rapid than in others. For most of human existence, our population grew slowly because predators and disease were common. Until a few decades ago, only half of the children in the world survived to adulthood, so families had many children to make sure that some would survive.

🔑 As you read, circle the answers to each Key Question. Underline any words you do not understand.

Academic Words

sanitation prevention of disease by removal of sewage and trash

☑ **List some ways that modern cities in developed countries have improved sanitation conditions over the last 200 years. You may use the Internet to research your answers.**

_____

_____

_____

_____

_____

_____

BUILD Vocabulary

demography scientific study of human populations

demographic transition change in a population from high birth and death rates to low birth and death rates

Prefixes The prefix _demo-_ comes from the Greek word _demos_, meaning "people." The same prefix is used in _democracy_. The demographic transition refers to a transition, or change, that is observed in human populations as countries become more developed.

☑ **What factors are measured to determine if a demographic change is occuring?**

_____

_____

_____

_____

_____

Exponential Human Population Growth As countries became more developed, food supplies became more reliable and the global human population grew more rapidly. Better <u>sanitation</u> and medicine reduced death rates. The combination of lower death rates and high birthrates led to exponential growth. It took 123 years for the human population to double from 1 billion in 1804 to 2 billion in 1927. Then it took only 33 years to grow by another billion. The time it took to add another billion continued to decrease until 1999, when it began to slowly rise.

The Predictions of Malthus Exponential growth cannot continue forever. Two centuries ago, Thomas Malthus suggested that only war (competition), famine (limited resources), and disease could limit human population growth.

World Population Growth Slows The global human population grew exponentially until the growth rate reached a peak around 1959. Since the mid-1960s, the growth rate has been slowly decreasing. The total human population continues to grow, but at a slower rate.

Patterns of Human Population Growth

🔍 **KEY QUESTION** _Why do population growth rates differ among countries?_

The scientific study of human populations is called **demography**. Demography examines characteristics of human populations and predicts how they will change. Birthrates, death rates, and the age structure of a population help predict why some countries have high growth rates while other countries' populations increase more slowly.

The Demographic Transition Population growth has slowed dramatically over the past century in the United States, Japan, and much of Europe. Demographers hypothesize that these countries have completed the demographic transition. The **demographic transition** is a change from high birthrates and death rates to low birthrates and death rates. There are three stages to the demographic transition. In Stage 1, human birthrates and death rates are high. This describes most of human history. Next, advances in nutrition, sanitation, and medicine lead to lower death rates in Stage 2. In Stage 2, birthrates remain high and greatly exceed the death rate. The United States passed through Stage 2 between 1790 and 1910. As living standards rise, families have fewer children and the birthrate falls, which leads to Stage 3. Lastly, the falling birthrate leads to slower population growth. The demographic transition is complete when the birthrate is roughly equal to the death rate.

Age Structure and Population Growth The age
structure of a population reveals how fast a population is
growing. A greater percentage of young people indicate a
growing population, and a greater percentage of older people
indicate a shrinking population. The United States has nearly
equal numbers of people in each age group. Demographers
believe that many factors predict human population growth.
The factors include age structure, the effects of deadly diseases,
and malnutrition.

Visual Reading Tool: Determining Age Structure Patterns

Use the Patterns of Population Change Graph to help you answer the following questions.

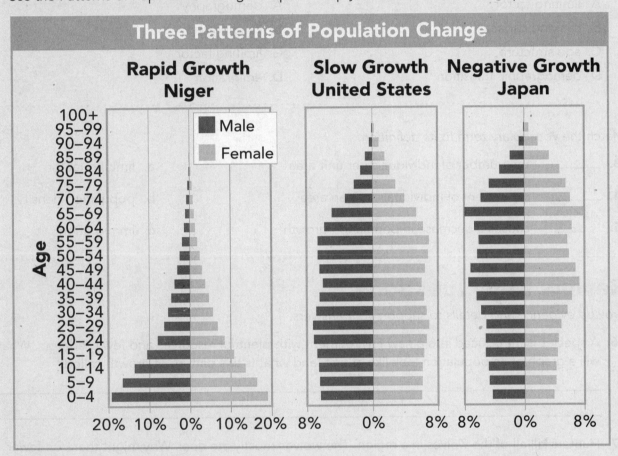

Source: United Nations, World Population Prospects

1. What percentage of Japan's population is between the ages of 0–4 years?

_____

2. Using the graph, explain why Niger's population is going through rapid growth.

_____

_____

3. What could cause Niger's rapid population growth?

_____

_____

Review Vocabulary

Choose the letter of the best answer.

1. the age and sex of members of a population

   A. limiting factor

   B. carrying capacity

   C. age structure

   D. demographic transition

2. the number of individuals an environment can support

   A. demography

   B. carrying capacity

   C. limiting factor

   D. emigration

Match the vocabulary term to its definition.

3. _____ the number of individuals per unit area

4. _____ movement of individuals into an area

5. _____ causes a decrease in population growth

   a. limiting factor

   b. population density

   c. immigration

Review Key Questions

Provide evidence and details to support your answers.

6. A species is introduced into a new environment with plentiful resources and few predators. What will a graph of its population look like at first, and what is this pattern of growth called?

_____

_____

7. Hunters kill all of the wolves in a region. The wolves mostly ate deer. Why might there be fewer deer a few years after the wolves are killed?

_____

_____

8. How could a drought reduce the carrying capacity of an environment for a predator?

_____

_____

9. How can you tell if a human population has passed through the demographic transition?

_____

_____

Habitats, Niches, and Species Interactions

READING TOOL **Compare and Contrast** For each section in this lesson, you will be comparing and contrasting key elements. Fill in the graphic organizer as you read. The first one has been started for you.

Elements	Similarities	Differences
Microhabitat vs. Microbiome	Both are very small.	Microbiome is microscopic; microhabitats are larger than that.
Habitat vs. Niche		
Predator-Prey Relationship vs. Herbivore-Plant Relationship		
Commensalism vs. Mutualism		

Lesson Summary

As you read, circle the answers to each Key Question. Underline any words you do not understand.

Habitat and Niche

KEY QUESTION *What factors determine and describe habitats and niches?*

A **habitat** is an area with a particular combination of physical and biological environmental factors that affect which organisms live within it. Simply put, it is an organism's "ecological address."

Microhabitats Examining environmental conditions on a smaller scale will reveal the microhabitats for organisms.

Microbiomes Microbiomes are microscopic communities too small for our eyes to comprehend. The organisms existing in these tiny habitats perform various functions.

Tolerance Each species has a range of **tolerance**, or variety of environmental conditions in which it can survive and reproduce.

The Niche A species' **niche** describes where an organism lives and what it does "for a living," including the way it interacts with biotic and abiotic factors.

Resources, Physical Aspects, and Biological Aspects of the Niche A **resource** is any necessity a species needs to live, and differs for each species. Each niche offers a special blend of resources allowing organisms living within it to thrive. The abiotic, or physical, factors that a species needs are also included in a specie's niche. The niche also encompases the biotic, or biological, factors needed to survive. Examples of a species' biotic factors include the food it eats, the way it obtains food, and how it reproduces.

Competition

KEY QUESTION *How does competition shape communities?*

Competition Competition occurs when two species attempt to use the same limited ecological resources in the same place at the same time. Competition among members of the same species is known as intraspecific competition.

Competitive Exclusion Principle The **competitive exclusion principle** states that no two species can occupy exactly the same niche in exactly the same habitat at exactly the same time. When this happens in nature, one species wins and the other dies out.

Dividing Resources Because of the competitive exclusion principle, species inhabiting the same niche within the same habitat can find success by dividing resources.

BUILD Vocabulary

habitat area where an organism lives including the biotic and abiotic factors that affect it

tolerance ability of an organism to survive and reproduce under circumstances that differ from their optimal conditions

niche full range of physical and biological conditions in which an organism lives and the way in which the organism uses those conditions

resource any necessity of life, such as water, nutrients, light, food, or space

competitive exclusion principle principle that states that no two species can occupy the same niche in the same habitat at the same time

Related Words As you learned previously, a biome is a large area with broadly similar environmental conditions that can house a variety of different ecosystems. ☑ **How is a habitat related to a biome?**

_____

_____

READING TOOL

Make Connections

Think of the yard at your home or the sports fields at your school.

☑ **How many different microhabitats can you name?**

_____

_____

_____

_____

Predation and Herbivory

🔍 **KEY QUESTION** *How does herbivory shape communities?*

Food webs identify which organisms feed on which other organisms, often distinguishing predator from prey. These relationships powerfully influence each other and are important in shaping communities. Any natural or human-caused environmental change that affects one population (predator or prey), will also greatly affect the other.

Predator-Prey Relationships The relationship between predators and their prey are tightly intertwined. This is especially true in areas where each prey species has only one predator and vice versa.

Herbivore-Plant Relationships Herbivores and the plants they eat share a similar relationship to predator and prey, though the plants can't run away from their predators. Herbivores affect how many plants will survive in an area, as well as how widespread they are in that area. When specific plants grow especially well in a location, they are sure to attract higher numbers of herbivores.

READING TOOL

Apply Prior Knowledge

Many people think that, by definition, predators must be large, powerful carnivores. ☑ **Explain how both predators and prey can be carnivores (meat-eaters), omnivores (meat-and-plant-eaters), or herbivores (plant-eaters).**

_____

_____

_____

_____

_____

_____

_____

Visual Reading Tool: Analyzing Herbivore-Plant Relationships

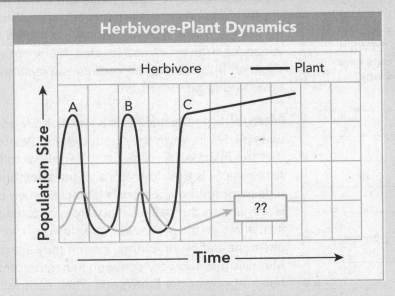

Herbivore-Plant Dynamics

Study the graph. Using what you have learned, explain what is happening at Point C and list three things that might happen at that time.

Explain Point C:

_____

_____

Three Things:

_____

_____

🔍 As you read, circle the answers to each Key Question. Underline any words you do not understand.

BUILD Vocabulary

keystone species single species that is not usually abundant in a community yet exerts strong control on the structure of a community

symbiosis (sim by oh sis) relationship in which two species live close together

commensalism (kuh men sul iz um) symbiotic relationship in which one organism benefits and the other is neither helped nor harmed

mutualism symbiotic relationship in which both species benefit from the relationship

parasitism a symbiotic relationship in which one organism lives on or inside another organism and harms it

Using Prior Knowledge Humans have symbiotic relationships with many organisms. Some live inside of our own bodies, and some we interact with externally. ☑ **Which type of symbiosis do pets have with their humans and why?**

_____

_____

_____

_____

_____

_____

_____

_____

Keystone Species

🔍 **KEY QUESTION** *How do keystone species shape communities?*

A **keystone species** plays a vital and unique role in maintaining structure, stability, and diversity in an ecosystem. These single species have a powerful influence on a community habitat. Changes in their population size can have dramatic effects on the entire ecosystem. If a keystone species is removed from an area, it can cause the ecosystem in that area to collapse entirely. Once an ecosystem has been changed in this way, returning the keystone species to the area may or may not help return it to its original condition.

Symbioses

🔍 **KEY QUESTION** *What are the three primary ways that organisms depend on each other?*

A particularly close, interdependent relationship between two species is called **symbiosis**. There are three types of symbiotic relationships among organisms: commensalism, mutualism, and parasitism.

Commensalism **Commensalism** is a symbiotic relationship in which one organism benefits and the other is neither helped nor harmed. This type of relationship occurs among a wide variety of large and small species. Many organisms living together in biomes share commensal relationships with each other and larger organisms.

Mutualism **Mutualism** is a symbiotic relationship between two species in which they both benefit. Another way to say it is that the relationship is mutually beneficial to both organisms. An example is the clownfish and sea anemone. The clownfish hides among the anemone's tentacles when threatened, and is immune to the painful stings from its tentacles that kill other fish. In return for protection, the clownfish will scare away anemone-eating predators, even if they are much bigger. Mutualism is also very common in microbiomes, like the human body or the Earth's soil. Their competition and other interactions help keep everything regulated.

Parasitism **Parasitism** is a symbiotic relationship in which one organism lives inside of or on another organism and harms it. The parasite takes what it needs from its host, and make the host sick or kill it.

LESSON 2 Succession

Cause and Effect Identify the effects of the elements listed below. Use the headings in your text as a guide. Be specific in your explanations. The causes are filled in for you.

Elements	Causes	Effects
Primary Succession	volcanic eruptions glaciers retreating	
Secondary Succession	natural disturbance human-caused disturbance	
Succession After Natural Disturbances	hurricane forest fire tsunami flood	
Succession After Human-Caused Disturbances	population expansion deforestation mining	

Lesson Summary

Primary and Secondary Succession

🔑 **KEY QUESTION** *How do communities change over time?*

Ecological succession is a series of somewhat predictable events that occur in a community over time. Ecosystems are constantly evolving, and experience major change after disturbances. New species move in, populations change, and other species die out. The diversity among species in an ecosystem increases as succession progresses.

Primary Succession Succession beginning on newly-formed rock or areas with no remnants of older communities is called **primary succession**. This typically happens after volcanic eruptions or as glaciers retreat, causing new, barren rock to be exposed. Ecological succession begins when **pioneer species**, or the first species to colonize barren areas, move in. They create an environment suitable for other organisms to move in and for the area to sustain growth.

🔑 As you read, circle the answers to each Key Question. Underline any words you do not understand.

BUILD Vocabulary

ecological succession series of gradual changes that occur in a community following a disturbance

primary succession succession that occurs in an area in which no trace of a previous community is present

pioneer species first species to populate an area during succession

Secondary Succession Secondary succession occurs when a disturbance affects an existing community but doesn't completely destroy it. This process happens faster than primary succession because parts of the original community still exist. Possible disturbances include: natural disasters like wildfires, hurricanes, and tsunamis, as well as human created disturbances.

Why Succession Happens Succession happens in different ecosystems for multiple reasons. Pioneer species prepare the area for other organisms to move in. Each new species makes the ecosystem more habitable for those species already there, as well as for additional species that would benefit the area. These processes become more complex over time as species diversity increases.

Climax Communities

🔍 **KEY QUESTION** *How do communities recover after a disturbance?*

Scientists understand that succession follows different paths, and that the communities that are the end results of succession, or climax communities, may not always be uniform or stable.

Succession After Natural Disturbances When natural disturbances happen in healthy ecosystems, the events and processes that occur during secondary succession often, but not always, reproduce the original climax community. Since natural disasters, like fires or floods, can happen to only a small part of a community, each community could be experiencing different stages of succession at the same time.

Succession After Human-Caused Disturbances Secondary succession can take different paths and produce many different communities. This all depends on the kind of disturbance, the season in which the disturbance occurs, and other factors. Sometimes this causes a change that prevents the regrowth of the original community. From some human-caused disturbances, ecosystems may or may not fully recover.

Studying Patterns of Succession Ecologists study succession by comparing different cases and looking for similarities and differences. For example, they learned that at both Mount Saint Helens and Krakatau, primary succession proceeded through stages. Pioneer species arrived via seeds, spores, or adult stages that traveled over long distances.

The pioneer species are important because they help stabilize loose volcanic debris. This allowed later species to take hold. Historical studies in Krakatau and ongoing studies on Mount Saint Helens confirm that early stages of primary succession are slow, and that chance can play a large role in determining which species colonize at different times.

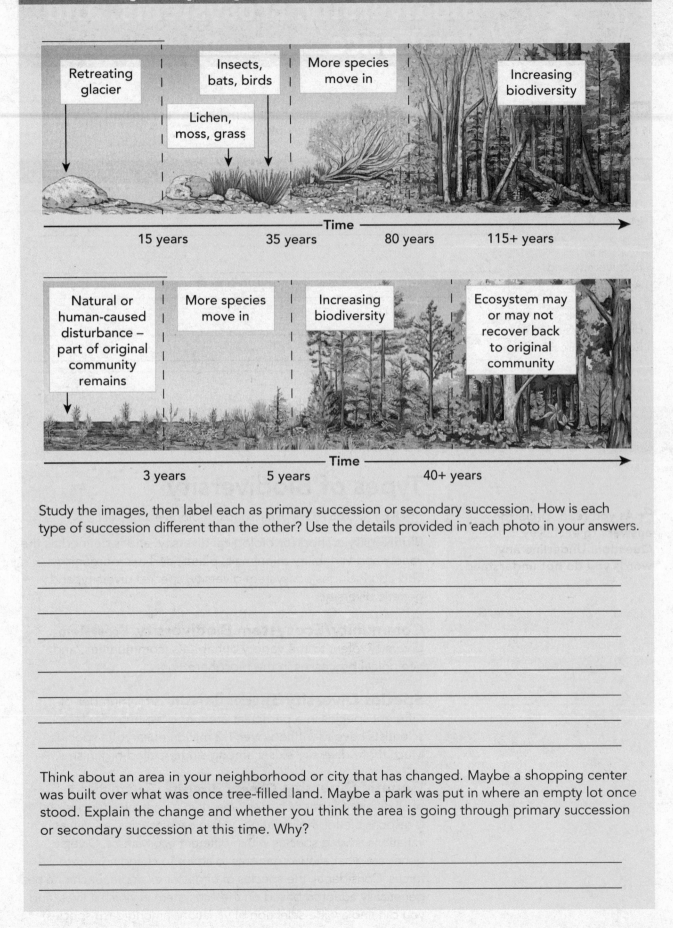

Retreating glacier

Insects, bats, birds

Lichen, moss, grass

More species move in

Increasing biodiversity

—— Time ——

15 years   35 years   80 years   115+ years

Natural or human-caused disturbance – part of original community remains

More species move in

Increasing biodiversity

Ecosystem may or may not recover back to original community

—— Time ——

3 years   5 years   40+ years

Study the images, then label each as primary succession or secondary succession. How is each type of succession different than the other? Use the details provided in each photo in your answers.

_____

_____

_____

_____

_____

_____

_____

_____

Think about an area in your neighborhood or city that has changed. Maybe a shopping center was built over what was once tree-filled land. Maybe a park was put in where an empty lot once stood. Explain the change and whether you think the area is going through primary succession or secondary succession at this time. Why?

_____

_____

LESSON 3 Biodiversity, Ecosystems, and Resilience

READING TOOL **Active Reading** As you read, list the many benefits that are gained when there is rich biodiversity within an ecosystem. Fill in the table below.

Benefit	Explanation
Biodiversity and Medicine	
Biodiversity and Agriculture	
Biodiversity and Ecosystem Resilience	

Lesson Summary

Types of Biodiversity

As you read, circle the answers to each Key Question. Underline any words you do not understand.

KEY QUESTION *What kinds of biodiversity exist?*

Biodiversity is short for biological diversity, and is defined as the variety and variability of animals, plants, and microorganisms. This also includes ecosystem diversity, species diversity, and genetic diversity.

Community/Ecosystem Biodiversity Ecosystem diversity refers to the variety of habitats, communities, and ecological processes in the biosphere.

Species Diversity Species diversity is the number of different species in a particular area, or biosphere. So far, scientists have identified over 1.2 million eukaryotic species. Much more diversity exists among single-celled organisms.

Genetic Diversity Genetic diversity refers to the total of all different forms of genes present in a particular species. It is responsible for the variations within each species, as well as variations among species within different ecosystems. Diverse genes are what allow organisms to adapt to changing external forces. Consider all the species of birds, for example. Each one has genetically adapted based on the ecosystem in which it lives, and you can find a wide selection of variations among each species.

Biodiversity Benefits

🔍 KEY QUESTION *What are the benefits of biodiversity?*

Biodiversity's benefits include offering invaluable contributions to medicine and agriculture, and enabling organisms and ecosystems to adapt to environmental change.

Biodiversity and Medicine A wide variety of plants and other organisms have long been used as medicines. Painkillers like aspirin and antibiotics like penicillin were among those first created from nature. Plant compounds are used to treat everything from depression to cancer.

Biodiversity and Agriculture Food or crop plants have closely-related versions in the wild. These wild plants may carry genes that promote disease resistance, pest resistance, or other useful traits. These genes could be transferred to crop plants through breeding to increase sustainability.

Biodiversity and Ecosystem Resilience An ecosystem's structure, stability, and function can be affected by changes to the biological diversity of an ecosystem. If you remember, the loss or reduction of a keystone species can dramatically affect the biodiversity and stability of an area. Additionally, some research shows that a decrease in species diversity in an ecosystem can also affect its resilience, or natural ability to recover after a disturbance.

Ecosystem Services and Biodiversity

🔍 KEY QUESTION *What are some important ecosystem services?*

Humans depend on healthy ecosystems in many ways. Ecosystem services are the benefits provided by ecosystems to humans. Important ecosystem services include production of food, cycling of nutrients, purifying water, storing carbon, regulating pests, pollinating crops, and buffering the effects of extreme weather events.

Food Production Diversity within ecosystems helps provide a resilient mix of food for livestock, while wild species preserve genes that may improve crops or livestock.

BUILD Vocabulary

biodiversity the total of the variety of organisms in the biosphere; also called biological diversity

ecosystem diversity variety of habitats, communities, and ecological processes in the biosphere

species diversity number of different species that makes up a particular area

genetic diversity sum total of all the different forms of genetic information carried by a particular species, or by all organisms on Earth

resilience a natural or human system's ability to recover after a disturbance

ecosystem services the benefits provided by ecosystems to humans

Related Words Another way to explain diversity is by calling it "variety." ☑ **Explain how biodiversity is different from genetic diversity.**

_____

_____

_____

_____

_____

Keystone species are important because they keep an entire ecosystem in balance. ☑ **What are two things that could happen to humans if keystone species died off and the Earth's biodiversity was significantly reduced?**

_____

_____

_____

_____

Nutrient Cycling and Soil Structure A resilient soil microbiome is one that nutrients are cycled through. This maintains soil fertility and structure as conditions change.

Purifying Water Soil microbiomes and other organisms play primary roles in filtering and purifying water.

Storing Carbon Healthy ecosystems with lots of plant life help remove carbon dioxide from the air. The healthier the ecosystem, the better it does this.

Regulating Pests and Pollinating Crops Diverse and resilient ecosystems keep the balance between predators and prey, and offer food and shelter to both.

Buffering Effects of Extreme Weather Events Diverse and resilient coastal wetlands or forests protect against erosion and shield shorelines from storms.

Visual Reading Tool: Ecosystem Services

Review the ecosystem services listed on the left side of the chart. List two benefits for humans for each ecosystem service.

Services Provided	Benefits to Humans
Purifying water	_____ _____ _____
Buffering effects of weather	_____ _____ _____
Pollinating	_____ _____ _____
Regulating pests	_____ _____ _____
Food production and Nutrient cycling	_____ _____ _____

Review Vocabulary

Match the vocabulary term to its definition.

1. _____ occurs in an area that was only partially destroyed by disturbances

a. primary succession

2. _____ occurs in an area in which no trace of a previous community is present

b. secondary succession

3. _____ where an organism lives and what it does "for a living"

c. niche

Fill in the blanks with the correct terms.

4. _____ is a symbiotic relationship in which one organism benefits and the other is neither helped nor harmed. _____ is a symbiotic relationship in which both species benefit from the relationship.

Review Key Questions

Provide evidence and details to support your answers.

5. Explain the similarities and differences between intraspecific competition among species and interspecific competition.

Similarities:

_____

_____

Differences:

_____

_____

6. Explain how pioneer species arrive in an area undergoing primary succession.

_____

_____

7. Explain what happens to species with lower resilience as compared to species with higher levels of resilience.

_____

_____

_____

Ecological Footprints

READING TOOL **Cause and Effect** Review Figure 7-1 and the lesson text to determine what makes up an individual's ecological footprint. For each of the items listed, identify two ways you can reduce the impact you make on the planet by reducing your ecological footprint.

Carbon Footprint Producers	Ways to Reduce
Energy use needed to create your home	
Energy use needed to sustain your home	
Agricultural processes used to create your food	
Processes used to get fresh water for you	
Processes used to take care of your waste products (trash, sewage)	
Processes used to create products you use	
Processes used to sustain your entertainment	
Fossil fuels used to power your vehicles	

Our Changing Ecological Footprints

KEY QUESTION *How do ecological footprints of typical Americans compare to the global average?*

Human population is climbing towards 9 billion. Because of this, changes we have made to Earth—so that we could feed, clothe, house, and entertain ourselves—are negatively affecting its atmosphere, climate, and oceans. This is why understanding, controlling, and adapting to human-caused global change are the greatest scientific challenges of this century. The view of global systems and model of global change we are developing will help us understand what humans are doing to Earth—and how we can slow down these changes.

Ecological Footprints Each person has an **ecological footprint**, which is the total area of healthy land and water ecosystems needed to provide the resources each person uses. This includes resources like energy, food, water, and shelter, as well as the production of wastes like sewage trash and greenhouse gases.

National and Global Ecological Footprints There is no universally-standard formula for calculating ecological footprints. To calculate a country's ecological footprint, scientists determine an average citizen's footprint, then multiply that by the country's population. We can learn a lot about how many resources a country uses by studying their ecological footprint. We can also learn about how many resources we use ourselves. According to some calculations, the average American has an ecological footprint over four times the global average. This ecological footprint is more than twice the size of an average person living in England or Japan, and more than six times the size of the average person in China. That incredible amount of human activity drives changes in global systems that affect environments worldwide. Learning how to reduce our ecological footprint is one of our greatest challenges.

The Age of Humans

KEY QUESTION *What is the Anthropocene?*

Humans' status on "spaceship Earth" has drastically changed since the Industrial Revolution of the 1800s, when we began harnessing the power of fossil fuels to run machinery.

As you read, circle the answers to each Key Question. Underline any words you do not understand.

BUILD Vocabulary

ecological footprint total amount of functioning ecosystem needed to both provide the resources a human population uses, and to absorb the wastes that population generates

anthromes globally significant ecological patterns created by long-term interactions between humans and ecosystems

Related Words Ecology is the scientific study of interactions among organisms and between organisms and their environment.
☑ **Why would a scientist studying ecological footprints be called an "ecologist"?**

_____

_____

_____

_____

_____

_____

READING TOOL

Connect to Visuals

Examine Figure 7-4 in your textbook to learn about the different anthromes that make up the continental United States.
☑ **Find your state on the map and list the different anthromes that exist there.**

_____

The Great Acceleration The 1950s was a period called "The Great Acceleration," when humans impact on planet Earth began greatly accelerating. Fewer people died and more people were born thanks to scientific advancements.

The Anthropocene Also called "the age of humans", the Anthropocene is the period during which human activity has become the major cause of global change.

Anthromes: Human-Altered Biomes Anthropogenic biomes, or **anthromes**, are globally significant ecological patterns created by long-term interactions between humans and ecosystems. These have replaced traditional biomes over much of the Earth.

Visual Reading Tool: The Impact of Humans

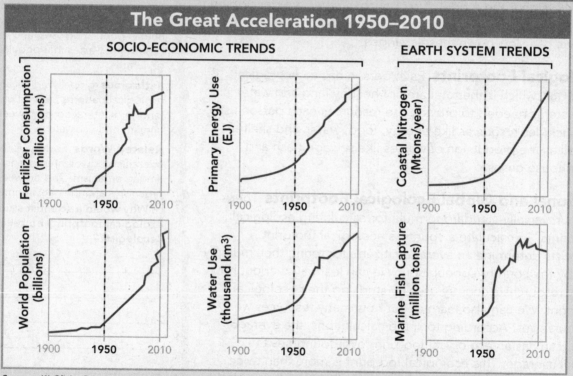

The Great Acceleration 1950–2010

Sources: (1) Olivier Rousseau, IFA; IFA database. (2) A Grubler, International Institute for Applied Systems Analysis (IIASA); Grubler et al. (2012). (3) M Flörke, Centre for Environmental Systems Research, University of Kassel; Flörke et al. (2013); aus der Beek et al. (2010); Alcamo et al. (2003). (4) HYDE database; Klein Goldewijk et al. (2010). (5) Mackenzie et al. (2002). (6) Data are from the FAO Fisheries and Aquaculture Department online database (Food and Agriculture Organization-FIGIS (FAO-FIGIS), 2013).

Review the charts and answer the following questions.

1. Describe the trends for world population and water use and compare them. Why do you think these trends are similar or different?

_____

_____

2. What other resources would also increase because of the increase in world population? Use the graph to justify your answer.

_____

_____

LESSON 2 Causes and Effects of Global Change

READING TOOL **Main Idea and Details** For each heading in this lesson, explain the main idea in the table below. Then, list details that support and explain the main idea.

Heading	Main Idea	Details
Human Causes of Global Change		
Changing Atmosphere and Climate		
Changes in Land Use		
Pollution		

Lesson Summary

Human Causes of Global Change

🔍 **KEY QUESTION** *How do human activities change the atmosphere and climate?*

The Understanding Global Change (UGC) model begins with global systems as they exist on Earth. Then, we add in human causes of global change and ecological interactions and processes in the biosphere (or non-human causes) of global change. Current human activities, like over-harvesting some species or changing the way we use land, stress ecosystems and the organisms living in them in ways that threaten biodiversity and ecosystem services. Often, single activities affect several global systems, rather than just one.

🔍 As you read, circle the answers to each Key Question. Underline any words you do not understand.

Atmospheric
carbon dioxide
(CO_2)

① _____

② _____

Dissolved
carbon dioxide + Water → Carbonic acid

Dissolved
carbon dioxide + Water + Carbonate ion → Two bicarbonate ions

③ _____

higher pH = less acidic

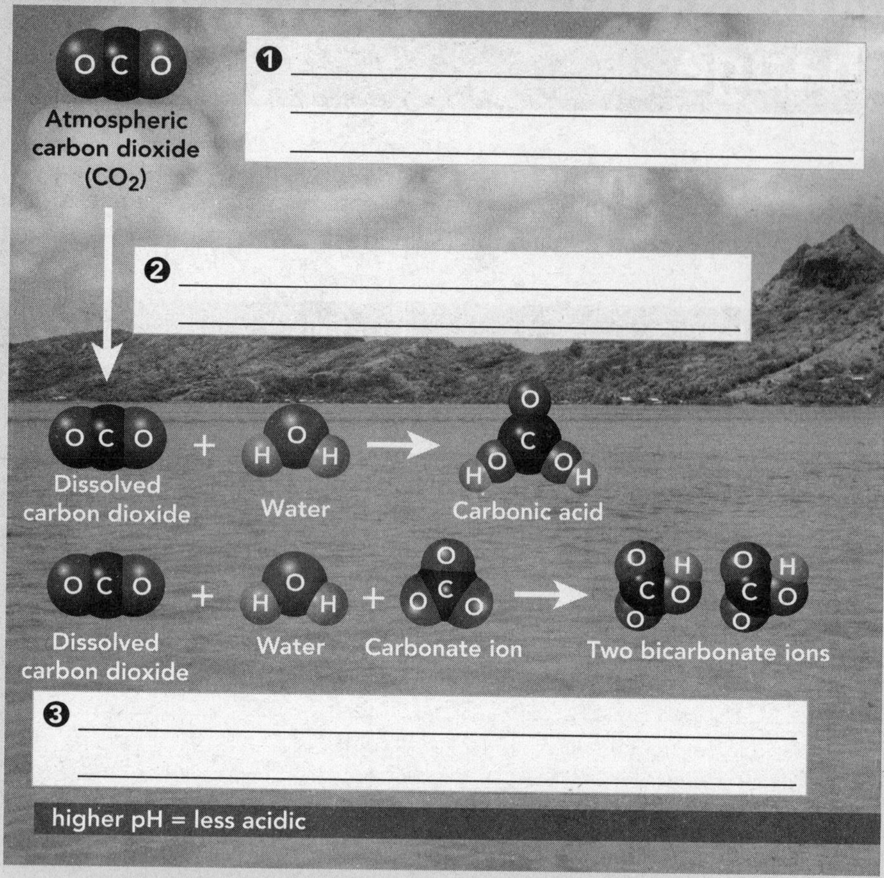

1. Describe how the diagram shows the ocean acidification process.

2. How do carbon dioxide levels change ocean chemistry?

_____
_____
_____
_____
_____
_____

BUILD Vocabulary

climate change measurable long-term changes in averages of temperature, clouds, winds, precipitation, and the frequency of extreme weather events

global warming increase in the average temperatures on Earth

Make Connections

You have learned that the environmental conditions on our planet usually remain stable, but have been changing since humans have begun to flourish and change our planet. One of the first noticeable changes on our planet was global warming. ☑ **What is the connection between global warming and climate change?**

_____
_____

Changing Atmosphere and Climate

KEY QUESTION *How do changes in the atmosphere drive climate change and other changes in global systems?*

Human activities that affect global systems are changing Earth's atmosphere faster than it has changed historically.

Fossil Fuels and the Atmosphere Scientists have confirmed that atmospheric carbon dioxide levels have been increasing since the Industrial Revolution.

Climate Change Ocean Acidification, Nitrogen Enrichment From Fossil Fuels Climate change is defined as measurable long-term changes in averages of temperature, clouds, winds, precipitation, and the frequency of extreme weather events. Global warming, or the increases in average global temperatures, is caused by climate change. Acid rain damages plant leaves and root systems by releasing metals from some soils. Ocean acidification is caused when carbon dioxide released from fossil-fuel burning dissolves in seawater and turns into acid. Nitrogen released from burning fossil fuels travels through the air and water falling far from its source and causing algal blooms.

Agriculture and the Atmosphere Methane is produced and released through cattle farming and the cultivation of rice in flooded paddies. Methane is a more powerful greenhouse gas than carbon dioxide.

Changes in Land Use

🔍 **KEY QUESTION** *How do the ways we use land drive change in global systems?*

Human activity has transformed about three-quarters of Earth's surface to provide food, housing, and energy.

Deforestation/Reforestation Healthy forests hold soil in place, protect freshwater quality, absorb carbon dioxide, and moderate local climates. When forests are lost, those ecosystems services disappear.

Deforestation Deforestation can affect water quality in streams and rivers. In mountainous areas, deforestation increases soil erosion, which can cause landslides.

Natural Regrowth Through Succession Many forests east of the Mississippi River are secondary forests that grew back after primary forests were cut. This is called secondary succession.

Reforestation Scientifically-guided reforestation, or replanting of forests, can replace areas that have been cleared of trees. Reforestation contributes to dependable, clean drinking water availability.

Agriculture Today, agricultural activities cover more of Earth's land surface than any other human activity.

Monoculture Monoculture involves planting large areas with a single highly-productive crop year after year. It requires large amounts of fertilizer and pesticide. When large areas are used for grazing, or to grow monocultures for long periods, fertilizers and pesticides can change soil structure and microbiomes in ways that degrade soil and prevent secondary succession.

Nitrogen Enrichment From Agriculture Today's fertilizer manufacturing and application has more than doubled the amount of biologically active nitrogen cycling through the biosphere, dramatically changing the natural nitrogen cycle.

Development/Urbanization Large amounts of sewage caused by urbanization can disrupt nutrient cycles and stimulate growth of toxic or ecologically damaging blooms of bacteria and algae.

Habitat Loss, Fragmentation, and Restoration Human-caused changes in natural habitats occur through habitat loss and fragmentation, or through restoration.

BUILD Vocabulary

deforestation destruction of forests

monoculture farming strategy of planting a single, highly productive crop year after year

Prefixes The prefix *de-* indicates removal, separation, or reversal. In the case of deforestation, the *de-* indicates the removal of trees.

☑ **What other words with the prefix *de* can you think of that indicate the removal of something helpful to humans?**

_____

_____

_____

READING TOOL

Make Connections

For many years, farmers only planted one crop type in the same field year after year. This monoculture has been shown to be harmful to the environment.

☑ **How should farmers change the agricultural production methods to avoid these dangers?**

_____

_____

_____

_____

_____

_____

BUILD Vocabulary

invasive species any non-native species whose introduction causes, or is likely to cause, economic harm, environmental harm, or harm to human health

pollutant harmful material that can enter the biosphere through the land, air, or water

ozone layer atmospheric layer in which ozone gas is relatively concentrated; protects life on Earth from harmful ultraviolet rays in sunlight

~~smog~~ gray-brown haze formed by a mixture of chemicals

biological magnification the increasing concentration of a harmful substance in organisms at higher trophic levels in a food chain or food web

Using Prior Knowledge Pollutants are harmful materials that can enter our ecosystem through a variety of ways. ☑ **Name three substances or products you use regularly that could be considered pollutants if they got into our air, water, or soil.**

_____

_____

_____

_____

Habitat Loss Habitats can be lost to urban, suburban, or industrial development, and to logging or agriculture. Species living there will move away or die off.

Habitat Fragmentation Habitat fragmentation causes biodiversity loss and makes ecosystems vulnerable to disturbances.

Habitat Restoration The right conditions and a lot of work are needed to restore damaged habitats, but it can be done. Ecological restoration aims to re-create conditions closely resembling the original ecosystem.

Hunting and Fishing Humans have hunted species to extinction and overfishing has caused significant declines in worldwide fish populations.

Invasive Species An **invasive species** is any non-native species whose introduction causes, or is likely to cause, economic harm, environmental harm, or harm to human health.

Pollution

🔍 **KEY QUESTION** _What kinds of pollutants are drivers of global change?_

A **pollutant** is any harmful material created as a result of human activity and released into the environment.

CFCs and Stratospheric Ozone (CFCs) are industrially-produced gases causing the destruction of the stratosphere, or upper section of our atmosphere. This layer, called the **ozone layer**, absorbs ultraviolet light and acts like global sunscreen.

Ground-Level Ozone **Smog** is a haze formed by chemical reactions among pollutants released by industrial processes and automobile exhaust.

Industrial and Agricultural Pollution Wastes from manufacturing and energy productions are discarded into air, water and soil. These chemicals enter the water supply as runoff.

Biological Magnification The process in which pollutants are concentrated as they pass through trophic levels of the food chain is called **biological magnification**.

DDT DDT was a widely-used pesticide that caused disastrous effects in organisms after entering the water supply, including reduction in fish-eating bird populations.

PCBs PCBs are toxic chemicals causing water pollution. Banned in the 1970s, they are still causing issues in our environment today.

Heavy Metals Heavy metals accumulate in food webs and pose health threats.

LESSON 3
Measuring and Responding to Change

READING TOOL **Cause and Effect** Complete the graphic organizer with the possible effects and possible solutions of each identified climate change. Several answers are filled in for you.

Identified Climate Changes		Possible Effects	Possible Solutions
Data shows that global temperatures are rising.	Species are forced to move to different areas to survive or face extinction.	Some species may not survive or may become extinct; species will need to adapt for survival.	Reduce rising global temperatures by reducing carbon emissions.
	Extreme weather events will occur more often.		
Data shows that global sea levels are rising.	Coastlines are receding.		
Data shows that global sea temperatures are rising.	Marine life is being negatively affected.		

⚲ As you read, circle the answers to each Key Question. Underline any words you do not understand.

READING TOOL

Active Reading

The IPCC has concluded that the atmosphere and the oceans are warming based upon climate data that has been collected over many years. ☑ **Based upon previous data, what are scientists predicting for the future regarding the average temperature on our planet?**

_____

_____

_____

_____

_____

_____

_____

_____

Climate Change: The Data

⚲ **KEY QUESTION** *What evidence supports the claims that the climate is changing?*

When a 5300-year-old ancient human emerged from melting glacial ice, the Worldwatch Institute noted to the world that our ancestors were telling us the Earth is getting warmer. Although it was a dramatic announcement, scientists needed data to back up that claim.

IPCC Climate Data The Intergovernmental Panel on Climate Change (IPCC) provides the world with the most reliable climate data available. This international organization was established to provide the best possible scientific information on climate change. Their reports contain data with analyses that are agreed upon and accepted by over 2500 international climate scientists and all governments participating in the research. They released their most recent report in 2014, which made a strong case that our global climate is undergoing change—and that human activity influences climate.

Climate Changes Through data collection and analyses, scientists have found that both the atmosphere and the oceans have been warming; that sea levels are rising; and that arctic sea ice, glaciers, and snow cover are all decreasing.

Human Activity Influences Change The latest IPCC report (from 2014) states firmly that "Human influence on the climate system is clear, and recent anthropogenic emissions of greenhouse gases are the highest in history." This states, in no uncertain terms, that humans are partly responsible for changes in our climate.

Modeling With Data Scientific researchers use data to construct computer-based models that help predict future climate trends. The most widely-accepted of these models predict that average global temperatures will rise somewhere between 0.3 and 1.7 degrees Celsius (or up to 3 degrees Fahrenheit) by the end of the twenty-first century if all the world's countries agree on very strong measures to curb greenhouse gas emissions. If countries continue to produce greenhouse gases at the rates they have been in recent years, global temperatures could rise somewhere between 2.6 and 4.8 degrees Celsius (or up to 4 degrees Fahrenheit) by the year 2100. Although seemingly small, these changes represent major consequences for the Earth and its inhabitants.

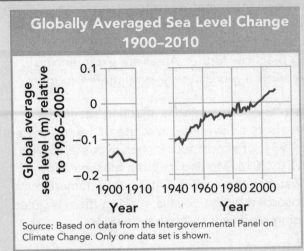

Globally Averaged Sea Level Change 1900–2010

Source: Based on data from the Intergovernmental Panel on Climate Change. Only one data set is shown.

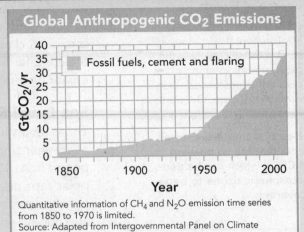

Global Anthropogenic CO₂ Emissions

Quantitative information of CH_4 and N_2O emission time series from 1850 to 1970 is limited.
Source: Adapted from Intergovernmental Panel on Climate Change.

1. On each chart, circle the date when the measured data steeply increased. How do these two dates relate to each other?

_____

2. What caused the sudden increase in CO_2 emissions?

_____

3. What causes sea levels to rise?

_____

4. How are CO_2 emissions and sea level rise related?

_____

_____

Climate Change Impacts

⚲ KEY QUESTION *What are some impacts of climate change?*

The 2014 IPCC report concludes that "changes in climate have caused impacts on natural and human systems on all continents and across oceans." Climate change includes much more than just the direct effects of global warming. Total rainfall and seasonal distribution of rainfall are changing. Heat waves are expected to become longer and more intense. Many areas will experience more episodes of extreme heat and storms. The temperatures are rising fastest in the Arctic Circle.

Ecological Impacts Small changes in climate or temperature can significantly affect organisms and ecosystems. Organisms each have a range of tolerance for temperature, humidity, and rainfall. If conditions move outside those tolerance zones, the organism must move to a more suitable location, or face extinction. Life cycles in many plants and animals are triggered by seasonal temperature changes, and data confirms that over 1700 species are experiencing shifts in these life cycles due to global temperature increases.

READING TOOL

Connect to Visuals

In 7.1, we saw a chart showing that America has one of the highest ecological footprints in the world. Compare that with Figure 7-19.

☑ **What connection could there be with increased temperatures in the Arctic Circle and the relative closeness of America?**

_____

_____

_____

_____

_____

_____

_____

_____

Sequence of Events

There have been many examples of environmental successes in the past. This usually involves the IPCC or governments creating plans to curb emissions based upon environmental data. Over time, a measurable improvement is seen.

☑ **Describe the sequence of events that led to phasing out CFCs, which has helped stratospheric ozone to begin recovering.**

_____

_____

_____

_____

_____

_____

_____

_____

_____

_____

_____

Impacts on Human Systems Changes in temperature and rainfall have begun to negatively affect crop cycles, like corn and wheat. Water availability is also changing and is expected to continue to become less available, directly affecting farming practices further. Areas are experiencing earlier or smaller snow run-offs as well as summer droughts.

Sea Level Rise Global warming is affecting sea levels. These levels have risen, on average, at a rate of 1.8 millimeters every year since 1961, or almost four inches over the 55-year period from 1961 to 2016. Melting ice from glaciers and polar caps add water to the oceans. Extra heat retained in the atmosphere is absorbed by the oceans, making them warmer and adding to rising sea levels through expansion.

Designing Solutions

🔍 **KEY QUESTION** _What is the role of science in responding to climate change?_

One of the goals of science is to help us understand our natural world and to apply that knowledge to improve the human condition. When scientific data is properly collected, analyzed, and applied, it helps us make important decisions that could positively affect the future of humanity. It also makes sense to note that when it is not collected, analyzed, or applied properly, it could negatively impact the future of our planet. Scientific research can have a positive impact on the global environment by (1) recognizing a problem in the environment, whether from human or other causes, (2) gathering data to document and analyze that problem and identify its cause, and then (3) guiding changes in our behavior based on scientific understanding.

Environmental Successes Research is vital for guiding us toward positive results on climate change. Several successes we've seen through science-applied changes include removing lead from gasoline, which has helped reduce water pollution, and the banning of CFCs, which has helped to repair the depleted ozone.

Climate Change Challenge Of all the ecological challenges humanity has faced, climate change is the most complicated and difficult to fix. Since the world still depends heavily on the burning of fossil fuels and methane-producing agriculture, efforts to address climate change will require major changes in the systems supporting human life. It is up to government policy-makers around the world to use science to inform their decisions on this vital issue.

LESSON 4 Sustainability

READING TOOL **Active Reading** For each section of this lesson, take notes on how sustainable development can be achieved.

Lesson Section	Connection to Sustainable Development
United Nations Sustainable Development Goals	
Renewable Resources	
Nonrenewable Resources	
Innovation	
Resilience	

Lesson Summary

Sustainable Development

🔍 **KEY QUESTION** *What criteria can be used to evaluate whether development is sustainable?*

Ecological science can help guide us in providing for human needs without causing long-term environmental harm, but science alone is not enough. Global planning requires input from economics, sociology, and other disciplines to affect the most positive change. Using resources in ways that preserve ecosystem services is called **sustainable development**.

🔍 As you read, circle the answers to each Key Question. Underline any words you do not understand.

BUILD Vocabulary

sustainable development strategy for using natural resources without depleting them and for providing human needs without causing long-term environmental harm

Sustainable development recognizes links between ecology, or the natural world, and economics, or the costs of processes. Sustainable development includes three nested spheres: Earth's life support system, society, and the economy. Our economy operates within our society, and our practices must be affordable for those operating those practices, as well as for those benefitting from them. For development to be sustainable, it needs to be cost-effective and non-harmful to our natural world.

United Nations Sustainable Development Goals

The United Nations has set and promoted 17 Sustainable Development Goals. Sustainable development should provide for human needs while preserving ecosystem services. It should cause no long-term harm to soil, water, and climate. It should consume as little energy and material as possible. Finally, sustainable development must take into account human needs and economic systems. It must do more than simply allow humans to survive; it should help them improve their situation.

Visual Reading Tool: Explaining Sustainable Development

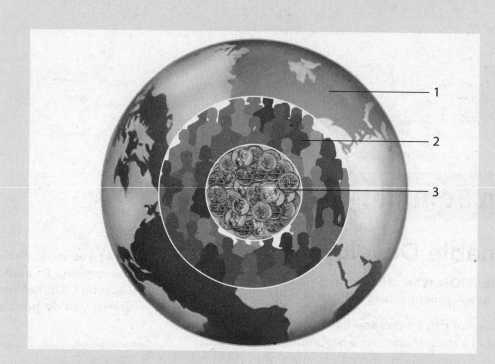

Identify each link in the chain of sustainable development.

1. _____   2. _____   3. _____

Explain why each link is equally important to sustainable development.

_____

_____

_____

Renewable Resources Sustainable development focuses on careful use of renewable ecosystem services. A **renewable resource** can be produced or replaced by a healthy ecosystem. Drinkable water provided by the Earth and filtered by wetlands is an example. If human-caused environmental changes impact ecosystems, water quality may fail. When this happens, mechanical or chemical treatment must occur to provide safe drinking water.

Nonrenewable Resources If natural processes cannot replenish resources within a reasonable time, they are considered **nonrenewable resources**.

Innovation Human intelligence and scientific creativity have improved our lives in many dramatic ways. Technology won't automatically solve our problems, unless it is guided by sustainable goals and practices. To evolve successfully, we need to be constantly innovating – new ideas and new engineering solutions that provide necessary services at reasonable costs. Solar panels are one example of human innovation that solves a problem (burning fossil fuels for energy). Although they've been on the market for over twenty years, before now, they were too expensive for most people to purchase. Engineering and manufacturing innovations of solar panels have dramatically lowered the price, and they are just now becoming affordable for the average consumer. Another example of an innovation is wind turbines that generate energy from wind, a renewable resource. Technological improvements in wind turbines have created smaller units that harness greater levels of energy.

Resilience Ecological scientists and many government agencies, like the US Military for example, recognize that life in the Anthropocene, or "age of humans", involves a high level of unpredictability. Some of that unpredictability involves loss of ecosystem services from biodiversity loss. More unpredictability will come from potential extreme weather events in the future. This is why sustainable development must include the element of **resilience**, which is the ability to deal with change and move on. Sustainable development practices must be flexible enough to deal with unknown environmental stresses and events, like cold snaps, droughts, floods, heat waves, and intense storms. Examples of solid resilience are US cities that are hit by strong hurricanes. These areas see loss of human life and major property damage, but are resilient enough (so far) to recover afterwards, even if it takes several years. Examples of areas with less resilience to hurricane damage are Haiti and Honduras. They have experienced a much greater loss of human life and more widespread destruction of property due to hurricanes. Often, this destruction is beyond their ability to handle on their own, and they must call for global assistance to recover.

> **BUILD Vocabulary**
>
> **renewable resource** resource that can be produced or replaced by healthy ecosystem functions
>
> **nonrenewable resource** resource that cannot be replenished by a natural process within a reasonable amount of time
>
> **resilience** the ability to deal with change and move on
>
> **Related Words** A resource is anything that is necessary for life.
> ☑ **Name three items that are necessary to your life that are considered renewable resources.**
>
> _____
>
> _____

Review Vocabulary

Match the vocabulary term to its definition.

1. _____ anthromes

   a. farming strategy of planting a single productive crop in the same field year after year

2. _____ monoculture

   b. an organism or community's ability to deal with change and successfully move on

3. _____ biological magnification

   c. ecological patterns created by human interactions with ecosystems

4. _____ resilience

   d. increasing concentration of harmful substances progressing through food chains

Fill in the blanks with the correct terms.

5. _____ are resources that can be reproduced or replaced by natural processes, while _____ cannot be reproduced or replaced by natural processes in a reasonable amount of time.

Review Key Questions

Provide evidence and details to support your answers.

6. Explain how the average Americans' ecological footprint compares to the average ecological footprint of people in other countries.

   _____

   _____

7. Identify two unsustainable agricultural practices currently in use in the United States.

   _____

8. Identify three ways unsustainable development practices have contributed to climate change.

   _____

   _____

   _____

9. Explain how the element of resilience affects two of the key factors needed for sustainable development: environment and society.

   _____

   _____

   _____

READING TOOL **Main Idea and Details** As you read your textbook, identify the main ideas along with details or evidence that supports the main ideas. Use the lesson headings to organize the main ideas and details. One example is entered for you. Record your work in the table.

Heading	Main Idea	Details/Evidence
The Discovery of the Cell		
Early Microscopes	The invention of the microscope led to the discovery of cells.	Microscopes show that cork consists of cells and that there are organisms present in pond water.
The Cell Theory		
Exploring the Cell		
Light Microscopes		
Electron Microscopes		
• Transmission Electron Microscopes		
• Scanning Electron Microscopes		
Prokaryotes and Eukaryotes		
Prokaryotes		
Eukaryotes		

The Discovery of the Cell

⚲ KEY QUESTION *What are the main points of the cell theory?*

The smallest living unit of any organism is a cell. Cells were unknown until the microscope was invented.

Early Microscopes Eyeglass makers in the late 1500s discovered that using several lenses in combination could magnify objects. They used their lenses to build the first microscopes. In 1665, Robert Hooke used a microscope to look at a slice of cork from a plant. The cork appeared to be made of many tiny empty chambers that Hooke called "cells." Around the same time Anton van Leeuwenhoek used a microscope to look at pond water. With the microscope, he saw many tiny living organisms in the water.

The Cell Theory In 1838, Matthias Schleiden stated that all plants are made of cells. In 1855, Theodor Schwann stated that all animals are made of cells. In 1885 Rudolf Virchow stated that new cells are produced only from the division of existing cells. These discoveries are summarized in the cell theory. The cell theory includes three main ideas:
- ➤ All living things are made up of cells.
- ➤ Cells are the basic units of structure and function in living things.
- ➤ New cells are produced from existing cells.

Exploring the Cell

⚲ KEY QUESTION *How do microscopes work?*

Modern biologists still use microscopes to study the cell. Microscopes work by using beams of light or beams of electrons to produce magnified images.

Light Microscopes You may be familiar with the compound light microscope. A light microscope uses light passing through a specimen and two lenses to form an image. The first lens, called the objective lens, is just above the specimen. The second lens, called the ocular lens, magnifies the image further. Due to the nature of light, light microscopes clearly magnify an object only about 1000 times. Chemical stains or dyes are used to help make parts of cells visible. Some dyes are fluorescent, meaning they give off light of a particular color.

Electron Microscopes Electron microscopes use beams of electrons instead of light. A light microscope can view something as small as 1 millionth of a meter. An electron microscope can view something as small as 1 billionth of a meter, such as viruses or a DNA molecule.

⚲ As you read, circle the answers to each Key Question. Underline any words you do not understand.

BUILD Vocabulary

cell basic unit of all forms of life

cell theory fundamental concept of biology that states that all living things are composed of cells; that cells are the basic units of structure and function in living things; and that new cells are produced from existing cells

cell membrane thin, flexible barrier that surrounds all cells; regulates what enters and leaves the cell

nucleus in cells, structure that contains the cell's genetic material in the form of DNA

eukaryote organism whose cells contain a nucleus

prokaryote unicellular organism that lacks a nucleus

Root Words *Karyo* comes from the Greek *karyon*, meaning "nut" or "kernel." It is used in words that refer to the nucleus. *Pro-* is a prefix that means "before," so prokaryotes have been around since before the nucleus appeared in living organisms.

☑ **What structure distinguishes eukaryotes from prokaryotes?**

Samples viewed on an electron microscope must be placed in a vacuum. Therefore, an electron microscope can only be used to examine nonliving samples. Images are black and white, but computers are used to add "false color" to structures.

Transmission Electron Microscopes Beams of electrons must pass through the sample, so samples of cells and tissues must be sliced extremely thin. Images appear flat and two-dimensional.

Scanning Electron Microscopes A beam of electrons scans the surface of a specimen, so samples do not have to be cut into thin slices. Images appear three-dimensional.

Prokaryotes and Eukaryotes

🔍 **KEY QUESTION** *How do prokaryotic and eukaryotic cells differ?*

Most cells range from 5 to 50 micrometers in diameter. All cells are surrounded by a thin flexible barrier called the **cell membrane** (also called the plasma membrane). Cells fall into two categories, depending on whether they contain a nucleus. The **nucleus** (plural: nuclei) is a large membrane-enclosed structure that contains genetic material in the form of DNA. **Eukaryotes** (yoo KAR ee ohts) are cells that have nuclei. **Prokaryotes** (pro KAR ee ohts) are cells that do not have nuclei.

Prokaryotes Prokaryotic cells do not enclose their genetic material within a nucleus. They are generally smaller and simpler than eukaryotic cells. Bacteria are prokaryotes. Prokaryotes carry out all of the activities associated with living things. Prokaryotes were the first photosynthetic organisms on Earth.

Eukaryotes In eukaryotic cells, the nucleus separates the genetic material from the rest of the cell. Most eukaryotic cells contain many structures and internal membranes. Some eukaryotes are unicellular organisms called protists. Others form multicellular organisms—plants, animals, and fungi. In multicellular organisms, cells are specialized and usually work together to perform specific tasks.

READING TOOL

Compare and Contrast
Transmission and scanning electron microscopy are both tools to examine biological structures. Each creates a very different type of image. ☑ **How do the final images of transmission and scanning electron microscopy differ?**

_____

_____

_____

_____

Visual Reading Tool: Prokaryotes and Eukaryotes

Read the section on prokaryotes and eukaryotes to identify the similarities and differences of each cell type. Use a green pencil to circle similarities, a blue pencil to circle prokaryotic cell characteristics, and a red pencil to circle eukaryotic cell characteristics. Then complete the table below.

	Prokaryotic Cell	Eukaryotic Cell
Cell membrane		yes
Nucleus		
Cell size	smaller	
Complexity		
Example of organism with this cell type		

LESSON 2 / Cell Structure

READING TOOL **Connect to Visuals** As you read, use the figures and diagrams to help you identify and describe each part of the cell, and what the function that part performs. Complete the graphic organizer.

Cellular Structure	Form and Function
Nucleus	
Ribosomes	
Endoplasmic reticulum	
Golgi apparatus	
Vacuoles	
Lysosomes	
Cytoskeleton	
Chloroplasts	
Mitochondria	
Cell wall	
Cell membrane	

Lesson Summary

Cell Organization

⚲ KEY QUESTION *What is the role of the cell nucleus?*

Eukaryotic cells can be divided into the nucleus and the cytoplasm. The **cytoplasm** is the part of the cell outside the nucleus. The interior of a prokaryotic cell, which lacks a nucleus, is also called the cytoplasm. Eukaryotic cells also have many specialized structures that are called **organelles**, which means "little organs."

Comparing the Cell to a Factory A eukaryotic cell functions much like a factory. The different organelles of a cell are like specialized machines and assembly lines. Organelles follow instructions and create biological molecules, like the people and machines in a factory create different products.

The Nucleus The nucleus is the control center of the cell. The nucleus contains nearly all of the DNA in the cell and, with it, the coded instructions for making proteins and other important molecules. In prokaryotic cells, there is no nucleus, and the DNA is found in the cytoplasm.

The nucleus is surrounded by the nuclear envelope, which is composed of two membranes. The nuclear envelope has thousands of nuclear pores, which allow material such as proteins and other molecules to move in and out of the nucleus. The genetic material in the nucleus is found in chromosomes. Most nuclei also contain a nucleolus, which is a region of the nucleus where ribosome assembly begins.

Organelles That Build Proteins

⚲ KEY QUESTION *What organelles help make and transport proteins and other macromolecules?*

Much of the cell is devoted to producing proteins, which are responsible for the synthesis of other macromolecules such as lipids and carbohydrates.

Ribosomes Proteins are assembled on ribosomes. **Ribosomes** are small particles of RNA and protein found throughout the cytoplasm in eukaryotes and prokaryotes. Ribosomes produce proteins by following instructions that come from DNA.

⚲ As you read, circle the answers to each Key Question. Underline any words you do not understand.

BUILD Vocabulary

cytoplasm fluid portion of the cell outside the nucleus

organelle specialized structure that performs important cellular functions within a eukaryotic cell

ribosome cell organelle consisting of RNA and protein found throughout the cytoplasm in a cell; the site of protein synthesis

Related Words The English word *organ* comes from the Latin word "organon," meaning tool or instrument. ☑ **Using this information, explain how an organ and organelles are related.**

_____

_____

_____

_____

_____

_____

_____

endoplasmic reticulum internal membrane system found in eukaryotic cells; place where lipid components of the cell membrane are assembled

Golgi apparatus organelle in cells that modifies, sorts, and packages proteins and other materials from the endoplasmic reticulum for storage in the cell or release outside the cell

vacuole cell organelle that stores materials such as water, salts, proteins, and carbohydrates

lysosome cell organelle that breaks down lipids, carbohydrates, and proteins into small molecules that can used by the rest of the cell

cytoskeleton network of protein filaments in a eukaryotic cell that gives the cell its shape and internal organization and is involved in movement

Chloroplast cell organelle that converts energy from sunlight into chemical energy through the process of photosynthesis

mitochondrion cell organelle that converts the chemical energy stored in food into compounds that are more convenient for the cell to use

cell wall strong, supporting layer around the cell membrane in most prokaryotes and some eukaryotes

Related Words *Plasm* is a root that appears in many biological terms related to cells and living things. It comes from a Greek word that means "something molded."

☑ **What two vocabulary terms in this lesson have *plasm* as a root?**

_____

_____

Endoplasmic Reticulum Eukaryotic cells contain an internal membrane system called the **endoplasmic reticulum** (en doh PLAZ mik reh TIK yoo lum), or ER. The portion of the ER involved in making proteins is called the rough ER, due to the ribosomes on its surface. Proteins made on the rough ER include those that will be released, or secreted, from the cell; many membrane proteins; and proteins destined for other specialized locations within the cell. Other proteins are made on ribosomes that are not attached to membranes.

The other part of the ER is called the smooth ER because ribosomes are not found on its surface. The smooth ER produces lipids and is involved in the detoxification of drugs and the synthesis of carbohydrates.

Golgi Apparatus In eukaryotic cells, proteins produced in the rough ER move into the **Golgi apparatus**, which appears as a stack of flattened membranes. The proteins are bundled into tiny membrane-enclosed structures called vesicles that bud from the ER and carry the proteins to the Golgi apparatus. The Golgi apparatus modifies, sorts, and packages proteins and other materials from the endoplasmic reticulum for storage in the cell or release from the cell.

Organelles That Store, Clean Up, and Support

🔍 **KEY QUESTION** *What are the functions of vacuoles, lysosomes, and the cytoskeleton?*

Vacuoles, vesicles, lysosomes, and the cytoskeleton represent the cellular factory's storage space, cleanup crew, and support structures.

Vacuoles and Vesicles Many cells contain **vacuoles**, which are large, saclike, membrane-enclosed structures. Vacuoles store materials like water, salts, proteins, and carbohydrates. Many plant cells have a single, large central vacuole. The pressure of the liquid in the central vacuole helps plants to support structures such as leaves and stems. In addition to vacuoles, most eukaryotic cells contain smaller membrane-enclosed structures called vesicles. Vesicles store and move materials between organelles, as well as to and from the cell surface.

Lysosomes **Lysosomes** break down lipids, proteins, and carbohydrates into small molecules that can be used by the cell. Lysosomes also break down and remove organelles and other things in the cell that are no longer needed. Lysosomes are found in animal cells and in some plant cells.

The Cytoskeleton Eukaryotic cells have a <u>network</u> of protein filaments called the **cytoskeleton**. The cytoskeleton helps to transport materials within the cell. The cytoskeleton helps the cell maintain its shape and is involved in movement.

Microfilaments Microfilaments are threadlike structures made from a protein called actin. They form a tough, flexible framework that supports the cell. Microfilaments also help cells move.

Microtubules Microtubules are hollow structures made from proteins called tubulins. In some cells they maintain cell shape. They are important in cell division, forming a structure called the mitotic spindle that separates chromosomes. Organelles called centrioles are also made from tubulins. Centrioles help to organize cell division in animal cells, but are not found in plant cells. Microtubules also help to build projections from the cell surface such as cilia (singular: *cilium*) and flagella (singular: *flagellum*) that allow cells to swim through liquid.

Organelles That Capture and Release Energy

🔑 **KEY QUESTION** *What are the functions of chloroplasts and mitochondria?*

Chloroplasts Plants and some other organisms contain chloroplasts (KLAWR uh plasts). Chloroplasts capture the energy from sunlight and convert it into chemical energy stored in food during photosynthesis. Chloroplasts are surrounded by two membranes and contain large stacks of additional membranes that contain the green pigment chlorophyll.

Mitochondria Nearly all eukaryotic cells, including plants, contain mitochondria (myt oh KAHN dree uh; singular *mitochondrion*). Mitochondria convert the chemical energy stored in food molecules into compounds that are more convenient for the cell to use. As with chloroplasts, mitochondria are surrounded by two membranes. The inner membrane is folded up inside the mitochondrion. All or nearly all of our mitochondria are inherited from our mothers.

Chloroplasts and mitochondria contain some of their own genetic information in the form of small DNA molecules. These organelles probably originated from prokaryotic cells that became part of eukaryotic cells in a mutualistic relationship. Genetic changes in human mitochondria can affect human health.

Cellular Boundaries

🔑 **KEY QUESTION** *What is the function of the cell membrane?*

Cell Walls The cell wall lies outside the cell membrane and supports, shapes, and protects the cell. Most prokaryotes and some eukaryotes, including plants and fungi, have cell walls. Animal cells do not have cell walls. Cell walls allow water, oxygen, carbon dioxide, and other substances to pass through. Cell walls provide much of the strength plants need to stand.

READING TOOL

Academic Words

network A network is a system of connected things. In a previous chapter you learned about food webs, which are another type of network.

☑ Based upon what you know about networks, explain why computers are more useful when they are connected to the internet.

_____

_____

_____

_____

_____

Cell Membranes All cells have cell membranes. Cell membranes are made up of a double-layered sheet called a **lipid bilayer**. The cell membrane regulates what enters and leaves the cell and also protects and supports the cell.

The Properties of Lipids Lipids have oily fatty chains that are attached to chemical groups that interact with water. The fatty acid portions of the lipid are hydrophobic (hy druh FOH bik), or "water hating," while the other end is hydrophilic (hy druh FIL ik), or "water loving." When the lipids are in water, their hydrophobic "tails" cluster together while the hydrophilic "heads" are attracted to water. This results in a lipid bilayer, with the fatty acid tails forming the interior of the membrane. Many substances can cross cell membranes, but some substances are too large or too strongly charged to cross the lipid bilayer. Cell membranes are **selectively permeable** (or semipermeable), meaning that some substances can cross the membrane and others cannot.

The Fluid Mosaic Model Proteins are embedded in the lipid bilayer of most cell membranes. Carbohydrate molecules are attached to many of these proteins. The proteins in the lipid bilayer can move around, "floating" among the lipids. Scientists describe the cell membrane as a "fluid mosaic." A mosaic is a type of art made up of different materials, just as the membrane is made up of different kinds of molecules. Some of these proteins form channels and pumps that move substances across the cell membrane. Some proteins attach to the cytoskeleton, enabling cells to use their membranes to move or change shape. Many of the carbohydrate molecules help cells to identify each other.

Visual Reading Tool: Eukaryotic Cell Structure

Write the name of the numbered structures.

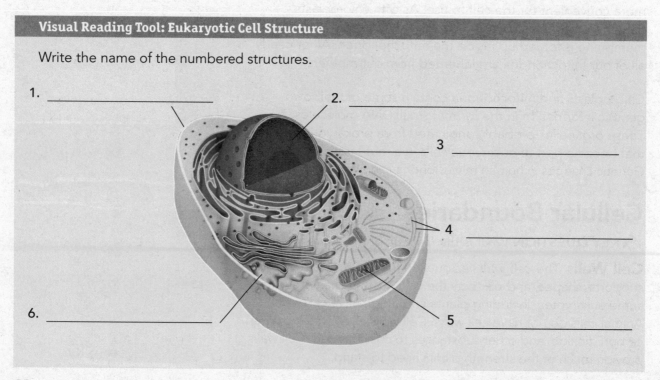

1. _____

2. _____

3. _____

4. _____

5. _____

6. _____

READING TOOL **Compare and Contrast** As you read, compare and contrast passive and active transport. Complete the Venn Diagram by filling in the similarities where the two circles overlap, and their differences on either side. Be sure to also include the types of passive transport and active transport.

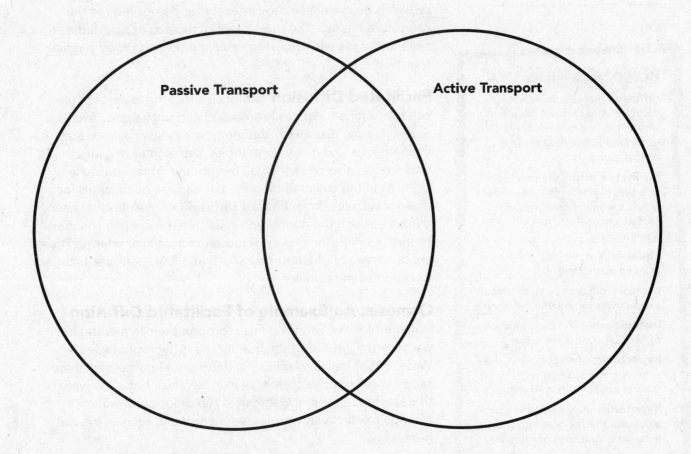

Passive Transport — Active Transport

Lesson Summary

Passive Transport

🔑 **KEY QUESTION** *How does passive transport work?*

Living cells must stay in **homeostasis**, which is a state of relatively constant internal physical and chemical conditions. One way that cells maintain homeostasis is by controlling the movement of molecules across the cell membrane.

🔑 As you read, circle the answers to each Key Question. Underline any words you do not understand.

BUILD Vocabulary

homeostasis relatively constant internal physical and chemical conditions that organisms maintain

passive *Passive* has multiple meanings. It can mean inactive, and it can also mean that something is unpowered, with no force behind it. ☑ *Passive transport* does not mean that a particle is inactive or not moving. It means that the particle can move without requiring what?

_____

_____

BUILD Vocabulary

diffusion process by which particles tend to move from an area where they are more concentrated to an area where they are less concentrated

facilitated diffusion process of diffusion in which molecules pass across the membrane through protein channels in the cell membrane

aquaporin water channel protein in a cell membrane

osmosis diffusion of water through a selectively permeable membrane

isotonic when the concentration of two solutions is the same

hypertonic when comparing two solutions, the solution with the greater concentration of solutes

hypotonic when comparing two solutions, the solution with the lesser concentration of solutes

osmotic pressure pressure that must be applied to prevent osmotic movement across a selectively permeable membrane

Prefixes *Iso-* means "equal." You may have encountered this prefix in the term *isosceles triangle* in a math class. An isosceles triangle has two equal sides. ☑ What quantity is equal between two solutions that are isotonic?

_____

_____

Diffusion In any solution, solute particles constantly move and collide with each other. The particles tend to move from an area where they are more concentrated to an area where they are less concentrated. This process is called **diffusion** (dih FYOO zhun). Diffusion is why many substances move across the cell membrane. For a substance that can cross the cell membrane, it will move to the side of the membrane where it is less concentrated. Equilibrium is reached when the concentration of the substance is the same on both sides of the membrane. Molecules will continue to move across the membrane, but the concentration will stay the same on both sides. Diffusion depends on molecular movements that do not require the cell to use energy. The movement of molecules across the cell membrane without using cellular energy is called <u>passive</u> transport.

Facilitated Diffusion Molecules that move across the cell membrane most easily are small and uncharged. Such molecules can dissolve in the membrane's lipid bilayer. But charged ions and many large molecules such as the sugar glucose can also cross the cell membrane. This is because proteins in the cell membrane act as carriers or channels for these molecules. In **facilitated diffusion**, molecules that cannot diffuse through the membrane pass through protein channels. Facilitated diffusion does not require any cellular energy. There are hundreds of different proteins that allow specific substances to cross cell membranes.

Osmosis: An Example of Facilitated Diffusion

Water molecules cannot diffuse through the cell membrane because the interior of the membrane is hydrophobic. Water enters cells by facilitated diffusion. Many cells contain proteins called **aquaporins** (ak wuh PAW rinz) that allow water to pass through them. **Osmosis** is the diffusion of water through a selectively permeable membrane, such as the cell membrane.

How Osmosis Works Think about two solutions of sugar in water separated by a membrane that is permeable to water, but not sugar. One solution has a higher concentration of sugar, which means there is a lower concentration of water. Water moves both ways across the membrane, but more water molecules will move from the side with more water and less sugar to the side with less water and more sugar until equilibrium is reached. Equilibrium is when the water and sugar concentrations are the same in both solutions. At equilibrium, the solutions are **isotonic**, meaning "same strength." Before equilibrium was reached, the solution with more sugar was **hypertonic**, or "above strength," and the solution with less sugar was **hypotonic**, or "below strength." The terms *isotonic, hypertonic,* and *hypotonic* refer the "strength," or concentration, of the sugar solute, not the water.

Osmotic Pressure The net movement of water into or out of a cell produces a force called **osmotic pressure**. Because cells contain salts, sugars, proteins and other dissolved molecules; they are almost always hypertonic to fresh water. As a result, water tends to move into a cell, increasing the osmotic pressure inside the cell and causing it to swell. This could cause the cell to burst. Most cells in large organisms are bathed in blood or other isotonic fluids, not water, so they are not in danger of bursting.

Visual Reading Tool: Passive Transport

Diffusion is the movement of particles from an area of high concentration to an area of low concentration. Osmosis is the diffusion of water through a selectively permeable membrane. Study the beakers at the right. The arrows between beakers tell you what process is occurring.

1. In the beakers on the right, draw the result of the described process. Draw changes in water levels. Draw changes in the number of solute particles. Remember to draw on both sides of the membrane.

2. Label each of the solutions on each side of the membrane as either hypertonic, hypotonic, or isotonic.

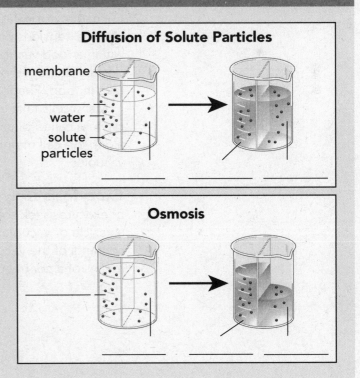

Diffusion of Solute Particles

membrane

water

solute particles

Osmosis

Cause and Effect Small molecules have the ability to move across the cell membrane by dissolving through the lipid bilayer. This is called diffusion and it happens without any energy input. ☑ **Why do some molecules need help moving across a cell membrane in the form of energy?**

_____

_____

_____

_____

_____

Active Transport

KEY QUESTION *How does active transport work?*

Sometimes cells transport materials against a concentration gradient, from an area of low concentration to an area of higher concentration. The movement of materials against a concentration difference is known as active transport, and it requires energy. The active transport of small molecules or ions across a cell membrane is usually carried out by membrane proteins called protein pumps. Larger molecules can be actively transported by processes known as endocytosis and exocytosis.

Molecular Transport
Many cells use protein pumps and cellular energy to move ions such as calcium, potassium, and sodium across membranes. This allows cells to store substances in a particular location even when diffusion would tend to move these substances in the opposite direction.

Bulk Transport
Large molecules and even clumps of material can be moved across the cell membrane by bulk transport.

Endocytosis
Endocytosis (en doh sy TOH sis) is the process of bringing material into a cell by means of parts of the membrane folding in, or forming pockets. The resulting pocket breaks away from the cytoplasmic side of the cell membrane, forming a vesicle or vacuole in the cytoplasm. Large molecules, clumps of food, and even whole cells can be taken up in this way.

Phagocytosis (fag oh sy TOH sis) is a kind of endocytosis in which extensions of the cell surround a particle and package it within a food vacuole. White blood cells use phagocytosis to destroy damaged or foreign cells. Amoebas use this method to take in food. Phagocytosis requires a lot of cellular energy.

Many cells take up liquid from the environment in a similar process called pinocytosis (py nuh sy TOH sis). Tiny pockets form along the cell membrane, fill with liquid, and pinch off to form vacuoles.

Exocytosis
Cells can also release material using the process of exocytosis (ek soh sy TOH sis). In exocytosis, the membrane of a vesicle or vacuole fuses with the cell membrane, forcing the contents of the vacuole out of the cell. Cells remove water by means of a contractile vacuole and exocytosis.

CHAPTER 8

LESSON 4

Homeostasis and Cells

READING TOOL **Make Connections** As you read the text, fill in the chart below to show how each idea is related to one another.

Specialized Cells
- Definition: ______________________
- Example: ______________________

Tissues
- Definition: ______________________
- Example: ______________________

Organs
- Definition: ______________________
- Example: ______________________

Organ System
- Definition: ______________________
- Example: ______________________

Lesson Summary

The Cell as an Organism

🔍 As you read, circle the answers to each Key Question. Underline any words you do not understand.

🔍 **KEY QUESTION** *How do single-celled organisms maintain homeostasis?*

Unicellular organisms, like all living things, must maintain homeostasis, or relatively constant internal physical and chemical conditions. To maintain homeostasis, unicellular organisms grow, respond to the environment, transform energy, and reproduce. Unicellular organisms include prokaryotes, such as bacteria. Many eukaryotes, such as amoebas, many algae, and yeasts, live as single cells.

Multicellular Life

🔍 **KEY QUESTION** *How do the cells of a multicellular organism work together to maintain homeostasis?*

The cells of humans and other multicellular organisms do not live on their own. They are interdependent. The cells of multicellular organisms are specialized for specific tasks and communicate with one another to maintain homeostasis.

Cell Specialization We each began life as a single cell. That cell grew and divided and gave rise to many other cells that became specialized to perform different roles. Each specialized cell in a multicellular organism contributes to homeostasis in the organism.

Levels of Organization In a multicellular organism, specialized cells are organized into tissues. Tissues are organized into organs, which are organized into organ systems. A **tissue** is a group of similar cells that perform a particular function. Different tissues may work together to form an **organ**. For example, the brain is an organ made of nerve and fat tissue and blood vessels. A group of organs that work together to perform a function is called an **organ system**. The brain, spinal cord, and nerves in the body work together as the nervous system.

Cellular Communication Cells in a large organism communicate using chemical signals. These signals can speed up or slow down the function of cells that receive them, or can cause the cell to change what it is doing. Some cells form connections or cellular junctions to neighboring cells. Some junctions hold cells together. Others allow molecules to carry chemical signals between cells. In order for cells to respond to a chemical signal, the cell must have a **receptor** that the chemical signal can bind to. Receptors can be on the cell membrane or inside the cytoplasm. In many animals, nerve cells carry messages from one part of the body to another.

BUILD Vocabulary

tissue group of similar cells that perform a particular function

organ group of tissues that work together to perform closely related functions

organ system group of organs that work together to perform a specific function

receptor on or in a cell, a specific protein that receives chemical signals from molecular messengers, such as hormones

Word Origins The English word *receive* is based upon the Latin word *recipere* which means "to take back." ☑ **What do receptors in cells receive from other cells?**

_____

_____

8 Chapter Review

Review Vocabulary

Choose the letter of the best answer.

1. Proteins that will be released from the cell are assembled at the

   A. central vacuole.

   B. mitochondria.

   C. rough endoplasmic reticulum.

2. The diffusion of water through a selectively permeable membrane is called

   A. homeostasis.

   B. pinocytosis.

   C. osmosis.

Match the vocabulary term to its definition.

3. _____ A cell that has DNA but no nucleus.

4. _____ A complex of protein and RNA that assembles proteins.

5. _____ A protein on or in a cell that binds a chemical signal.

a. receptor

b. prokaryote

c. ribosome

Review Key Questions

Provide evidence and details to support your answers.

6. What are the three main parts of the cell theory?

_____

_____

_____

7. Plants and animals are both made up of eukaryotic cells. Does this mean they have the same kinds of organelles? Why or why not?

_____

_____

_____

8. A cell makes and secretes a certain protein. Explain where it is made, how it is secreted from the cell, and what kind of transport is used.

_____

_____

9. Why do prokaryotes not have cell specialization?

_____

_____

CHAPTER 9

Energy and Life

READING TOOL **Main Idea** As you read the lesson, complete the main idea table for each heading. The first one has been completed for you.

Heading	Main Idea
Chemical Energy and ATP	Chemical energy is contained in the bonds between atoms. ATP is the molecule that organisms use to temporarily store energy.
• Storing Energy	
• Releasing Energy	
• How Cells Use ATP	
Heterotrophs and Autotrophs	

Lesson Summary

Chemical Energy and ATP

🔑 As you read, circle the answers to each Key Question. Underline any words you do not understand.

🔑 **KEY QUESTION** *Why is ATP useful to cells?*

Cells require energy to perform work, and energy makes life possible. We humans cannot use sunlight as a source of energy, but must take in food made by other organisms, plant or animal, to acquire energy. We are heterotrophs.

Energy comes in many forms, including light, heat, and electricity. Energy can be stored in chemical compounds, too. For example, when you light a candle, the wax melts, soaks into the wick, and is burned. As the candle burns, chemical bonds between carbon and hydrogen atoms in the wax are broken. New bonds then form between these atoms and oxygen, producing CO_2 and H_2O (carbon dioxide and water). These new bonds are at a lower energy state than the original chemical bonds in the wax. The energy is released as heat and light in the glow of the candle's flame.

Storing Energy All living cells store energy in the chemical bonds of certain compounds. Of these compounds, one of the most important is adenosine triphosphate **(ATP)**. ATP consists of adenine, a 5-carbon sugar called ribose, and three phosphate groups. The phosphate groups are the key to ATP's ability to store and release energy. Adding a phosphate group to adensosine diphosphate (ADP) adds energy to the molecule and changes it to ATP. When a cell requires this energy, it removes the third phosphate group from ATP, changing it to ADP again.

Releasing Energy ATP can release energy by breaking the bonds between its phosphate groups. This characteristic of ATP makes it exceptionally useful as a basic energy source for all cells. ATP is the most immediate source of energy for cells.

How Cells Use ATP Cells use the energy provided by ATP to carry out active transport. Many cell membranes contain sodium-potassium pumps, which are membrane proteins that pump sodium ions (Na^+) out of the cell and potassium ions (K^+) into the cell. ATP provides the energy that keeps this pump working, which involves maintaining a carefully-regulated balance of ions on both sides of the cell membrane. The energy stored in ATP also enables cells to move, providing power for motor proteins that contract muscles and generate the wavelike movement of cilia and flagella.

Energy from ATP can be transferred to other molecules in the cell to power processes such as protein synthesis. The chemical energy from ATP can even be converted to light. In fact, the blink of a firefly comes from an enzyme that is powered by ATP!

Most cells have only enough ATP to last for a few seconds of activity. ATP is not a good molecule for storing large amounts of energy over the long term. A single molecule of the sugar glucose, for example, stores more than 90 times the energy required to add a phosphate group to ADP to produce ATP. Therefore, it is more efficient for cells to keep only a small supply of ATP on hand. Cells regenerate ATP from ADP as needed by using the energy in sugars and other sources.

BUILD Vocabulary

adenosine triphosphate (ATP) compound used by cells to store and release energy

Word Origins The name photosynthesis comes from the Greek words *phós* (light) and *synthesis* (putting together).

☑ **What other words do you know that begin with the prefix *photo-*?**

_____

_____

Heterotrophs and Autotrophs

BUILD Vocabulary

photosynthesis process used by plants and other autotrophs to capture light energy and store it in energy-rich carbohydrates such as sugars and starches

READING TOOL

Compare and Contrast

Heterotrophs cannot make their own energy, so they obtain it from eating other living organisms, such as autotrophs. ☑ **What are the two different types of autotrophs, and which is more common on our planet?**

_____

_____

_____

_____

_____

_____

🔍 **KEY QUESTION** *What happens during the process of photosynthesis?*

All animals obtain the chemical energy they need from the food they consume. Animals are known as heterotrophs, which are organisms that obtain energy by consuming other organisms.

Some heterotrophs eat plants and are known as herbivores. Others, such as the heron, consume other animals and are known as carnivores. Animals that eat both plants and other animals are known as omnivores. Decomposers are heterotrophs that consume dead organisms and the wastes of living organisms. A mushroom is one example of a decomposer.

Autotrophs are organisms that make their own food using an external source of energy. Most autotrophs use sunlight as a source of energy and are known as photoautotrophs. Chemoautotrophs use chemicals as a source of energy, and are found only near vents on the ocean floor. **Photosynthesis** is the process by which photoautotrophs convert light energy into chemical energy. Photosynthetic organisms include plants, algae, and bacteria known as cyanobacteria. Nearly all life on Earth depends on autotrophs that capture sunlight energy and synthesize high-energy carbohydrates—sugars and starches—that can be used as food.

Visual Reading Tool: Adenosine Triphosphate

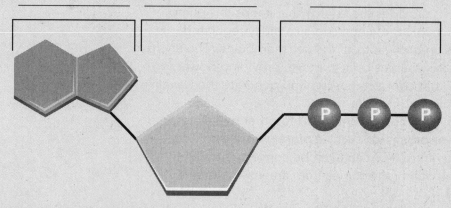

1. Label the ATP shown above.

2. Which part of the structure is a type of sugar? _____

3. Which part contains important bonds that store energy? _____

4. How does ADP get converted to ATP? _____

_____

5. Which molecule has a higher potential energy. ADP or ATP? _____

Photosynthesis: An Overview

READING TOOL **Make Connections** Fill in the concept map to show the organization of a chloroplast. Then below, answer the questions to describe how the different parts are related to each other.

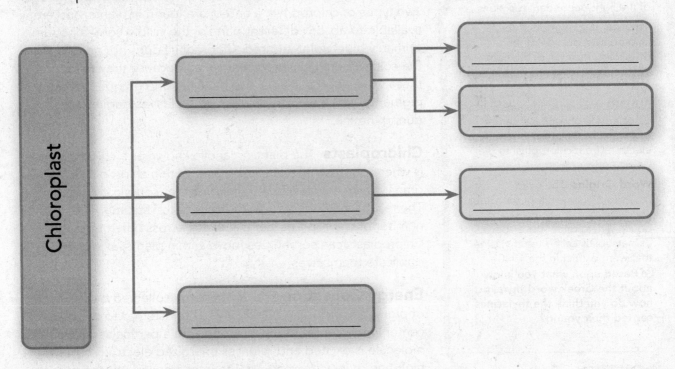

Complete each of the following sentences.

Saclike membranes that contain chlorophyll are known as _____ .

_____ is a stack of thylakoids.

_____ is the fluid portion of the chloroplast outside of the thylakoids.

Two _____ surround and enclose the chloroplasts.

Lesson Summary

Chlorophyll and Chloroplasts

KEY QUESTION *What role do pigments play in the process of photosynthesis?*

Our lives, and the lives of nearly every living thing on the surface of Earth, are made possible by the sun and the process of photosynthesis. In order for photosynthesis to occur, light energy from the sun must somehow be captured.

As you read, circle the answers to each Key Question. Underline any words you do not understand.

Light The sun's energy travels to Earth in the form of light. Sunlight, which our eyes perceive as "white" light, is actually a mixture of different wavelengths. Our eyes see the different wavelengths of the visible spectrum as different colors: shades of red, orange, yellow, green, blue, indigo, and violet.

Pigments Light-absorbing compounds are known as **pigments**. Photosynthetic organisms primarily use the pigment chlorophyll to capture the energy in sunlight. The principal pigment of green plants is known as **chlorophyll**. Two types of chlorophyll, *a* and *b*, are found in plants, and are available to absorb different parts of the visible light spectrum, primarily blue-violet and red. Chlorophyll does not absorb the color green. Leaves appear green because they reflect these wavelengths. Plants also have red and orange carotene pigments, which we can only see when leaves begin to die during the fall.

Chloroplasts The plant organelle known as a chloroplast is where photosynthesis takes place. Within chloroplasts are grana, which are stacks of **thylakoids** that contain chlorophyll. The rest of the fluid outside of this is called **stroma**. The number of chloroplasts per cell varies across different plants. Chloroplasts can sometimes move within plants, as well as duplicate themselves.

Energy Collection The light energy collected by a cluster of pigments, including chlorophyll, is transferred to the reaction center in the center of the cluster where a particular chlorophyll molecule is excited and releases energized electrons. These high-energy electrons are vital to later steps of photosynthesis.

High-Energy Electrons

🔍 **KEY QUESTION** *What are electron carrier molecules?*

Specific molecules called electron carriers are necessary to convey the highly reactive and high-energy electrons that are produced by chlorophyll. The electron carrier moves the electrons with their energy to other molecules where they are needed.

Nicotinamide adenine dinucleotide phosphate, or **NADP⁺**, is one such electron carrier. When it accepts two high-energy electrons, NADP⁺ also bonds a hydrogen ion, which turns it into NADPH. Now the captured energy can be moved to the location in the chloroplast where sugars are manufactured.

An Overview of Photosynthesis

⚲KEY QUESTION *What are the reactants and products of photosynthesis?*

Photosynthesis uses the energy of sunlight to convert water and carbon dioxide (low-energy reactants) into high-energy sugars and oxygen (products).

Light-Dependent Reactions The **Light-dependent Reactions** need sunlight. The sunlight energy is captured by pigments in the thylakoid membrane. The energy is used to convert ADP into ATP and NADP⁺ into NADPH. These sources of energy are important for other steps in photosynthesis. Also, water is split apart, which makes more electrons available, and produced oxygen (O_2) and hydrogen ions (H^+).

Light-Independent Reactions The **Light-independent Reactions** (Calvin cycle) occur in the stroma and do not use sunlight. The energy in ATP and NADPH, produced in the light-dependent reactions, is used to "fix" carbon dioxide. That is, carbon dioxide (CO_2) is combined with H^+ to produce sugars, primarily glucose ($C_6H_{12}O_6$). The plant makes these sugars as food for itself.

BUILD Vocabulary

light-dependent reactions set of reactions in photosynthesis that use energy from light to produce ATP and NADPH

light-independent reactions set of reactions in photosynthesis that do not require light; energy from ATP and NADPH is used to build high-energy compounds such as sugar

Visual Reading Tool: Inside a Chloroplast

1. Fill in the reactants and products of the light-dependent and light-independent reactions of photosynthesis.

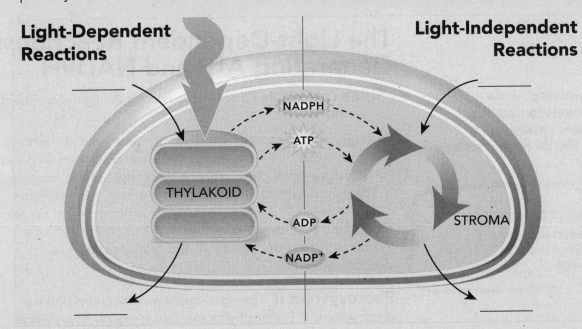

Light-Dependent Reactions

Light-Independent Reactions

2. What is the NADPH responsible for? _____

_____

3. Where do the "light" reactions (light-dependent) take place? _____

The Process of Photosynthesis

READING TOOL **Main Idea** As you read the lesson, complete the main idea table for the primary headings below.

Heading	Main Idea
The Light-Dependent Reactions: Generating ATP and NADPH	
The Light-Independent Reactions: Producing Sugars	
Factors Affecting Photosynthesis	

Lesson Summary

The Light-Dependent Reactions: Generating ATP and NADPH

As you read, circle the answers to each Key Question. Underline any words you do not understand.

BUILD Vocabulary

photosystem cluster of chlorophyll and proteins found in thylakoids

KEY QUESTION *What happens during the light-dependent reactions?*

The light-dependent reactions use solar energy to convert ADP and NADP$^+$ into the energy and electron carriers ATP and NADPH. Oxygen is produced as a by-product of this reaction.

The light-dependent reactions occur across the thylakoids of chloroplasts. Thylakoids are saclike membranes that contain most of the machinery needed to carry out photosynthesis, including clusters of chlorophyll and proteins known as **photosystems**.

Photosystem II The light-dependent reactions begin in photosystem II. Chlorophyll molecules in the photosystem absorb light. This absorption of light raises electrons in chlorophyll to a higher energy level, and these high-energy electrons (e–) are passed from chlorophyll to the electron transport chain.

Electron Transport Chain The Electron Transport Chain (ETC) uses energy from the electrons to pump protons (H^+) through the proteins in the chain from the stroma to the inside of the thylakoid sac. At the end of the electron transport chain, the electrons themselves pass to a second photosystem called photosystem I.

Photosystem I In Photosystem I the low-energy electrons from the ETC are passed to chlorophyll molecules and re-energized using light energy. The energized electrons are passed on to an enzyme that facilitates the production of NADPH from NADP+ and hydrogen ions. The NADPH can now move on to the light-independent reactions.

Hydrogen Ion Movement and ATP Formation All of the prior steps involved some increasing of H^+ concentration inside the thylakoids. Now there is a concentration gradient between the inside and outside of the thylakoid. Because molecules tend to move from a high to low concentration, the H^+ ions will move back across the thylakoid, if given the opportunity. ATP synthase provides a pathway for the hydrogen ions. As H^+ ions move across the thylakoid, through the ATP synthase protein, ADP is converted into ATP by the addition of a phosphate group.

Summary of Light-Dependent Reactions Light energy is used to convert ADP to ATP, and NADPH+ to NADPH. Water is split apart to make electrons available to PS II, which produces O_2 and hydrogen ions.

The Light-Independent Reactions

⚷ **KEY QUESTION** *What happens during the light-independent reactions?*

During the light-independent reactions, ATP and NADPH from the light-dependent reactions are used to synthesize high-energy sugars. The light-independent reactions are commonly referred to as the Calvin cycle. The Calvin cycle occurs in the stroma of the chloroplast.

Carbon Dioxide Enters the Cell Carbon dioxide that has entered the leaves through the stomata is used in the Calvin cycle to produce higher energy sugars. An enzyme called RuBisCO "grabs" the CO_2 and brings it into the cycle where the energy from ATP and NADPH is used, through a series of steps, to produce a simple 3-carbon sugar for every 3 carbon dioxides that enter the cycle.

Sugar Production The two 3-carbon compounds are vital later on, helping to make other carbon-based compounds. One glucose molecule is a 6-carbon compound and would require 6 "turns" of the Calvin cycle.

BUILD Vocabulary

electron transport chain series of electron carrier proteins that shuttle high-energy electrons in preparation for ATP-generating reactions

ATP synthase enzyme that spans the thylakoid membrane and produces ATP from ADP when hydrogen ions (H^+) pass through it

Calvin Cycle the light-independent reactions of photosynthesis in which energy from ATP and NADPH is used to build high-energy compounds such as sugar

Suffixes When words end in *-ase* this usually indicates an enzymatic protein. ATP synthase is an enzymatic protein that creates ATP.

☑ **What molecules need to travel through ATP synthase to help it create ATP?**

Apply Prior Knowledge Think about how you would care for a houseplant. It needs water, access to sunlight, and a supply of air.
☑ **Now that you know more about the specific processes of photosynthesis, explain exactly why a plant needs carbon dioxide from the air.**

_____

_____

_____

_____

_____

_____

Summary of the Calvin Cycle Six carbon dioxide molecules are needed to produce a 6-carbon sugar molecule, glucose. ATP and NADPH provided energy for these reactions to occur. The plant uses the sugars for growth and maintenance. Animals access the sugars when they eat the plant.

The End Results High energy sugars and O_2 gas are the end products of photosynthesis. The basic photosynthetic steps consisting of the light reactions and Calvin cycle is known as the C3 photosynthetic pathway. It is labeled as C3 because the first molecule generated during the Calvin cycle contains 3 carbon atoms.

Factors Affecting Photosynthesis

🔍 **KEY QUESTION** *What factors affect photosynthesis?*

Many factors affect the rate of chemical reactions, including those that occur during photosynthesis.

Temperature, Light, and Water The reactions of photosynthesis function best within a certain range of environmental conditions. The enzymes that carry out the Light-Dependent and Light-Independent reactions function best between 0°C and 35°C. Above or below that, it slows the rate of photosynthesis and can even stop it completely. Plants also need access to sunlight. High intensity light increases the rate of photosynthesis up to a certain point where plants reach their maximum photosynthetic rate. The last factor that affects photosynthesis is water availability. A shortage of water can halt photosynthesis. Some plants that live in dry conditions, such as desert plants and conifers, have waxy coatings on their leaves that reduce water loss.

Photosynthesis Under Extreme Conditions Plants have openings on the underside of their leaves that are called stomata. They allow for CO_2 to enter the leaf and excess O_2 to leave. Unfortunately these openings also allow water to leave the leaf. Under hot and dry conditions the rate of water loss can be very high and the plant can run low on water. Plants have many adaptations to conserve water, including the physiological adaptations of C4 plants and CAM photosynthesis.

C4 Plants Dry conditions force plants to close their stomata in order to conserve water. Photosynthesis in C3 plants quickly comes to a stop because there is not enough CO_2 inside the leaves. However, C4 plants are able to fix CO_2 at much lower concentrations because they have an extra enzyme that assists RuBisCO. The name "C4" comes from the fact that the first compound formed in this pathway contains four carbon atoms instead of three. C4 plants include important crop plants like corn, sugar cane, and sorghum.

CAM Plants Crassulacean acid metabolism (CAM) plants open their stomata at night to allow for gas exchange when water loss will be minimized. They store the CO_2 that they collect at night as in an organic acid. When day comes, they then release the CO_2 in order to perform photosynthesis as usual. This evolved in some plants as an adaptation to arid conditions. The jade plant is one example of the Crassulacea family.

Visual Reading Tool: The Light-Independent Reactions

1. Label the diagram with the four molecules that carry energy through photosynthesis.

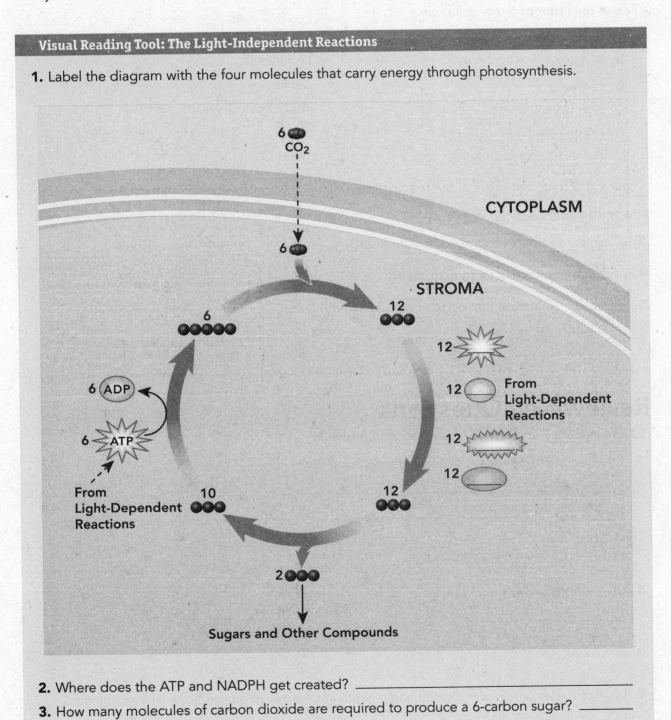

2. Where does the ATP and NADPH get created? _____

3. How many molecules of carbon dioxide are required to produce a 6-carbon sugar? _____

Review Vocabulary

Choose the letter of the best answer.

1. The main pigment of green plants is:

   A. thylakoid

   B. carotene

   C. chlorophyll

   D. chloroplast

2. What concentration gradient powers ATP synthase?

   A. O_2

   B. CO_2

   C. H^+

   D. H_2O

Match the vocabulary term to its definition.

3. _____ material that absorbs light energy

4. _____ source of temporary energy

5. _____ reactions that occur in the thylakoid membrane

6. _____ fluid matrix of chloroplasts

a. stroma

b. pigment

c. ATP

d. light-dependent

Review Key Questions

Provide evidence and details to support your answers.

7. What is the importance of photosynthesis for all life?

   _____

   _____

   _____

8. How is energy captured from the sun?

   _____

   _____

9. In what stages are carbon dioxide and oxygen involved in photosynthesis ATP production?

   _____

   _____

CHAPTER 10

LESSON 1

Cellular Respiration: An Overview

READING TOOL **Active Reading** As you read your textbook, record key ideas on the summary table for each heading in the chapter. The first one is done for you.

Heading	Summary
Chemical Energy and Food	Heterotrophs get the energy they need from the food they eat. In food it is measured in units called Calories.
Overview of Cellular Respiration	
• Stages of Cellular Respiration	
• Oxygen and Energy	
Comparing Photosynthesis and Cellular Respiration	

Lesson Summary

Chemical Energy and Food

🔑 **KEY QUESTION** *Where do organisms get energy?*

Heterotrophs get the energy they need from the food they eat. Energy is stored in a variety of macromolecules in the body, including fats, proteins, and carbohydrates. The energy is measured in a unit known as a **calorie**. A calorie is the amount of energy needed to raise the temperature of 1 gram of water by 1 degree Celsius. There are 1000 of these calories in 1 food Calorie (that is seen on a food label). When measuring calories, fats tend to have 9000 calories (9 food Calories) of energy per gram, while proteins and carbohydrates have 4000 calories (4 food Calories). The cells in the body release and use this energy over time using the process of cellular respiration.

🔑 As you read, circle the answers to each Key Question. Underline any words you do not understand.

BUILD Vocabulary

calorie the amount of energy needed to raise the temperature of 1 gram of water by 1 degree Celsius

Overview of Cellular Respiration

⚲ KEY QUESTION *How does cellular respiration work?*

Energy is released from food in the presence of oxygen during a complex process known as cellular respiration. There are many reactions in this process, but simply put, the process takes oxygen and glucose and converts it into carbon dioxide, water, and energy. This process happens over time, and energy is released gradually in the form of ATP.

In Symbols:

$$6O_2 + C_6H_{12}O_6 \rightarrow 6CO_2 + 6H_2O + \text{Energy}$$

In Words:

Oxygen + Glucose → Carbon Dioxide + Water + Energy

If cellular respiration took place in just one step, all of the energy from glucose would be released at once, and most of it would be lost in the form of heat.

Stages of Cellular Respiration There are three stages of cellular respiration. During the first stage, called glycolysis, glucose is broken down and small amounts of ATP are produced. In the next stage, the Krebs cycle, pyruvic acid that was produced during glycolysis is broken down, and energy carriers are produced. These energy carriers move into the final stage of cellular respiration, the electron transport chain. Here the electron carriers release their stored energy and produce ATP.

Oxygen and Energy Oxygen is required at the very end of the electron transport chain. Any time a cell's demand for energy increases, its use of oxygen increases, too. The double meaning of respiration points out a crucial connection between cells and organisms.

High energy–yielding pathways in cells require oxygen, and that is the reason we need to breathe, or respire. Pathways of cellular respiration that require oxygen are said to be aerobic ("in air"). The Krebs cycle and the electron transport chain are both aerobic processes. Glycolysis, however, does not directly require oxygen, nor does it rely on an oxygen-requiring process to run. Glycolysis is therefore said to be anaerobic ("without air"). Even though glycolysis is anaerobic, it is considered part of cellular respiration because its products are key reactants for the aerobic stages.

Glycolysis occurs in the cytoplasm. In contrast, the Krebs cycle and electron transport chain, which generate the majority of ATP during cellular respiration, take place inside the mitochondria. If oxygen is not present, another anaerobic pathway, known as fermentation, makes it possible for the cell to keep glycolysis running, generating ATP to power cellular activity.

BUILD Vocabulary

cellular respiration process that releases energy from food in the presence of oxygen

aerobic process that requires oxygen

anaerobic process that does not require oxygen

Prior Knowledge You have probably encountered the term *Calorie* before when reading food labels. ☑ **How does a Calorie on a food label relate to a calorie that is produced in cellular respiration?**

_____

_____

Comparing Photosynthesis and Cellular Respiration

As you read, circle the answers to each Key Question. Underline any words you do not understand.

KEY QUESTION *How does cellular respiration work?*

Photosynthesis and cellular respiration are both important processes in the harnessing and extraction of energy. In fact, they work in opposite ways. Photosynthesis is a process that deposits energy, while cellular respiration is a way to withdraw energy. Photosynthesis removes carbon dioxide from the atmosphere, while cellular respiration adds it to the atmosphere. Photosynthesis releases oxygen, while cellular respiration uses it.

The global balance between cellular respiration and photosynthesis is essential to maintain Earth as a living planet. Another necessity is a constant input of energy into the system. This input comes from the sun. You can trace the flow of energy from the sun to organisms that perform photosynthesis and then to a series of organisms that perform cellular respiration.

READING TOOL

Compare and Contrast

Photosynthesis and cellular respiration are necessary to maintain Earth as a living, healthy planet. ☑ **How do these two processes work in tandem?**

_____

_____

_____

_____

_____

_____

_____

Visual Reading Tool: Cellular Respiration: An Overview

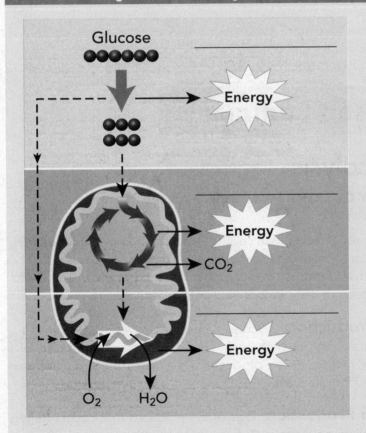

Glucose

Energy

Energy

CO_2

Energy

O_2 H_2O

1. On the diagram, label each stage of cellular respiration: *Electron Transport Chain, Glycolysis, Krebs Cycle.*

2. What is the difference between aerobic and anaerobic processes?

_____

_____

3. Circle the two stages of cellular respiration that are aerobic.

_____

_____

4. In what organelle do the Krebs cycle and the electron transport chain occur in?

_____

5. Where does glycolysis take place in the cell?

_____

Sequence of Events As you read your textbook, record the sequences of the three main events involved in cellular respiration. Use transition words like *first, next,* and *last* to explain these events. The first stage has an introductory sentence to get you started. Elaborate on stage one, and then fill in the rest of the flowchart, keeping in mind where each stage takes place and what is created.

STAGE ONE: GLYCOLYSIS

First, glycolysis occurs in the cytoplasm.

▼

STAGE TWO: KREBS CYCLE

▼

STAGE THREE: ELECRON TRANSPORT

Lesson Summary

Glycolysis

 As you read, circle the answers to each Key Question. Underline any words you do not understand.

 KEY QUESTION *What happens during the process of glycolysis?*

The first set of reactions in cellular respiration is known as **glycolysis**, which literally means "sugar breaking." During glycolysis, 1 molecule of glucose, a 6-carbon compound, is transformed into 2 molecules of the 3-carbon compound pyruvic acid.

ATP Production Glycolysis requires two ATP molecules to begin breaking down glucose. Throughout glycolysis a total of four ATP molecules are produced. As a result, there is a net gain of two ATP molecules.

NADH Production One of the reactions that occurs during glycolysis removes four electrons. These electrons are in a high-energy state and are transported to **NAD⁺**, also known as nicotinamide adenine dinucleotide. Each NAD⁺ molecule accepts a pair of high-energy electrons and a hydrogen ion.

BUILD Vocabulary

Glycolysis [gli-koli-sis] first set of reactions in cellular respiration during which one molecule of glucose (a 6-carbon compound) is transformed into 2 molecules of pyruvic acid (a 3-carbon compound)

NAD⁺ (nicotinamide adenine dinucleotide) carrier molecule that transfers high-energy electrons from glucose to other molecules

This molecule, now known as NADH, holds the electrons until they can be transferred to other molecules. In the presence of oxygen, these high-energy electrons can be used to produce even more ATP molecules.

The Advantages of Glycolysis One advantage of glycolysis is that it occurs so quickly that thousands of ATP molecules are created in milliseconds. This is helpful when the energy needed by a cell increases. A second advantage is that glycolysis does not require the use of oxygen. As a result, it can provide usable energy to the cell when oxygen is not available. However, if oxygen is available, the pyruvic acid and NADH that are created from glycolysis can be used for other processes in cellular respiration to produce additional ATP molecules.

Krebs Cycle

🔑 **KEY QUESTION** *What happens during the Krebs cycle?*

The Krebs cycle is the second stage of cellular respiration. It occurs when the pyruvic acid that is formed from glycolysis is broken down in a series of reactions. These reactions extract energy and produce the reactant that allows the cycle to start again.

Citric Acid Production At the beginning of the Krebs cycle, the three-carbon compound known as pyruvic acid created from glycolysis passes through the two membrane walls of the mitochondrion. As a result, it moves into a region located in the matrix. One carbon atom splits off from the pyruvic acid and forms carbon dioxide. This is eventually released into the air. The other two carbon atoms form acetic acid and combine with a compound called coenzyme A to form acetyl CoA. As the Krebs cycle unfolds, this acetyl CoA transfers the two carbon atoms to a four-carbon molecule that is already present in the cycle. This results in the formation of citric acid.

Energy Extraction Through a series of many reactions, citric acid is broken down into a 5-carbon compound, and then a 4-carbon compound (releasing 2 CO_2 molecules along the way). This 4-carbon compound can then start the cycle over again by combining with acetyl CoA. Energy released by the breaking and rearranging of carbon bonds is captured in the forms of ATP, NADH, and $FADH_2$.

Electron Transport and ATP Synthesis

🔑 **KEY QUESTION** *How does the electron transport chain use high energy electrons from glycolysis and the Krebs cycle?*

The final step of cellular respiration is the electron transport stage. The electron transport chain uses the high-energy electrons from glycolysis and the Krebs cycle to synthesize ATP from ADP.

> **BUILD Vocabulary**
>
> **Krebs cycle** second stage of cellular respiration in which pyruvic acid is broken down into carbon dioxide in a series of energy-extracting reactions
>
> **matrix** innermost compartment of mitochondrion
>
> **Multiple Meanings** The word *matrix* can be used to describe things shaped in a pattern of lines and spaces. ☑ **How does this relate to a mitochondrion?**
>
> _____
>
> _____
>
> _____

Make Connections Two carrier molecules are used in cellular respiration to transport high energy electrons: NADH and FADH₂.

☑ **In what molecule does the energy from these high-energy electrons end up?**

_____

Electron Transport NADH and FADH₂ transport electrons to the electron transport chain. This chain is located in the inner membrane of the mitochondrion in eukaryotic cells and in the cell membrane in prokaryotic cells. The electrons travel through this chain, and the resulting energy transports hydrogen ions through the membrane and into the intermembrane space. Oxygen will accept the electrons at the end of the chain and combine with hydrogen ions to form water.

ATP Production The inner membrane of the mitochondrion contains enzymes known as ATP synthases. The hydrogen ions are forced through the ATP synthases, causing the base of the enzymes to spin. As the enzyme molecules spin, they grab an ADP molecule and it attaches to a phosphate group, forming ATP.

The Totals Cellular respiration occurs in three phases. When the phases are complete, the end result is 36 ATP molecules that are created with each molecule of glucose. This represents about 36% of the total energy of glucose. The rest of the energy is released as <u>heat</u>. When it comes to a way of extracting energy, the process of cellular respiration is more efficient than an automobile engine that runs on gasoline.

Visual Reading Tool: ATP Synthase

1. What stage of cell respiration is being shown above?

_____

2. Which molecule has higher energy: ADP or ATP?

_____

3. What do cells use ATP for?

_____

4. When four hydrogen atoms bind with oxygen and four electrons, what molecule is created?

_____

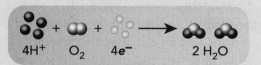

$$4H^+ + O_2 + 4e^- \rightarrow 2\ H_2O$$

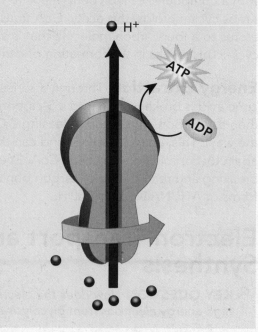

H⁺

ATP

ADP

READING TOOL **Compare and Contrast** As you read your textbook, compare and contrast fermentation and cellular respiration using the Venn diagram. Make sure to list the similarities in the center of the diagram.

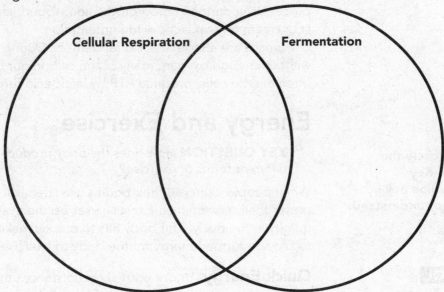

Cellular Respiration   Fermentation

Lesson Summary

Fermentation

🔍 **KEY QUESTION** *How do organisms generate energy when oxygen is not available?*

When oxygen is not present, glycolysis is maintained by a pathway that makes it possible to continue to produce ATP without oxygen. The combined process of this pathway and glycolysis is called **fermentation**. In the absence of oxygen, fermentation releases energy from food molecules by producing ATP.

During fermentation, cells convert NADH to NAD⁺ by passing high-energy electrons back to pyruvic acid. This allows glycolysis to keep going and to produce a steady supply of ATP. Fermentation is an anaerobic process that occurs in the cytoplasm of cells. Sometimes, glycolysis and fermentation are together referred to as anaerobic respiration. There are two slightly different forms of the process: alcoholic fermentation and lactic acid fermentation.

Alcoholic Fermentation The process of alcoholic fermentation is conducted by yeast. In this process, NADH combines with pyruvic acid to form alcohol, carbon dioxide, and NAD⁺.

🔍 **As you read, circle the answers to each Key Question. Underline any words you do not understand.**

BUILD Vocabulary

fermentation process by which cells release energy in the absence of oxygen

Suffixes Suffixes are endings added to a word to change the meaning of a word. When the suffix *tion* is added to a word, the meaning "action" or "act of" is added to the word. So *fermentation* is the "act of fermenting." Make a list of three other scientific words that have *-tion* as a suffix.

_____

_____

The NAD⁺ allows glycolysis to continue without oxygen. One common way to see this process is in the baking of bread. The yeast release carbon dioxide, which are the air pockets you see in bread. The alcohol that forms evaporates when the bread is baked.

Lactic Acid Fermentation Lactic acid fermentation is carried out by bacteria. These bacteria convert pyruvic acid and NADH into lactic acid and NAD⁺. As with alcoholic fermentation, the NAD⁺ allows glycolysis to continue. This process is common in food production. Yogurt, cheese, and sour cream rely on lactic acid fermentation.

Humans are also lactic acid fermenters. During brief periods without enough oxygen, many of the cells in our bodies, most often muscle cells, produce ATP by lactic acid fermentation.

Energy and Exercise

🔑 **KEY QUESTION** *How does the body produce ATP during different forms of exercise?*

When people exercise, their bodies use chemical energy to power their movements. Exercise uses up the available ATP quickly in the body. The body has to quickly make ATP in order to provide further energy for the body to exercise.

Quick Energy Under normal circumstances the body is able to take in enough oxygen to fuel cellular respiration. But sometimes, exercise involves rapid movements that occur in fast spurts. In these circumstances, the body uses the supply of ATP in the muscles quickly. While normal aerobic respiration cannot supply enough ATP to flood the muscles quickly, lactic acid fermentation can because it does not require oxygen and is a quicker process. Lactic acid fermentation can provide the muscles enough ATP for short bursts. However, the consequence is the person might need extra oxygen to help remove the excess lactic acid. This is sometimes called oxygen debt. This is why people who exercise rapidly, like sprinters, often huff and puff after exercising.

Long-Term Energy For exercise longer than about 90 seconds, cellular respiration is the only way to continue generating a supply of ATP. Cellular respiration releases energy more slowly than fermentation does, which is why even well-conditioned athletes have to pace themselves during a long race or over the course of a game. Your body stores energy in muscle cells and other tissues in the form of the carbohydrate glycogen. These stores of glycogen are usually enough to last for 15 or 20 minutes of activity. After that, your body begins to break down other stored molecules, including fats, for energy. Athletes competing in long-distance events, such as the marathon, depend on the efficiency of their respiratory and circulatory systems to provide their muscles with oxygen to support long periods of aerobic exercise.

🔑 As you read, circle the answers to each Key Question. Underline any words you do not understand.

READING TOOL

Make Connections When sprinting, the cells in your legs need more ATP to power the rapid muscle movements. ☑ **What substance builds up in the muscles, which can cause a burning feeling?**

_____

Write labels to show where each process is occurring and the name of each process. Then answer the questions below.

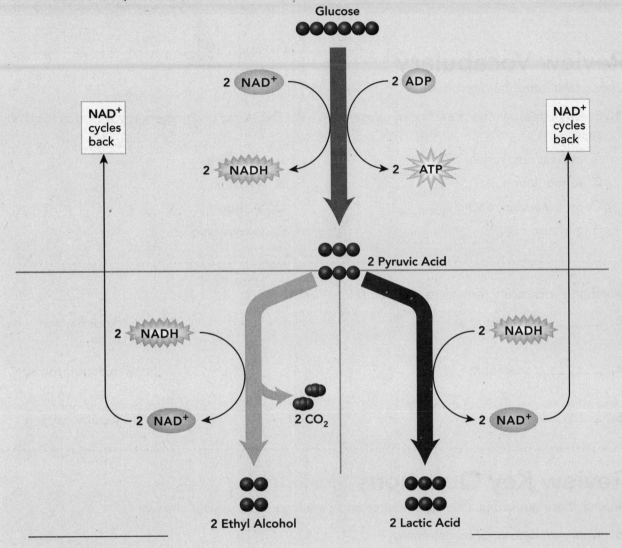

1. In what part of the cell does glycolysis take place?

_____

2. What is the importance of NAD+ cycling back up to glycolysis?

_____

_____

3. What foods are created using lactic acid fermentation?

_____

4. What type of organisms can carry out alcoholic fermentation?

_____

5. How many ATP are created by fermentation?

_____

Review Vocabulary

Choose the letter the best answer.

1. Energy release in the presence of oxygen is called

   A. cellular respiration.

   B. fermentation.

   C. an anaerobic reaction.

   D. a matrix.

2. The name given to energy stored in food is

   A. glycolysis.

   B. a matrix.

   C. a calorie.

   D. fermentation.

Match the vocabulary term to its definition.

3. _____ aerobic

4. _____ anaerobic

5. _____ NAD⁺

   a. without oxygen

   b. an electron carrier

   c. to require oxygen

Review Key Questions

Answer these questions. Provide evidence and details to support your answer.

6. Where do heterotrophs get energy?

_____

_____

7. What happens during the process of glycolysis?

_____

_____

_____

8. How do organisms generate energy when oxygen is not available?

_____

_____

_____

_____

Cell Growth, Division, and Reproduction

READING TOOL **Compare and Contrast** As you read, identify the similarities and differences between sexual and asexual reproduction. Include the advantages and disadvantages of each method. Take notes in the Venn diagram below.

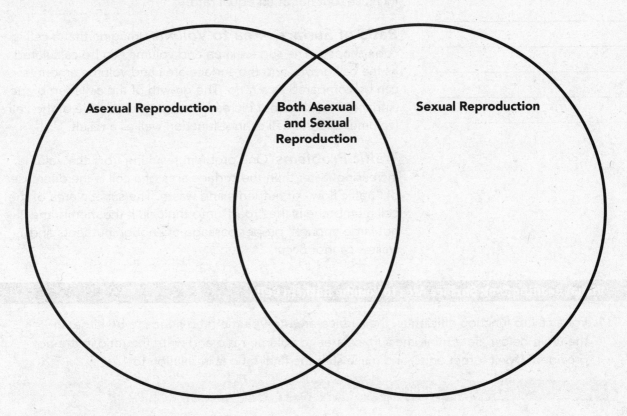

Asexual Reproduction

Both Asexual and Sexual Reproduction

Sexual Reproduction

In the space provided, describe an organism that uses both asexual and sexual reproduction.

_____

_____

Lesson Summary

Limits to Cell Size

KEY QUESTION *What are some of the difficulties a cell faces as it increases in size?*

As a cell becomes larger, it is less efficient at moving nutrients into the cell and waste material out of the cell because the surface area does not grow as quickly as the volume. In addition, as a cell grows, it places increasing demands on its own DNA. Therefore, complex living things grow in size by producing more cells rather than by increasing cell size.

As you read, circle the answers to each Key Question. Underline any words you do not understand.

Cause and Effect

Cells can only grow so big until they become inefficient. ☑ **Using a cause-and-effect statement, explain the cause of limited cell size.**

_____

_____

_____

_____

_____

_____

A Problem of Size The larger a cell becomes, the less efficient it is in moving nutrients and wastes across its cell membrane. Food, oxygen, and water enter through the cell membrane, and waste products leave the cell the same way. The total area of the cell membrane, known as the surface area, determines how fast this transportation of materials occurs. The volume of the cell determines how much food material is needed and how much waste is produced. As the cell gets larger, both the surface area and the volume of the cell increase, but not at an equal rate.

Ratio of Surface Area to Volume Imagine that a cell is cube shaped. The surface area and volume can be calculated as the cell grows, and the surface area and volume amounts can be compared as a ratio. The growth of the cell membrane (surface area) does not increase as fast as the inside of the cell (volume) and the cell cannot function well as a result.

Traffic Problems One problem resulting from the volume increasing faster than the surface area of a cell is the decrease of "traffic flow" of nutrients and waste. The surface area of the cell membrane is the "road" into the cell. If the membrane is not large enough, proper passage of enough nutrients and wastes cannot occur.

Visual Reading Tool: Surface Area to Volume Ratio in Cells

1. For a cell to function efficiently, the surface-area-to-volume ratio needs to be large. In the table below, determine the surface area to volume ratio and write the ratio in the box provided. Don't forget units, and make sure the final ratio is in relation to 1.

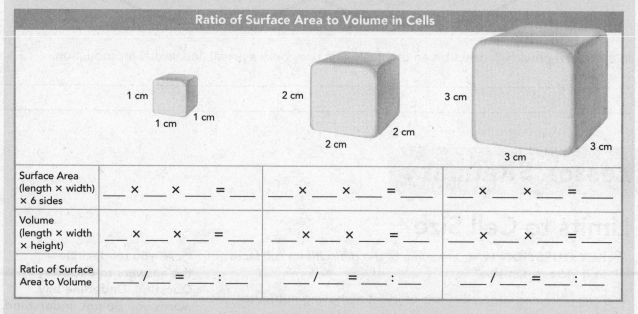

Ratio of Surface Area to Volume in Cells

Surface Area (length × width) × 6 sides	___ × ___ × ___ = ___	___ × ___ × ___ = ___	___ × ___ × ___ = ___
Volume (length × width × height)	___ × ___ × ___ = ___	___ × ___ × ___ = ___	___ × ___ × ___ = ___
Ratio of Surface Area to Volume	___ / ___ = ___ : ___	___ / ___ = ___ : ___	___ / ___ = ___ : ___

2. What happens to the surface-area-to-volume ratio as the cell increases in size? Will the cell continue to function efficiently as the cell size gets larger and larger?

_____

Information Overload Referring to the town analogy in Figure 11-3, access to information is critical to run the town efficiently. If the town grows quickly but its library stays the same, there will not be enough information to serve the population. Cells store critical information in a molecule known as DNA. The information in DNA directs all the cell's functions, but it does not increase in size as the cell increases in size. The cell solves this "information crisis" by creating a duplicate copy of the DNA and dividing it among two new cells so that each new cell has its own copy of the DNA.

Cell Division To function efficiently, the cell divides into two new daughter cells through a process called **cell division**. First, DNA is copied through a process called DNA replication, resulting in a complete set of the DNA for each new daughter cell. Then the cell splits in two. Cell division reduces the cell volume, resulting in efficient exchange of materials between the cell membrane and its environment. Cells easily obtain nutrients like oxygen, water, and food and quickly eliminate cellular waste products.

Cell Division and Reproduction

🔍 **KEY QUESTION** *How do asexual and sexual reproduction compare?*

Both sexual and asexual reproduction result in new individuals. Asexual reproduction produces offspring identical to the parent by cell division. In sexual reproduction, reproductive cells from two parents are fused to form a new individual.

To form new individuals, all organisms must be able to reproduce. There are two types of reproduction, asexual and sexual reproduction.

Asexual Reproduction **Asexual reproduction** is the production of genetically identical offspring from a single parent. Asexual reproduction in single-celled organisms occurs through cell division.

Sexual Reproduction **Sexual reproduction** involves the fusion of two reproductive cells from each of two parents. Offspring produced by sexual reproduction inherit some of their genetic information from each parent.

Comparing Asexual and Sexual Reproduction The advantages of asexual reproduction include quick and successful reproduction when conditions are ideal, which allows offspring to survive when in competition with other organisms. The lack of genetic diversity may prevent them from surviving if conditions change.

Sexual reproduction produces genetic diversity. If an environment changes, genetic diversity in a species may help to ensure that the individual members of the population contain the right combination of characteristics needed to survive.

Build Vocabulary

cell division process in which a cell divides into two new identical daughter cells

asexual reproduction process of reproduction involving a single parent that results in offspring that are genetically identical to the parent

sexual reproduction type of reproduction in which cells from two parents unite to form the first cell of a new organism

Word Origins The word *divide* is based upon the Latin word *dividere*, which means "to force apart or remove." ☑ **What needs to be duplicated before a cell can go through cell division?**

The Process of Cell Division

READING TOOL **Sequence of Events** In the cell cycle diagram below, each section represents the relative time the cell spends in each stage. In the following diagram, write in each of the following phases:

a. Interphase
b. G_1 phase
c. S
d. G_2
e. M phase
f. Mitosis
g. Cytokinesis
h. Cell division

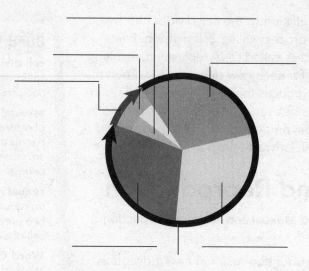

Lesson Summary

Chromosomes

🔍 As you read, circle the answers to each Key Question. Underline any words you do not understand.

🔑 **KEY QUESTION** *What is the role of chromosomes in cell division?*

Cells must divide to function efficiently. Each new daughter cell needs a complete set of genetic information for cell growth and function. The genetic information is bundled into packages of DNA called **chromosomes**. When DNA is organized into chromosomes, it is easier for the cell to divide the genetic material equally between the two daughter cells.

Prokaryotic Chromosomes The circular chromosome found in prokaryotic cells contains almost all of the genetic information and is not enclosed in a nucleus.

Eukaryotic Chromosomes The DNA strands in eukaryotic cells are tightly bound to proteins called histones, creating a complex called **chromatin**. Histones and DNA coil tightly together, forming beadlike structures called nucleosomes, which condense to form thick fibers called chromosomes. The X-like chromosome is actually a duplicated chromosome connected together.

BUILD Vocabulary

chromosome threadlike structure within the nucleus that contains genetic information that is passed on from one generation to the next

chromatin substance found in eukaryotic chromosomes that consists of DNA tightly coiled around histones

The Cell Cycle

KEY QUESTION *What are the main events of the cell cycle?*

During the **cell cycle**, a cell grows, prepares for division, and then divides to form two daughter cells. There are 4 main phases of the cell cycle: G_1, S, G_2, and M.

Prokaryotic Cell Cycle The prokaryotic cell cycle takes place very quickly when conditions are ideal. As the cell grows and functions, it reaches a certain size and begins to copy its DNA. When DNA replication is complete, the cell divides by binary fission, which is a form of asexual reproduction. The two copies of the DNA attach to different regions of the cell membrane. The cell membrane then pinches inward between the two regions to divide the cytoplasm. The two resulting daughter cells have identical copies of the DNA and equal amounts of cytoplasm.

Eukaryotic Cell Cycle The four stages of the eukaryotic cell cycle are G_1, S, G_2, and M. The longest period of the cell cycle, called **interphase**, includes the G_1, S, and G_2 phases.

G_1: Cell Growth Cell Growth is the period of cell growth in which the cell increases in size and makes new organelles.

S: DNA Replication DNA replication is the stage of the cell cycle that results in two complete sets of DNA ready to be divided between the daughter cells.

G_2: Preparing for Cell Division The preparation time for cell division is when the organelles and molecules needed to carry out cell division are made.

M phase: Cell Division Mitosis is the division of the cell nucleus, and the division of the cytoplasm is called **cytokinesis**.

Mitosis

KEY QUESTION *What happens during the phases of mitosis?*

Mitosis is the segment of the cell cycle during which the division of the cell nucleus occurs. Mitosis is divided into four phases: prophase, metaphase, anaphase, and telophase.

During prophase, the duplicated chromosomes become visible. In metaphase, the centromeres of the duplicated chromosomes line up. In anaphase, the chromosomes separate and move to opposite ends of the cell. During telophase, the chromosomes spread out into a tangle of chromatin.

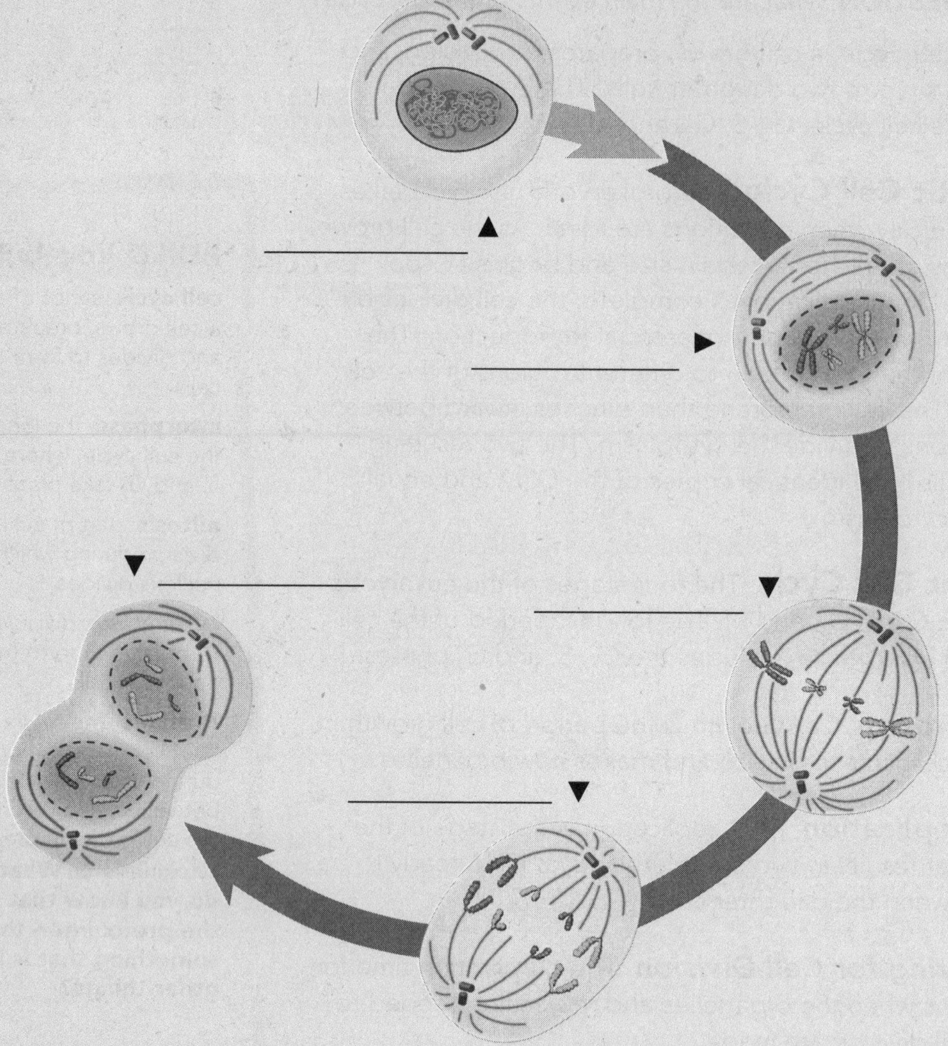

Label the diagram above with the four stages of mitosis. Then, in the space provided below, describe what happens in each stage of mitosis.

Prophase: _____

_____

_____

Metaphase: _____

_____

Anaphase: _____

_____

Telophase: _____

_____

Prophase The genetic material inside the nucleus condenses and the duplicate chromosomes become visible during the first stage of mitosis called prophase. At the beginning of prophase, the sister chromatids, or strands of condensed chromosomes, become visible. They are attached to each other at a point called the centromere. In the cytoplasm, two tiny organelles, called centrioles, are involved in developing spindle fibers that span across the cell.

Metaphase During metaphase, the spindle fibers move the centromeres of the duplicated chromosomes to the center of the cell. These spindle fibers are connected to the two poles near the centrioles and are ready to separate the sister chromatids.

Anaphase During anaphase, the chromosomes separate and move along the spindle fibers to opposite ends of the cell. Anaphase ends when the sister chromatids, now considered individual chromosomes, are completely separated into two groups and the spindle fibers have almost disappeared.

Telophase During telophase, the chromosomes, which were distinct and condensed, begin to spread out into a tangle of chromatin. This is the final stage of mitosis. The nuclear envelope is reconstructed and the nucleolus becomes visible in each new cell.

Cytokinesis

🔍 **KEY QUESTION** *How do daughter cells split apart after mitosis?*

In plants, cytokinesis separates the cells by forming a cell plate between the divided nuclei. In animals, cytokinesis draws the membrane inward to separate the cells.

During the M phase of the cell cycle, mitosis forms two nuclei, each with a complete set of the DNA. The last segment of the M phase is cytokinesis. Cytokinesis completes the process of cell division by dividing one cell into two.

Cytokinesis in Animal Cells The cell membrane is drawn inward and pinched into two new daughter cells. Each cell contains the new nucleus formed during mitosis and an equal amount of cytoplasm.

Cytokinesis in Plants Because of the rigid cell wall surrounding the cell membrane in plant cells, pinching from the outside inward cannot occur. A cell plate forms halfway between the two nuclei and gradually expands toward and fuses with the existing cell membranes. A new cell wall then forms to separate the two daughter cells.

BUILD Vocabulary

prophase first and longest phase of mitosis in which the genetic material inside the nucleus condenses and the chromosomes become visible

chromatid one of two identical "sister" parts of a duplicated chromosome

centromere region of a chromosome where the two sister chromatids attach

centriole structure in an animal cell that helps to organize cell division

metaphase phase of mitosis in which the chromosomes line up across the center of the cell

anaphase phase of mitosis in which the chromosomes separate and move to opposite ends of the cell

telophase phase of mitosis in which the distinct individual chromosomes begin to spread out into a tangle of chromatin

Prefixes In biology, the prefix *telo-* means "end" or "completion."

☑ **What occurs during telophase that signifies the end of mitosis?**

_____

_____

_____

READING TOOL

Compare and Contrast

☑ **How do chromosomes differ in prokaryotes and eukaryotes?**

_____

_____

_____

_____

_____

Regulating the Cell Cycle

READING TOOL **Make Connections** In the graphic organizer below, fill in each box with headings from this unit to help you understand the concepts.

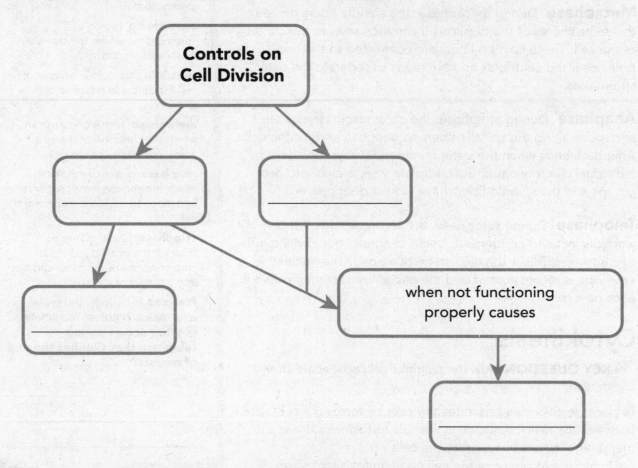

Lesson Summary

Controls on Cell Division

🔍 As you read, circle the answers to each Key Question. Underline any words you do not understand.

🔍 **KEY QUESTION** *How is the cell cycle regulated?*

The cell cycle is controlled by regulatory proteins both inside and outside the cell.

How do cells know when it is time to divide? Cell growth and cell division are highly controlled in multicellular organisms. Some cells grow and divide very quickly, like skin and blood cells, whereas other cells grow to a certain size and never divide, like muscle and nerve cells. Without precise regulation of cell growth and division, serious diseases like cancer can result. Controls on cell growth and division can be influenced, and scientists have identified many of these controlling factors.

Regulatory Proteins   For many years, biologists searched for a signal that might regulate the cell cycle—something that would "tell" the cell when it was time to divide, duplicate its chromosomes, or enter another phase of the cell cycle. They found out that there is not just one signal, but many. Scientists have identified dozens of proteins that help to regulate the cell cycle. The cell cycle is controlled by many different regulatory proteins located inside and outside of the cell.

Internal Regulators   Internal regulatory proteins control events of the cell cycle by responding to events inside the cell. These "checkpoint proteins" assure that cell activities, like DNA replication or spindle fiber production, are completed before the next phase is triggered.

External Regulators   External regulatory proteins control events of the cell cycle by responding to events outside the cell. Growth factors are proteins that stimulate the growth and division of cells. Some regulatory proteins, found on the surface of neighboring cells, encourage slowing or even deactivation of the cell cycle to ensure that excessive growth does not occur.

Cyclins   Biologists had been searching for years for the signal that regulates the cell cycle because they realized that it could help them treat diseases. Learning that there is not just one signal but many has made that job more complicated. Cyclin is a kind of internal regulatory protein that regulates the cell cycle. When this protein is present, the mitotic spindle forms and the mitosis phase of the cell cycle is activated.

Apoptosis   The process of programmed cell death is called apoptosis. The steps include shrinking chromatin, cell membrane fragmentation, and cell debris clean up by neighboring cells. This process is important in growth and development because it shapes and restructures the developing parts of the organism. Uncontrolled apoptosis leads to diseases like AIDS and Parkinson's.

Cancer: Uncontrolled Cell Growth

⚘ **KEY QUESTION** *How do cancer cells differ from other cells?*

Cancer cells do not respond to the signals that regulate the growth of most cells. As a result, the cell cycle is disrupted, and cells grow and divide uncontrollably.

Cancer is a disorder in which body cells lose the ability to control growth. Cancer cells do not respond to the signals that regulate the growth of most cells. As a result, the cell cycle is disrupted, and cells grow and divide uncontrollably. Consequently, a mass of cells forms, called a tumor. Benign tumors, or noncancerous tumors, do not spread to surrounding tissues. Malignant tumors, or cancerous tumors, spread to surrounding tissues and destroy the healthy functioning of those tissues. As cancerous cells spread, they interfere with the other cells by absorbing necessary nutrients, blocking nerve connections, and preventing the organs they invade from functioning properly.

Build Vocabulary

growth factor   one of a group of external regulatory proteins that stimulate the growth and division of cells

cyclin   one of a family of proteins that regulates the cell cycle in eukaryotic cells

apoptosis   the process of programmed cell death

cancer   disorder in which some of the body's cells lose the ability to control growth

tumor   mass of rapidly dividing cells that can damage surrounding tissue

Root Words   The root of cyclin, *cycl*, is the Greek word for "circle." ☑ **How does the concept of a circle relate to cyclins?**

_____

_____

_____

_____

READING TOOL

Prefixes

The prefix *bene-* means "well" or "good," and the prefix *mal-* means "bad" or "evil." ☑ **Which type of tumor, benign or malignant, causes more damage to the body?**

_____

What Causes Cancer? All cancerous cells have lost control over the cell cycle because of defects in the genetic material that regulates cell growth and division. The defects in the DNA can be prompted by smoking, chewing tobacco, radiation exposure, and viral infections. Some cancer cells do not respond to external regulatory proteins, and others stop responding to internal regulatory proteins.

Treatments for Cancer Some cancerous tumors can be removed by surgery, but others need to be treated with radiation and/or chemotherapy. The most severe form of skin cancer, melanoma, can be treated by surgery, especially when detected early. In radiation therapy, high-energy, carefully targeted beams of radiation are used to kill the cancerous cells because the radiation damages the genetic material of these cells. Chemotherapy is the use of chemical compounds that target and kill rapidly dividing cells, but a side effect of these drugs is the interference with division of normal, healthy cells in parts of the body such as hair or the stomach lining.

Visual Reading Tool: Cyclin Levels

The MPF (mitosis-promoting factor) enzyme is present during the entire cell cycle. When MPF cyclin is also present, mitosis occurs. View the chart and answer the questions below.

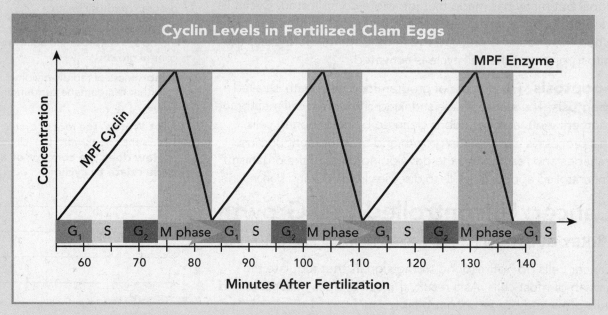

Cyclin Levels in Fertilized Clam Eggs

1. About how long does one cell cycle last in fertilized clam eggs?

_____

2. What occurs when MPF cyclin levels are highest?

_____

3. What are the four steps that occur during the M phase?

_____

_____

LESSON 4 Cell Differentiation

READING TOOL Main Idea and Details In the chart below, fill in the details that support the main ideas from this lesson.

Main Idea	Details
From One Cell to Many	
Defining Differentiation	
Mapping Differentiation	
Differentiation in Mammals	
Stem Cells and Development	
Human Development	
Stem Cells	
Frontiers in Stem Cell Research	
Ethical Issues	
Induced Pluripotent Stem Cells	
Regenerative Medicine	

Lesson Summary

From One Cell to Many

KEY QUESTION *How do cells become specialized for different functions?*

Multicellular organisms start as one cell, and then grow through the developmental stage called an **embryo**, which gradually becomes the adult organism. As this process proceeds, cells become different from one another and perform different functions for the organism.

As you read, circle the answers to each Key Question. Underline any words you do not understand.

BUILD Vocabulary

embryo developing stage of a multicellular organism

Defining Differentiation During development, cell **differentiation** is the process by which cells become specialized for specific functions.

Mapping Differentiation Biologists have determined the pathway of cell differentiation in a microscopic worm, *C. elegans*. The identity of each cell from the point of fertilization to the 959-celled adult has been mapped and identified.

Differentiation in Mammals Differentiation in mammals is more complicated and influenced by many interwoven factors. However, there is a specific point in the development of the organism when cell differentiation is complete.

Stem Cells and Development

⚲ KEY QUESTION *What are stem cells?*

Stem cells are the unspecialized cells from which differentiated cells develop.

How the differentiated cells develop from the single cell made from the fertilized egg is one of the secrets of developing organisms that biologists are still investigating. The zygote, or the fertilized egg, is **totipotent** because it is the single cell that is able to develop into any type of cell in the body.

Human Development Human development begins as a zygote, then after a few cell divisions, the embryo is formed. The **blastocyst** is formed next, which is a hollow ball of cells with another group of cells in the center. The outer cells of the blastocyst will eventually become the tissues that attach to the placenta of the mother, and the inner cell mass will become the actual embryo. The inner cells are **pluripotent** because they can develop into any of the cell types of the body, but they cannot form the tissues surrounding the embryo like the totipotent zygote.

Stem Cells **Stem cells** are unspecialized cells from which differentiated cells develop. They are found in the developing embryo and also in specific places of the adult body.

Adult Stem Cells Adult stem cells are **multipotent** because the types of cells that they form are restricted to the tissue type in which they are found.

Embryonic Stem Cells Embryonic stem cells are pluripotent because they are able to produce any cell in the body.

Frontiers in Stem Cell Research

🔑 KEY QUESTION *What are some possible benefits and issues associated with stem cell research?*

Stem cells may be useful to repair cell damage from heart attacks, strokes, or spinal cord injuries. Human embryonic stem cell research involves ethical issues.

Basic research on stem cells takes on a special urgency in light of the importance it might have for human health. Heart attacks destroy cells in the heart muscle, strokes injure brain cells, and spinal cord injuries cause paralysis by breaking connections between nerve cells. Not surprisingly, the prospect of using stem cells to repair such cellular damage has excited medical researchers.

Ethical Issues Human embryonic stem cell research is controversial because the arguments for it and against it both involve ethical issues of life and death. Adult stem cells are harvested from people who are willing to go through the process of donating the cells. However, obtaining embryonic stem cells involves the destruction of a human embryo.

Induced Pluripotent Stem Cells Shinya Yamanaka, a Japanese Nobel Prize–winning stem cell researcher, converted human fibroblasts, cells that make proteins in skin, into induced pluripotent stem cells. These modified fibroblasts may be able to replace embryonic stem cells, potentially solving the ethical problems.

Regenerative Medicine Some organisms regenerate lost body parts. Scientists continue to study the steps of regeneration and hope to replicate the steps in the human body.

READING TOOL

Pros and Cons

People have many different opinions on stem cell research, including whether or not it is ethical. ☑ Determine the benefits and issues regarding stem cell research.

Benefits:

_____

_____

_____

_____

Issues:

_____

_____

_____

_____

Visual Reading Tool: Future Treatment for Heart Disease

The diagram below shows how stem cells can be used to repair damaged heart tissue. Fill in the three steps doctors would take.

❶ _____

❷ _____

❸ _____

Review Vocabulary

Match the vocabulary word with the corresponding definition.

1. _____ a disorder in which cells do not respond to regulatory factors, resulting in uncontrolled growth and division

2. _____ the process by which cells become specialized

3. _____ the process by which a cell divides into two new daughter cells

4. _____ a mass of cancerous cells that can be benign or malignant

a. cell division

b. cancer

c. tumor

d. cell differentiation

Review Key Questions

Provide evidence and details to support your answers.

5. Describe the differences between asexual and sexual reproduction.

_____

_____

_____

6. List the four phases of mitosis in the order in which they occur and describe what happens in each.

_____

_____

_____

_____

_____

_____

7. Describe two types of tumors, and indicate which type is harmful and which is not.

_____

_____

_____

8. What are the benefits and issues regarding embryonic stem cell research?

_____

_____

The Work of Gregor Mendel

Sequence of Events As you read your textbook, identify the sequence of events that influenced Mendel's conclusions about genetics. Pay attention to his experiments with the F_1 and F_2 generations. The first event is filled in for you.

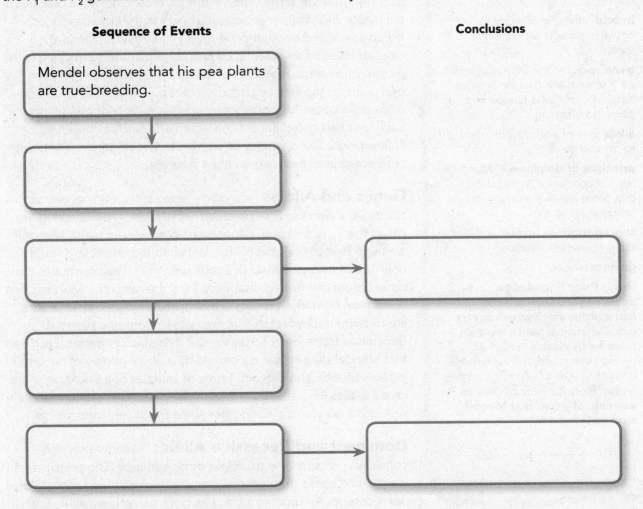

Sequence of Events

Conclusions

Mendel observes that his pea plants are true-breeding.

Lesson Summary

Mendel's Experiments

KEY QUESTION *Where does an organism get its unique characteristics?*

All living organisms have characteristics that are inherited from their parent or parents. The scientific study of biological inheritance is called **genetics**. Modern genetics began with the work of Gregor Mendel in the 1800s. Mendel studied inheritance in peas, which produce hundreds of offspring.

As you read, circle the answers to each Key Question. Underline any words you do not understand.

The Role of Fertilization During sexual reproduction, male and female reproductive cells join in a process called **fertilization** to produce a new cell. In peas, this cell develops into an embryo encased in a seed. Peas are normally self-pollinating, which means that the male and female reproductive cells come from within the same flower. Plants like this inherit all of its characteristics from its single parent. Mendel had stocks of pea plants with different specific characteristics, or **traits**. The stocks were true-breeding, meaning that when self-pollinated, the offspring had the same traits as the parents. One stock produced tall plants and another produced short plants. One produced green seeds and another produced yellow seeds. Mendel crossed his stocks of plants, causing one plant to reproduce with a plant from another stock. He did this by placing pollen from one plant on the female part of another. This process is called cross-pollination. Mendel examined seven traits of pea plants. Each trait had two different characteristics, such as green or yellow pods. The offspring of crosses between parent plants with different characteristics are called **hybrids**.

Genes and Alleles In genetic crosses, the original pair of plants are called the P, or parental, generation. Their offspring are called the F_1, or first filial, generation. In one experiment, Mendel was surprised to find that his F_1 plants had the characteristics of only one of their parents. For each cross, the characteristics of the other parent seemed to disappear from the offspring. Mendel's first conclusion from these results is that an individual's characteristics are determined by factors that are passed from one parental generation to the next. Today we call these factors **genes**. Each trait that Mendel studied was controlled by a single gene that occurred in two varieties. The different forms or varieties of a single gene are called **alleles** (uh LEELZ). For the gene for pea plant height, one allele produced tall plants and another allele produced short plants.

Dominant and Recessive Alleles Mendel's second conclusion is called the **principle of dominance**. The principle of dominance states that some alleles are dominant and some alleles are recessive. An organism that has both a dominant allele and a recessive allele for a trait will show the dominant characteristic. Mendel found that the allele for tall plants was dominant over the recessive allele for short plants, and the allele for yellow pods was dominant over the recessive allele for green pods.

Segregation

🔑 **KEY QUESTION** *How are different forms of a gene distributed to offspring?*

Mendel had another question: Had the recessive alleles disappeared, or were they still present in the new plants? To find out, he allowed all seven kinds of F_1 hybrids to self-pollinate. This cross of the F_1 generation produced the F_2 (second filial) generation.

The F₁ Cross When Mendel examined the F₂ plants, he found that traits produced by the recessive alleles reappeared in this generation. About one fourth of the F₂ plants showed the trait controlled by the recessive allele. Why did these traits appear to disappear in the F₁ generation and then reappear in the F₂ generation?

Explaining the F₁ Cross Mendel assumed that a dominant allele had masked the corresponding recessive allele in the F₁ generation. However, the recessive trait did appear in the F₂ generation. This indicates that at some point the allele for yellow pods had separated, or segregated, from the allele for green pods. Mendel suggested that the **segregation** of the alleles for yellow and green pods occurred during the formation of the reproductive cells, or **gametes** (GAM eetz).

The Formation of Gametes All of the F₁ plants inherited an allele (*G*) for green pods from the green parent and an allele (*g*) for yellow pods from the yellow parent. (For each trait, we use a capital letter to represent the dominant allele, and the same letter in lowercase to represent the recessive allele). Because the allele for green pods is dominant, all of the F₁ plants (*Gg*) have green pods. During gamete formation, the alleles for each gene segregate from each other, so that each gamete carries only one allele for each gene. Each F₁ plant produces two kinds of gametes, those with the green pod allele (*G*) and those with the yellow pod allele (*g*). When a gamete with the allele for yellow pods pairs with another gamete with the allele for yellow pods, the resulting F₂ plant (*gg*) has yellow pods. If one or both gametes that pair have the allele for green pods (*GG* or *Gg*), an F₂ plant with green pods is produced.

Visual Reading Tool: Segregation

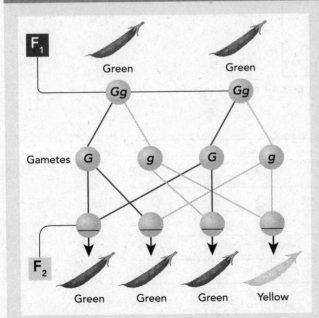

A cross between yellow-pod and green-pod pea plants results in only green-pod plants in the F₁ offspring. When the F₁ offspring are crossed with themselves, the yellow pods reappear in the F₂ generation. Use the figure to answer the questions.

1. In the figure, label each individual in the F₂ generation with the alleles it inherited from the F₁ generation.

2. What color is a pod with the *gg* alleles? _____

3. What color is a pod with the *GG* or *Gg* alleles? _____

4. Describe in your own words how a plant with a yellow pod can have two green-pod parents.

_____

_____

Applying Mendel's Principles

READING TOOL **Connect to Visuals** Before you read, preview **Figure 12-7**. Try to infer the purpose of this diagram. As you read, compare your inference to the text. After you read, revise your statement if needed or write a new one about the diagram's purpose. Take notes on the lines provided. Then view the Punnett square and answer the questions below regarding the genotypes and phenotypes.

Inference:

_____

_____

Revision:

_____

_____

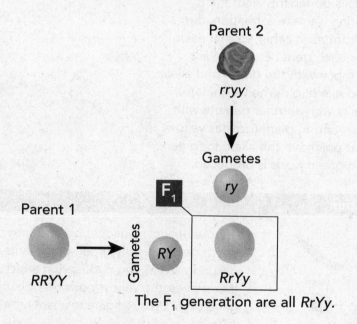

Parent 2

rryy

Gametes

ry

F$_1$

Parent 1

Gametes

RY

RrYy

RRYY

The F$_1$ generation are all *RrYy*.

1. What is the phenotype of parent 1? _____

2. What is the genotype of parent 1? _____

3. What is the phenotype of parent 2? _____

4. What is the genotype of parent 2? _____

5. What is the phenotype of the F$_1$ offspring? _____

6. What is the genotype of the F$_1$ offspring? _____

7. What kind of cross does this figure describe? _____

Lesson Summary

Probability and Heredity

🔑 **KEY QUESTION** *How can we use probability to predict traits?*

By analyzing his data, Mendel realized that the principles of probability could explain the results of his crosses. **Probability** is the likelihood that a particular event will occur.

Using Segregation to Predict Outcomes During gamete formation, alleles segregate randomly. Therefore, the principles of probability can predict the outcomes of genetic crosses, similar to the way probability is used to predict the outcomes of coin tosses. In Mendel's F_1 cross, each F_1 plant (*Gg*) has one green pod allele and one yellow pod allele, so $\frac{1}{2}$ of the gametes produced by the F_1 plants have yellow alleles (*g*). Because the yellow pod (*g*) allele is recessive, the only way to produce a plant with yellow pods (*gg*) is for two gametes, each carrying the *g* allele, to combine. Each gamete produced by the F_1 plants has a one in two, or $\frac{1}{2}$, chance of carrying the *g* allele. Since each plant is formed from two gametes, the probability of both gametes carrying the *g* allele is $\frac{1}{2} \times \frac{1}{2} = \frac{1}{4}$. Therefore, roughly one fourth of the F_2 offspring should have yellow pods, and the remaining three fourths should have green pods. Both the *GG* and *Gg* allele combinations result in green pea pods. Organisms that have two identical alleles for a particular gene, such as *GG* or *gg*, are said to be **homozygous**. Organisms that have two diffe*rent* alleles for the same gene, such as *Gg*, are said to be **heterozygous**.

Probabilities Predict Averages Probabilities predict the average outcome of a large number of events. In genetics, the predicted ratios may only occur when observing a large number of offspring. An F_2 generation with only a few offspring may not match Mendel's predicted ratios, but if there are hundreds or thousands of offspring, the results should come close to the predicted ratios.

Genotype and Phenotype One of Mendel's most important insights is that every organism has a genetic makeup as well as observable physical characteristics. The physical traits are called the **phenotype**, and the genetic makeup is called the **genotype**. Mendel's F_2 plants had three different genotypes—*GG*, *Gg*, and *gg*—but only two phenotypes: green or yellow pods. The *GG* and *Gg* genotypes have the same phenotype, green pods.

🔑 As you read, circle the answers to each Key Question. Underline any words you do not understand.

BUILD Vocabulary

probability likelihood that a particular event will occur

homozygous having two identical alleles for a particular gene

heterozygous having two different alleles for a particular gene

phenotype physical characteristics of an organism

genotype genetic makeup of an organism

Using Prior Knowledge In math class, you have studied probability using coin tosses. Flipping a coin is like studying the genetics of a gene with two different alleles. Each coin flip has a probability of $\frac{1}{2}$ of landing heads up. The probability of flipping two coins and getting heads on both tosses is $\frac{1}{2} \times \frac{1}{2} = \frac{1}{4}$. ☑ **If you flip a coin 50 times, about how many times would you expect to get heads?**

_____

Using Punnett Squares

Using Punnett Squares Punnett squares are one good way to predict the outcome of genetic crosses. **Punnett squares** use mathematical probability to help predict the genotype and phenotype combinations in genetic crosses. The number of possible alleles from each parent determines the number of rows and columns in the Punnett square.

Independent Assortment

KEY QUESTION *How do alleles segregate when more than one gene is involved?*

Mendel wondered if the segregation of one pair of alleles affects another pair. For example, does the gene that determines the shape of a seed affect the gene for seed color? This type of experiment is known as a two-factor, or dihybrid, cross because it involves two different genes. Single-gene crosses are monohybrid crosses.

Visual Reading Tool: Two-Factor Cross: F_2

The Punnett square shows the results of self-crossing the F_1 generation of a cross between round yellow peas and wrinkled green peas.

1. List the different genotypes in the F_2 generation. What is the frequency of each genotype? One is filled out for you.

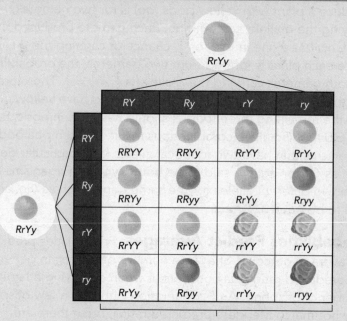

F_2 Generation

Genotype	Frequency
RRYY	$\frac{1}{16}$
rryy	$\frac{1}{16}$

2. List the different phenotypes in the F_2 generation. What is the frequency of each phenotype? One is filled out for you.

Phenotype	Frequency
wrinkled, green	$\frac{1}{16}$

The Two-Factor Cross: F₁ First, Mendel crossed true-breeding plants that produced only round, yellow peas with plants that produced only wrinkled, green peas.

The genotype is *RRYY* for the round, yellow peas and *rryy* for the wrinkled, green peas. All of the F₁ offspring produced round yellow peas. This shows that the alleles for yellow and round peas are dominant and the alleles for green and wrinkled peas are recessive. The genotype of the F₁ plants is *RrYy*. The F₁ plants are all heterozygous for seed shape and color.

The Two-Factor Cross: F₂ Mendel then crossed the F₁ plants to produce F₂ offspring. Each F₁ plant was formed from the fusion of a gamete with the dominant *RY* alleles with a gamete carrying the recessive *ry* alleles. Would the two dominant alleles always stay together or would they segregate independently, forming new combinations? If they segregated independently, a Punnett square shows that there will be a 9:3:3:1 ratio of round, yellow seeds to round, green seeds to wrinkled, yellow seeds to wrinkled, green seeds. In Mendel's experiment, the F₂ plants produced 556 seeds in a roughly 9:3:3:1 ratio. There were 315 round, yellow seeds, and 32 wrinkled, green seeds. However there were 209 seeds that had round, green seeds or wrinkled, yellow seeds. These were phenotypes that were not found in either parent. Therefore, the alleles for seed shape segregate independently from the alleles for seed color. Genes that segregate independently do not influence each other's inheritance. The principle of <mark>independent assortment</mark> states that genes for different traits can segregate independently during the formation of gametes. Independent assortment explains much of the variation observed in organisms that have the same parents.

A Summary of Mendel's Principles

🔑 **KEY QUESTION** *What did Mendel contribute to our understanding of genetics?*

Mendel's principles of heredity, observed through patterns of inheritance, form the basis of modern genetics. The following principles of heredity apply to many organisms, not just pea plants.

➤ The inheritance of biological characteristics is determined by individual units called genes.

➤ Where two or more forms (alleles) of the gene for a single trait exist, some alleles may be dominant and others may be recessive.

➤ In most sexually reproducing organisms, each adult has two copies for each gene—one from each parent. These genes segregate from each other when gametes are formed.

➤ Alleles for different genes usually segregate independently of each other.

BUILD Vocabulary

Punnett square diagram that can be used to predict the genotype and phenotype combinations of a genetic cross

independent assortment one of Mendel's principles that states that genes for different traits can segregate independently during the formation of gametes

Word Origins The Punnett square is named after Reginald Punnett, a British geneticist from the early 1900s. ☑ How many squares are in a Punnett square for a one-factor cross?

_____

How many for a two-factor cross?

_____

READING TOOL

Use Structure Mendel's principles of heredity are listed on this page in a bulleted list. Read the list carefully and answer the question below. ☑ Two offspring from the same parents can have different phenotypes. How is this possible?

_____

_____

_____

_____

_____

_____

Other Patterns of Inheritance

READING TOOL **Main Idea and Details** As you read your textbook, identify the five different types of nontraditional inheritance. In each box in the graphic organizer below, give an example of that main idea from the text.

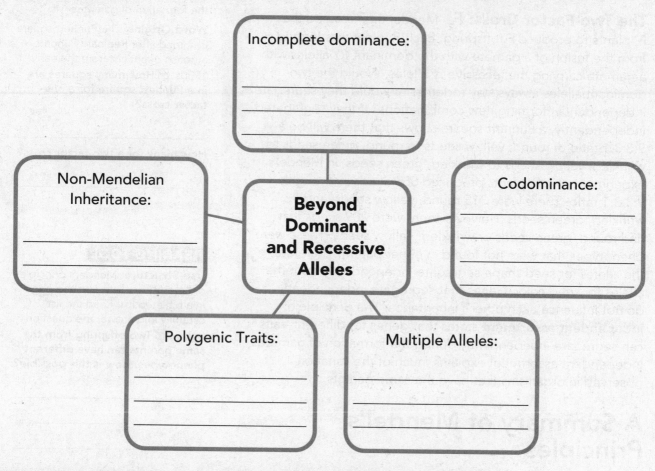

Incomplete dominance:

_____

_____

_____

Non-Mendelian Inheritance:

_____

_____

Beyond Dominant and Recessive Alleles

Codominance:

_____

_____

_____

Polygenic Traits:

_____

_____

_____

Multiple Alleles:

_____

_____

_____

Lesson Summary

Beyond Dominant and Recessive Alleles

🔍 As you read, circle the answers to each Key Question. Underline any words you do not understand.

🔍 **KEY QUESTION** *What are some exceptions to Mendel's principles?*

Incomplete Dominance Some alleles are neither completely dominant nor recessive. In the four o'clock plant (*Mirabilis jalapa*), a cross between a red-flowered (*RR*) plant and a white-flowered (*rr*) plant produces F$_1$ plants with pink flowers (*Rr*). This situation is called incomplete dominance. In **incomplete dominance**, the heterozygous phenotype lies somewhere between the two homozygous phenotypes.

Codominance Codominance is when the phenotypes produced by both alleles are clearly expressed. In some chickens, the allele for black feathers is codominant with the allele for white feathers. Heterozygous chickens have a mixture of black and white feathers. Unlike the blending of red and white colors in heterozygous four o'clock flowers, the black and white colors remain separate in chickens.

Multiple Alleles In nature, many genes have more than two alleles. Many genes exist in several different forms and are therefore said to have **multiple alleles**. A gene with more than two alleles has multiple alleles. An individual usually has two copies of each gene, but in a population there are many different alleles. A rabbit's coat color is determined by a single gene with at least four different alleles, and the four alleles display a pattern of dominance that can produce four different coat colors.

Polygenic Traits Many traits are produced by the interaction of several genes. Traits controlled by two or more genes are said to be **polygenic traits**. Polygenic means "many genes." There may be as many as a dozen genes that are responsible for the many different shades of human eye colors.

Non-Mendelian Inheritance Some traits follow non-Mendelian patterns of inheritance. Leaf color in *Mirabilis jalapa* is determined by the leaf color in the maternal parent. This pattern, known as maternal inheritance, would not be predicted from Mendel's principles. Maternal inheritance occurs because chloroplasts and mitochondria are inherited from the maternal gamete, or egg cell. Chloroplasts and mitochondria contain genes on small DNA molecules. Genes in the chloroplast determine leaf color in *Mirabilis*. Therefore, this trait shows maternal inheritance. Another source of non-Mendelian inheritance is genetic imprinting. In genetic imprinting, certain genes have been chemically modified in one parent in a way that prevents their expression in the next generation.

Genes and the Environment

🔑 **KEY QUESTION** *Does the environment have a role in how genes determine traits?*

An organism's characteristics are not only determined by the genes it inherits. Environmental conditions can affect gene expression and influence genetically determined traits. In some butterflies, the amount of pigmentation in the wing is influenced by the length of daylight during the time of year the larva hatches. Butterflies hatched when there is less daylight have more pigmentation, and therefore darker markings, than butterflies hatched when there is more daylight.

BUILD Vocabulary

incomplete dominance situation in which one allele is not completely dominant over another allele

codominance situation in which the phenotypes produced by both alleles are completely expressed

multiple alleles a gene that has more than two alleles

polygenic trait trait controlled by two or more genes

Prefixes *Poly-* is a prefix that means "many." Many roots that can use the prefix *poly-* can also use the prefix *mono-*, which means "one." ☑ **What would be a word for a trait controlled by a single gene?**

_____

READING TOOL

Connect to Visuals In four o'clock plants, the gene for flower color is inherited by incomplete dominance. View the Punnett square below that shows the cross of a pink plant with a white plant.

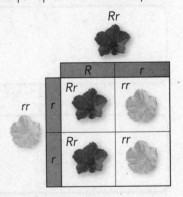

☑ **What is the probability that the offspring of this cross has white flowers?**

_____

READING TOOL **Sequence of Events** Identify the sequence of events in the process of meiosis. Take notes in the chart.

MEIOSIS I

MEIOSIS II

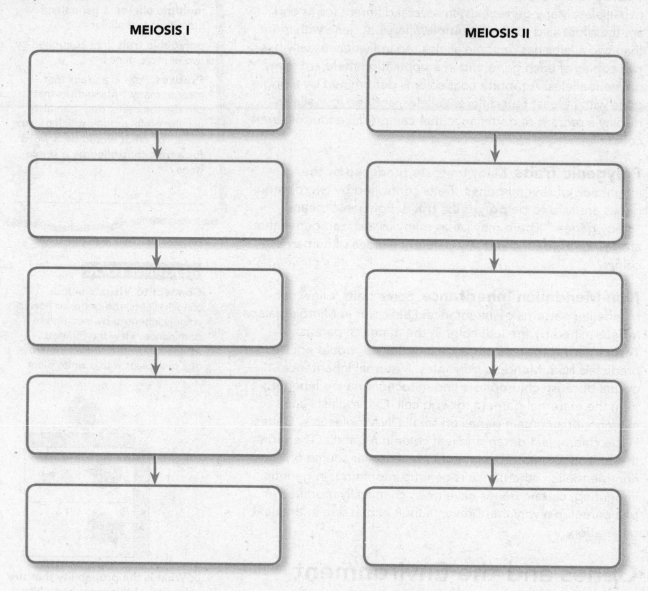

Lesson Summary

Chromosome Number

⚲ **KEY QUESTION** *How many sets of genes are found in most adult organisms?*

Mendel's principles require at least two events to occur. First, an organism with two parents must inherit one copy of every gene from each parent. Then, when the organism reproduces, its two sets of genes must be separated so that each gamete contains just one set of genes. Genes are located on chromosomes, strands of DNA and proteins in the cell.

Diploid Cells Each cell of the fruit fly *Drosophila melanogaster* has eight chromosomes. Four of these chromosomes come from the male parent and four from the female parent. The two sets of chromosomes are **homologous**, meaning that each chromosome from the male parent has a corresponding chromosome from the female parent. A cell with two sets of homologous chromosomes is **diploid**, meaning "double." The diploid cells of most adult organisms contain two complete sets of inherited chromosomes and two complete sets of genes. The diploid number of chromosomes can be represented by the symbol 2N. For *Drosophila*, the diploid number is 8, or 2N = 8.

Haploid Cells Some cells, such as gametes, have a single set of chromosomes and therefore a single set of genes. Such cells are **haploid**, meaning "single." The haploid number of chromosomes is represented by N.

Phases of Meiosis

⚲ **KEY QUESTION** *What events occur during each phase of meiosis?*

Sexually reproducing organisms produce haploid (N) gamete cells from diploid (2N) cells in meiosis (my OH sis). **Meiosis** is a process in which the homologous chromosomes of a diploid cell are separated from each other. Meiosis involves two distinct cell divisions called meiosis I and meiosis II. Through meiosis, a single diploid cell produces four haploid cells.

Meiosis I Prior to meiosis I, the cell replicates its chromosomes during interphase. Each replicated chromosome consists of two identical chromatids joined at the center.

⚲ As you read, circle the answers to each Key Question. Underline any words you do not understand.

BUILD Vocabulary

homologous type of chromosomes in which one set comes from the male parent and one set comes from the female parent

diploid a cell that contains two sets of homologous chromosomes

haploid a cell that contains only a single set of genes

meiosis process in which the number of chromosomes per cell is cut in half through the separation of homologous chromosomes in a diploid cell

Prefixes The prefix *homo-* means "same," and, in general usage, means "same position," or "same structure." *Homologous* chromosomes are two chromosomes from different parents that have the same genes and structure. ☑ **What other word from this unit has the prefix *homo-* and means to have two copies of the same allele?**

_____

Prophase I After interphase I, the chromosomes pair up. In prophase I of meiosis, each replicated chromosome pairs with its corresponding homologous chromosome. This pairing forms a structure with four chromatids called a **tetrad**. As the chromosomes pair, they sometimes exchange pieces of the homologous chromosomes in a process called **crossing-over**. Crossing-over produces new combinations of alleles on each chromosome.

Metaphase I and Anaphase I As prophase I ends, a spindle forms and attaches to each tetrad. During metaphase I of meiosis, paired homologous chromosomes line up across the center of the cell. Then the homologous pairs of chromosomes separate. During anaphase I, spindle fibers pull each homologous chromosome pair toward opposite ends of the cell.

Telophase I and Cytokinesis When anaphase I is complete, the separated chromosomes cluster at opposite ends of the cell. The next phase is telophase I, in which a nuclear membrane forms around each cluster of chromosomes. Cytokinesis follows, forming two new cells. Meiosis I produces two daughter cells. Since each pair of homologous chromosomes are separated, neither cell has the two complete sets of chromosomes found in a diploid cell. The two sets of chromosomes have been shuffled, so that the sets of chromosomes and alleles differ from those in the diploid cell that started meiosis I.

Meiosis II The two cells now enter a second meiotic division called meiosis II. Neither cell replicates its chromosomes before entering meiosis II.

Prophase II As cells enter prophase II, their chromosomes— each consisting of two chromatids—become visible. The chromosomes do not pair, because the homologous pairs were already separated during meiosis I.

Metaphase II, Anaphase II, Telophase II, and Cytokinesis During metaphase of meiosis II, the chromosomes line up in the center of each cell. As the cells enter anaphase, the paired chromatids separate. The final four phases of meiosis II are similar to those in meiosis I. However, the result is four haploid cells that contain the haploid number (N) of chromosomes. The haploid cells produced by meiosis develop into the gametes for sexual reproduction. The male gametes are usually called sperm, and the female gametes are called egg cells.

Comparing Meiosis and Mitosis

⚲ KEY QUESTION *How is meiosis different from mitosis?*

Meiosis and mitosis are very different. Mitosis can be a form of asexual reproduction. Meiosis is an early step in sexual reproduction. Mitosis and meiosis also differ in the way chromosomes are divided between daughter cells and in their number of cell divisions.

Replication and Separation of Genetic Material

A cell replicates, or copies, all of its chromosomes before entering either mitosis or meiosis. In mitosis, each daughter cell receives a complete diploid set of chromosomes. In meiosis, homologous chromosomes are separated, and each daughter cell receives only a haploid set of chromosomes. In meiosis, the two alleles for each gene are segregated and end up in different gamete cells. The sorting and recombination of genes in meiosis increases genetic variation.

Visual Reading Tool: Gene Map

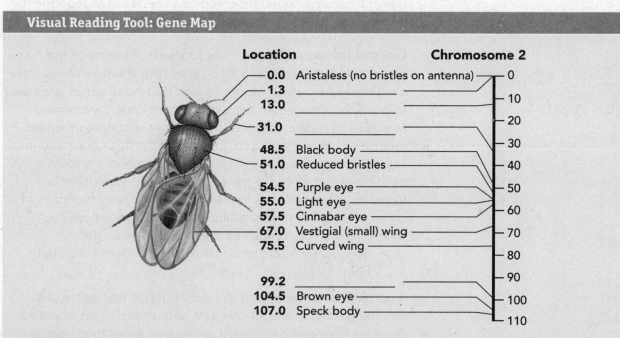

Location	
0.0	Aristaless (no bristles on antenna)
1.3	
13.0	
31.0	
48.5	Black body
51.0	Reduced bristles
54.5	Purple eye
55.0	Light eye
57.5	Cinnabar eye
67.0	Vestigial (small) wing
75.5	Curved wing
99.2	
104.5	Brown eye
107.0	Speck body

This gene map shows the locations of genes on chromosome 2 of the fruit fly *Drosophila melanogaster*.

1. Write in the following genes at their listed location on the gene map.
   Arc (bent wings): 99.2   Dumpy wing: 13.0
   Dachs (short legs): 31.0   Star eye: 1.3

2. Which pair of genes are closer together on the chromosome—*dachs* and *dumpy wing*, or *arc* and *star eye*? _____

3. Which pair of genes are more likely to assort independently—*dachs* and *dumpy wing*, or *arc* and *star eye*? _____

4. What process can lead to genes on the same chromosome assorting independently?
   _____

5. When does the process from question 4 occur during meiosis? _____

Compare and Contrast

Mitosis and *meiosis* are two similar biological processes with important differences. They both start with a diploid cell, but end up with very different products. ☑ **What is the final product for each process?**

_____

_____

_____

_____

_____

Changes in Chromosome Number Mitosis does not change the chromosome number of the original cell. This is not the case for meiosis, which reduces the chromosome number by half. A diploid cell that enters mitosis with eight chromosomes will produce two diploid daughter cells, each with eight chromosomes. A diploid cell that enters meiosis with eight chromosomes will pass through two meiotic divisions to produce four haploid daughter cells, each with four chromosomes.

Number of Cell Divisions Mitosis is a single cell division. Meiosis requires two rounds of division. Mitosis results in the production of two genetically identical diploid cells, whereas meiosis produces four genetically different haploid cells.

Gene Linkage and Gene Maps

🔍 **KEY QUESTION** *How can two alleles from different genes be inherited together?*

Genes located on different chromosomes assort independently. What about genes on the same chromosome?

Gene Linkage Thomas Hunt Morgan's research on the *Drosophila* fruit fly showed that genes on the same chromosome are inherited together. Morgan found that many genes appeared to be "linked" together and are not independently assorted. Morgan and others observed many genes that were inherited together. They were able to group all of the fly's genes into four linkage groups. The linkage groups assorted independently from each other, but all of the genes in one group were inherited together. *Drosophila* has four linkage groups, and four pairs of chromosomes. Morgan's results led to two conclusions.
➤ First, each chromosome is a group of linked genes.
➤ Second, Mendel's principle of independent assortment holds true.

It is the chromosomes, not the individual genes, that assort independently. Alleles of different genes tend to be inherited together from one generation to the next when those genes are located on the same chromosome. Mendel missed gene linkage, because several of the genes he studied are on different chromosomes. Others are on the same chromosome, but are so far apart that they also assort independently.

Gene Mapping One of Morgan's students, Alfred Sturtevant, reasoned that the farther apart two genes were on a chromosome, the more likely it was that crossing-over would occur between them. If genes are far apart and more likely to cross-over, then they are more likely to assort independently. Sturtevant used the frequency of crossing-over between genes to determine their distances from each other. Sturtevant produced in one night a gene map showing the relative locations of each known gene on one of the *Drosophila* chromosomes.

Review Vocabulary

Choose the letter of the best answer.

1. A diagram to predict the outcome of a genetic cross is a/an

   A. independent assortment.

   B. Punnett square.

   C. polygenic trait.

2. The exchange of genetic information between homologous chromosomes during meiosis is called

   A. segregation.

   B. a polygenic trait.

   C. crossing-over.

Match the vocabulary term to its definition.

3. _____ the offspring of parents with contrasting characteristics

   a. hybrid

4. _____ structure formed by paired homologous chromosomes

   b. genotype

5. _____ the genetic makeup of an organism

   c. tetrad

Review Key Questions

Provide evidence and details to support your answers.

6. How are alleles segregated in sexually reproducing organisms?

_____

_____

7. In a Punnett square for a two-factor cross, is it possible for all of the offspring to be identical? Explain why or why not.

_____

_____

8. A parent with blood type A (genotype AO) and a parent with blood type B (genotype BO) have children with blood types A, B, and AB. What type of inheritance pattern is shown by the child with type AB blood and why?

_____

_____

9. How does meiosis increase genetic variation?

_____

_____

CHAPTER 13

LESSON 1

Identifying the Substance of the Gene

READING TOOL **Sequence of Events** As you read, pay attention to the experiments that were carried out to help scientists understand genes and how DNA affects living things. Take notes on the importance of each experiment in the graphic organizer below.

Griffith	Avery	Hershey-Chase

Lesson Summary

Bacterial Transformation

As you read, circle the answers to each Key Question. Underline any words you do not understand.

KEY QUESTION *What clues did bacterial transformation yield about the gene?*

Through experimentation and watching the process of transformation in bacteria, scientists learned that DNA stores and transmits genetic information from one generation to the next.

About a century ago, scientists who wanted to understand genetics better began experimenting to learn the chemical nature of genes. In 1928, the British scientist Frederick Griffith was investigating how certain types of bacteria produce pneumonia, a serious lung disease. Griffith had isolated two very similar types of bacteria from mice. Both types grew very well in culture plates in Griffith's lab, but only one of them caused pneumonia. The disease-causing bacteria (the "S" type) grew into smooth-edged colonies on culture plates, whereas the harmless bacteria (the "R" type) produced colonies with rough edges. The difference in appearance made the two types easy to tell apart.

Griffith's Experiments When Griffith injected mice with disease-causing bacteria, they developed pneumonia, while those injected with harmless bacteria remained healthy. An injection combining heat-killed, disease-causing bacteria and harmless bacteria still made the test mice sick.

Transformation Griffith identified that a chemical factor turned dead and harmless bacteria into disease-causing bacteria through a process called transformation. He determined that the disease-causing ability was transferred to the bacteria's offspring; thus transformation was caused by a gene.

The Molecular Cause of Transformation In 1944, Oswald Avery and a team of scientists tried to repeat Griffith's experiments to identify the molecule in the heat-killed bacteria that caused the transformation. They first removed molecules from heat-killed bacteria and used enzymes that destroyed their proteins, lipids, carbohydrates, and RNA. Despite this, transformation still occurred. A second experiment, where enzymes were used to destroy DNA, proved that when this happened, transformation did not occur. Their experiment proved that DNA must be responsible for the process of transformation.

Bacterial Viruses

🔍 **KEY QUESTION** *What role did bacterial viruses play in identifying genetic material?*

Experiments with bacterial viruses demonstrated that DNA and not the cell's protein coat carried genetic material.

Bacteriophages A bacteriophage is a virus that infects bacteria. One way bacteriophages infect bacteria is by inserting genetic information into a cell and reproducing until the bacteria bursts.

The Hershey-Chase Experiment To determine which part of the virus entered the bacterium, Hershey and Chase grew viruses with radioactive isotopes. These identified which molecules entered the bacteria—showing that DNA, not the protein coat, held the genetic material.

READING TOOL

Active Reading

During his experiments, Griffith figured out that the "S" type bacteria caused pneumonia in mice, and the "R" type did not.

☑ **Why was Griffith surprised when the mice injected with both harmless and heat-killed bacteria developed pneumonia and died?**

_____

_____

_____

_____

_____

_____

BUILD Vocabulary

transformation process in which one strain of bacteria is changed by a gene or genes from another strain of bacteria

bacteriophage (bak-tir-ē-∂-fāj) type of virus that infects bacteria

ROOT WORDS If you break the term *bacteriophage* down into two parts—*bacterio* and *phage*—it may help you understand it better. From the definition, you can see that *phage* is a type of virus. With *bacterio* at the beginning of it, you can see the relation between the two parts of the word. ☑ **What does a bacteriophage inject into a bacterial cell?**

_____

The Role of DNA

🔑 KEY QUESTION *What is the role of DNA in heredity?*

DNA stores and copies genetic information, and then transmits it to offspring. Through DNA, genes are expressed and cells develop with specific characteristics.

Storing Information DNA's primary job is to store genetic information. It is the heredity molecule, and it controls cell development. All information for a single cell to develop into a complex organism is stored in DNA.

Copying Information DNA's second job is to copy all of its genetic information exactly.

Gene Expression DNA's third job is to express the genetic information into other cells so they develop into exactly what they are coded to be.

Visual Reading Tool: Bacteriophages and the Hershey-Chase Experiment

T4 Bacteriophage

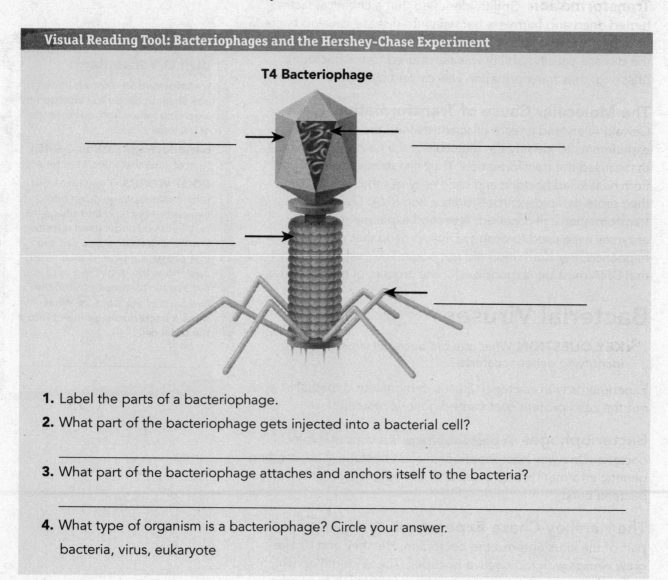

1. Label the parts of a bacteriophage.
2. What part of the bacteriophage gets injected into a bacterial cell?

_____

3. What part of the bacteriophage attaches and anchors itself to the bacteria?

_____

4. What type of organism is a bacteriophage? Circle your answer.

   bacteria, virus, eukaryote

The Structure of DNA

READING TOOL **Connect to Visuals** Refer to the given scientists and the associated textbook figure numbers to help you understand the events that led to solving the structure of DNA. In the boxes, write the names of the scientists and a short description of the experiment or discovery.

Scientist	Summary of Experiment
Chargaff (Figure 13-10)	
Franklin (Figure 13-7)	
Watson and Crick (Figure 13-8)	

Lesson Summary

The Components of DNA

KEY QUESTION *What are the chemical components of DNA?*

DNA is a nucleic acid made of nucleotides joined into long strands or chains by covalent bonds.

Nucleic Acids and Nucleotides The monomer of nucleic acids is a nucleotide. They are long chains that are somewhat acidic. Nucleotides include three basic components: a 5-carbon sugar molecule, a phosphate group, and a nitrogenous base. Nucleotides join together to form strands of DNA.

Nitrogenous Bases The nucleotides that make up DNA have four types of nitrogenous bases: adenine, guanine, cytosine, and thymine. Each of these is often referred to by its first initial: A, G, C, or T. Covalent bonds connect the sugar of one nucleotide with the phosphate group of another nucleotide—and these can join in any sequence.

Solving the Structure of DNA

KEY QUESTION *What clues helped scientists to determine the structure of DNA?*

The data in Franklin's X-ray pattern enabled Watson and Crick to build a model that explained the specific structure and properties of DNA.

Chargaff's Rule Biochemist Erwin Chargaff discovered similarities in the percentages of bases in DNA. He identified that each sample of DNA included an equal percentage of adenine (A) and thymine (T), as well as an equal percentage of guanine (G) and cytosine (C). This realization created what's known as Chargaff's rule: [A] = [T], and [G] = [C].

Franklin's X-Rays Scientist Rosalind Franklin used X-ray diffraction to study the structure of DNA molecules. After stretching the DNA fibers to make the strands as parallel as possible, she X-rayed the samples and recorded the patterns they created. Although she was not able to fully determine the structure of the molecule, her work provided insight into the helix shape of DNA strands.

The Work of Watson and Crick James Watson and Francis Crick were studying the structure of DNA at the same time as Franklin. Although they were able to build three-dimensional models of DNA, they still could not explain its properties. After seeing Franklin's X-ray of DNA, they determined that its structure was that of a double helix.

As you read, circle the answers to each Key Question. Underline any words you do not understand.

READING TOOL

Cause and Effect Let's explore cause and effect for a moment.

☑ **If Franklin had never used X-ray technology to take pictures of DNA, how might Watson and Crick's work have been different?**

_____

_____

_____

_____

The Double-Helix Model

KEY QUESTION *What does the double-helix model show about DNA?*

The double-helix model explains Chargaff's rule of base pairing and how two strands of DNA are held together.

Antiparallel Strands The two strands of DNA's double helix run antiparallel, or in opposite directions. This structure connects the nitrogenous bases on each strand, and allows DNA to carry nucleotides in a specific sequence.

Hydrogen Bonds DNA strands are held together by hydrogen bonds formed between nucleotides. Nitrogenous bases bond with certain other bases in a process called base pairing. For DNA, adenine (A) bonds with thymine (T), and guanine (G) bonds with cytosine (C).

Base Pairing Base pairing clarified how Chargaff's rule applied to DNA, and why (A) = (T) and (G) = (C). This led to a Nobel Prize for Watson, Crick, and Franklin. Although base pairing explained DNA structure and sequences, it did not explain how DNA carried or used the genetic information.

> **BUILD Vocabulary**
>
> **base pairing** principle that bonds in DNA can form only between adenine and thymine and between guanine and cytosine
>
> **Related Words** In genetics, the word *base* is shorthand for *nitrogenous base* and generally refers to A's, T's, C's, and G's.
>
> ☑ **What are the three main parts of a nucleotide?**
>
> _____
>
> _____

Visual Reading Tool: Identifying Base Pairs

1. Fill in the missing nucleotides in the diagram.

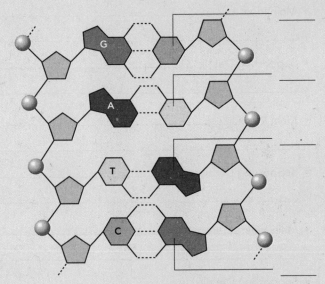

2. What do you notice about the number of hydrogen bonds that exist between the nucleotides?

_____

3. Who was the scientist who discovered the rule of base pairing? _____

4. On the diagram, what do the pentagons and spheres represent?

_____

_____

DNA Replication

READING TOOL **Main Idea and Details** As you read through this lesson, write the main ideas and supporting details in the chart below.

Copying the Code	• Main Idea: _____ _____ • Supporting Detail: _____ _____
The Replication Process	• Main Idea: _____ • Supporting Detail: _____ _____ _____
The Role of Enzymes	• Main Idea: _____ • Supporting Detail: _____ _____ _____
Telomeres	• Main Idea: _____ _____ • Supporting Detail: _____ _____
Replication of Living Cells	• Main Idea: _____ _____ • Supporting Detail: _____ _____
Prokaryotic DNA Replication	• Main Idea: _____ _____ • Supporting Detail: _____ _____
Eukaryotic DNA Replication	• Main Idea: _____ _____ • Supporting Detail: _____ _____

Lesson Summary

Copying the Code

KEY QUESTION *What is the role of DNA polymerase in copying DNA?*

DNA polymerase, or the main enzyme involved in DNA replication, joins nucleotides to synthesize a new complementary strand of DNA.

The Replication Process The DNA duplication process is called replication. During replication, DNA strands separate, and two complementary strands are created—one from each matching the opposite. Each new DNA molecule has one original and one new strand, making it identical to the original.

The Role of Enzymes An enzyme disconnects bonds between base pairs and unwinds the strands. Each strand becomes the model for the complementary strand. Then an enzyme called **DNA polymerase** creates the bonds connecting nucleotides, and ensures that each new strand is an exact copy of its original.

Telomeres The tips of eukaryotic chromosomes are called **telomeres**. These are hard to replicate, so the telomerase enzyme makes this happen. Telomerase adds short, repeated DNA sequences to telomeres during replication, and helps prevent the genes near the ends of chromosomes from getting lost or damaged during replication.

As you read, circle the answers to each Key Question. Underline any words you do not understand.

BUILD Vocabulary

replication process of copying DNA prior to cell division

DNA polymerase principal enzyme involved in DNA replication

telomere repetitive DNA at the end of a eukaryotic chromosome

Using Prior Knowledge There are three main differences between prokaryotes and eukaryotes. One difference is that one does not have a nucleus while the other does. Another difference is that the prokaryote is unicellular, while the eukaryote can be either unicellular or multicellular. ☑ **What is the third difference that you have learned about in this lesson?**

_____

_____

Visual Reading Tool: Structure Identification

1. Identify the following structures on the diagram: *DNA polymerase, new strand, nitrogenous bases, old strand, replication fork.*

2. On each side of the diagram, draw arrows to show the direction in which DNA replication is moving.

3. What is the job of DNA polymerase?

_____

_____

_____

_____

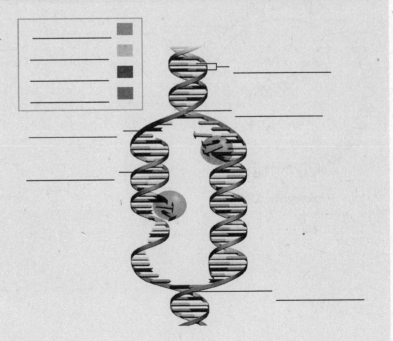

_____

Replication in Living Cells

🔍 **KEY QUESTION** *How does DNA replication differ in prokaryotic cells and eukaryotic cells?*

DNA replication in prokaryotic cells starts from one point and continues in two directions until replication is complete. In eukaryotic cells, it begins at multiple points and continues outward until complete.

Prokaryotic DNA Replication

Replication in most prokaryotes begins at a single point and moves in two directions until the entire chromosome is copied. Regulatory proteins bind at a single point on a chromosome, sparking the S phase and DNA replication. The two chromosomes produced in this process are connected to separate points within a cell's membrane and get separated during cell division.

Eukaryotic DNA Replication

Replication in eukaryotes is more complex and begins at multiple places on the DNA molecule, fanning out in two directions. Proteins ensure that base pairs are matched correctly and no damage occurs. Sometimes these proteins fail, and damaged sections of DNA are replicated. This causes changes to DNA base sequences and may have serious consequences for cell development.

Visual Reading Tool: Compare and Contrast

On each diagram below, label the following structures: *New DNA, Origin of replication, Replication fork, Unreplicated DNA.*

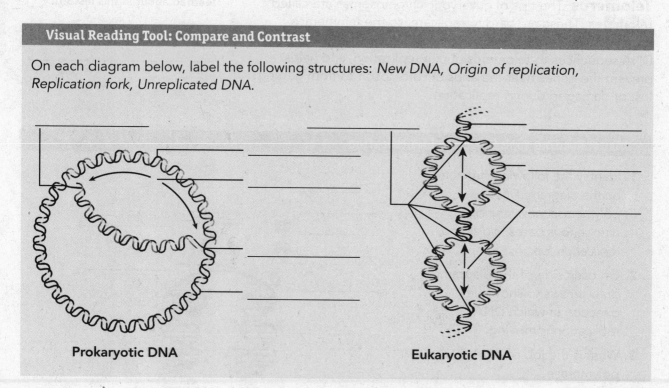

Prokaryotic DNA

Eukaryotic DNA

Review Vocabulary

Match the vocabulary term to its definition.

1. _____ a kind of virus that infects bacteria

2. _____ the process in which bacteria is changed by a gene

3. _____ principle that explains how bonds in DNA will form between specific nucleotides

4. _____ process of copying DNA prior to cell division

a. transformation

b. bacteriophage

c. base pairing

d. replication

Fill in the blanks with the correct terms to complete the sentence.

5. _____ are unicellular organisms that have circular DNA, while _____ have linear DNA and can be unicellular or multicellular.

Review Key Questions

Provide evidence and details to support your answers.

6. Explain how studying viruses led to the discovery that DNA contains genetic material.

_____

_____

7. If DNA is charged with storing, copying, and expressing genetic traits, what might happen if DNA got damaged?

_____

_____

8. Explain how the sugars, phosphate groups, and nitrogenous bases in one strand of DNA connect to a complementary strand during replication.

_____

_____

9. Enzymes serve several functions during DNA replication. Name two of these functions.

_____

_____

_____

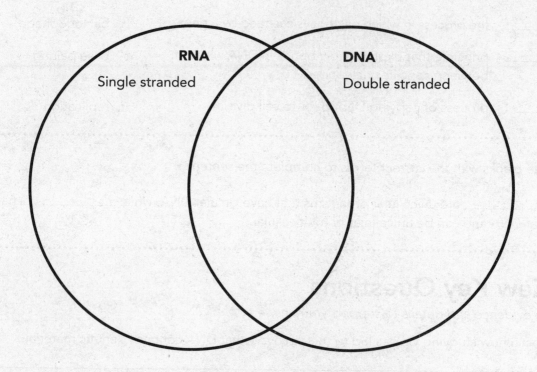

RNA

Single stranded

DNA

Double stranded

Lesson Summary

The Role of RNA

🔍 As you read, circle the answers to each Key Question. Underline any words you do not understand.

🔍**KEY QUESTION** *How does RNA differ from DNA?*

DNA contains a genetic code that living cells can read, understand, and express. DNA is made of just four nucleotides joined together in double-stranded molecules that can be millions of bases in length. What exactly do those bases code for, and how does the cell "read" that code? That's where RNA comes in. RNA helps to put the genetic code into action. RNA, like DNA, is a nucleic acid that consists of a long chain of nucleotides.

BUILD Vocabulary

ribonucleic acid (RNA) single-stranded nucleic acid that contains the sugar ribose

Genes contain coded DNA instructions that tell cells how to build proteins. The first step in decoding these genetic instructions is to copy part of the base sequence from DNA into RNA. RNA then uses these instructions to direct the production of proteins, which help to determine an organism's characteristics.

Comparing RNA and DNA Like DNA, RNA is made up of nucleotides. Each nucleotide consists of a 5-carbon sugar, a phosphate group, and a nitrogenous base. However, DNA and RNA differ in three important ways. RNA uses the sugar ribose instead of deoxyribose, RNA generally is single stranded, and RNA contains uracil in place of thymine. These chemical differences make it easy for enzymes in the cell to tell DNA and RNA apart.

The differences between DNA and RNA allow them to perform separate functions in the cell. The information in DNA is always around, stored safely in the cell's nucleus, where it serves as a template to make multiple RNA copies. In contrast, RNA is synthesized when the products of a particular gene are needed. RNA copies travel to the ribosomes, which then put the coded instructions into action by assembling proteins in the cytoplasm.

Three Main Types of RNA RNA has many roles, one of which is protein synthesis. RNA controls the assembly of amino acids into proteins. There are three main types of RNA involved in protein synthesis: messenger RNA, ribosomal RNA, and transfer RNA. Each type of RNA molecule specializes in a different aspect of the job.

Messenger RNA (mRNA) Most genes encode instructions for assembling amino acids into proteins. The molecules of RNA that carry copies of these instructions from the nucleus to ribosomes in the cytoplasm are known as **messenger RNA** (mRNA).

Ribosomal RNA (rRNA) Proteins are assembled on ribosomes, which are small organelles composed of two subunits. The subunits are made of several **ribosomal RNA** (rRNA) molecules and as many as 80 different proteins.

Transfer RNA (tRNA) During the assembly of a protein, a third type of RNA molecule known as **transfer RNA** (tRNA) carries amino acids to the ribosome and matches them to the coded mRNA message.

RNA Synthesis

🔑**KEY QUESTION** *How does the cell make RNA?*

A single DNA molecule may contain hundreds or even thousands of genes. However, only those genes being expressed are copied into RNA at any given time.

Transcription The process of copying a base sequence from DNA to RNA is known as **transcription**. In transcription, segments of DNA serve as templates to produce complementary RNA molecules.

BUILD Vocabulary

messenger RNA (mRNA) type of RNA that carries copies of instructions for the assembly of amino acids into proteins from DNA to the rest of the cell

ribosomal RNA (rRNA) type of RNA that combines with proteins to form ribosomes

transfer RNA (tRNA) type of RNA that carries each amino acid to a ribosome during protein synthesis

transcription synthesis of an RNA molecule from a DNA template

RNA polymerase enzyme that links together the growing chain of RNA nucleotides during transcription, using a DNA strand as a template

promoter specific region of a gene where RNA polymerase can bind and begin transcription

intron sequence of DNA that is not involved in coding for a protein

exon expressed sequence of DNA; codes for a protein

Prefixes *In-* is a prefix of Latin origin that can mean "in, on, or not."

☑ **Which meaning does *in-* have in the word *intron*? Explain your answer.**

_____

_____

_____

_____

_____

Academic Words

splice to join together

☑ **Why do exons have to be spliced together?**

_____

_____

_____

_____

_____

Transcription is carried out by an enzyme called **RNA polymerase**. RNA polymerase first binds to DNA and separates the DNA strands. It then uses one strand of DNA as a template to assemble nucleotides into a complementary strand of RNA. A single gene can produce hundreds, or even thousands, of RNA molecules.

Promoters RNA polymerase does not bind to DNA just anywhere. The enzyme binds only to **promoters**, which are regions of DNA with specific base sequences that can bind to RNA polymerase. Other regions of DNA cause transcription to stop when an RNA molecule is completed.

RNA Editing New RNA molecules sometimes require editing before they are ready to be read. These pre-mRNA molecules have pieces cut out of them before they can go into action. The portions that are cut out and discarded are called **introns**. The remaining pieces, known as **exons**, are then <u>spliced</u> back together to form the final mRNA.

Visual Reading Tool: Introns and Exons

1. Use colored pencils to color the parts of pre-mRNA as it goes through the editing process to become RNA. Color the cap green, the introns blue, the exons purple, and the tail red.

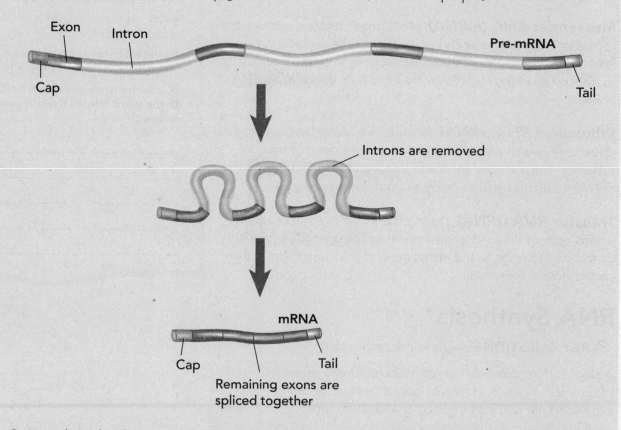

Exon   Intron   Pre-mRNA

Cap   Tail

Introns are removed

mRNA

Cap   Tail

Remaining exons are spliced together

2. How does the diagram show the difference between pre-mRNA and completed mRNA?

_____

_____

LESSON 2
Ribosomes and Protein Synthesis

READING TOOL **Sequence of Events** As you read your textbook, identify the steps of translation and protein synthesis. Complete the flowchart by writing the steps in the correct order. Use sequence words such as *first*, *then*, *next*, *after*, and *finally* to show the relationship between the steps. The first step has been entered for you.

First, a ribosome attaches to the mRNA molecule in the cytoplasm.

Lesson Summary

⚲ As you read, circle the answers to each Key Question. Underline any words you do not understand.

BUILD Vocabulary

polypeptide long chain of amino acids that makes proteins

genetic code collection of codons of mRNA, each of which directs the incorporation of a particular amino acid into a protein during protein synthesis

codon group of three nucleotide bases in mRNA that specify a particular amino acid to be incorporated onto a protein

Root Words The root word of the word *codon* is the word *code*.
☑ **Why does this root word make sense?**

_____

_____

_____

The Genetic Code

⚲ **KEY QUESTION** *How does the genetic code work?*

Cells use the code in mRNA to build proteins, one amino acid after another. The first step in the process of decoding genetic messages is transcription, which is the copying of a nucleotide base sequence from DNA to mRNA. The next steps lead to the assembly of a protein. Proteins are made by joining amino acids together into chains called **polypeptides**. The specific order in which amino acids are joined together in a polypeptide chain determines the shape, chemical properties, and, ultimately, function of a protein.

The four bases of RNA form a kind of language with just four letters: A, C, G, and U. We call this language the genetic code. The **genetic code** is read three bases at a time. Each "word" of the code is three bases long and corresponds to a single amino acid. This three-base "word" is known as a codon. A **codon** consists of three consecutive bases that specify a single amino acid to be added to the polypeptide chain.

Visual Reading Tool: Reading Codons

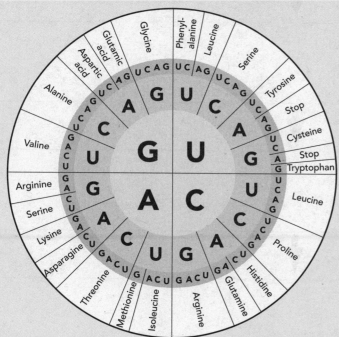

To interpret this diagram, read each codon starting at the inner circle and going toward the outer circle. For example, the codon CAC codes for the amino acid called histidine.

1. What amino acid does the codon AAU code for? _____

2. What three codons signal that translation should stop? _____

3. Is it possible for a codon to code for more than one amino acid? _____

4. In RNA, uracil replaced what nitrogenous base that is found in DNA? _____

170 Chapter 14 RNA and Protein Synthesis

How to Read Codons Because there are four different bases in RNA, there are 64 possible three-base codons (4 × 4 × 4 = 64) in the genetic code. Most amino acids can be <u>specified</u> by more than one codon. For example, UUA, UUG, CUU, CUC, CUA, and CUG all code for leucine.

Start and Stop Codons The methionine codon AUG serves as the "start" codon for protein synthesis. Following the start codon, mRNA is read three bases at a time, until it reaches one of three different "stop" codons, which end translation.

Translation

🔍 **KEY QUESTION** *What role does the ribosome play in assembling proteins?*

The sequence of bases in an mRNA molecule gives the order in which amino acids should be joined to produce a polypeptide. Once the polypeptide is complete, it then folds into its final shape or joins with other polypeptides to become a functional protein.

Ribosomes carry out the protein assembly tasks. Ribosomes use the sequence of codons in mRNA to assemble amino acids into polypeptide chains. The decoding of an mRNA message into a protein is a process known as **translation**.

Steps in Translation Translation begins when a ribosome attaches to an mRNA molecule in the cytoplasm. As each codon passes through the ribosome, several molecules of tRNA bring the proper amino acids into the ribosome. One at a time, the ribosome attaches these amino acids to a growing chain. Each tRNA molecule carries just one kind of amino acid. In addition, each tRNA molecule has a group of three unpaired bases that is called an **anticodon**. Each anticodon is complementary to a codon on mRNA. The polypeptide chain grows until the ribosome reaches a "stop" codon on the mRNA molecule. Then the ribosome releases both the newly synthesized polypeptide and the mRNA molecule.

The Roles of tRNA and rRNA in Translation The three major forms of RNA are all involved in the process of translation. The mRNA molecule carries the coded message that directs the process. tRNA molecules deliver the amino acids, enabling the ribosome to "read" the mRNA's message. Ribosomes themselves are composed of roughly 80 proteins and three or four different rRNA molecules. These rRNA molecules hold ribosomal proteins in place and carry out the chemical reactions that join amino acids together.

READING TOOL
Academic Words

specify To *specify* is to "identify precisely." Because each codon identifies only one amino acid, the genetic code can be accurately translated.

☑ What is the "start" codon, and which amino acid does it specify?

_____

_____

_____

_____

BUILD Vocabulary

translation process by which the sequence of bases of an mRNA is converted into the sequence of amino acids of a protein

anticodon group of three bases on a tRNA molecule that are complementary to the three bases of a codon of mRNA

Multiple Meanings The word *translation* is also used to describe the process of changing speech or text from one language to another.

☑ How is the translation of mRNA like the translation of a language?

_____

_____

_____

_____

_____

_____

_____

_____

Fill in the missing labels on the diagram of protein synthesis.

1. _____

C G T G C A G A T DNA strand

NUCLEUS

mRNA

CYTOPLASM

2. _____

6. _____

Lysine

5. _____

7. _____

U A C

A A G U U U

A U G U U C A A A

3. _____

4. _____

Molecular Genetics

🔍 **KEY QUESTION** *How does molecular biology relate to genetics?*

Most genes contain nothing more than instructions for assembling proteins. Many proteins are enzymes, which catalyze and regulate chemical reactions, thereby affecting the expression of genetic traits. In short, proteins are microscopic tools, each specifically designed to build or operate a component of a living cell.

Once scientists explained the genetic code, a new scientific field called molecular biology was established. Molecular biologists seek to understand living organisms by studying them at the molecular level, using molecules like DNA and RNA. Molecular biology provides a way to understand the links between genes and the characteristics they influence.

One of the most interesting discoveries of molecular biology is the near-universal nature of the genetic code. Although some organisms show slight variations in the amino acids assigned to particular codons, the code is always read three bases at a time, is always read in the same direction, and is always translated on ribosomes composed of RNA and protein.

LESSON 3

Gene Regulation and Expression

READING TOOL **Main Ideas and Details** As you read your textbook, identify the main ideas and details or evidence that support the main ideas. Use the lesson headings to organize the main ideas and details. Record your work in the table. Two examples are entered for you.

Heading	Main Idea	Details/Evidence
Prokaryotic Gene Regulation		
The *Lac* Operon	The *lac* operon controls the production of proteins needed for *E. coli* to use lactose for food.	
Promoters and Operators • The *lac* repressor blocks transcription • Lactose turns the operon "on"		
Eukaryotic Gene Regulation		
Transcription Factors		Some transcription factors block access to genes so they are not expressed.
Cell Specialization		
Genetic Control of Development		
Homeotic Genes		
Epigenetics		
Environmental Influences		

Lesson Summary

Prokaryotic Gene Regulation

BUILD Vocabulary

operon in prokaryotes, a group of adjacent genes that share a common operator and promoter and are transcribed into a single mRNA

operator short DNA region, adjacent to the promoter of a prokaryotic operon, that binds repressor proteins responsible for controlling the rate of transcription of the operon

Root Words The Latin root word *oper* means "work." Similar words include *operate* or *operator*.

☑ How does the operator region of DNA work to regulate gene expression?

_____

_____

_____

_____

_____

_____

_____

_____

KEY QUESTION *How are prokaryotic genes regulated?*

By regulating gene expression, bacteria can respond to changes in their environment. DNA-binding proteins in prokaryotes regulate genes by controlling transcription. Some of these regulatory proteins switch genes on, while others turn genes off.

How does an organism know when to turn a gene on or off? *E. coli* provides us with an example. Three genes must be turned on together before the bacterium can break apart lactose, a type of sugar, for food. Because the three genes are "operated" together, they are called the *lac* operon. An **operon** is a group of genes that are regulated together.

The *Lac* Operon To use lactose for food, the bacterium must have the proteins coded for by the genes of the *lac* operon. The bacterium seems to "know" when the products of the *lac* operon genes are needed and when they're not needed. For example, if the bacterium grows in a medium where lactose is the only food source, the genes are transcribed to produce the proteins. If the environment changes to another food source, then the genes are not transcribed.

Promoters and Operators On one side of the operon's three genes, there are two regulatory regions. The first is a promoter (P), which is a site where RNA polymerase can bind to begin transcription. The other region is called the **operator** (O). The O site is where a DNA-binding protein known as the *lac* repressor can bind to DNA.

The *Lac* Repressor Blocks Transcription When lactose is not present, the *lac* repressor binds to the O region and RNA polymerase cannot reach the *lac* genes to begin transcription. The binding of the repressor protein switches the operon "off" by preventing the transcription of its genes.

Lactose Turns the Operon "On" When lactose is present, some of it attaches to the *lac* repressor and causes it to fall off the operator. RNA polymerase can bind to the promoter and transcribe the genes of the operon. As a result, in the presence of lactose, the operon is automatically switched on. Many other prokaryotic genes are switched on or off by similar mechanisms.

Eukaryotic Gene Regulation

⚲ KEY QUESTION *How are genes regulated in eukaryotic cells?*

The general principles of gene expression in prokaryotes also apply to eukaryotes, but the regulation of many eukaryotic genes is much more complex.

Transcription Factors DNA-binding proteins known as transcription factors play an important part in regulating gene expression. By binding DNA sequences in the regulatory regions of eukaryotic genes, transcription factors control gene expression. A transcription factor can activate scores of genes at once, thereby dramatically affecting patterns of gene expression. Eukaryotic gene expression can also be regulated by many other factors.

Cell Specialization Gene regulation in eukaryotes is more complex than in prokaryotes because of the way in which genes are expressed in a multicellular organism. Cell differentiation requires genetic specialization, yet most of the cells in a multicellular organism carry the same DNA in their nucleus. Complex gene regulation in eukaryotes makes it possible for cells to be differentiated and specialized. Gene regulation also allows multicellular organisms to reproduce. Complex changes in gene expression allow the single cell of a new organism to develop into a functioning multicelluar organism.

Genetic Control of Development

⚲ KEY QUESTION *What controls the development of cells and tissues in multicellular organisms?*

The activation of genes in different parts of an embryo cause cells to differentiate. The process of **differentiation** gives rise to specialized tissues and organs.

Homeotic Genes A set of master control genes, known as **homeotic genes**, regulates organs that develop in specific parts of the body. Homeotic genes share a very similar 180-base DNA sequence, the *homeobox*. **Homeobox genes** code for transcription factors that activate other genes that are important in cell development and differentiation. In flies, homeobox genes known as **Hox genes** are located side by side in a single cluster. Hox genes determine the identities of each segment of a fly's body. They are arranged in the order in which they are expressed, from anterior to posterior. Hox genes exist in the DNA of other animals, including humans. These genes are also arranged from head to tail, and they tell the cells of the body how to differentiate as the body grows. This means that nearly all animals share the same basic tools for building the different parts of the body.

BUILD Vocabulary

differentiation process in which cells become specialized in structure and function

homeotic gene class of regulatory genes that determine the identity of body parts and regions in an animal embryo. Mutations in these genes can transform one body part into another.

homeobox genes genes that code for transcription factors that activate other genes that are important in cell development and differentiation

Hox gene group of homeotic genes clustered together that determine the head-to-tail identity of body parts in animals. All Hox genes contain the homeobox DNA sequence.

Word Origins The word part *homeo* comes from the Latin and Greek part *homio*, meaning "similar to" or "the same kind." Homeobox genes are a group of similar genes that regulate specific structures.

☑ How are Hox genes, a type of homeotic gene, similar across species?

_____

_____

_____

_____

Make Connections The prefix *epi-* means "over." Epigenetic changes, such as the addition of markers, occur *above*, or *over*, the level of the genome. ☑ If epigenetic changes take place above the level of the genome, what would be an example of a change at the level of the genome?

_____

_____

_____

Common patterns of genetic control exist because all these genes have descended from the genes of common ancestors. Master control genes are like switches that trigger particular patterns of development and differentiation in cells and tissues. The details can vary from one organism to another, but the switches are nearly identical.

Epigenetics In places where chromatin is tightly packed, gene expression is blocked. In regions where chromatin is opened up, gene expression is enhanced. Cells can regulate the state of chromatin by enzymes that attach chemical groups to DNA and to histone proteins.

These chemical marks on chromatin are epigenetic, or above the level of the genome. Epigenetic marks do not change DNA base sequences. Instead, they influence patterns of gene expression over long periods of time.

Environmental Influences In prokaryotes and eukaryotes, environmental factors can regulate gene expression. The environment can often influence how and when epigenetic marks are attached to chromatin. Environmental factors can also directly affect the expression of other genes.

Visual Reading Tool: Effect of Chemical Marks on Gene Expression

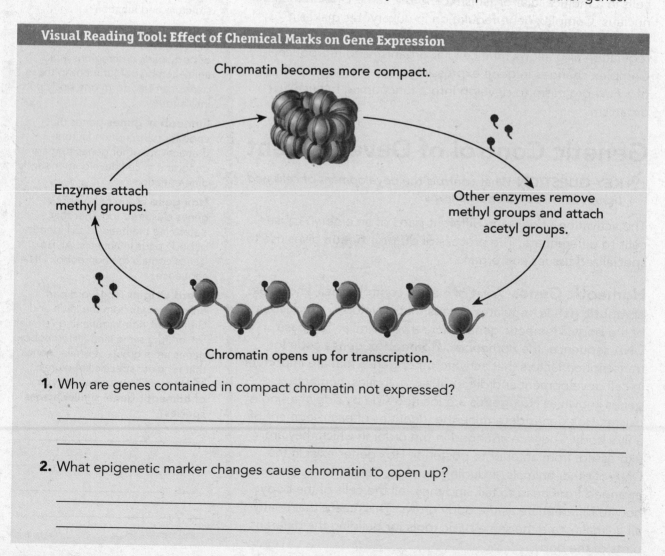

Chromatin becomes more compact.

Enzymes attach methyl groups.

Other enzymes remove methyl groups and attach acetyl groups.

Chromatin opens up for transcription.

1. Why are genes contained in compact chromatin not expressed?

_____

_____

2. What epigenetic marker changes cause chromatin to open up?

_____

_____

LESSON
4 Mutations

READING TOOL **Cause and Effect** As you read your textbook, find a brief description of each cause, or mutation, provided. Then identify its possible effect(s). Record your work in the table. An example is entered for you.

Mutation (Cause)	Description	Effect(s)
Silent Mutation	A changed codon of mRNA results in the same amino acid.	None; the amino acid sequence is unchanged and the protein is normal.
Missense Mutation		
Nonsense Mutation		
Frameshift Mutation		

Lesson Summary

Types of Mutations

As you read, circle the answers to each Key Question. Underline any words you do not understand.

KEY QUESTION *In what ways do mutations change genetic information?*

When cells make mistakes in copying their own DNA, the resulting variations are called **mutations**. Mutations are heritable changes in genetic information. Mutations can involve changes in the sequence of nucleotides in DNA or changes in the number or structure of chromosomes.

Point Mutations Mutations that change a single base pair are **point mutations**. Point mutations usually involve a substitution, in which one base is changed to a different base. Substitutions usually affect no more than a single amino acid, and sometimes have no effect at all. Mutations that don't affect amino acid sequence are known as *silent mutations*. Mutations that change the amino acid specified by a codon can be more significant and are called *missense mutations*.

If a mutation changes an mRNA codon to result in a stop codon, it is known as a *nonsense mutation* because it causes translation to stop before the protein is finished. This can result in the production of a defective protein.

Insertions and Deletions Mutations in which one base or many bases are inserted or removed from the DNA sequence are called insertions and deletions. Insertions and deletions are also called **frameshift mutations** because they shift the "reading frame" of the genetic message. Frameshift mutations can change every amino acid that follows the point of the mutation. They can alter a protein so much that it is unable to perform its normal functions.

Chromosomal Mutations Chromosomal mutations involve changes in the number or structure of chromosomes. These mutations can change the location of genes on chromosomes and can even change the number of copies of some genes. There are four types of chromosomal mutations: deletion, duplication, inversion, and translocation. Deletion involves the loss of all or part of a chromosome, duplication produces an extra copy of all or part of a chromosome, and inversion reverses the direction of parts of a chromosome. Translocation occurs when part of one chromosome breaks off and attaches to another.

BUILD Vocabulary

mutation change in the genetic material of a cell

point mutation gene mutation in which a single base pair in DNA has been changed

frameshift mutation mutation that shifts the "reading frame" of the genetic message by inserting or deleting a nucleotide

Word Origins The word *mutation* comes from the Latin word *mutare*, meaning "to change." ☑ **Which types of point mutations typically cause the most significant changes?**

_____

_____

_____

_____

On the diagrams below, label each type of mutation.

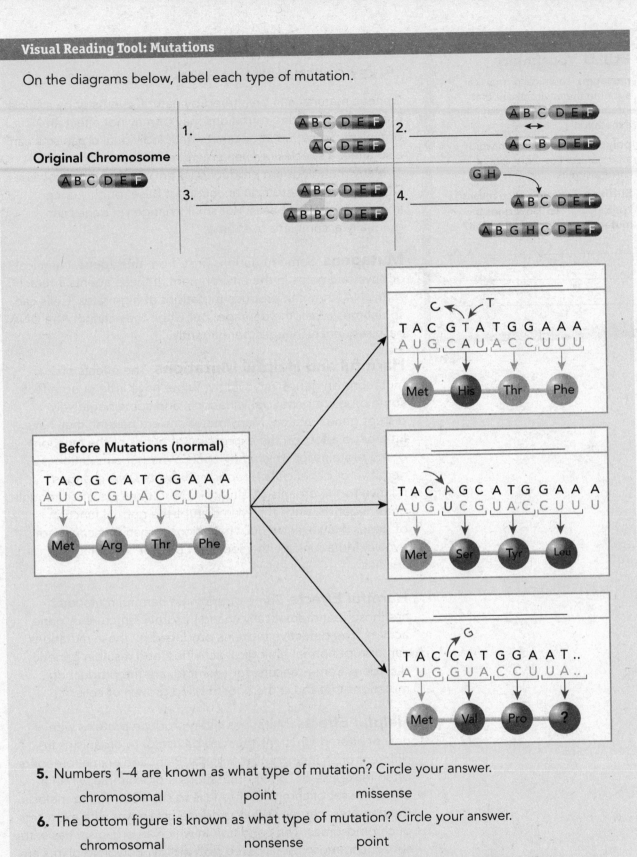

Original Chromosome

A B C D E F

1. _____

A B C D E F

A C D E F

2. _____

A B C D E F

A C B D E F

3. _____

A B C D E F

A B B C D E F

4. _____

G H

A B C D E F

A B G H C D E F

Before Mutations (normal)

T A C G C A T G G A A A
A U G C G U A C C U U U

Met — Arg — Thr — Phe

_____

C ← ↓ T
T A C G T A T G G A A A
A U G C A U A C C U U U

Met — His — Thr — Phe

_____

T A C A G C A T G G A A A
A U G U C G U A C C U U U

Met — Ser — Tyr — Leu

_____

G
T A C C A T G G A A T..
A U G G U A C C U U A..

Met — Val — Pro — ?

5. Numbers 1–4 are known as what type of mutation? Circle your answer.

     chromosomal   point   missense

6. The bottom figure is known as what type of mutation? Circle your answer.

     chromosomal   nonsense   point

7. What is the difference between point mutations and chromosomal mutations?

_____

_____

_____

Effects of Mutations

🔍 KEY QUESTION *How do mutations affect genes?*

Genetic material can be altered by natural events or by artificial means. The resulting mutations may or may not affect an organism. Some mutations that affect individual organisms can also affect a species or even an entire ecosystem.

Many mutations are produced by errors in genetic processes. DNA replication results in an incorrect base roughly once in every 10 million bases. But small changes in genes can gradually accumulate over time.

Mutagens Some mutations arise from **mutagens**, chemical or physical agents in the environment. If these agents interact with DNA, they can produce mutations at high rates. Cells can sometimes repair the damage, but when they cannot, the DNA base sequence changes permanently.

Harmful and Helpful Mutations The effects of mutations on genes vary widely. Some have little or no effect, some produce beneficial variations, and some negatively disrupt gene function. Many mutations are neutral; they have little or no effect on the expression of genes or the function of the proteins for which they code. Whether a mutation is negative or beneficial depends on how its DNA changes relative to the organism's situation. Mutations are often thought of as negative, since they can disrupt the normal function of genes. However, without mutations, organisms could not evolve. Mutations are the source of genetic variability in a species.

Harmful Effects Some of the most harmful mutations are those that dramatically change protein structure or gene activity. The defective proteins produced by these mutations can disrupt normal biological activities, and result in genetic disorders. Some cancers, for example, are the product of mutations that cause the uncontrolled growth of cells.

Helpful Effects Mutations often produce proteins with new or altered functions that can be useful to organisms in different or changing environments. Plant and animal breeders often make use of "good" mutations. For example, when a complete set of chromosomes fails to separate during meiosis, the gametes that result may produce organisms with extra sets of chromosomes. The condition in which an organism has extra sets of chromosomes is called **polyploidy**. Polyploid plants are often larger and stronger than diploid plants. Important crops have been produced this way.

Review Vocabulary

Choose the letter of the best answer.

1. The molecule that carries amino acids to the ribosome is called

A. transfer RNA.

B. ribosomal RNA.

C. messenger RNA.

2. Insertions and deletions are also known as

A. silent mutations.

B. nonsense mutations.

C. frameshift mutations.

Match the vocabulary term to its definition.

3. _____ the process of decoding an mRNA message into a protein   a. transcription

4. _____ the process of copying a base sequence from DNA to RNA   b. mutation

5. _____ the process by which variations are introduced into DNA   c. translation

Review Key Questions

Provide evidence and details to support your answers.

6. How are both DNA and RNA involved in the process of protein synthesis?

_____

_____

_____

7. Describe gene regulation in prokaryotes.

_____

_____

_____

8. How can mutations affect organisms?

_____

_____

_____

CHAPTER 15

LESSON 1

Human Chromosomes

READING TOOL **Apply Prior Knowledge** Before you read this lesson, think about what you have learned about human chromosomes from your study of cell division, genetics, and other biology concepts in previous chapters. Consider, too, what questions about human chromosomes you still have. Record your answers in the **Know** and **Want to Know** sections of the chart below. Once you have read the lesson, return to this page to complete the **Learned** section.

Know	Want to Know	Learned

Lesson Summary

🔍 **As you read, circle the answers to each Key Question. Underline any words you do not understand.**

BUILD Vocabulary

genome entire set of genetic information that an organism carries in its DNA

karyotype micrograph of the complete diploid set of chromosomes grouped together in pairs, arranged in order of decreasing size

Karyotypes

🔍 **KEY QUESTION** *How are human karyotypes used?*

To find what makes us uniquely human, we have to explore the human genome. A **genome** is the full set of genetic information that an organism carries in its DNA. The analysis of any genome starts with chromosomes. To see human chromosomes clearly, cell biologists photograph the chromosomes using a microscope. Scientists then arrange images of each chromosome to produce a **karyotype**. A karyotype shows the complete diploid set of chromosomes grouped together in pairs, arranged in order of decreasing size. The karyotype from a typical human cell contains 46 chromosomes, arranged in 23 pairs.

Sex Chromosomes Two of the 46 chromosomes in the human genome are known as **sex chromosomes**, because they determine an individual's sex. Females have two copies of the X chromosome. Males have one X chromosome and one Y chromosome. More than 1400 genes are found on the X chromosome. The Y chromosome, which is smaller, contains only about 158 genes.

Autosomal Chromosomes The remaining 44 human chromosomes are autosomal chromosomes, or **autosomes**.

Transmission of Human Traits

KEY QUESTION *What patterns of inheritance do human traits follow?*

Human genes follow the same patterns of inheritance as the genes of other organisms.

Dominant and Recessive Alleles Many human traits follow a pattern of simple dominance. A trait that displays simple dominance is the Rhesus, or Rh, blood group. The allele for Rh factor comes in two forms: Rh+ and Rh−. Rh+ is dominant, so an individual with both alleles (Rh+/Rh−) is said to have Rh-positive blood. Rh-negative blood is found in individuals with two recessive alleles (Rh−/Rh−).

Codominant and Multiple Alleles The alleles for many human genes display codominant inheritance. One example is the ABO blood group, determined by a gene with three alleles: I_A, I_B, and i. Alleles I_A and I_B are codominant. Individuals with alleles I_A and I_B are blood type AB. The i allele is recessive. Individuals with alleles $I_A I_A$ or $I_A i$ are blood type A. Those with $I_B I_B$ or $I_B i$ alleles are type B. Those homozygous for the i allele (ii) have blood type O. If a person has AB-negative blood, it means the individual has I_A and I_B alleles from the ABO gene and two Rh− alleles from the Rh gene.

Sex-Linked Inheritance Because the X and Y chromosomes determine sex, the genes located on them show a pattern of inheritance called sex-linkage. A **sex-linked gene** is a gene located on a sex chromosome. Genes on the Y chromosome are found only in males and are passed directly from father to son. Genes located on the X chromosome are found in both sexes, but the fact that men have just one X chromosome leads to some interesting <u>consequences</u>.

In males, a recessive allele on the single X chromosome is usually expressed. In order for a recessive allele to be expressed in females, it must be present on both of the X chromosomes. This means that the recessive phenotype of a sex-linked genetic disorder tends to be much more common among males than among females.

BUILD Vocabulary

sex chromosome one of two chromosomes that determines an individual's sex

autosome chromosome that is not a sex chromosome; also called autosomal chromosome

sex-linked gene a gene located on a sex chromosome

Prefixes *Auto-* is a prefix of Greek origin that means *self* or *same*. In diploid cells, each autosome pairs with another autosome that has the same shape and the same genes.

☑ Why are sex chromosomes not called autosomes? Use the definition of the prefix *auto-* in your explanation.

_____
_____
_____
_____
_____
_____
_____
_____
_____

READING TOOL

Academic Words

consequence a result or an effect of a condition or an action

☑ Explain why the presence of a recessive allele on one X chromosome often has different consequences for a man than for a woman.

_____
_____
_____
_____
_____
_____
_____
_____

X-Chromosome Inactivation In female cells, most of the genes in one of the X chromosomes are inactivated, forming a condensed region in the nucleus known as a Barr body. A special RNA molecule binds to the inactivated chromosome and keeps it in the condensed state.

Human Pedigrees

🔍 **KEY QUESTION** *How can pedigrees be used to analyze human inheritance?*

To analyze the pattern of inheritance followed by a particular trait, you can use a **pedigree** chart that shows the relationships within a family. A pedigree shows the presence or absence of a trait according to the relationships among parents, siblings, and offspring.

By analyzing a pedigree, we can infer genotypes and predict future outcomes by applying the principles of Mendelian genetics to humans. The information gained from pedigree analysis makes it possible to determine the nature of genes and alleles associated with inherited human traits. Based on a pedigree, you can often determine if an allele for a trait is dominant or recessive, as well as if it is autosomal or sex-linked.

Visual Reading Tool: How to Use a Pedigree

The sample pedigree below shows an example of how a dominant trait might pass through three generations of a family. Fill in the blanks to complete a key that explains how to read a pedigree.

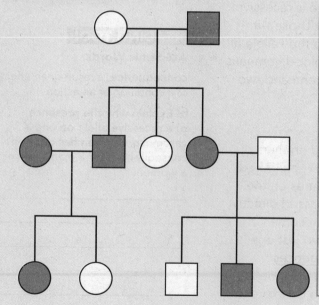

Key
1. A _____ represents a female.
2. A _____ represents a male.
3. A vertical line and bracket connect _____
4. A horizontal line connecting a male and female represents _____
5. Shading indicates _____
6. No shading indicates _____

Human Genetic Disorders

READING TOOL **Main Idea and Details** As you read your textbook, identify the main ideas and details or evidence that support the main ideas. Use the lesson headings to organize the main ideas and details. Record your work in the table. Two examples are entered for you.

Heading	Main Idea	Details/Evidence
Chromosomal Disorders	Nondisjunction, the failure of homologous chromosomes to separate during meiosis, can lead to chromosome number disorders.	
From Molecule to Phenotype		A difference of one DNA base in a single gene determines whether a person has dry earwax or wet earwax.
Disorders Caused by Individual Genes		
Genetic Advantages		

Lesson Summary

Chromosomal Disorders

KEY QUESTION *What are the effects of errors in meiosis?*

Most of the time, the process of meiosis works perfectly and each human gamete gets exactly 23 chromosomes. Every now and then, however, something goes wrong. The most common error in meiosis occurs when homologous chromosomes fail to separate. This mistake is known as **nondisjunction**, which means "not coming apart."

As you read, circle the answers to each Key Question. Underline any words you do not understand.

If nondisjunction occurs during meiosis, gametes with an abnormal number of chromosomes may result, leading to a disorder of chromosome numbers. For example, if two copies of an autosomal chromosome fail to separate during meiosis, an individual may be born with three copies of that chromosome. Down syndrome, a condition where an individual has three copies of chromosome 21, is associated with a range of cognitive disabilities and certain birth defects.

Nondisjunction of the X chromosomes can lead to a disorder known as Turner's syndrome. A female with Turner's syndrome usually inherits only one X chromosome. In males, nondisjunction may cause Klinefelter's syndrome, resulting from the inheritance of an extra X chromosome.

From Molecule to Phenotype

🔍 **KEY QUESTION** *How do small changes in DNA affect human traits?*

Genes are made of DNA and interact with the environment to produce an individual organism's characteristics, or phenotype. However, when a gene fails to work or works improperly, serious problems can result.

Visual Reading Tool: Nondisjunction

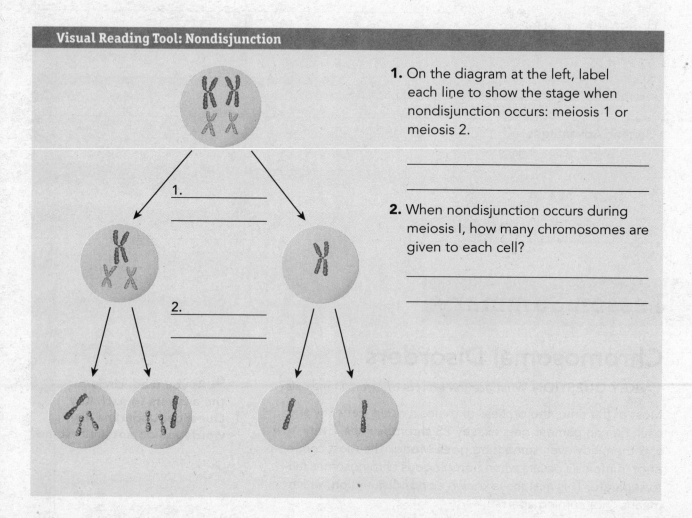

1. On the diagram at the left, label each line to show the stage when nondisjunction occurs: meiosis 1 or meiosis 2.

_____

_____

2. When nondisjunction occurs during meiosis I, how many chromosomes are given to each cell?

_____

_____

The connection between molecule and trait, and between genotype and phenotype, is often simple and direct. Changes in a gene's DNA sequence can change proteins by altering their amino acid sequences, which may directly affect an individual's phenotype. Sometimes, however, these effects are more subtle. For example, certain alleles are associated with tendencies to develop conditions such as diabetes, heart disease, and cancer. Many other factors, such as behavior, diet, and environment, can have a profound effect on whether these conditions actually develop.

Disorders Caused by Individual Genes Thousands of genetic disorders are caused by changes in individual genes. These changes often affect specific proteins associated with important cellular functions.

Sickle Cell Disease Sickle cell disease is a hereditary disease caused by a defective recessive allele for beta-globin, one of two polypeptides in hemoglobin. The defective polypeptide causes hemoglobin to clump into long fibers that push against the membranes of red blood cells and distort their shape. Sickle-shaped cells are more rigid than normal red blood cells, so they tend to get stuck in capillaries.

Cystic Fibrosis Cystic fibrosis (CF) usually results from the deletion of just three bases in the gene for a protein. The loss of these bases removes a single amino acid, causing the protein to fold improperly. Two copies of the defective allele are needed to produce the disorder, which means the CF allele is recessive. Children with CF have serious digestive problems and produce thick, heavy mucus that clogs their lungs and breathing passageways.

Huntington's Disease Huntington's disease is caused by a dominant allele for a protein found in brain cells. The allele for this disease contains a long string of bases in which the codon for the amino acid glutamine repeats over and over again. The symptoms of Huntington's disease, mental deterioration and uncontrollable movements, usually do not appear until middle age.

Genetic Advantages Disorders such as sickle cell disease and CF are still common in human populations. Why are these alleles still around if they can be fatal for those who carry them?

CF Allele and Typhoid Typhoid is caused by a bacterium that enters the body through cells in the digestive system. The protein produced by the CF allele helps block the entry of this bacterium. Individuals who are heterozygous for CF have an advantage against typhoid. Because they also carry the normal allele, these individuals do not suffer from cystic fibrosis.

Sickle Cell Allele and Malaria Malaria is a mosquito-borne infection caused by a parasite that lives inside red blood cells. Individuals with just one copy of the sickle cell allele are generally healthy and are also highly resistant to the parasite. This resistance gives them a great advantage against malaria.

READING TOOL

Apply Prior Knowledge In previous chapters you have read about dominant and recessive alleles. Generally, the dominant allele overpowers the recessive allele and the recessive allele is not expressed. However, in some disorders, having one copy of the recessive allele gives the individual a genetic advantage.
☑ **How do scientists describe a genotype that has one copy of the dominant allele and one copy of the recessive allele?**

READING TOOL **Use Structure** As you read, fill in the graphic organizer that explains how scientists manipulate DNA to read nucleotide sequences. Fill in the boxes to explain the process as you read the text. Some examples have been filled in for you.

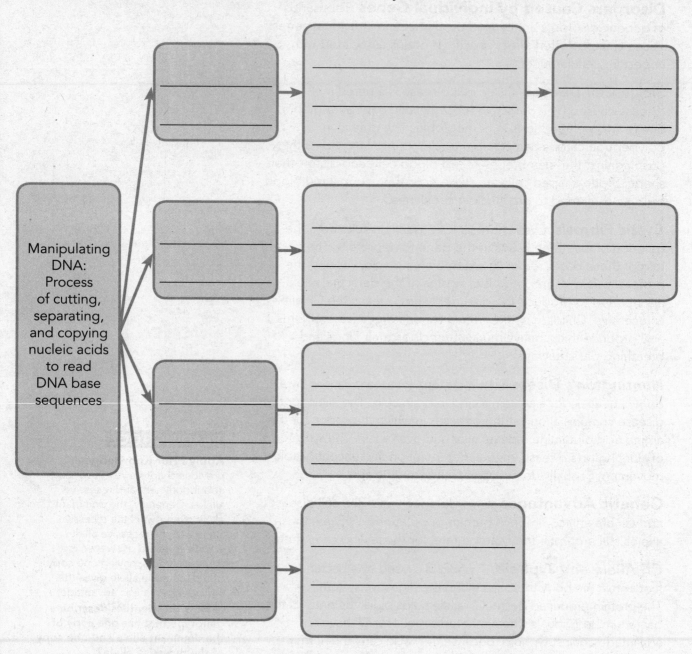

Manipulating DNA: Process of cutting, separating, and copying nucleic acids to read DNA base sequences

Lesson Summary

Manipulating DNA

KEY QUESTION *How can scientists read DNA base sequences?*

In the late 1960s, scientists discovered special prokaryote enzymes, called **restriction enzymes**, that could cut DNA at specific sites. By using tools that cut, separate, and copy nucleic acids, scientists can now read DNA base sequences. Such techniques have made it possible to study the genomes of living organisms, including humans, in great detail.

Cutting DNA DNA molecules must first be cut into smaller pieces for analysis. Many bacteria produce restriction enzymes that cut DNA at a very specific short sequence that is 4–8 pairs long. Each restriction enzyme can only recognize one base sequence. It cuts the strand of DNA between specific bases, leaving single-stranded overhangs. The overhangs are called "sticky ends" because they can bond, or "stick," to a DNA fragment with the complementary base sequence.

Separating DNA Once DNA has been cut by restriction enzymes, scientists can use **gel electrophoresis** to separate the fragments. DNA fragments are placed in wells on one end of a porous gel. When an electric voltage is applied to the gel, DNA molecules—which are negatively charged—move toward the positive end of the gel. The smaller the DNA fragment, the faster and farther it moves. The result is a pattern of bands based on fragment size. Researchers can then remove individual restriction fragments from the gel and study them further.

Reading DNA After the DNA fragments have been separated, researchers sequence them. The single-stranded DNA fragments are placed in a test tube containing DNA polymerase and the four nucleotide bases, A, T, G, and C. The enzyme uses the unknown strand as a template to make new DNA strands. The researchers also add a small number of bases that have a chemical dye attached. Each time a dye-labeled base is added to a new DNA strand, the synthesis of that strand stops. When DNA synthesis is completed, the result is a series of color-coded DNA fragments of different lengths. Researchers can then separate these fragments, often by gel electrophoresis. The order of colored bands on the gel tells the exact sequence of bases in the DNA.

As you read, circle the answers to each Key Question. Underline any words you do not understand.

BUILD Vocabulary

restriction enzyme enzyme that cuts DNA at a specific sequence of nucleotides

gel electrophoresis procedure used to separate and analyze DNA fragments by placing a mixture of DNA fragments at one end of a porous gel and applying an electrical voltage to the gel

Make Connections DNA is placed in gel that is *porous*, meaning that it has many small spaces or holes that air and liquids can pass through.

☑ **Why is it important that the substance DNA is placed in for electrophoresis be porous?**

_____

_____

_____

_____

_____

_____

_____

_____

_____

Using the figure shown, label the different parts of a gel electrophoresis setup.

1. _____

_____

2. _____

_____

3. _____

4. _____

5. _____

6. _____

7. Why is a restriction enzyme important in gel electrophoresis?

_____

8. Why do the DNA fragments move from the negative end of the gel toward the positive end?

_____

_____

Assembling the Sequence Most DNA sequencing techniques read fragments no more than a few hundred bases in length. These short "reads" of DNA are put together through a technique known as "shotgun" sequencing. Fragments are sequenced automatically, and the information is fed into a computer. A computer program analyzes the data by searching for matching sequences among the fragments, and aligns them to reassemble the fragments and complete the sequence.

The Human Genome—What's Inside?

🔍**KEY QUESTION** *How large is the human genome?*

In 2003, an international effort known as the Human Genome Project finished the first complete human DNA sequence. Labs around the world now study which regions of DNA are transcribed into RNA, which bind to proteins, which are marked with epigenetic tags, and which vary from one individual to the next.

How Many Genes? Human cells contain approximately 20,000 genes. The functions of about a quarter of human genes are unknown. The genes that we do understand fall into categories such as transcription factors, metabolic enzymes, components of the cell membrane, receptors, and regulatory factors.

The Large and Small of It The human haploid genome is larger than the genome of many other organisms. However, the cells of many organisms contain far more DNA than our cells do! Only about 2 percent of the human genome actually codes for proteins. What does the rest of the DNA code for? Some of it is involved in the regulation of gene expression. However, all of these sequences taken together account for only about 10 percent of the genome. Approximately 50 percent of the human genome is composed of highly repetitive DNA sequences. The functions of these regions remain unknown.

The Personal Genome On average, about one base in 1200 will not match between two individuals. Biologists refer to these single-base differences as single nucleotide polymorphisms (SNPs, or "snips"). Researchers have discovered that certain sets of closely linked SNPs occur together time and time again. Some of these are associated with certain traits, including the susceptibility to particular diseases or medical conditions. High-speed DNA sequencing is making it possible to rapidly pinpoint SNPs and their associated alleles, enabling physicians to tailor medical treatments to a patient's genome. In addition, many private companies now offer "personal genome" services that analyze one's DNA for a modest price.

Genome Privacy Rapid advances in the gathering and analyzing of genomic data have raised a number of ethical and legal questions. Who owns and controls genetic information? Who should have access to personal genetic information? In response to some of these issues, in 2008, the U.S. Congress passed the Genetic Information Nondiscrimination Act. This act makes it illegal for insurance companies and employers to discriminate based on information from genetic tests.

Gene Imprinting Epigenetic chemical marks can be attached to DNA and histone proteins in a way that affects gene expression by altering chromatin structure. This process is known as **genomic imprinting**. Some of these marks can be passed from one generation to the next through either the mother or the father. This means there are some genes that are only expressed if they came from a male parent and there are some genes that are only expressed if they came from a female parent. Nearly 100 known genes in humans are imprinted in this way.

Review Vocabulary

Choose the letter of the best answer.

1. Which shows patterns of traits among members of a family?

A. genome

B. pedigree

C. personal genome

2. Which is/are used to "cut" DNA into fragments?

A. gel electrophoresis

B. restriction enzymes

C. genomic imprinting

Match the vocabulary term to its definition.

3. _____ full set of genetic information in an organism's DNA

4. _____ process used to separate DNA fragments by size

5. _____ when homologous chromosomes fail to separate during meiosis

a. nondisjunction

b. genome

c. gel electrophoresis

Review Key Questions

Provide evidence and details to support your answers.

6. How does human blood type show both simple dominance and codominant inheritance patterns?

7. Explain the difference between disorders of chromosome number and disorders caused by individual genes.

8. What steps must scientists follow in order to "read" a sequence of DNA?

LESSON 1

Changing the Living World

Make Connections While you read this lesson, fill in the graphic organizer below. Explain the two ways that scientists carry out selective breeding practices, and the two ways they create increased variation within a population. Use examples from your text to support your explanations.

Hybridication: _____
_____
_____
_____

Inbreeding: _____
_____
_____
_____

Selective Breeding

Bacterial Mutation: _____
_____
_____
_____

Polypoid Plants: _____
_____
_____
_____

Increasing Variation

Selective Breeding

🔑 **KEY QUESTION** *What is selective breeding used for?*

Allowing only those organisms with desired characteristics to produce the next generation is called **selective breeding**. Selective breeding takes advantage of naturally occurring genetic variation to pass desired traits on to the next generation. This is one example of **biotechnology**, which has been practiced for thousands of years in developing animals, such as dog breeds, and plants, such as corn and potatoes. Corn was selectively bred from the wild grass teosinte nearly 10,000 years ago.

🔑 As you read, circle the answers to each Key Question. Underline any words you do not understand.

BUILD Vocabulary

selective breeding method of breeding that allows only those organisms with desired characteristics to produce the next generation

biotechnology the process of manipulating organisms, cells, or molecules, to produce specific products

Hybridization Hybridization is the crossing of dissimilar individuals to bring together the best of both organisms. American botanist Luther Burbank's hybrid crosses combined the disease resistance of one plant with the food-production capacity of another. This resulted in a new line of plants that led to increased food production. In fact, the Russet Burbank potato is one example of a new line of plants.

Inbreeding To maintain desirable characteristics in a line of organisms, breeders will continually breed individuals with similar characteristics. This technique is known as **inbreeding**. Inbreeding helps ensure that the characteristics that make each breed unique are preserved. Many breeds of dogs are maintained this way. Although inbreeding is useful in preserving certain traits, it also brings along some risks. Most of the members of a breed are genetically similar, which increases the chance that a cross between two individuals will bring together two recessive alleles for a genetic defect.

Increasing Variation

🔍 **KEY QUESTION** *How do people increase genetic variation?*

Breeders can increase the genetic variation in a population by introducing mutations, which are the ultimate source of biological diversity.

Bacterial Mutations Mutations, which are heritable changes in DNA, occur spontaneously, but breeders can increase the mutation rate of an organism by using radiation or chemicals. While many mutations are harmful, breeders can select those mutations that produce useful characteristics not found in the original population.

This technique has been very useful with bacteria. Because they are small, millions of bacteria can be treated with radiation or chemicals at the same time. This increases the chances of producing a useful mutant. This technique has allowed scientists to develop hundreds of useful bacterial strains.

For instance, it is been known for decades that certain strains of oil-digesting bacteria are effective for cleaning up oil spills. Today, scientists are working to produce bacteria that can clean up radioactive substances and metal pollution in the environment.

Polyploid Plants Drugs that prevent the separating of chromosomes during meiosis are useful in plant breeding. These drugs can produce cells that have many times the normal number of chromosomes. Plants grown from these cells are called polyploid because they have many sets of chromosomes. Polyploidy is usually fatal in animals. But, for reasons that are not clear, plants are much better at tolerating extra sets of chromosomes.

Polyploidy can quickly produce new species of plants that are larger and stronger than their diploid relatives. A number of important crop plants, such as bananas and many types of citrus fruits, have been produced in this way.

Visual Reading Tool: Mutations Timeline

Complete the timeline shown by first identifying the two plants shown, and then determining the time when they occurred. Use Figure 16-1 in the textbook to help you.

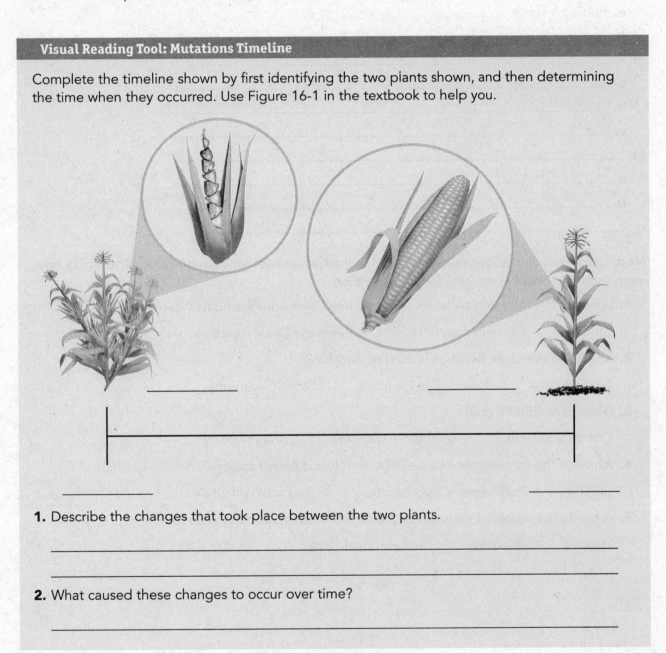

1. Describe the changes that took place between the two plants.

_____

_____

2. What caused these changes to occur over time?

_____

LESSON 2

The Process of Genetic Engineering

READING TOOL **Use Structure** Before you read, skim through the lesson and fill in the outline below with the section headings. The first one is shown for you as an example. Then, using your outline, answer the questions below.

I. Analyzing DNA

   a. Finding a Gene

   b. _____

II. _____

   a. _____

   b. _____

   c. _____

III. _____

   a. _____

   b. _____

   c. _____

Next, Use the outline above to help you chose the best answer for each question. There may be more than one possible solution for each question.

1. Which of the following biotechnologies is used to rewrite the human genome?

   CRISPR   Recombinant DNA   Polymerase Chain Reaction

2. A Polymerase Chain Reaction is used to do what?

   Analyze DNA   Rewrite the Genome   Clone Organisms

3. What does CRISPR do?

   Clone Organisms   Rewrite the Genome   Analyze DNA

4. Which of the following combines DNA from two different sources?

   CRISPR   Polymerase Chain Reaction   Recombinant DNA

5. What do scientists call the small circular DNA sequences found in bacteria?

   Markers   Plasmids   Recombinant DNA

Lesson Summary

Analyzing DNA

🔑 **KEY QUESTION** *How do scientists copy the DNA of living organisms?*

Genes can be engineered to change the characteristics of living organisms. Scientists can isolate single genes from among millions of fragments.

Finding a Gene Scientists analyze the nucleotide sequences of genes to screen for specific genes. The gene for the green fluorescence protein (GFP) in a species of jellyfish was isolated by a method in which DNA fragments are separated by a gel so as to isolate the fragment containing the actual gene for GFP.

Polymerase Chain Reaction Once a gene has been isolated, scientists can take a small sample and make multiple copies of specific DNA sequences using a technique known as **polymerase chain reaction**.

Rewriting the Genome

🔑 **KEY QUESTION** *How is recombinant DNA used?*

Recombinant DNA Not only can scientists isolate genes but they can make changes in the genome by inserting new or foreign DNA molecules into living cells. The combined molecules are known as **recombinant DNA**, and they change the genetic composition of a living organism.

Plasmids and Genetic Markers Some bacteria contain small circular DNA molecules known as **plasmids**, which are widely used in recombinant DNA studies. Plasmid DNA contains a signal for replication, but it also has a **genetic marker** that makes it possible to distinguish bacteria that carry the plasmid from those that don't. Using plasmids, recombinant DNA technology has been used to transform a bacterial cell so that it can manufacture human growth hormones.

CRISPR and DNA Editing CRISPR (clustered regularly interspersed short palindromic repeats) technology enables scientists to rewrite the base sequence of nearly any gene in a cell, transforming disease-causing genes and reengineering genes to perform new functions.

🔑 As you read, circle the answers to each Key Question. Underline any words you do not understand.

BUILD Vocabulary

polymerase chain reaction the technique used by biologists to make many copies of a particular gene

recombinant DNA DNA produced by combining DNA from two or more different sources

plasmid small, circular piece of DNA located in the cytoplasm of many bacteria

genetic marker alleles that produce detectable phenotypic differences useful in genetic analysis

Prefixes

The prefix *trans* means "across," and generally refers to things being moved from one area to another. For example: transporting goods from one side of a country to the other side. ☑ How does this prefix express the meaning of the word *transgenic*?

_____

_____

_____

Transgenic Organisms and Cloning

🔍 **KEY QUESTION** *How are transgenic organisms produced?*

The universal nature of the genetic code makes it possible to construct organisms that contain genes from other species. These **transgenic** organisms can be produced by the insertion of recombinant DNA into the genome of a host organism.

Transgenic Plants Plant cells can be transformed using different methods: inserting a bacterium that contains a small DNA tumor-producing plasmid, removing plant cell walls, or injecting DNA directly into the cell.

Transgenic Animals Egg cells of many animals are large enough that DNA can be inserted directly into the nucleus. Enzymes normally responsible for DNA repair and recombination may help to insert the foreign DNA into the chromosomes of the cell.

Cloning A **clone** is a population of genetically identical cells produced from a single cell. The technique of cloning uses a single cell from an adult organism to grow an entirely new individual that is genetically identical to the organism from which the cell was taken.

Cloned colonies of bacteria and other microorganisms are easy to grow, but this is not always true of multicellular organisms, especially animals.

Visual Reading Tool: Analyze a Sequence: Cloning

Use the steps listed below to explain the process of creating a cloned sheep. Match each step or description with the appropriate letter on the diagram.

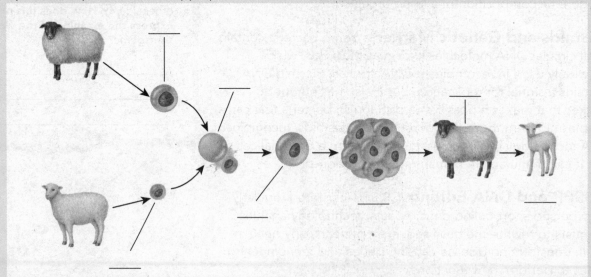

Cloned Lamb	Donor Nucleus	Egg Cell
Embryo	Foster Mother	Fused Cell
Nucleus of Egg Cell is Removed		

Lastly, circle the two sheep on the diagram that represent two genetically identical sheep.

Applications of Biotechnology

READING TOOL **Main Idea and Details** As you read, identify the main idea and supporting details under each main heading from the text.

Main Idea	Evidence and Details
Agriculture and Industry	
GM Crops	
GM Animals	
Health and Medicine	
Genetic Testing	
Medical Research	
Preventing and Treating Disease	
Examining Active Genes	
Personal Identification	
Forensic Science	
Fallen Heroes	
Establishing Relationships	

Lesson Summary

⚲ As you read, circle the answers to each Key Question. Underline any words you do not understand.

READING TOOL

Make Connections Scientists can modify the DNA of plants or animals. ☑ **What are two ways that scientists use genetically modified animals to benefit humans?**

_____

_____

_____

_____

Agriculture and Industry

⚲ **KEY QUESTION** *How can genetic engineering benefit agriculture and industry?*

Genetic engineering can benefit agriculture by producing better, less expensive, and more nutritious foods as well as making manufacturing processes less harmful.

GM Crops Since their introduction in 1996, genetically modified (GM) plants have become an important component of our food supply. For example, corn is often modified with bacterial genes that produce a protein called Bt toxin. The Bt toxin inserted in plants makes them resistant to insects, making spraying with pesticides unnecessary, and often produces higher crop yields. Resistance to insects is just one useful characteristic being engineered into crops. Others include resistance to viral infections and herbicides, resistance to rotting, and the production of plastics.

GM Animals Transgenic animals can be made larger and faster growing, which also makes them more productive. Cows have been injected with hormones produced by recombinant-DNA techniques to increase milk production. Pigs can be genetically modified (GM) to produce more lean meat or higher levels of healthy omega-3 acids.

Health and Medicine

⚲ **KEY QUESTION** *How can biotechnology improve human health?*

Genetic Testing Genetic tests diagnose hundreds of disorders, such as cystic fibrosis. Because the CF allele has slightly different DNA sequences from its normal counterpart, genetic tests using labeled DNA probes can distinguish the presence of CF. Like many genetic tests, the CF test uses specific DNA sequences that detect the complementary base sequences found in the disease-causing alleles.

Medical Research Transgenic animals are often used as model test subjects in medical research, simulating human disorders, such as Alzheimer's disease and arthritis.

Preventing and Treating Disease Bioengineering can prevent and treat human diseases in a variety of different ways, from making our food more nutritious to creating strains of mosquitos that are incapable of transmitting particular pathogens.

Examining Active Genes Although each cell in a person contains the same genetic material, the same genes are not active in every cell. Scientists use **DNA microarray** technology to study hundreds or thousands of genes at once, to understand their activity levels.

Personal Identification

🔍 **KEY QUESTION** *How is DNA used to identify individuals?*

The variation of the human genome ensures that no individual is exactly like any other, except in the case of twins. **DNA fingerprinting** analyzes sections of DNA that may have little or no function but that vary widely from one individual to another. Because only identical twins share the same genome, DNA can be used to determine a person's identity.

Forensic Science In **forensics**—the scientific study of crime scene evidence—DNA fingerprinting has been used to solve crimes, convict criminals, and even overturn wrongful convictions. DNA forensics has also been used to conserve wildlife. Officials can use DNA fingerprinting to identify the African elephant herds where the animals were poached for their tusks to help stop the illegal ivory trade.

Fallen Heroes The U.S. military requires all personnel to provide a sample of their DNA when they begin their service. Those DNA samples are kept on file and used, if needed, to identify the remains of individuals who perish in the line of duty.

Establishing Relationships DNA fingerprinting can also be used to establish paternity and trace ancestry. For example, DNA fingerprinting makes it easy to find alleles carried by the child that do not match those of the mother. Any such alleles must come from the child's biological father, and they will show up in his DNA fingerprint.

Visual Reading Tool: Compare and Contrast: DNA Fingerprints

Compare Suspect 1 (S1) and Suspect 2 (S2) to the DNA evidence sample (E). Based upon the DNA fingerprints, which suspect was likely at the crime scene and why?

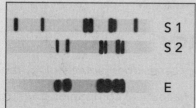

DNA fingerprint

_____

_____

_____

_____

CHAPTER 16

LESSON 4

Ethics and Impacts of Biotechnology

READING TOOL **Benefits and Drawbacks** As you read, identify the opposing views on each ethical issue. Take notes in the two-column chart shown below.

Issue	Benefits	Drawbacks
Patenting life		
Genetic privacy		
GM foods		
New biology		

Lesson Summary

Profits and Privacy

As you read, circle the answers to each Key Question. Underline any words you do not understand.

KEY QUESTION *What privacy issues does biotechnology raise?*

Private biotechnology and pharmaceutical companies do much of the research involving genetically modified (GM) plants and animals. They have often sought to protect their research by placing a patent on their discoveries. A patent is a legal tool that gives an individual or a company the exclusive right to profit from innovations for a number of years.

Patenting Life Patents have been used for years for new machines and devices. Now patents are also being used for molecules and biotechnology procedures. At times, disputes over biotechnology procedures arise—and these disputes have slowed the research of other biotechnological advancements.

One such dispute was brought to the United States Supreme Court. In 2013, the U.S. Supreme Court unanimously ruled that genes found in nature cannot be patented. Altered, or synthetic genes, however, could be patented, allowing companies to protect <u>novel</u> biotechnology products.

Genetic Privacy DNA can reveal personal information, including ethnic heritage, the chances of developing certain diseases, and evidence for criminal cases. The revelation of this information does raise questions of privacy. For example, it may be considered unfair for an employer to pass on a possible candidate if certain conclusions were made based on information from the candidate's DNA. As science advances, legal experts will debate ways to keep personal genetic information safe and confidential.

Safety of Transgenic Organisms

⚲ **KEY QUESTION** *What are some of the pros and cons of transgenic organisms?*

The presence of GM products in the marketplace has raised concerns from consumers. While nearly half of the GM crops today are grown in the United States, farmers around the world are now using GM technology. Many public-interest groups have argued that GM foods should be labeled. The U.S. Department of Agriculture is currently attempting to develop guidelines for this labeling. There are supporters and opponents of GM foods, with each side having very important points to support its opinions.

Arguments for GM Foods Those who support the use and growth of GM foods and crops argue that GM plants are actually better and safer than other crops. Farmers choose GM plants because they produce higher yield reducing the amount of land and energy that must be devoted to agriculture and lowering the cost for everyone. Supporters also argue that insect-resistant GM plants need little, if any, insecticide to grow successfully. Thus, GM crops could reduce the chance of chemical residue entering our food supply and lessen the effects of or damage to the environment. Finally, supporters point to the fact that the scientific community generally regards foods made from GM plants as safe to eat.

Below, use your own words to describe what the graph shows about the use of genetically modified crops between 1996 and 2016.

_____

_____

_____

_____

_____

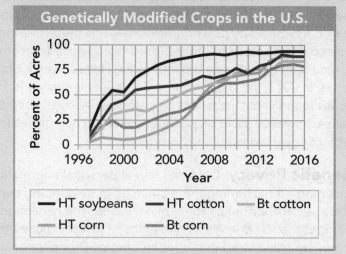

Genetically Modified Crops in the U.S.

Legend: HT soybeans, HT cotton, Bt cotton, HT corn, Bt corn

Data for each crop category include varieties with both HT and Bt (stacked) traits.
Sources: USDA, Economic Research Service using data from Fernandez-Cornejo and McBride (2002) for the years 1996–1999 and USDA, National Agriculture Statistics Service, *June Agriculture Survey* for years 2000–16.

Arguments Against GM Foods On the other hand, opponents of GM foods have raised concerns about the possible unintended consequences for agriculture of a shift to GM farming and ranching. One concern is that insect resistance may threaten beneficial insects (such as honeybees) as well as crop pests. Another concern is that patents held on GM seeds may raise the cost of seeds to the point that small farmers would go out of business, especially in the developing world.

In the United States, many public interest groups have argued that GM foods should be identified and labeled so that consumers would be fully aware of what they are eating. In 2016, Vermont passed a law that required labeling on GM foods. However, Congress later overrode that law, but did request that the United States Department of Agriculture develop rules for GM food labeling. The rules would then be implemented across all of the United States.

Ethics of the New Biology

🔑 **KEY QUESTION** *What are some of the ethical issues around new biotechnology?*

With the new knowledge we gain about ourselves using biotechnology, there is also a great responsibility. We can alter life forms for any purpose, scientific or nonscientific. Scientists could cure diseases such as cystic fibrosis or hemophilia. But should they try to engineer taller people or change their eye color, hair texture, sex, blood group, or appearance? The goal of biology is to gain a better understanding of the nature of life. Everyone is responsible for ensuring that the tools science has given us are used wisely.

Review Vocabulary

Choose the letter of the best answer that defines the word.

1. Biotechnology

    A. the science of computers

    B. the evolution of animal species

    C. manipulation of organisms or cells to produce desired products

    D. computer programs for creating life

2. Hybridization

    A. creation of mutations for gene modification

    B. crossing of dissimilar organisms to combine the best traits of each

    C. development of transport using alternative fuels

Match the vocabulary term to its definition.

3. _____ small, circular piece of DNA located in the cytoplasm of many bacteria

4. _____ use of DNA in the study of crime scene evidence

5. _____ member of a population of genetically identical cells produced from a single cell

    a. clone

    b. plasmid

    c. forensics

Review Key Questions

Provide evidence and details to support your answers.

6. Why do scientists, farmers, and animal breeders use selective breeding practices?

_____

_____

7. What is recombinant DNA and how is it used?

_____

_____

8. How is DNA used in forensics?

_____

_____

_____

9. List some of the benefits and drawbacks of GM organisms.

_____

_____

A Voyage of Discovery

Main Ideas and Details As you read the lesson, complete the main ideas and details table. One row is completed for you.

Heading	Main Idea	Details
Darwin's Epic Journey	What did Darwin contribute to science?	Darwin developed the theory of evolution.
Observations from the Voyage		
• Species Vary Globally		
• Species Vary Locally		
• Species Vary Over Time		
• Putting the Puzzle Together		

Darwin's Epic Journey

🔍 **KEY QUESTION** *What did Charles Darwin contribute to science?*

Charles Darwin was born in England in 1809. In 1831, he started a five-year voyage on the ship HMS *Beagle*. The voyage of the *Beagle* took place at a time of new scientific ideas. Geologists suggested that Earth was ancient and had changed over time. Biologists suggested that life had also changed, through a process they called **evolution**. However, no scientist before Darwin had offered a scientific explanation of how evolution could occur.

Darwin developed a theory of biological evolution that offered a scientific explanation for the unity and diversity of life, by proposing how modern organisms evolved through descent from common ancestors.

Observations from the Voyage

🔍 **KEY QUESTION** *What three patterns of biodiversity did Darwin observe?*

Darwin saw much diversity of life during the voyage. He saw how well suited plants and animals were to their environment. Darwin wanted to explain the diversity of life in a scientific way, so he kept observing, asking questions, and formulating hypothesis. Darwin focused on three patterns of diversity: (1) species vary globally, (2) species vary locally, and (3) species vary over time.

Species Vary Globally In South America, Darwin saw flightless, ground-dwelling birds called rheas. Rheas look and act a lot like ostriches. Yet rheas only live in South America, and ostriches only live in Africa. Then, in Australia, Darwin saw another large flightless bird, the emu. Darwin also noticed that rabbits and other grassland species in Europe did not live in the grasslands of South America and Australia. In Australia, Darwin saw kangaroos and other grassland species that are found nowhere else. Darwin noticed that different, yet ecologically similar, species inhabited separate, but ecologically similar, habitats around the globe.

Species Vary Locally Darwin noticed that different, yet related, species often occupied different habitats within a local area. Darwin saw two species of rheas in South America. One lived in the grasslands while a smaller species lived in a colder scrubland. Darwin also observed local variation in the Galápagos Islands off the Pacific coast of South America. The islands are relatively close to each other but are ecologically different. People who lived there could tell which island a tortoise came from just by looking at the shape of its shell.

BUILD Vocabulary

evolution change over time; the process by which modern organisms have descended from ancient organisms

fossil preserved remains or traces of ancient organisms

Word Origins *Evolution* comes from the Latin *volvere:* "turn, roll, revolve." With the prefix *e-*, meaning "away" or "out of," *evolution* means unfolding or unrolling. ☑ **What was Darwin's key contribution to science?**

_____

_____

_____

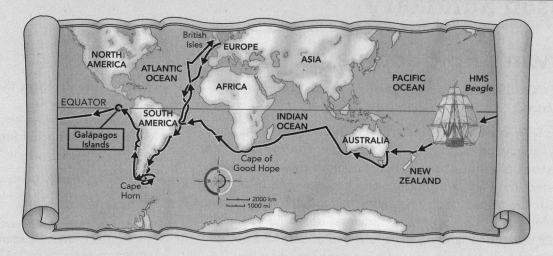

1. List the three species of flightless birds Darwin observed and draw a line to where he saw them.

   _____

2. List three different animals Darwin observed in the Galápagos.

   _____

Make Connections Darwin observed many species of small finches in the Galápagos that had beaks of different shapes and sizes. ☑ **What do birds use their beaks for, and why would there be differences between species?**

_____

_____

_____

_____

Species Vary Over Time In addition to collecting specimens of living species, Darwin also collected fossils. **Fossils** are preserved remains or traces of ancient organisms. In Darwin's time, scientists knew that fossils formed a record of extinct organisms, but did not know how to interpret that record. Darwin observed that the fossil record included many extinct animals that were similar to, yet different from, living species. One fossil he collected was from an extinct animal called a glyptodont. Why had glyptodonts disappeared, and why did modern armadillos resemble them? Could glyptodonts and armadillos have had a common ancestor?

Putting the Puzzle Together When Darwin returned home, experts identified his samples. The Galápagos mockingbirds were three separate species found nowhere else. The small brown birds were species of finches that lived nowhere else, but resembled South American species. This was true of Galápagos tortoises, iguanas, and many plants. Darwin wondered if species were really fixed and unchanging as many thought. Could organisms change over time through natural processes? Could Galápagos species have evolved from South American ancestors?

Ideas That Influenced Darwin

READING TOOL **Use Structure** As you read, use the structure of the lesson to identify the science concepts and ideas that influenced Darwin. Complete the graphic organizer by writing the concepts and ideas in the box on the left side with the scientist's name, and in the boxes on the right, fill in how those ideas influenced Darwin.

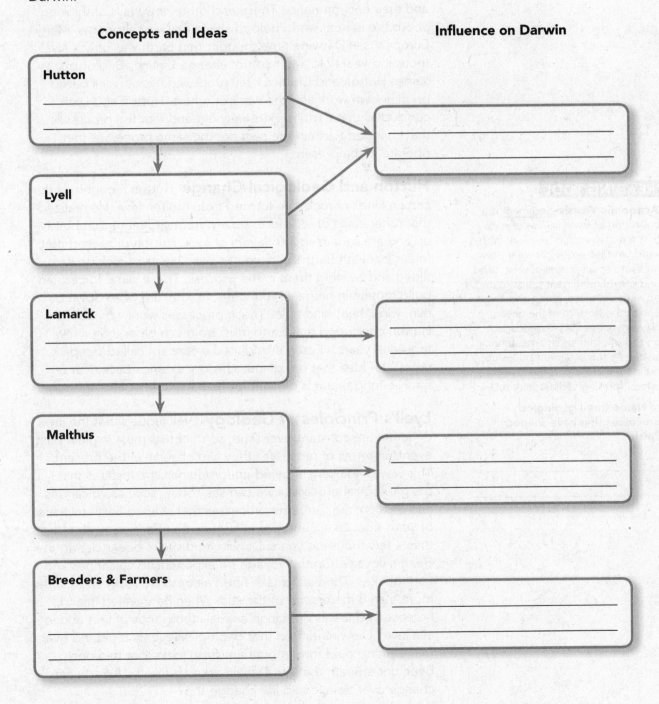

Concepts and Ideas

Influence on Darwin

Hutton
_____
_____

Lyell
_____
_____

Lamarck
_____
_____

Malthus
_____
_____
_____

Breeders & Farmers
_____
_____
_____

_____
_____

_____
_____

_____
_____

_____
_____

Lesson Summary

An Ancient, Changing Earth

🔍 As you read, circle the answers to each Key Question. Underline any words you do not understand.

🔍 **KEY QUESTION** *What did Hutton and Lyell conclude about Earth's history?*

Darwin was influenced by the work of other scientists. At the time of the *Beagle's* voyage, geologists were making new observations about forces that have shaped our planet. Naturalists were analyzing connections between organisms and their environments. These and other new ways of thinking about the natural world helped shape Darwin's thoughts. Many Europeans in Darwin's time thought that Earth was only a few thousand years old and had not changed much. Geologists James Hutton and Charles Lyell proposed hypotheses based on their own work and the work of others. Hutton and Lyell concluded that Earth is extremely old and that the processes that changed Earth in the past are the same processes that operate in the present.

Hutton and Geological Change Hutton recognized that certain kinds of rocks are formed from molten lava. He realized that other kinds of rock form slowly, from **sediment** that builds up and are squeezed into layers of rock. Hutton proposed that forces beneath Earth's surface can push layers of rock upward, tilting and twisting them in the process. These same forces can build mountain ranges. Mountains, in turn, are worn down by rain, wind, heat, and cold. These processes work very slowly. Hutton concluded that Earth must be much older than a few thousand years. Hutton introduced a concept called *deep time*—the idea that our planet's history extends back over a time so long that it is difficult for humans to imagine.

Lyell's *Principles of Geology* Lyell argued that the laws of nature are constant over time, so scientists must explain past events in terms of processes they can observe in the present. This way of thinking is called *uniformitarianism*. It states that the geological processes we can see today, such as volcanoes and erosion, are the same processes that shaped Earth millions of years ago. Like Hutton, Lyell argues that Earth is much older than a few thousand years. Darwin read Lyell's books during the *Beagle* voyage. On the voyage he experienced volcanoes and earthquakes. The earthquake lifted a stretch of rocky shorelines more than 3 meters out of the sea. When he traveled inland, he observed fossils of marine animals thousands of feet above sea level. Darwin realized that geological events repeated over many years could form mountains from rocks that had once been underneath the sea. Darwin asked himself, "If Earth can change over time, could life change too?"

READING TOOL

Academic Words <u>Sediment</u> is a collection of small pieces of rock that are the result of erosion. Water, wind, and ice erode, or wear down, rock into small pieces of dust, sand, and gravel. Sediment tends to end up in river valleys, along coastlines, and at the bottom of the ocean. Newer sediments are deposited on top of older sediments, forming layers. As the sediment builds up, pressure increases in the lower layers, forming sedimentary rocks.

☑ **Name three geological processes that have shaped Earth.**

_____

_____

Lamarck's Evolutionary Hypothesis

🔍 **KEY QUESTION** *How did Lamarck propose that species evolve?*

Darwin wasn't the first to suggest that species could evolve. The fossil record provided strong evidence that life had changed over time. Jean-Baptiste Lamarck proposed two of the first hypotheses about how species could change. Lamarck suggested that individual organisms could change during their lifetimes by selectively using or not using various parts of their bodies. He also suggested that individuals could pass these acquired traits on to their offspring, enabling species to change over time.

Lamarck's Ideas Lamarck proposed that all organisms have an inborn urge to become more complex and perfect. Organisms change and acquire features that help them live more successfully in their environments. According to Lamarck, water birds could have acquired long legs by wading in deeper water looking for food. Or, if a bird stopped flying, its wings would become smaller. Lamarck called traits altered by individual organisms during their lifetime *acquired characteristics*. Lamarck also suggested that acquired traits, such as longer legs, could be passed on to offspring. This principle is called *inheritance of acquired characteristics*.

Evaluating Lamarck's Hypotheses Today we know that Lamarck's hypotheses are wrong. Organisms do not have an inborn drive to become perfect. Evolution does not mean that a species becomes "better" over time. Evolution does not progress in a predetermined direction. Traits acquired by individuals during their lifetime (such as the loss of a limb) are not inherited by their offspring. However, Lamarck was one of the first naturalists to argue that species are not fixed and unchanging. Lamarck recognized that organisms' adaptations are related to their environment and the way they live. Lamarck's hypotheses were wrong, but his ideas paved the way for Darwin's ideas.

Thomas Malthus recognized that our planet can only support a certain amount of people before it gets overcrowded, and there are not enough resources for everyone. The graph below represents the population of Earth and the available resources over time.

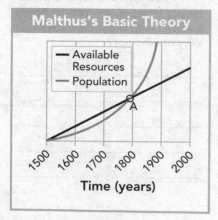

Malthus's Basic Theory

☑ What happens after point A in regard to the population and resources available at that point in time?

_____

_____

_____

BUILD Vocabulary

artificial selection selective breeding of plants and animals to promote the occurrence of desirable traits in offspring

Root Word *Artificial* has the root *artifice*, from *art*, meaning "skillful, creative," and *facere*, meaning "doing, making." *Artificial* means "made or done by humans."

☑ Why is animal and plant breeding by farmers artificial?

_____

_____

_____

Population Growth

KEY QUESTION *How did Malthus explain population growth?*

Before Darwin's time, the economist Thomas Malthus recognized that people were being born faster than people were dying, causing overcrowding. Malthus reasoned that if the human population grew unchecked, there wouldn't be enough living space and food for everyone. The forces that work against population growth, he suggested, include war, famine, and disease. Darwin realized that if Malthus's reasoning applied to people, it applied even more to other organisms. Many organisms can produce many more offspring than humans. Darwin realized that if all descendants of just one pair of oysters, which produce millions of eggs, were to survive, oysters would overrun Earth. However, many die and only a few survive to reproduce. This is known as differential reproductive success. This idea was important to Darwin in determining the mechanism, or natural process, that could produce evolutionary change. Darwin wanted to know which individuals survive, and why.

Artificial Selection

KEY QUESTION *How is inherited variation used in artificial selection?*

Some plants have larger or smaller fruit than average for their species. Some cows produce more or less milk than others in their herd. Farmers told Darwin that some of these differences were inherited variation—meaning they were traits that were passed from parents to offspring. Farmers would select for breeding only the plants that produced the largest fruit or cows that produced the most milk. Darwin called this selective breeding **artificial selection**. In artificial selection, nature provides the inherited variations, and humans select those variants they find useful. Darwin did not know how heredity worked, but he knew that inherited variation occurred in wild species as well as in domesticated plants and animals. Unlike earlier scientists, Darwin recognized that inherited variation was important, because it could provide the material for a natural process that could drive evolution.

Darwin's Theory: Natural Selection

Make Connections As you read your textbook, complete the natural selection concept map by entering an explanation for each term or concept.

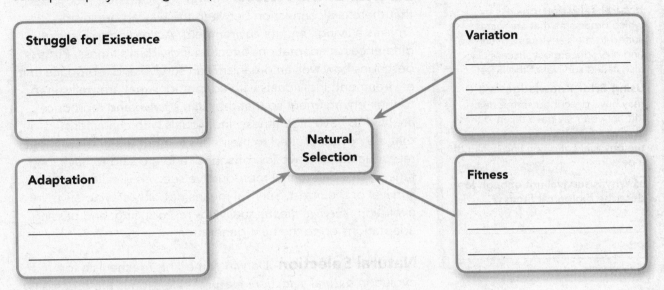

Struggle for Existence

_____

_____

_____

Variation

_____

_____

_____

Natural Selection

Adaptation

_____

_____

_____

Fitness

_____

_____

_____

Lesson Summary

Evolution by Natural Selection

🔑**KEY QUESTION** *Under what conditions does natural selection occur?*

Darwin worked out his theory of evolution by natural selection soon after reading Malthus, but did not publish his ideas for another 20 years. Darwin knew that many scientists ridiculed Lamarck's ideas, and Darwin's theory was even more radical. Darwin wanted to gather as much evidence as he could before making his ideas public.

In 1858, Alfred Russel Wallace published his ideas about evolution, which were almost identical to Darwin's. Darwin's ideas and Wallace's essay were presented together at a scientific meeting in 1858. Darwin then moved forward with his own work. He published his ideas in *On the Origin of Species* in 1859. Although both had the right idea, Darwin had more data to support his hypotheses than Wallace. Darwin's contribution was to describe a natural process that could operate like artificial selection.

The Struggle for Existence Malthus's work convinced Darwin that members of a population compete for a finite supply of resources. Darwin described this as *the struggle for existence.* Which individuals would succeed in surviving and reproducing?

🔑 As you read, circle the answers to each Key Question. Underline any words you do not understand.

Variation and Adaptation Darwin hypothesized that some individuals inherited traits that made them better suited, or better adapted, than other individuals to life in their environment. Any heritable characteristic that increases an organism's ability to survive and reproduce in its environment is called an **adaptation**. Adaptations can involve body parts or structures, physiology, or behaviors.

Survival of the Fittest Darwin, like Lamarck, recognized that there is a connection between the way an organism "makes a living" and its environment. According to Darwin, differences in adaptations affect an individual's fitness. **Fitness** describes how well an organism can survive and reproduce in its environment. Individuals with adaptations that are well suited to their environment so that they can survive and reproduce are said to have high fitness. Individuals with characteristics that are not well suited to their environment either die without reproducing, or leave few offspring, and are said to have low fitness. This differential reproductive success is called by some *survival of the fittest*. Survival means not only staying alive. In evolution, *survival* means surviving, reproducing, and passing adaptations on to the next generation.

Natural Selection Darwin named his mechanism for evolution *natural selection*. **Natural selection** is the process by which organisms in nature with variations most suited to their environment survive and leave more offspring. The different conditions of the environment influence fitness. Natural selection occurs in any situation in which:

➤ more individuals are born than can survive (the struggle for existence),

➤ natural heritable variation affects the ability to survive and reproduce (variation and adaptation), and

➤ fitness varies among individuals (differential reproductive success).

Well-adapted individuals survive and reproduce. Populations continue to change from generation to generation as they become better adapted or as their environment changes.

Natural selection only acts on inherited traits, because those are the only characteristics that parents can pass on to offspring. Natural selection does not make organisms "better." Adaptations only have to be good enough to enable an organism to pass on its genes. Natural selection does not move in one fixed direction. If the environment changes, this may change which traits are adaptive. This leads to a great diversity of adaptations in different environments. A species may become extinct if it cannot adapt to a changing environment fast enough. Natural selection is not the only mechanism that leads to evolutionary change.

Common Ancestry

⚲ KEY QUESTION *What does evolutionary theory suggest about the unity and diversity of life?*

Every organism is descended from parents who survived and reproduced. Those parents also descended from their parents, and so forth back through time. Just as well-adapted individuals survive, well-adapted species survive over time. Darwin proposed that living species descended with changes over time from common ancestors, an idea called *descent with modification*. Over many generations, changing environmental conditions lead to adaptations that cause a single species to split into two or more new species. Darwin supported this theory using the fossil record and Hutton and Lyell's work on deep time.

The idea that natural selection and adaptation can produce new species explains both the unity and the diversity of life. Darwin used a sketch of a branching tree to show descent from common ancestors. Look back in time and you can find common ancestors for similar species of mammals. Farther back is the common ancestor of all mammals. Farther back is the common ancestor of all animals and, farther back, of all living things. According to the principle of common descent, all species—living and extinct—are united by descent from ancient common ancestors, and they exhibit diversity due to natural selection and adaptation.

Visual Reading Tool:

The diagram below shows a tree diagram like the one Darwin used to show relationships between different species of finches on the Galápagos Islands.

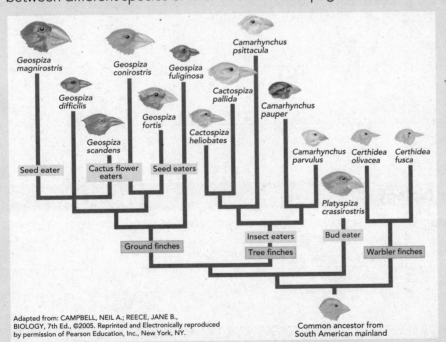

Adapted from: CAMPBELL, NEIL A.; REECE, JANE B., BIOLOGY, 7th Ed., ©2005. Reprinted and Electronically reproduced by permission of Pearson Education, Inc., New York, NY.

1. On the diagram, circle all the species that eat seeds.

2. All of these birds descended from a common ancestor. Is the common ancestor shown at the bottom or the top of the tree diagram?

_____

3. What caused the different species to evolve separately of each other if they lived on the same islands?

_____

_____

Evidence of Evolution

READING TOOL **Active Reading** As you read, complete the chart to describe the evidence of evolution.

Concept	How Concept Supports Evolution
Biogeography	
Closely Related but Different	
Distantly Related but Similar	
The Age of Earth and Fossils	
The Age of Earth	
Recent Fossil Finds	
Comparing Anatomy and Development	
Homologous Structures	
Analogous Structures	
Development	
Genetics and Molecular Biology	
Life's Common Genetic Code	
Molecular Homology	
Testing Natural Selection	
The Grants' observations of finches on the Galápagos Islands	

Lesson Summary

Scientists in Darwin's time did not have the knowledge or technology to test his ideas. However, every scientific test since then has supported Darwin's basic ideas about evolution.

Biogeography

🔍 **KEY QUESTION** *How does geographic distribution of species today relate to their evolutionary history?*

Darwin recognized the importance of patterns in where organisms live. The study of where organisms live now and where they and their ancestors lived in the past is called **biogeography**. Patterns in the distribution of fossils and living species tell us how modern organisms evolved from their ancestors. Darwin made two observations involving biogeography. First, closely related species can evolve diverse adaptations in different environments. Second, distantly related species can evolve similar adaptations if they live in similar environments.

Closely Related but Different The biogeography of Galápagos bird species suggested to Darwin that different island species evolved from a mainland species. Natural selection on different islands selected individuals with different inherited variations. The populations on different islands evolved into different, but closely related, species.

Distantly Related but Similar Darwin noted that ground-dwelling birds in ecologically similar grasslands in South America, Australia, and Africa resembled one another, although they were not closely related. Natural selection in similar habitats led to similar adaptations, such as legs and feet adapted for running.

The Age of Earth and Fossils

🔍 **KEY QUESTION** *How do fossils help document descent of modern species?*

The Age of Earth Darwin, along with Hutton and Lyell, knew that the Earth must be very old. The discovery of radioactivity and radioactive dating enabled geologists to determine the age of certain rocks and fossils. This data indicates that Earth is about 4.5 billion years old, old enough for evolution by natural selection to have taken place.

Recent Fossil Finds Scientists in Darwin's time had not found enough fossils to show the evolution of modern species from their ancestors. More recently discovered fossils now show clearly how modern species evolved from extinct ancestors. All records are incomplete, but many intermediate forms have been found. The fossil evidence tells an unmistakable story of evolutionary change.

🔍 As you read, circle the answers to each Key Question. Underline any words you do not understand.

BUILD Vocabulary

biogeography study of past and present distribution of organisms

Prefixes The prefix *bio-* means "life," and the prefix *geo-* means "Earth." The study of biogeography combines Earth science and life science. ☑ **What caused the island finch species to diversify over time?**

_____

_____

_____

_____

Connect to Visuals Examine Figure 17-14 in your textbook. This shows the evolution of whales from animals that walked on land, and highlights some of the changes that occurred in the front limbs (forelimbs) and rear limbs (hind limbs) as these animals evolved.

☑ *Artiodactyl* has legs for walking on land. *Dorudon* has flippers for swimming. The flippers of *Dorudon* and the legs of *Artiodactyl* are what kinds of structures?

_____

_____

BUILD Vocabulary

homologous structure structure that is similar in different species of common ancestry

vestigial structure structure that is inherited from ancestors but has lost much or all of its original function

analogous structure body part that shares a common function, but not a common structure

Word Roots *Homologous* and *analogous* share the Greek root *logos*, meaning "speech" or "reason." With the prefix *homo-*, *homologous* means "the same," and with the prefix *ana-*, *analogous* means "said to be similar."

☑ How are homologous and analagous structures different?

_____

_____

_____

_____

Comparing Anatomy and Development

🔍 **KEY QUESTION** *What do homologous structures and similarities in development suggest about the process of evolutionary change?*

By Darwin's time, scientists knew that the bones in all vertebrate limbs resembled each other. The same basic bone structure is used for climbing, running, and flying.

Homologous Structures Similar structures, like the bones of vertebrate limbs, that are shared by species and inherited from a common ancestor are called **homologous structures**. Evolutionary theory explains the existence of homologous structures adapted to different purposes as the result of descent with modification from a common ancestor. Biologists determine that structures are homologous by studying anatomical details, the way the structures develop in embryos, and their appearance over evolutionary history.

The degree of similarity in homologous structures is related to how recently species shared a common ancestor. Many bones of reptiles and birds are more similar to one another in structure and development than they are to homologous bones in mammals. This is evidence that reptiles and birds had a common ancestor that lived more recently than the common ancestor of mammals, reptiles, and birds. The key to identifying homology is common structure and origin during development, not function. Homology occurs in plants, too. Groups of plants share homologous stems, roots, leaves, and flowers.

Some homologous structures don't serve important functions. **Vestigial structures** are inherited from ancestors but have lost much of their original size and function. An example is the hipbone of a dolphin, or remnants of limbs in legless lizards. These structures may persist because they don't affect an organism's fitness. Therefore, natural selection does not fully eliminate them.

Analogous Structures Body parts that serve similar functions, but do not share a similar structure and development, are called **analogous structures**. The wing of a bee and the wing of a bird are examples of analogous structures. Both are used for flight, but they develop from different embryonic tissues.

Development Scientists noticed long ago that early developmental stages of many vertebrates look similar. Recent studies show that the same groups of embryonic cells develop in the same order in vertebrates to produce many homologous tissues and organs. Darwin realized that similar patterns of embryological development provide evidence that organisms have descended from a common ancestor.

Genetics and Molecular Biology

🔑 KEY QUESTION *How can molecular biology be used to trace the process of evolution?*

Genetics provides strong evidence supporting evolutionary theory. At the molecular level, similarities in the genetic code of all organisms, along with homologous genes and molecules, provide evidence of common descent. Mutation and gene shuffling during sexual reproduction produce the heritable variation on which natural selection works.

Life's Common Genetic Code All living organisms use information coded in DNA and RNA to carry information from one generation to the next. This genetic code is nearly identical in all organisms, including bacteria, fungi, plants, and animals. This is evidence that all organisms evolved from common ancestors that had the same code.

Molecular Homology Homology resulting from common ancestors is seen at the molecular level too. One example of homologous genes is the set of Hox genes that determine the development of body parts. Hox genes determine which parts of an embryo become the head and which become the tail. In vertebrates, Hox genes direct the growth of the front and hind limbs. Small changes or mutations in the Hox genes can produce major changes in an organism's structure. Some homologous Hox genes are found in almost all multicellular animals, from fruit flies to humans. The Hox genes must have been inherited from ancient common ancestors.

Testing Natural Selection

🔑 KEY QUESTION *What does recent research of the Galápagos finches show about natural selection?*

Darwin did not think it was possible to observe natural selection in nature because evolutionary change happens very slowly. Recently biologists have designed experiments to study natural selection in the wild.

Back to Galápagos The longest-running study of evolution in a natural environment is the ongoing work on Darwin's finches by Peter and Rosemary Grant. The Grants have been studying the finches on the island Daphne Major in the Galápagos. For over 40 years the Grants have been capturing, identifying, and measuring every finch on the island. When new birds hatch, the Grants note the parents and tag the birds. The Grants and their assistants also count and measure all the different kinds of seeds the birds use for food. They created a device to measure the hardness of the seeds.

A Testable Hypothesis Darwin had observed that different Galápagos finch species have beaks of different sizes and shapes. He hypothesized that natural selection shaped the beaks of different populations as they adapted to eat different foods. The Grants realized this hypothesis rested on two testable assumptions. First, in order for beak size and shape to evolve, there must be heritable variation in those traits. Second, if the beak differences were involved in natural selection, birds with different beak sizes and shapes should show differential survival and reproduction.

Natural Selection The Grants found a lot of heritable variation in beak size and shape in finch populations. During their study, a severe drought occurred. Plants produced fewer seeds. As the drought continued, birds ate the smaller and softer seeds first. Over time, only the largest and hardest seeds remained. Many birds starved and the finch population decreased. The Grants showed that birds with the largest beaks were more likely to survive, which gave them higher evolutionary fitness. The drought caused the average beak size in this finch population to change greatly in a few years. If the finch population did not have enough variation for natural selection to operate, they would not have been able to adapt and change.

Evolutionary Theory Evolves Many scientific discoveries have confirmed and expanded Darwin's hypotheses. Like any scientific theory, evolutionary theory is reviewed as new data are collected. Any questions that remain are about *how* evolution works, not *whether* evolution occurs.

Visual Reading Tool: Data from the Galápagos

Seed Abundance and Hardness	Bird Survival Based on Beak Size
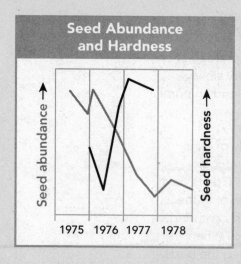	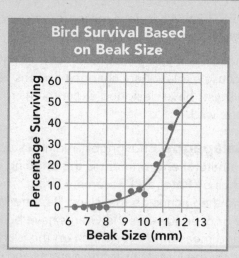

1. What caused seed abundance to decrease from 1975 to 1978? _____

2. What do you think the effect of the decrease in seed abundance was? _____

3. What is the connection between the change in seed hardness and the characteristic in the second graph? _____

17 Chapter Review

Review Vocabulary

Choose the letter of the best answer.

1. An inherited structure that has lost much of its original function is called a/an

   A. fossil.

   B. adaptation.

   C. vestigial structure.

   D. analogous structure.

2. The study of past and present distribution of organisms is called

   A. evolution.

   B. adaptation.

   C. fossils.

   D. biogeography.

Match the vocabulary term to its definition.

3. _____ process by which organisms survive and reproduce

4. _____ body parts similar in structure in different species

5. _____ body parts similar in function but not in structure

6. _____ heritable characteristic that increases fitness

   a. analogous structures

   b. homologous structures

   c. adaptation

   d. natural selection

Review Key Questions

Provide evidence and details to support your answers.

7. What three patterns of biodiversity did Darwin observe?

_____

8. What are two ways that Lamarck's ideas paved the way for later biologists such as Darwin?

_____

_____

9. Why is heritable variation important for both artificial and natural selection?

_____

_____

10. List three forms of evidence for descent from a common ancestor.

_____

_____

11. How does the work of Peter and Rosemary Grant illustrate natural selection?

_____

_____

Genes and Variation

Use Structure Use the section headings and bulleted lists below to help understand the information. What distinguishes and defines each of the list items from each other?

Genetics Joins Evolutionary Theory
➤ Species: _____

➤ Population: _____

➤ Gene Pool: _____

   ○ Allele frequency: _____

➤ Genotype vs. Phenotype: _____

Sources of Genetic Variation
➤ Mutations: _____

➤ Genetic Recombination during Sex: _____

_____

➤ Lateral Gene Transfer: _____

_____

Genes and Traits
➤ Single-gene Traits: _____

➤ Polygenic Traits: _____

_____

Lesson Summary

Genetics Joins Evolutionary Theory

🔑 As you read, circle the answers to each Key Question. Underline any words you do not understand.

🔑 **KEY QUESTION** *How is evolution defined in genetic terms?*

Heritable traits are controlled by genes carried on chromosomes. Changes in genes and chromosomes generate variation within populations. Molecular genetic techniques can now test hypotheses about variation and selection, and help us understand evolutionary change better than Darwin ever could. Studies in population genetics reinforce Darwin's understanding that populations—not individual organisms—evolve over time. All these discoveries give biologists a deeper understanding of how evolution works.

Genes, Populations, and Species The genetic definition of a species is a group of organisms that are physically similar and able to interbreed, but that do not interbreed with other groups. The genetic definition of a population is a group of individuals of the same species that mate and produce offspring.

Populations and Gene Pools The gene pool of a population is made up of all genes within that group's members. This includes all alleles for each gene. The allele frequency is how often a specific allele occurs within the gene pool. This number is expressed as a percentage of all the alleles for that gene in the population. Allele frequency has nothing to do with whether the allele is dominant or recessive. Sometimes, the recessive allele occurs more frequently than the dominant allele. Evolution involves any change in the frequency of alleles in a population over time. Remember, populations evolve, not individuals!

Genotype, Phenotype, and Evolution The combination of all the alleles in an individual organism is called its genotype. The phenotype encompasses all of the physical aspects of the organism. Evolution only acts on the phenotype, not the genotype. Individuals with genes that produce phenotypes that increase their survival and the number of their offspring in a particular environment will pass the genes for those traits on to their more numerous offspring. This change in the frequency of a trait in a population is known as evolution.

Sources of Genetic Variation

🔍 **KEY QUESTION** *What are the sources of genetic variation?*

Genetic variation is produced in three main ways: mutation, genetic recombination during sexual reproduction, and lateral gene transfer. Genetic variation must be present in a population for evolution to take place.

Mutations Occasionally an error occurs in gene replication. When this happens, the gene is considered mutated. Mutations in the germ line can be inherited by an individual's offspring. Sometimes an inherited mutation can be fatal to the individual. Other times, this can have neutral or even positive effects on the individual's fitness. Mutations are important because they provide a regular source of variation for natural selection to operate on the population.

Genetic Recombination During Sexual Reproduction The special aspect of sexual reproduction is the random association of individual chromosomes of homologous pairs during meiosis and the combination of different alleles coming from two parents. This is why you appear different from your siblings, and parents. You are a combination of alleles from both parents, half from each.

Lateral Gene Transfer The gene flow that occurs between individuals who may or may not be the same species is termed lateral gene flow. It is important for generating diversity among species. Many bacteria swap their genes on plasmids. This is how antibiotic resistance spreads.

Single-Gene and Polygenic Traits

🔍 **KEY QUESTION** *What determines the number of phenotypes for a given trait?*

The number of phenotypes produced for a trait depends on how many genes control the trait.

Single-Gene Traits Genes control traits in different ways. When only one gene controls one trait, this is called a **single-gene trait**. The trait may express itself as one or more phenotypes depending on how many alleles are present for the gene and whether alleles are dominant and recessive, incomplete, or codominant.

Polygenic Traits When multiple genes control a trait, it is referred to as a **polygenic trait**. The influence of the environment is often important in polygenic traits. Examples of polygenic traits in humans include hair, eye, or skin color.

Visual Reading Tool: Allele Frequencies

1. Calculate the allele frequency for black fur (B) and brown fur (b) in the mice population based on the number of each type of allele. Answer the questions below.

Sample Population

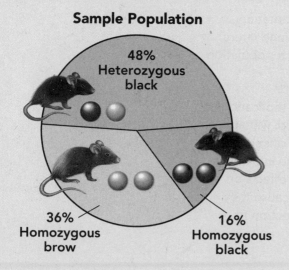

48% Heterozygous black

36% Homozygous brow

16% Homozygous black

Frequency of Alleles

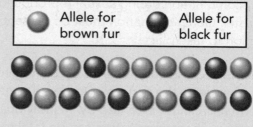

Allele for brown fur   Allele for black fur

Brown allele frequency: _____

Black allele frequency: _____

2. Which allele frequency is higher? _____

3. What is the genotype of a homozygous brown mouse? _____

4. In a population of 200 mice, how many would be homozygous black? _____

LESSON 2

Evolution as Genetic Change

READING TOOL **Compare and Contrast** Focus on the similarities and differences of the subjects in this section. Use the titles and subtitles in the chart below to take notes differentiating the concepts for each section.

Natural Selection

Directional	Stabilizing	Disruptive

Genetic Drift

Bottleneck Effect	Founder Effect

Hardy-Weinberg Principle

Nonrandom Mating	Small Populations	Gene Flow	Mutations	Natural Selection

Lesson Summary

How Natural Selection Works

⚲ KEY QUESTION *How does natural selection affect single-gene and polygenic traits?*

Individuals have inherited differences. Some better suited individuals will reproduce more successfully than others and pass those genes on to their more plentiful offspring.

Natural Selection on Single-Gene Traits Natural selection on single-gene traits can produce changes in allele frequencies that may be reflected by simple changes in phenotype frequencies.

⚲ As you read, circle the answers to each Key Question. Underline any words you do not understand.

directional selection form of natural selection when individuals at one end of a distribution curve have higher fitness than individuals in the middle or at the other end of the curve

stabilizing selection form of natural selection in which individuals near the center of a distribution curve have higher fitness than individuals at either end of the curve

disruptive selection natural selection in which individuals at the upper and lower ends of the curve have higher fitness than individuals near the middle of the curve

genetic drift random change in allele frequency caused by a series of chance occurrences that cause an allele to become more or less common in a population

bottleneck effect a change in allele frequency following a dramatic reduction in the size of a population

founder effect change in allele frequencies as a result of the migration of a small subgroup of a population

genetic equilibrium situation in which allele frequencies in a population remain the same from one generation to the next

Using Prior Knowledge The bottleneck effect occurs when a significant portion of a population is killed off. ☑ **List 3 events that could cause a dramatic decrease in a population size.**

_____

_____

_____

Natural Selection on Polygenic Traits Natural selection on polygenic traits can affect the relative fitness of phenotypes in directional selection, stabilizing selection, or disruptive selection.

Directional Selection When a preferred phenotype at one end of the distribution curve of phenotypes is favored, this type of selection is **directional selection**. The overall curve will shift toward that direction.

Stabilizing Selection If an intermediate phenotype comes under selection, then a **stabilizing selection** will take place. Extreme variations in the specific trait at both ends of the population will have less success, and so the bell curve becomes taller and narrower.

Disruptive Selection If the opposite scenario to stabilizing selection occurs, where extremes of the trait are selected for, then **disruptive selection** occurs. Thus the phenotype at both extremes become more successful, increasing the population diversity.

Genetic Drift

🔑 **KEY QUESTION** *What is genetic drift?*

In small populations, individuals that carry a particular allele may leave more descendants over time than other individuals by chance. These random changes in allele frequency are called **genetic drift**.

Genetic Bottlenecks When a large proportion of a given population is killed off, this can cause a restriction in the gene pool, which is called the **bottleneck effect**. A severe population bottleneck can result in decreased diversity.

The Founder Effect Sometimes a fraction of a population breaks away and colonizes a new habitat. Because the individuals in this group can contain a very different frequency of the alleles compared to the original population, it causes a **founder effect**.

Evolution Versus Genetic Equilibrium

🔑 **KEY QUESTION** *What conditions are required to maintain genetic equilibrium?*

Genetic equilibrium is a theoretical condition in which evolution is not occurring and the gene pool does not change. No population is ever in perfect genetic equilibrium.

Sexual Reproduction and Allele Frequency Because meiosis and fertilization do not change the proportions of allele occurrences, sexual reproduction alone does not lead to evolution.

The Hardy-Weinberg Principle

The Hardy-Weinberg principle predicts that five conditions can disturb genetic equilibrium and cause evolution to occur.

Nonrandom Mating Sexual selection is a common occurrence in sexually reproducing species, as individuals will seek out mates with the highest fitness. Phenotypic traits such as size or color will often play a role.

Small Population Size Large populations are less likely to be affected by genetic drift than small populations, because their size buffers them against random changes in allele frequencies.

Gene Flow from Immigration or Emigration The movement of genes into or out of a population is called gene flow. If animals come and go, this will change what alleles are available in the gene pool of the population of interest.

Mutations Just as it is a source of genetic variation, the existence of mutations means that allele frequencies will change.

Natural Selection Varying fitness levels mean that some individuals will survive better than others, leading to changing allele frequencies.

Visual Reading Tool: Polygenic Trait Selection

Label the different patterns of selection appropriately. Answer the questions below.

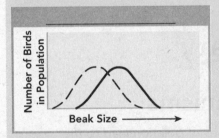
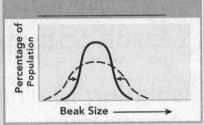
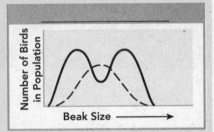

- - Original distribution
— New distribution as a result of selection

1. Darwin's finches vary in size from 10–20 cm and 8–38 g. Warbler-finches are the smallest species of them all. At some time in history, which selection led to their evolution?

_____

2. In the large cactus finch, some males have shorter beaks and other males have longer beaks. Which type of selection probably operated on this species?

_____

CHAPTER 18

LESSON 3

The Process of Speciation

READING TOOL **Cause and Effect** As you read, think about the three types of reproductive isolation and what causes them. Fill in the flow chart below.

Effect: Behavioral Isolation	Effect: Geographic Isolation	Effect: Temporal Isolation
Cause:	Cause:	Cause:

Lesson Summary

Isolating Mechanisms

As you read, circle the answers to each Key Question. Underline any words you do not understand.

KEY QUESTION *What types of isolation lead to the formation of new species?*

Speciation is the process by which new species evolve. Sexual reproduction allows for genes to be passed along in a population. If some individuals stop breeding with other individuals, eventually this can lead to a split in the population. As evolution continues, if two groups stop reproducing together, the gene pool will not be shared, resulting in **reproductive isolation**. Reproductive isolation can develop in several ways, including behavioral isolation, geographic isolation, and temporal isolation.

BUILD Vocabulary

speciation formation of a new species

reproductive isolation separation of a species or population so that they no longer interbreed

Behavioral Isolation If an important behavior, such as a mating ritual, evolves differently in two groups, then this type of reproductive isolation is termed **behavioral isolation**.

Geographic Isolation Geography can be a barrier that leads to reproductive isolation. If individuals cannot physically reach each other, this is known as **geographic isolation**. Any type of isolated habitat can result in this, whether they be mountaintops or actual islands. Natural disasters can also play a part as barriers or connectors.

Temporal Isolation When two or more species experience mating seasons that do not match up, then time is the divisive factor here, and it is known as **temporal isolation**.

Speciation in Darwin's Finches

🔍 **KEY QUESTION** *What is a current hypothesis about Galápagos finch speciation?*

Using research-based understanding of the finch populations on the Galápagos Islands, we can begin to piece together the historical events that led to Darwin's finches as the species they are today. Speciation in Galápagos finches occurred by founding a new population, geographic isolation, changes in the new population's gene pool, behavioral isolation, and ecological competition.

Founders Arrive A founding population of finches migrated to one of the Galápagos Islands from the South American mainland. A founder effect occurred, because these individuals would have only had certain alleles compared to the larger gene pool of the overall species back on the mainland.

Geographic Isolation Finding themselves on an island, the finches would have been geographically isolated from other populations, which would minimize the opportunity for interbreeding. If members of this founding population migrated to other islands, these new populations would become isolated.

Changes in Gene Pools Over time, each population of finch would evolve to adapt to the environment of each island. Food type and availability would be important in determining the most fit beak shape and size. Evolution continues.

Behavioral Isolation After more time, if any individuals manage to return to the original founding colony on the first island, behavioral isolation would have occurred. It is likely that courtship rituals and sexual selection would prevent birds with different-sized beaks from choosing to mate with one other.

BUILD Vocabulary

behavioral isolation form of reproductive isolation in which two populations develop differences in courtship rituals or other behaviors that prevent them from breeding

geographic isolation form of reproductive isolation in which two populations are separated by geographic barriers such as rivers, mountains, or bodies of water, leading to the formation of two separate subspecies

temporal isolation form of reproductive isolation in which two or more species reproduce at different times

Root Words The word temporal is based on the Latin word *tempus* which means "time." ☑ **Do you know any other word that has a similar root that relates to time?**

_____

_____

_____

Competition and Continued Evolution Competition between birds with different phenotypes (beak size and shape) would result in further evolution and speciation. This process would repeat until modern times, when 13 distinct species are found among the island system.

1. Fill in the diagram below with the five events that caused speciation of the finches of the Galápagos Islands.

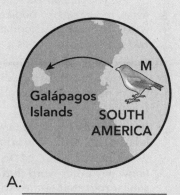

A._____

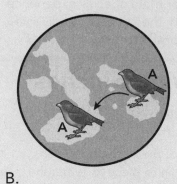

B. _____

C. _____

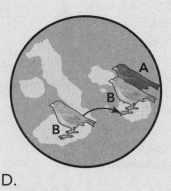

D. _____

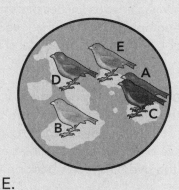

E. _____

_____

2. Behavioral isolation occurs when one population stops breeding with another population, perhaps because of physiological differences and behaviors. In which event has behavioral isolation occurred? How can you tell?

_____

_____

_____

3. At what stage did the founder effect take place?

_____

_____

_____

Molecular Evolution

READING TOOL **Main Idea and Details** As you read, identify the details that describe the headings listed below.

Heading	Notes
Gene Duplication	
Genetic Rearrangement	
Hox Genes and Evolution	
Neutral Mutations	
Calibrating the Clock	

Lesson Summary

New Genes, New Functions

KEY QUESTION *Where do new genes come from?*

The human genome is made up of about 25,000 genes. How do genes change over time? One way new genes can evolve is through duplication, followed by modification, of existing genes.

Gene Duplication During meiosis, crossing-over occurs between homologous chromosomes. If extra genes get copied on to one of the chromosomes, gene duplication has occurred. If this happens without any harmful effects, these gene copies can mutate and take on new functions while one copy maintains the original function.

Genetic Rearrangement DNA sequence can be modified by insertions, deletions, duplications, and rearrangements. This changing of the DNA code can produce modified proteins, and the duplication and modification results in the formation of gene "families." These gene families allow geneticists to trace evolutionary relationships between species and groups of species.

Developmental Genes and Body Plans

KEY QUESTION *How may Hox genes be involved in evolutionary change?*

Evo-devo is a field of biology that connects evolutionary genetics with development of organisms. Studying the relationship between the two leads to better understanding of gene function.

Hox Genes and Evolution The regulatory genes that determine which embryonic parts will grow into adult body parts are known as **Hox genes**. Small changes in Hox gene activity during embryological development can produce large changes in adult animals.

Timing Is Everything When growth occurs is critical to the development of an animal. Genetic changes affecting how long or when this growth occurs will directly affect the body plan of an animal.

As you read, circle the answers to each Key Question. Underline any words you do not understand.

BUILD Vocabulary

Hox gene regulatory genes that determine which parts of an embryo develop into arms, legs, or wings.

Word Origins The word gene was coined by Wilhelm Johannsen, a Danish botanist, in 1905. It is based upon the greek word *genos* which means "race, kind, or offspring."

☑ What other famous botanist worked with pea plants and is responsible for many important discoveries in the field of genetics?

_____

_____

Molecular Clocks

⚲ KEY QUESTION *How do molecular clocks work?*

Because related species should have similar genomes, the differences that do exist between their genomes will provide an estimate of how long the two species have been evolving independently.

Neutral Mutations as "Ticks" Molecular clocks are based on the relatively constant rate at which mutations occur. In particular, mutations that are not subject to selection (neutral mutations) are used as the "ticks" of the clock. More mutations, and a greater difference between the two species, means that they have been separate species for a greater amount of time.

Calibrating the Clock There are many different molecular clocks, because the rate of mutation happens differently for different DNA. If scientists already know the age of a particular species, they can use that information to calibrate the neutral mutation "ticks" in a particular gene, and determine that particular molecular clock's accuracy.

Visual Reading Tool: Gene Duplication

1. Write the sequence of events by which gene duplication occurs.

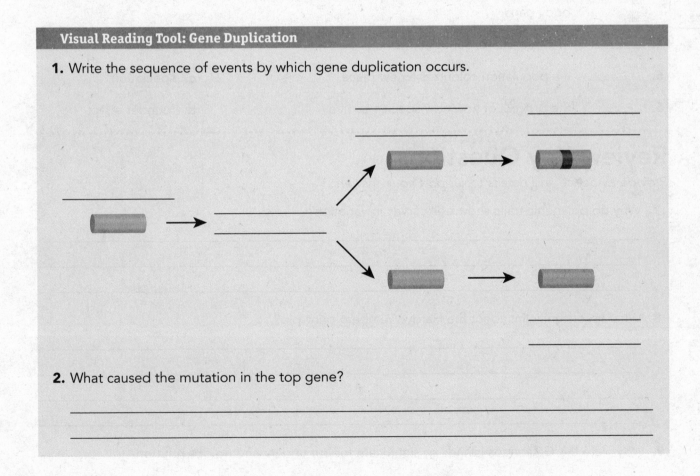

2. What caused the mutation in the top gene?

_____

_____

Review Vocabulary

Choose the letter of the best answer.

1. The movement of genes in or out of a population is called:

   A. gene transfer

   B. gene flow

   C. gene pool

   D. genetic drift

2. When two populations are separated by physical barriers:

   A. reproductive isolation

   B. temporal isolation

   C. geographical isolation

   D. behavioral isolation

Match the vocabulary term to its definition.

3. _____ genes determining the development of animal body parts

4. _____ multiple alleles/genes control one trait

5. _____ if a population colonizes a new place

6. _____ the process of how new species evolve

a. polygenic trait

b. Hox gene

c. speciation

d. founder effect

Review Key Questions

Provide evidence and details to support your answers.

7. Why do polygenic traits show bell curves in variation?

   _____

   _____

   _____

8. What is so significant about the Hardy-Weinberg principle?

   _____

   _____

   _____

   _____

9. Why were the Galápagos Islands so significant for our understanding of evolution?

   _____

   _____

   _____

READING TOOL **Sequence of Events** Determine the order of the following events, and number each event in the left column. The first one has been completed for you.

Order	Event Descriptions
1	As European scientists traveled the world, they discovered plants and animals they had never seen before. Though they wanted to communicate with each other about their discoveries, the names of organisms varied greatly from place to place, which made it hard for them to share their findings.
	The only known differences among living things were the characteristics that separated animals from plants. As a result, the two kingdoms of this time were Animalia and Plantae.
	As scientists continued to research the differences between organisms, they found that prokaryotes and eukaryotes were even more different from each other than recently thought, so they established the idea of a domain, which is larger than a kingdom.
	Carolus Linnaeus developed a naming system called binomial nomenclature. In binomial nomenclature, each species is assigned a two-part scientific name.
	Early scientists began to use Latin and Greek names to describe species, but these names often described the species in great detail, so this wasn't a useful way to classify living things.
	Researchers found that organisms were more complex than what they had thought initially, so they developed a system of classification that included the six kingdoms: Eubacteria, Archaebacteria, Protista, Fungi, Plantae, and Animalia.

Lesson Summary

Assigning Scientific Names

KEY QUESTION *What are the goals of binomial nomenclature and taxonomy?*

At first, European scientists tried to assign Latin or Greek names to each species, but the names were too long because they were described in detail, so this system did not work well. Biologists now identify and organize biodiversity through a standardized system that everyone can understand and agree upon. Taxonomy is a system of naming and classifying organisms based on shared characteristics and universal rules. Each scientific name must refer to only one species.

Binomial Nomenclature In the 1730s, Swedish botanist Carolus Linnaeus developed a naming system called **binomial nomenclature**, which is used today. In binomial nomenclature, each species is assigned a two-part scientific name, which is written in italics.

As you read, circle the answers to each Key Question. Underline any words you do not understand.

BUILD Vocabulary

taxonomy system of naming and classifying organisms based on shared characteristics and universal rules

binomial nomenclature classification system where each species is assigned a two-part scientific name

The first part of that name is the **genus** to which the species belongs. A genus is a group of similar species. The second part of a scientific name describes an important trait or the organism's habitat.

Classifying Species into Larger Groups The science of naming and grouping organisms is called **systematics**. The goal of systematics is to organize living things into groups that have biological meaning. Biologists often refer to these groups as many **taxa** or a taxon.

The Linnaean Classification System

🔍 **KEY QUESTION** *How did Linnaeus group species into larger taxa?*

Linnaeus developed a classification system that organized species into seven taxa based on similarities and differences: species, genus, family, order, class, phylum, and kingdom.

Species and Genus The scientific name of a camel with two humps is *Camelus bactrianus*. The genus *Camelus* also includes other species of camels that only have one hump.

Family The genera *Camelus* (camels) and *Lama* (llamas) are grouped with other genera that share many similarities into a larger taxon, the **family**, Camelidae.

Order Closely related families are grouped into an **order**. Camels and llamas are grouped with other animal families, including deer and cattle, forming the order Artiodactyla, which includes hoofed animals with an even number of toes.

Class Similar orders are grouped into a **class**. The order Artiodactyla is in the class Mammalia, which includes animals that are warm-blooded, have body hair, and produce milk for their young.

Phylum Classes are grouped into a **phylum**, which includes organisms that can look different, but share important characteristics. The class Mammalia is placed in the phylum Chordata, in which all of the animals have a nerve cord.

Kingdom The largest and most inclusive traditional taxonomic category is the **kingdom**. All multicellular animals are placed in the kingdom Animalia.

Classification Changes with New Discoveries

Organisms belong to the same species if they can mate and produce fertile offspring. A species is the smallest taxon. Higher taxa, in contrast, are defined by rules created by researchers and ongoing discoveries in genetics, cell biology, development, and Darwinian theory.

Changing Ideas About Kingdoms

🔍 KEY QUESTION *What are the six kingdoms of life as they are now identified?*

During Linnaeus's time, there were two kingdoms—Animalia and Plantae—because the only known differences among organisms were those that separated animals from plants.

From Two to Six Kingdoms Because single-celled organisms were significantly different from plants and animals, researchers placed all microorganisms in kingdom Protista. Yeasts, molds, and mushrooms were placed in the kingdom Fungi. Because bacteria lack nuclei, mitochondria, and chloroplasts, all prokaryotes were placed in kingdom Monera, while single-celled eukaryotic organisms remained in kingdom Protista. By the 1990s, researchers learned that monerans were genetically and biochemically different, so they were separated into Eubacteria and Archaebacteria, forming six kingdoms.

Three Domains To account for new differences among prokaryotes, biologists established a new taxon, the **domain**, which is larger than a kingdom. The three domains are Bacteria, Archaea, and Eukarya.

> **BUILD Vocabulary**
> **domain** taxonomic category that is even larger than a kingdom

Visual Reading Tool: Analyzing Data

Use the classification table below to answer the questions about the 3 domains of living things.

Classification of Living Things

DOMAIN	Bacteria	Archaea	Eukarya			
KINGDOM	Eubacteria	Archaebacteria	"Protista"	Fungi	Plantae	Animalia
CELL TYPE	Prokaryote	Prokaryote	Eukaryote	Eukaryote	Eukaryote	Eukaryote
CELL STRUCTURES	Cell walls with peptidoglycan	Cell walls without peptidoglycan	Cell walls of cellulose in some; some have chloroplasts	Cell walls of chitin	Cell walls of cellulose; chloroplasts	No cell walls or chloroplasts
NUMBER OF CELLS	Unicellular	Unicellular	Most unicellular; some colonial; some multicellular	Most multicellular; some unicellular	Most multicellular; some green algae unicellular	Multicellular
MODE OF NUTRITION	Autotroph or heterotroph	Autotroph or heterotroph	Autotroph or heterotroph	Heterotroph	Autotroph	Heterotroph
EXAMPLES	*Streptococcus, Escherichia coli*	Methanogens, halophiles	*Amoeba, Paramecium*, slime molds, giant kelp	Mushrooms, yeasts	Mosses, ferns, flowering plants	Sponges, worms, insects, fishes, mammals

1. What are the key differences between the three domains? _____

_____

2. Which kingdom or kingdoms have only heterotrophs? _____

LESSON 2

Modern Evolutionary Classification

READING TOOL **Cause and Effect** As you read Chapter 19, Lesson 2, explain how derived characters can be lost by defining the terms and providing examples of each.

	Derived Character	Lost Trait
DEFINITION		
EXAMPLES		

Lesson Summary

BUILD Vocabulary

phylogeny study of the evolutionary relationships among organisms

clade evolutionary branch of a cladogram that includes a single ancestor and all its descendants

🔍 As you read, circle the answers to each Key Question. Underline any words you do not understand.

Darwin's "tree of life" suggests a way to classify organisms based on how closely related they are. When taxa are rearranged this way, some old Linnaean classifications no longer work. For example, the Linnaean class Reptilia isn't valid unless birds are included—which means birds are reptiles and are descended from dinosaurs.

Evolutionary Classification

🔍 **KEY QUESTION** *What is the goal of evolutionary classification?*

Darwinian theory gave birth to **phylogeny**, the study of the evolutionary history of lineages of organisms. Phylogeny, in turn, led to evolutionary classification, which groups species into larger categories that reflect lines of evolutionary descent, rather than similarities and differences. The larger a taxon is, the farther back in time all of its members shared a common ancestor.

When organisms are grouped this way, they are called clades. A **clade** is a group of species that includes a single common ancestor and all descendants of that ancestor, living and extinct.

Cladograms

🔍 KEY QUESTION *What is a cladogram?*

Modern evolutionary classification uses cladistic analysis to compare selected traits to determine the order in which organisms branched off from their common ancestors. This information is then used to build a **cladogram**.

Building Cladograms Refer to Figure 19-6. Part 1 represents how one ancestral species branches into two species, each of which could found a new lineage. In part 2, the bottom represents the common ancestor shared by all organisms in the cladogram. The branching pattern shows how closely related various lineages are. Each branch point represents the last point at which species in lineages above that point shared a common ancestor.

Derived Characters Cladistic analysis focuses on certain kinds of characters, called **derived characters**. A derived character is a trait that arose in the most recent common ancestor of a lineage and was passed to its descendants.

Losing Traits Snakes are reptiles, which are tetrapods, but they don't have four limbs! The ancestors of snakes, however, did have four limbs. Somewhere in the lineage, that trait was lost. Because distantly related groups can sometimes lose a character, systematists are cautious about using the absence of a trait as a character in their analyses.

Interpreting Cladograms Look at Figure 19-8, which shows a simplified phylogeny of the cat family. The lowest branching point represents the last common ancestor of all four-limbed animals (clade Tetrapoda). The forks in this cladogram show the order in which various groups branched off from the tetrapod lineage. The positions of various characters in the cladogram reflect the order in which those characteristics arose. Each derived character listed along the main trunk of the cladogram defines a clade. Retractable claws is a derived character shared only by the clade Felidae. Derived characters that occur "lower" on the cladogram than the branch point for a clade are not derived for that particular clade.

Clades and Traditional Groups A true clade must contain an ancestral species and *all* of its descendants, with no exceptions. It also must exclude all species that are not descendants of the original ancestor.

BUILD Vocabulary

cladogram diagram showing patterns of shared characteristics among species

derived character trait that arose in the most recent common ancestor of a lineage and was passed to its descendants

Suffixes The suffix *-gram* means "something written or drawn," and usually refers to a visual representation of a concept.

☑ **Based upon what you know about clades, explain what a cladogram is in your own words.**

_____

_____

_____

Anatomical describes the structural characteristics of an organism

☑ **Circle the characteristic of a bird that is anatomical.**

1. Birds lay eggs.

2. Birds eat seeds.

3. Birds have wings.

DNA in Classification

🔍 **KEY QUESTION** *How are DNA sequences used in classification?*

The goal of modern systematics is to understand the evolutionary relationships of all life on Earth, including bacteria, plants, worms, and octopuses.

Genes and Derived Characters All organisms carry genetic information in DNA. They inherit genes from earlier generations. A wide range of organisms share genes that can be used to determine evolutionary relationships. Because all genes mutate over time, shared genes contain differences that can be treated as derived characters in cladistic analysis. For that reason, similarities and differences in DNA can be used to explain evolutionary relationships.

New Techniques Suggest New Trees DNA analysis has helped to make evolutionary trees more accurate. Often, scientists use DNA evidence when **anatomical** traits alone cannot provide clear answers.

Visual Reading Tool: Analyze Cladograms

Use the cladogram at the right to answer the following questions.

1. Circle the clade that includes both amphibians and snakes.

2. What is something that all organisms in that clade have in common?

_____

3. What kingdom does this cladogram fit into?

_____

4. Who are the lizards most closely related to on this cladogram?

_____

5. On the cladogram, star the organism that has wings as a derived character.

Clade or Not?

The Tree of All Life

🔑 **KEY QUESTION** *What does the tree of life show?*

Modern evolutionary classification is changing rapidly and aims to show all life on one evolutionary tree. As discoveries are made, biologists change the way organisms are grouped. Currently, organisms are grouped in three domains.

Domain Bacteria Members of the domain Bacteria (formerly Eubacteria) are unicellular and prokaryotic. Their cells have thick, rigid walls that surround a cell membrane, and their cell walls contain peptidoglycan. These bacteria range from free-living soil organisms to deadly parasites. Some photosynthesize, some need oxygen to survive, and others are killed by oxygen.

Domain Archaea Members of the domain Archaea (formerly Archaebacteria) are also unicellular and prokaryotic, but live in some of the most extreme environments on Earth, such as volcanic hot springs. Many archaea can only survive in the absence of oxygen. Their cell walls lack peptidoglycan, and their cell membranes contain unusual lipids that aren't found in other organisms.

Domain Eukarya Eukarya consists of all organisms that have a nucleus. It includes kingdoms Protista, Fungi, Plantae, and Animalia.

"Protists": Unicellular Eukaryotes Protists differ greatly from one another and are part of several evolutionary lineages. They are divided into at least five clades, with most being unicellular (the brown algae is multicellular), some photosynthetic, and others heterotrophic.

Fungi Members of the kingdom Fungi are heterotrophs with cell walls containing chitin. Examples include mushrooms and yeast.

Plantae Members of the kingdom Plantae are autotrophs with cell walls that contain cellulose. They photosynthesize using chlorophyll.

Animalia Members of the kingdom Animalia are multicellular and heterotrophic, and lack cell walls. Most animals can move about at some point during their life cycle.

A Revised Tree of Life The tree in Figure 19-12 illustrates current hypotheses about relationships among organisms; however, it gives some incorrect impressions. To more accurately portray the living world, that kind of tree would spread organisms out to reflect their genetic diversity. However, it would be difficult to read because it would span several pages. One solution, proposed by biologist David Hillis, is shown in Figure 19-13. It provides a truer representation of the full diversity of living organisms.

READING TOOL

Apply Prior Knowledge

Earlier in the book you learned about prokarytes vs. eukaryotes. Eukaryotes contain membrane-bound organelles, and prokaryotes do not. ☑ **What is another difference between prokaryotes and eukaryotes?**

_____

_____

_____

_____

_____

Review Vocabulary

Choose the letter of the best answer.

1. The largest taxon is called

A. domain.

B. kingdom.

C. species.

D. clade

2. The study of the evolutionary history of lineages of organisms is known as

A. a genus.

B. binomial nomenclature.

C. phylogeny.

D. systematics.

Review Key Questions

Provide evidence and details to support your answers.

5. Use the cladogram below to answer the following questions.

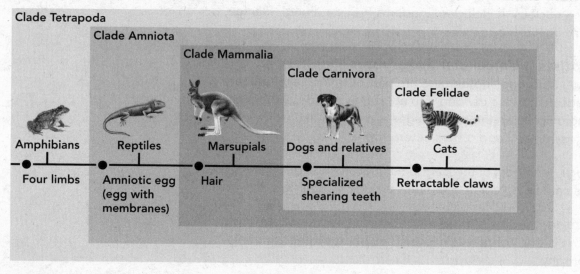

a. Which clades contain animals that have specialized shearing teeth?

_____

b. Marsupials belong to which clades? _____

6. What are the advantages of classifying species according to their evolutionary relationships, instead of their physical similarities?

_____

_____

_____

_____

The Fossil Record

Active Reading Fossils can tell us a lot about the history of our planet. As you read through this lesson, pay special attention to how fossils form. Fill in the graphic organizer below to outline the steps that create fossils.

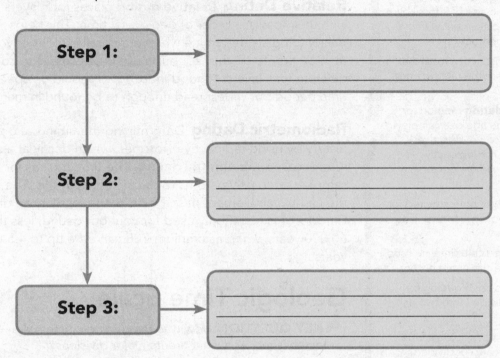

Step 1: _____

Step 2: _____

Step 3: _____

Lesson Summary

Fossils and Ancient Life

🔑 **KEY QUESTION** *What do fossils reveal about ancient life?*

We know dinosaurs once existed because they are preserved in fossils. Extinct species—those with no living members—are known to us because of fossils.

Types of Fossils The fossils preserved today vary greatly in size and completeness. Trace fossils are only impressions, but these can still be informative, showing details such as an animal's behavior or diet.

Fossils in Sedimentary Rock Sedimentary rock is formed when particles of eroded rocks and other materials become compacted together. Because organic material decomposes, shells, bones, and teeth can be mineralized into rocks.

🔑 As you read, circle the answers to each Key Question. Underline any words you do not understand.

BUILD Vocabulary

extinct condition of a species that has died out and has no living members

Evaluating Evidence in the Fossil Record Fossils reveal information about the structures of ancient organisms, the sequential nature of groups in the fossil record, the evolution from common ancestors, and the ecology of ancient environments.

Dating Earth's History

🔑 **KEY QUESTION** *How do we date events in Earth's history?*

Relative Dating Relative dating places rock layers with their fossils in order of geological time. This helps paleontologists determine whether a fossil is older or younger than others. To do this, scientists use index fossils to compare different rock layers. A good index fossil should be specific to a time period but widespread enough to be found in many places.

Radiometric Dating Determining the timing of geological history by using radioactive isotopes, which decay at a steady rate, is called radiometric dating. The time it takes for half of a sample's radioactive atoms to decay is its half-life. The longer the half-life an element has, the older the fossil it can date. Carbon-14 is commonly used for younger dating, less than 60,000 years, whereas uranium-238 can date up to 4.5 billion years ago.

Geologic Time Scale

🔑 **KEY QUESTION** *How was the geologic time scale established, and what are its major divisions?*

An overall timeline of the Earth's history is called the geologic time scale. The geologic time scale is based on both relative and absolute dating. The major divisions of the geologic time scale are eons, eras, and periods.

Establishing the Time Scale Paleontologists first decided the different periods of time scale based on distinct rock layer boundaries.

Divisions of the Geologic Time Scale Geologists then broke down time into four eons. These eons were then subdivided into eras. Eras were then further divided into periods, which are millions of years long.

Naming the Divisions The divisions were named for a variety of reasons. The Precambrian Period, which was named simply because nothing older than the Cambrian Period had been discovered until then, covers about 90 percent of Earth's history.

Comparing Time If all geologic time were imagined in the form of a 24-hour clock, humans would only fall into the last minute of that clock.

BUILD Vocabulary

relative dating method of determining the age of a fossil by comparing its placement with that of fossils in other rock layers

index fossil distinctive fossil that is used to compare the relative ages of fossils

radiometric dating method for determining the age of a sample from the ratio of a radioactive isotope to the nonradioactive isotope of the same element in a sample

half-life length of time required for half of the radioactive atoms in a sample to decay

geologic time scale timeline used to represent Earth's entire history

era major division of geologic time; usually divided into two or more periods

period division of geologic time into which eras are subdivided

plate tectonics geologic processes, such as continental drift, volcanoes, and earthquakes, resulting from plate movement

Multiple Meanings Indexes are used to organize or compare events. For the fossil index, they are used to show when organisms from fossils were alive based upon their location in rock layers. ☑ **Where else can you find indexes that help organize concepts?**

Life on a Changing Planet

🔍 **KEY QUESTION** *How have Earth's physical and biological environments shaped the history of life?*

The environment has affected life, and life has affected the environment in turn.

Changes in Climate Earth's environment and climate have changed greatly over time, including global climate change from human and nonhuman causes. Not a lot of temperature change is required to have serious effects in the form of an ice age or a "heat wave."

Geologic Forces Geological forces move very slowly, but to sometimes dramatic effect. The theory that explains how and where continents and oceans have moved is **plate tectonics**. This includes when Pangaea formed and broke apart.

Effects on Life Global climate change, mountain building, the emergence of islands, continental drift, changes in levels of continents and oceans, and meteor impacts have altered Earth's habitats, with major effects on the history of life.

Biological Forces Life has played a role in changing the environment, biologically, geologically, and chemically. The actions of living organisms over time have changed conditions in the atmosphere, the oceans, and the land.

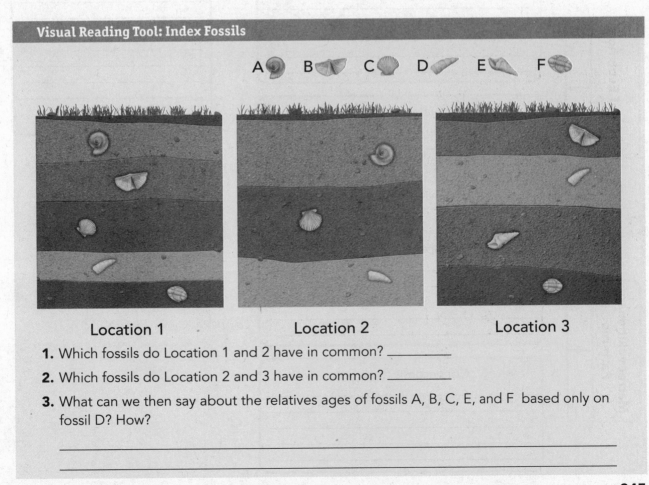

Visual Reading Tool: Index Fossils

A   B   C   D   E   F

Location 1   Location 2   Location 3

1. Which fossils do Location 1 and 2 have in common? _____

2. Which fossils do Location 2 and 3 have in common? _____

3. What can we then say about the relatives ages of fossils A, B, C, E, and F based only on fossil D? How?

_____

_____

READING TOOL **Use Structure** Use section headings and the graphic organizer below to fill in information about each item that connects it to the overall lesson.

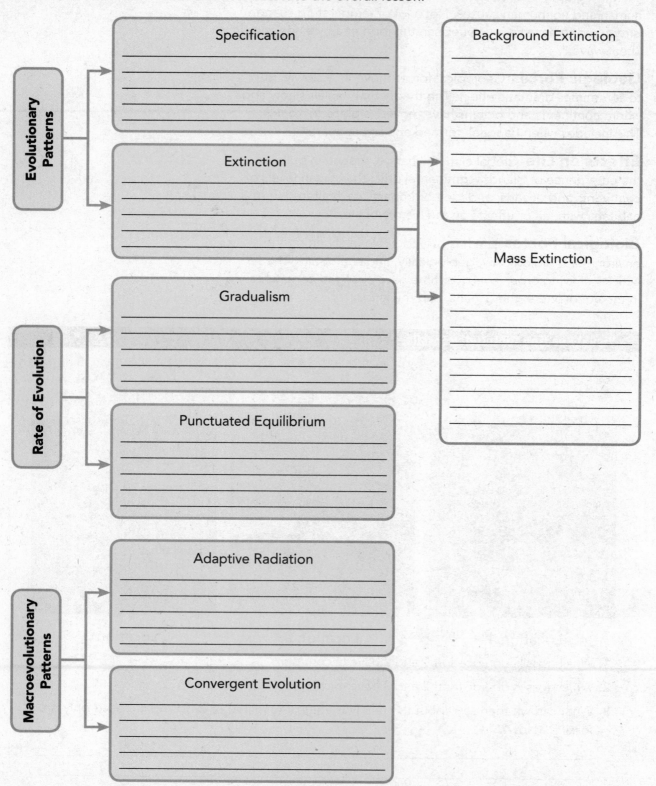

Evolutionary Patterns

Specification
_____
_____
_____
_____
_____

Extinction
_____
_____
_____
_____
_____

Background Extinction
_____
_____
_____
_____
_____
_____
_____
_____

Mass Extinction
_____
_____
_____
_____
_____
_____
_____
_____
_____

Rate of Evolution

Gradualism
_____
_____
_____
_____
_____

Punctuated Equilibrium
_____
_____
_____
_____
_____

Macroevolutionary Patterns

Adaptive Radiation
_____
_____
_____
_____
_____

Convergent Evolution
_____
_____
_____
_____
_____

Speciation and Extinction

KEY QUESTION *What patterns describe the sequential nature of groups in the fossil record?*

As you read, circle the answers to each Key Question. Underline any words you do not understand.

More than 99 percent of all life forms that ever lived are now extinct, based on fossils. The emergence, growth, and extinction of larger clades, such as dinosaurs, mammals, or flowering plants, are examples of **macroevolutionary patterns.**

Macroevolution and Cladistics Cladograms are a way to visualize how related different species are, living and extinct, and what common ancestors they might have had.

Adaptation and Extinction The rate at which different species adapt and go extinct varies between clades and geological periods. High species diversity is important for clade survival.

Patterns of Extinction The **background extinction** rate is considered to be the "normal" amount of extinction that occurs. When a dramatic event affects species on a global scale, a **mass extinction** can occur, in which a large proportion of species go extinct relatively rapidly.

Rate of Evolution

KEY QUESTION *What does the fossil record show about periods of stasis and rapid change?*

Fossil evidence supports the hypothesis that evolution can occur at different rates in different clades, and at different times.

Gradualism Slow and steady evolution is called **gradualism**. This idea was championed by Darwin, and is supported by fossil evidence that shows species evolving gradually over time.

Punctuated Equilibrium Now and then, the fossil record shows that equilibrium can be interrupted by brief periods of geologically rapid change. When this happens, we call it **punctuated equilibrium**. Over thousands or millions of years, rapid bursts of speciation can occur.

Rapid Evolution After Equilibrium Two ways evolution can rapidly occur are through genetic drift and mass extinctions.

Genetic Drift In small populations, random chance can lead to certain genes' becoming more or less prevalent.

Mass Extinction Because mass extinctions mean many species disappear, many ecological niches become available. Because of a lack of competition, evolution and speciation can occur relatively rapidly.

BUILD Vocabulary

macroevolutionary patterns changes in anatomy, phylogeny, and behavior that take place in clades larger than a single species

background extinction extinction caused by the slow and steady process of natural selection

mass extinction event during which many species become extinct during a relatively short period of time

gradualism evolution of a species by gradual accumulation of small genetic changes over long periods of time

punctuated equilibrium pattern of evolution in which long, stable periods are interrupted by brief periods of more rapid change

Word Origins

The word *equilibrium* is based on two Latin words, *aequi*, which means "equal," and *libra*, which means "balance." *Equilibrium* is a common concept in biology and can be used under many different contexts. ☑ **When else have you used the word** *equilibrium* to describe a biological concept?

_____

_____

_____

_____

Macroevolutionary Patterns

🔍 **KEY QUESTION** *What are two patterns of macroevolution?*

Two important patterns of macroevolution are adaptive radiation and convergent evolution.

Adaptive Radiation One species may evolve into several species; this is known as **adaptive radiation**. Dinosaurs, mammals, and Darwin's finches have all undergone adaptive radiation before.

Convergent Evolution When unrelated organisms develop similar physical characteristics to adapt to comparable ecological niches, **convergent evolution** has occurred.

Coevolution

🔍 **KEY QUESTION** *What evolutionary characteristics are typical of coevolving species?*

When two species evolve tightly together, we call it **coevolution**. The relationship between coevolving organisms often becomes so specific that neither organism can survive without the other.

Flowers and Pollinators Flowers and their pollinators are a good example of coevolving to perfectly complement one another in nature.

Plants and Herbivorous Insects Some herbivores have coevolved to tolerate plants that use specific defenses to protect themselves from general consumption.

Visual Reading Tool: Lineage of Modern Birds

1. Label the clades by completing the figure with the following terms: crocodiles, modern birds, *Tyrannosaurus rex*.

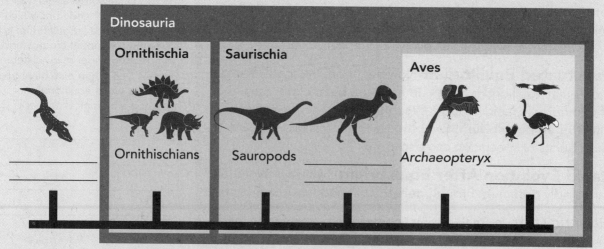

2. Which clade is not part of the Dinosauria clade? _____

3. Which clade contains Archaeopteryx? _____

4. What is the only surviving clade within Dinosauria? _____

Earth's Early History

READING TOOL **Sequence of Events** List events described in the text in the order in which they occur. Words such as *first*, *next*, *after*, and *finally* are clues to the sequence. Use the titles below to organize your events.

1. Earth's Early Atmosphere _____
_____
_____

2. Miller-Urey Experiment _____
_____
_____

3. Formation of Protocells _____
_____
_____
_____

4. RNA World Hypothesis _____
_____
_____

5. Life Changes the Atmosphere _____
_____
_____
_____

6. Earliest Eukaryotes _____
_____
_____

7. Endosymbiotic Theory _____
_____
_____

Lesson Summary

Mysteries of Life's Origins

🔍 As you read, circle the answers to each Key Question. Underline any words you do not understand.

READING TOOL

Make Connections Cell membranes are made of lipids, and are necessary for cells because they separate them from the external environment. Protocells were the first examples of membrane-like vesicles that scientists can create in a lab. ☑ **What role do cell membranes and protocells play in the "RNA world" hypothesis?**

_____

_____

_____

🔍 **KEY QUESTION** *What do scientists hypothesize about early Earth and the origin of life?*

Geological and astronomical evidence suggest that our planet was formed when cosmic debris collided 4.2 billion years ago. Earth finally cooled enough to form the solid rock we know today. Condensing water formed rain, which led to oceans. Earth's early atmosphere contained little or no oxygen. It was mainly composed of carbon dioxide, water vapor, and nitrogen, with smaller amounts of carbon monoxide, hydrogen sulfide, and hydrogen cyanide. Breathing oxygen was not yet possible.

Organic Molecules in Space Some basic building blocks for life, like amino acids, can be found in the solar system. Thus, these molecules were probably around in Earth's early years.

The Miller-Urey Experiment In 1953, two scientists attempted to simulate how organic compounds first formed on Earth. They combined liquid water with gaseous methane, ammonia, and hydrogen, and applied electric "lightning" sparks, which produced multiple amino acids. Although their hypotheses were incorrect, recent experiments have validated their conclusion. Miller and Urey's experiment suggests that organic compounds necessary for life could have arisen from simpler compounds on a primitive Earth.

Formation of Protocells Molecules similar to fatty acids can sometimes form spontaneously. Thus, these molecules might have been able to form membrane-like vesicles. The protocells could then form around RNA, which could then provide information for replication to occur.

RNA First? The "RNA world" hypothesis proposes that RNA existed before DNA. From this simple RNA-based system, several steps could have led to today's DNA-directed protein synthesis. There are many pieces of evidence to support this hypothesis. All proteins originate from RNA; even DNA nucleotides are first synthesized as RNA nucleotides.

Life Changes the Atmosphere Prokaryotes have been fossilized for 3.5 billion years, but it was not until 2.2 billion years ago that photosynthetic bacteria evolved. Photosynthesis resulted in an oxygen-rich atmosphere, which developed the ozone layer and killed off anaerobic creatures living up till then.

Origin of the Eukaryotic Cell

🔍 **KEY QUESTION** *What theory explains the origin of eukaryotic cells?*

Eukaryotic cells contain several complex organelles. They differ from prokaryotic cells, like bacteria.

The Earliest Eukaryotes Eukaryotes can be traced to fossils from 2.1 billion years ago. A leading theory for how eukaryotic cells evolved is the **endosymbiotic theory**. Much evidence now supports this theory that many of the complex features of eukaryotic cells evolved through endosymbiosis. Mitochondria are a significant organelle supporting this hypothesis, because they contain their own DNA, among other reasons. A similar case could be made for chloroplasts, a special organelle reminiscent of ancient photosynthetic bacteria.

The Ribosome The ribosomes are a piece of evidence for the "RNA world" hypothesis, as one step in the origin of life on Earth. They build proteins in all cells, but use RNA, not DNA, to link amino acids together. Specifically, the ribosome translates mRNA instructions into amino acids for proteins. Their RNA is mainly responsible for the protein synthesis. Proteins were probably later added to ribosomes to improve their efficiency in production.

Cilia and Flagella These are complex structures involved in the cell's movement. The flagellum aids cell motility in some cells, but all flagella contain multipurpose protein subunits. Thus, cells probably "borrowed" proteins to evolve flagella.

Do We Understand the Cell Completely? Many uncertainties remain in our current understanding of cellular complexity. The study of cell function remains an interesting challenge.

BUILD Vocabulary

endosymbiotic theory theory that proposes that eukaryotic cells formed from a symbiotic relationship among several different prokaryotic cells

Word Origins The word symbiosis comes from the Greek *syn* meaning "together," and *biosis* "living." The Greek *endon* also means "within."

☑ Based on that, how does endosymbiotic theory relate to symbiosis?

_____

_____

_____

Visual Reading Tool: The Endosymbiotic Theory

1. What distinguishing organelle does the photosynthetic eukaryote evolve to contain? _____

2. From which cell type do fungi evolve? _____

Review Vocabulary

Choose the letter of the best answer.

1. Two species evolve in response to each other over time in

   A. convergent evolution.

   B. coevolution.

   C. adaptive radiation.

2. Determining a fossil's age by its placement with other fossils within rock layers is called

   A. the geologic time scale.

   B. radiometric dating.

   C. relative dating.

Match the vocabulary term to its definition.

3. _____ time for half of radioactive atoms to decay   a. half-life

4. _____ species that has died out and has no living members   b. period

5. _____ division of geologic time into which eras are subdivided   c. extinct

Review Key Questions

Provide evidence and details to support your answers.

6. Have changes in climate occurred in the past? Give examples.

_____

_____

_____

_____

7. What defines a mass extinction? What are the immediate biodiversity effects?

_____

_____

_____

_____

8. What pieces of evidence support the RNA world hypothesis?

_____

_____

_____

_____

LESSON 1 Viruses

READING TOOL **Compare and Contrast** After you read this lesson, make notes of the similarities and differences between viruses and cells. Complete the Venn diagram below.

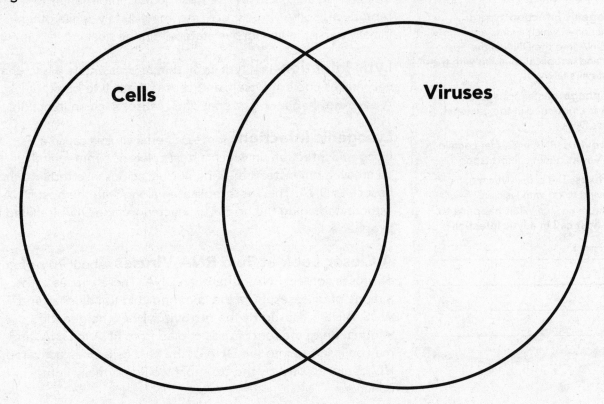

Cells

Viruses

Lesson Summary

What Is a Virus?

KEY QUESTION *How do viruses reproduce?*

In 1892, a scientist named Dmitri Ivanovski tried to determine what was causing a disease called tobacco mosaic in plants.

Discovery of Viruses It took scientists almost 50 years to determine that viruses, which are not truly living, were causing the tobacco mosaic. A **virus** is a nonliving particle made of proteins, nucleic acids, and sometimes lipids.

As you read, circle the answers to each Key Question. Underline any words you do not understand.

BUILD Vocabulary

virus particle made of proteins, nucleic acids, and sometimes lipids that can replicate only by infecting living cells

Structure and Composition Viruses differ widely in terms of size and structure. They contain genetic information in the form of RNA or DNA, surrounded by a protein coat known as a **capsid**. Viruses can only reproduce by infecting living cells.

Viral Infections

🔑 **KEY QUESTION** *What happens after a virus infects a cell?*

Inside living cells, viruses use their genetic information to reproduce. Some viruses replicate immediately, while others initially persist in an inactive state within the host.

Lytic Infection In a **lytic infection**, a virus enters a bacterial cell, makes copies of itself, and causes the cell to burst, or lyse. A **bacteriophage**, or bacterial virus, causes such an infection.

Lysogenic Infection Some bacterial viruses cause a **lysogenic infection**, in which a host cell is not immediately taken over, but instead the viral nucleic acid is inserted into the host cell's DNA. There it is replicated along with the host DNA without damaging the host. This bacteriophage DNA is called a **prophage**.

A Closer Look at Two RNA Viruses About 70 percent of viruses contain RNA rather than DNA. These viruses cause a range of diseases, from the common cold to influenza and AIDS. AIDS is caused by the **retrovirus** HIV. The genetic information of the retrovirus is copied from RNA to DNA, and may be inserted into the DNA of the host cell. Once activated, HIV begins to destroy the cells that would normally fight infections.

Viral Diseases

🔑 **KEY QUESTION** *How do viruses cause disease?*

Viruses produce disease by disrupting the body's normal homeostasis.

Disease Mechanism Viruses cause disease by directly destroying living cells or by affecting cellular processes in ways that upset homeostasis.

Prevention and Treatment Many viral diseases can be prevented by vaccines, which stimulate the body's immune system to recognize and destroy viruses before they can cause disease. Cold and flu viruses are often transmitted by hand-to-mouth contact, so washing hands and controlling coughs and sneezes can help prevent the spread of viruses.

Viruses and Cells

🔍 **KEY QUESTION** *Can viruses be considered living things?*

Besides needing a host to reproduce, viruses have many of the characteristics of living things. They can regulate gene expression and evolve just like traditional cells.

Visual Reading Tool: Analyze a Diagram

The diagram below shows the two different ways that bacteriophages infect cells. Label the two different types.

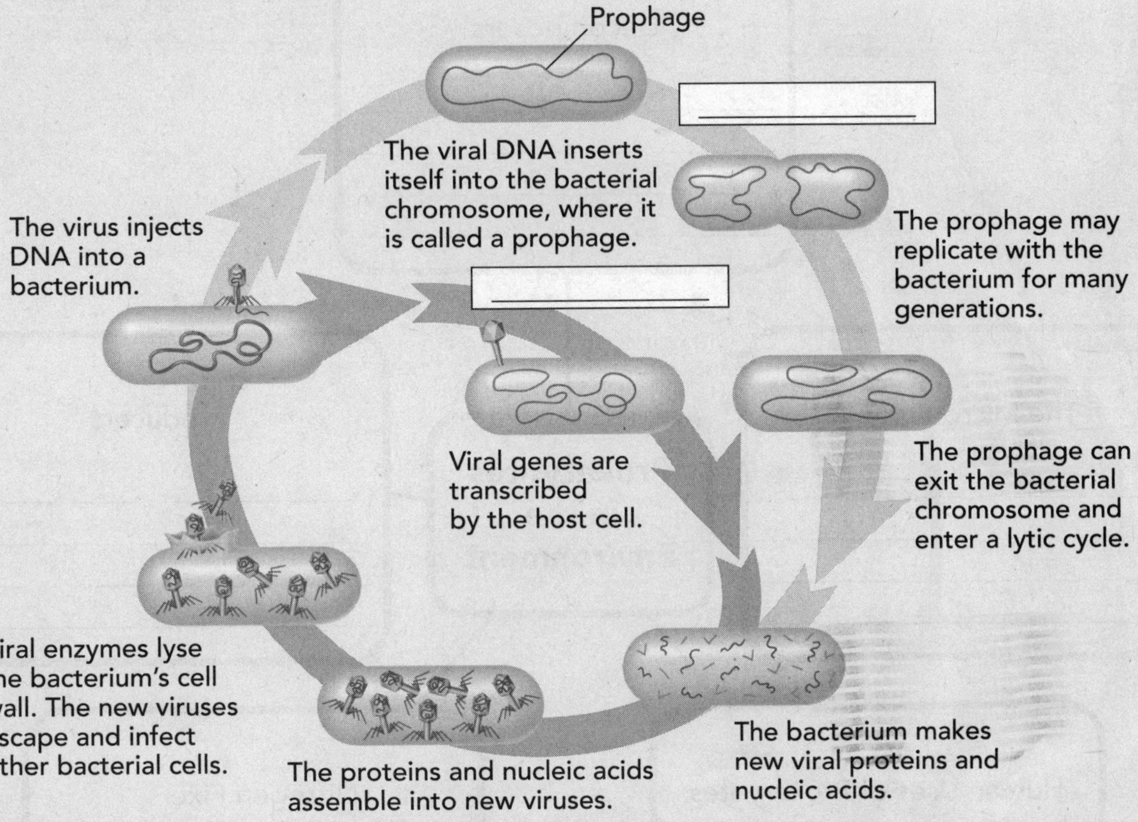

Prophage

The virus injects DNA into a bacterium.

The viral DNA inserts itself into the bacterial chromosome, where it is called a prophage.

The prophage may replicate with the bacterium for many generations.

Viral genes are transcribed by the host cell.

The prophage can exit the bacterial chromosome and enter a lytic cycle.

Viral enzymes lyse the bacterium's cell wall. The new viruses escape and infect other bacterial cells.

The proteins and nucleic acids assemble into new viruses.

The bacterium makes new viral proteins and nucleic acids.

Explain the differences between the two ways bacteriophages infect cells.

_____

_____

_____

_____

_____

_____

_____

_____

READING TOOL **Active Reading** As you read this lesson, explain the many different ways that prokaryotes function on our planet. Fill in each category on the graphic organizer below.

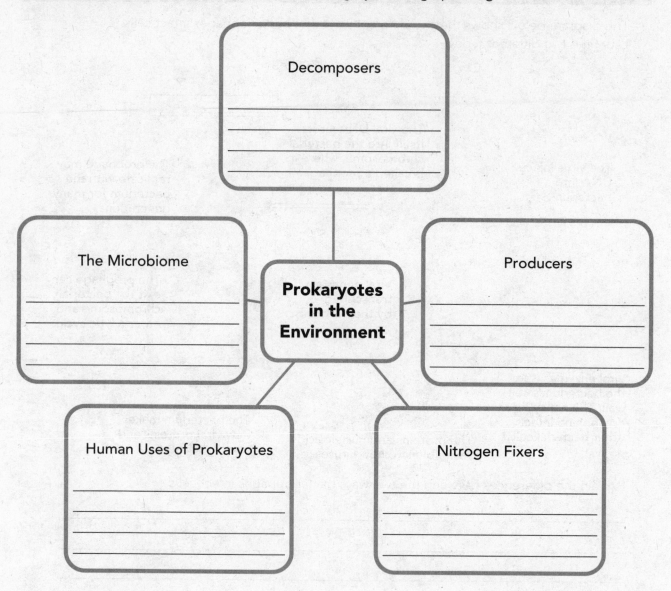

Decomposers

_____

_____

_____

The Microbiome

_____

_____

_____

Prokaryotes in the Environment

Producers

_____

_____

_____

Human Uses of Prokaryotes

_____

_____

_____

_____

Nitrogen Fixers

_____

_____

_____

_____

Lesson Summary

What Are Prokaryotes?

⚲ **KEY QUESTION** *How are prokaryotes classified?*

The smallest and most abundant microorganisms are prokaryotes—unicellular organisms that lack a nucleus. Prokaryotes are classified as Bacteria or Archaea—two of the three domains of life.

Bacteria The larger of the two domains of prokaryotes is the Bacteria. The domain Bacteria includes a wide range of organisms that live almost everywhere, even within the bodies of humans as well as other prokaryotes. The cell walls of bacteria usually contain peptidoglycan, and some bacteria, such as *E. coli*, have a second membrane outside the cell wall that makes the cell resistant to damage.

Archaea Archaea look similar to Bacteria, but their cell walls don't contain peptidoglycan, and their membranes contain different lipids. The DNA sequences of key genes are more like those of eukaryotes than those of bacteria. They survive in extremely harsh environments, such as those with little or no oxygen or in temperatures close to the boiling point of water.

Structure and Function of Prokaryotes

⚲ **KEY QUESTION** *How do prokaryotes vary in their structure and function?*

Prokaryotes vary in their size and shape, in the way they move, and in the way they obtain and release energy.

Nutrition and Metabolism Prokaryotes release energy by cellular respiration, fermentation, or both. They capture energy in many ways, from chemical self-feeding through feeding on other organisms or organic molecules. Some can also use light energy to convert CO_2 into carbon compounds.

Growth, Reproduction, and Recombination Most prokaryotes reproduce by the process of binary fission, in which an organism replicates its DNA and divides in half, producing two daughter cells. When growth conditions become unfavorable, many prokaryotic cells form an endospore—a thick internal wall that encloses the DNA and a portion of the cytoplasm. This allows the cell to remain dormant for months or even years.

⚲ As you read, circle the answers to each Key Question. Underline any words you do not understand.

BUILD Vocabulary

prokaryote (pro KAR ee oht) unicellular organism that lacks a nucleus

binary fission type of asexual reproduction in which an organism replicates its DNA and divides in half, producing two identical daughter cells

endospore structure produced by prokaryotes in unfavorable conditions; a thick internal wall that encloses the DNA and a portion of the cytoplasm

Prefixes The prefix *bi-* means two. In *binary fission*, a prokaryotic cell copies itself and then splits into two identical cells. ☑ What other words do you know with the prefix *bi-* that refers to two of something?

_____

_____

Mutations Mutations are one of the main ways prokaryotes evolve. The heritable changes in DNA are inherited by daughter cells produced by binary fission.

Conjugation Many prokaryotes exchange genetic information by a process called **conjugation**, in which a hollow bridge forms between two bacterial cells, and genetic material, usually in the form of plasmids, moves from one cell to the other.

Prokaryotes in the Environment

🔍 **KEY QUESTION** *What roles do prokaryotes play in the living world?*

Prokaryotes are essential in maintaining every aspect of the ecological balance of the living world. In addition, some species have specific uses in human industry.

Decomposers By breaking down, or decomposing, dead organisms, prokaryotes supply raw materials to the environment. Bacterial decomposers are essential in sewage treatment, helping to produce pure water and chemicals that can be used as fertilizers.

Producers Food chains everywhere are dependent on photosynthetic prokaryotes as producers of food and biomass.

Nitrogen Fixers All organisms need nitrogen to grow. Only a few prokaryotes can convert the nitrogen gas in the atmosphere to forms useful to organisms. This process is known as nitrogen fixation.

Human Uses of Prokaryotes Some prokaryotes, especially bacteria, are used in the production of a wide variety of foods, such as yogurt. Some bacteria can digest petroleum and remove wastes and poisons from water. Others are used to synthesize drugs and chemicals through genetic engineering.

The Microbiome More than 150 different species of bacteria inhabit the human body, forming the "microbiome"—a huge collection of prokaryotic genomes that rivals the human genome in complexity. This great diversity of microorganisms helps us to maintain balance that is important to good health.

Bacterial Diseases

🔍 **KEY QUESTION** *How do bacteria cause disease?*

Often relationships among prokaryotes and viruses are highly beneficial, but in a few cases, sharing doesn't work and disease is the result. Disease-causing agents are called **pathogens**. Nearly all known prokaryotic pathogens are bacteria.

Disease Mechanisms Bacteria disrupt health and cause disease by destroying living cells or by releasing chemicals that upset homeostasis.

Controlling Bacteria Most bacterial infections can be controlled by washing hands and surfaces and using disinfectants. Sanitation processes to protect drinking water are essential to a safe environment. Safe food storage, food processing, and sterilization by heat can control the spread of harmful bacteria.

Preventing Bacterial Diseases Many bacterial diseases can be prevented by stimulating the body's immune system with vaccines. A **vaccine** is a preparation of weakened or killed pathogens that prompt the body to produce immunity to the disease.

Treating Bacterial Diseases A number of drugs can be used to attack a bacterial infection. These drugs include **antibiotics**, which disrupt proteins or cell processes that are specific to bacterial cells.

"Superbugs" Evolution of bacteria has led to antibiotic resistance, which has resulted in "superbugs" such as *Staphylococcus aureus*. Such superbugs can cause infections that are especially difficult to control.

Emerging Disease

⚲ **KEY QUESTION** *What are emerging diseases?*

A previously unknown disease that appears in a population for the first time or a well-known disease that suddenly becomes harder to control is called an emerging disease.

The Threat Today Changes in lifestyle and commerce have made the health disruptions from emerging diseases even more of a threat. The Zika virus was first discovered in monkeys in Africa, but it eventually made the jump to humans and spread across southeast Asia, to the islands of the Pacific, and then to South America. Public health officials are also worried about the flu virus, which has emerged as a dangerous "bird flu" similar to the strain that killed millions of people in the 1918 pandemic.

Prions Other infections in animals are cause for concern. Clumps of tiny protein particles called prions, short for "protein infectious particles," were identified in sheep and have also infected humans. Accumulations of prions can damage nerve cells.

Apply Prior Knowledge When the human body is exposed to certain pathogens, it learns how to fight them off. If the pathogen appears again, the body is able to easily remember how to defeat it. Scientists create vaccines to prepare the body to fight off certain infections, such as chickenpox or measles, without allowing the individual to get sick. ☑ **When are vaccines given to humans? Why do you think this is so?**

_____

_____

_____

_____

On the diagram below, label the major structures of bacteria.

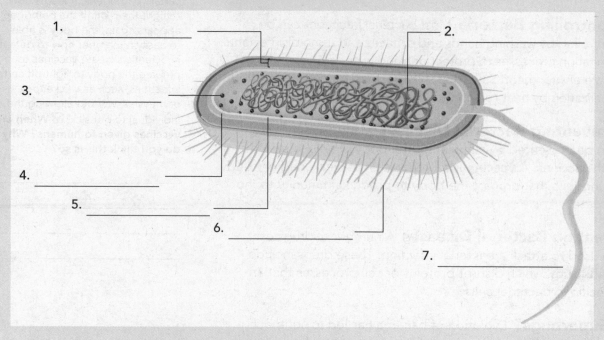

1. _____

2. _____

3. _____

4. _____

5. _____

6. _____

7. _____

1. What type of bacteria is shown above? Circle your answer.

   bacilli   cocci   spirilla

2. What purpose do the flagella serve?

_____

_____

3. Some bacteria, like the *E. coli* shown above, have pilli on their outer surface. What do these structures do for the bacteria?

_____

_____

_____

4. What do the cell walls of bacteria contain?

_____

_____

5. Explain why the bacteria shown (*E. coli*) have a second membrane outside the peptidoglycan.

_____

_____

_____

CHAPTER 21

LESSON 3 Protists

READING TOOL **Outline** Preview the headings in this lesson to construct an outline. As you read, fill in supporting details for each heading in the outline below.

1. What Are Protists?

A. Protists: The First Eukaryotes ______________________

B. The "Protist" Dilemma ______________________

C. What "Protist" Means Today ______________________

2. Structure and Function of Protists

A. Movement ______________________

B. Reproduction ______________________

3. Protists in the Environment

A. Autotrophic Protists ______________________

B. Mutualists ______________________

C. Parasites ______________________

Lesson Summary

What Are Protists?

KEY QUESTION *How are protists classified?*

Protists are eukaryotes that are not members of the plant, animal, or fungi kingdoms.

As you read, circle the answers to each Key Question. Underline any words you do not understand.

Protists: The First Eukaryotes Microscopic fossils of eukaryotic cells have been found in rocks as old as 1.5 billion years. Genetic and fossil evidence indicates that eukaryotes evolved from prokaryotes and are more closely related to present-day Archaea than to Bacteria.

The "Protist" Dilemma Recent studies of protists divide them into six major clades, each of which could be considered a living kingdom in its own right. Plant, animal, and fungi kingdoms fit into these six clades, with the animal and fungi kingdoms emerging from the same protist ancestors.

What "Protist" Means Today "Protists" are not a single kingdom but a collection of organisms that includes several distinct clades. This is why the term is sometimes surrounded by quotation marks. The six major groups, or clades, are Excavata; Chromalveolata; Cercozoa, Foraminifera, and Radiolaria; Rhodophyta (red algae); Amoebozoa; and Choanozoa.

Structure and Function of Protists

⚘ **KEY QUESTION** *How do protists move and reproduce?*

Some protists move by changing their cell shape, and some move by means of specialized organelles. Other protists do not move actively but are carried by wind, water, or other organisms.

Movement Many unicellular protists move like amoebas, changing their shape in a process that makes use of pseudopods (SOO doh pahdz).

Cillia and Flagella Many protists move by means of cilia and flagella. Cilia are short structures that move somewhat like oars on a boat. Flagella are relatively long and can spin or move in a wavelike motion. They usually number only one or two per cell.

Passive Movement Some protists are nonmobile, depending on air or water currents and other organisms to carry them around.

Reproduction Some protists reproduce asexually by mitosis. Others have life cycles that combine asexual and sexual forms of reproduction.

Asexual Reproduction Most protists reproduce by mitosis, simply dividing themselves in two. Paramecia and most ciliates reproduce asexually by mitotic cell division. Under stress they can reproduce by conjugation, a process in which two organisms exchange genetic material.

Build Vocabulary

cilium short hairlike projection that produces movement like oars on a boat

flagellum structure used by protists for movement; produces movement in a wavelike motion

alternation of generation life cycle that has two alternating phases—a haploid (N) phase and a diploid (2N) phase

Suffixes In Latin, -*um* is a singular ending, and -*a* or -*ae* are plural endings. Latin suffixes are often used in the naming of biological structures. ☑ **What are the plural forms of *cilium* and *flagellum*?**

Sexual Reproduction Many protists have sexual life cycles in which they switch between a diploid and a haploid phase, a process known as **alternation of generations**.

Protists in the Environment

⚲ KEY QUESTION *What role do protists play in the environment?*

Autotrophic Protists Photosynthetic protists include many phytoplankton species, red and brown algae, euglenas, and dinoflagellates. These organisms use energy from light to make a carbohydrate food source. The position of photosynthetic protists at the base of the food chain makes much of the diversity of aquatic life possible.

Mutualists Many protists are involved in mutualistic symbioses, in which they and their hosts both benefit. For example, the protist *Trichonympha* lives within the digestive systems of termites and helps to produce enzymes that enable the termites to digest wood.

Parasites Parasitic protists are responsible for some of the world's most deadly diseases, including several kinds of debilitating intestinal diseases, African sleeping sickness, and malaria.

READING TOOL

Connect to Visuals

Photosynthetic protists are vital to keeping the biosphere in equilibrium. ☑ **Using Figure 21-20 in your textbook, describe some of the ways that protists support ecosystems.**

_____

_____

_____

_____

_____

_____

_____

_____

_____

_____

Visual Reading Tool: Complete a Diagram

Label the Plantae, Animalia, and Fungi kingdoms on the figure below. Explain what the location suggests about how they evolved.

Six Major Groups

 Excavata

 Chromalveolata

 Cercozoa, Foraminifera, and Radiolaria

 Rhodophyta (red algae)

 Amoebozoa

 Choanozoa

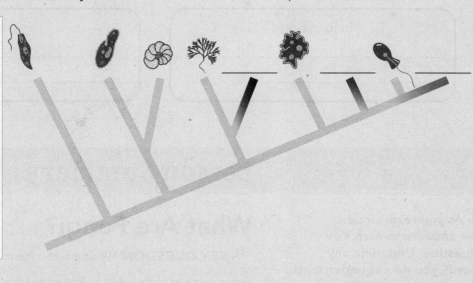

_____

_____

READING TOOL **Make Connections** The chart shown lists some of the key terms in this lesson related to fungi structure and organization. As you read, complete the chart with a definition in your own words.

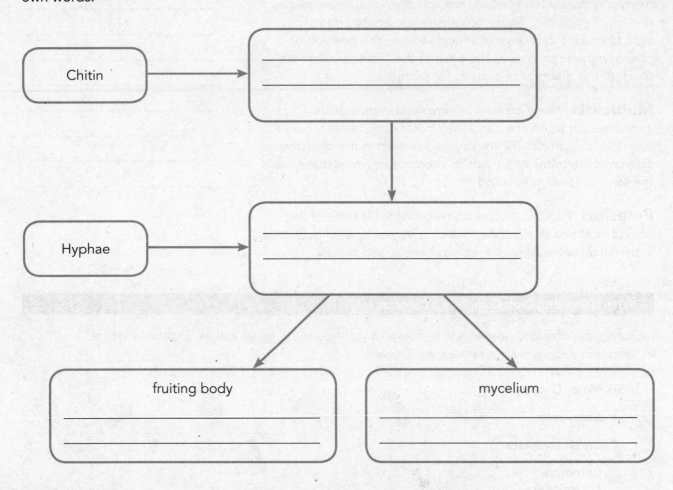

Chitin →

Hyphae →

fruiting body

mycelium

Lesson Summary

🔑 As you read, circle the answers to each Key Question. Underline any words you do not understand.

BUILD Vocabulary

chitin complex carbohydrate that makes up the cell walls of fungi: also found in the external skeletons of arthropods

What Are Fungi?

🔑 **KEY QUESTION** *What are the basic characteristics of fungi?*

Fungi are heterotrophic eukaryotes with cell walls that contain chitin. **Chitin** is a polymer made of modified sugars that is also found in the external skeletons of insects.

Structure and Function Some fungi, known as yeasts, live most of their lives as single cells. Mushrooms and other fungi grow much larger. Their bodies are made up of long branching filaments called **hyphae**. The body of the mushroom is the **fruiting body**, which grows from the **mycelium**, the mass of branching hyphae below the soil.

Reproduction Fungi can reproduce asexually by releasing spores or simply breaking off a hypha or budding off a cell. Most fungi can also reproduce sexually.

Diversity of Fungi More than 100,000 species of fungi are known.

Fungi in the Environment

🔍 **KEY QUESTION** *How do fungi affect homeostasis in other organisms and the environment?*

Fungi play an essential role in maintaining ecosystem health and equilibrium. But some species disrupt health by causing disease in plants and animals.

Decomposition Fungi help ecosystems maintain homeostasis by breaking down dead organisms and recycling essential elements and nutrients.

Parasitism Parasitic fungi can cause serious diseases in plants and animals by disrupting homeostasis.

Plant and Animal Diseases A number of parasitic fungi cause diseases such as corn smut and wheat rust that threaten food crops. Amphibians worldwide have been impacted by a deadly fungus known as *Bd*. The fungus invades the outer layer of the skin, disrupting the immune system and causing death. It poses a threat to up to one third of the world's amphibian population. Fungal infections in humans include athlete's foot, thrush, and vaginal yeast infections.

Lichens A **lichen** is a symbiotic association between a multicellular fungus, a yeast, and a photosynthetic organism. Lichens are often the first organisms to enter barren environments, gradually breaking down the rocks on which they grow.

Build Vocabulary

hyphae long, slender filaments that make up the body of a fungus

fruiting body reproductive structure of a fungus that grows from the mycelium

mycelium densely branched network of the hyphae of a fungus

lichen symbiotic association between a fungus and a photosynthetic organism

Prefixes The prefix *myco-* denotes a relationship to fungus, and is based upon the Greek word *mykes*, which means "fungus." ☑ **What purpose does the mycelium serve for the fungus?**

_____

_____

_____

_____

Mycorrhizae Fungi form mutualistic relationships with plant roots. The symbiotic webs of plant roots and fungal mycelia are called **mycorrhizae**. Mycorrhizae gather water and nutrients from the soil, and are essential for the growth of many plants.

Human Uses of Fungi Humans have used mushrooms and other fungi as food for thousands of years. Many mushrooms are highly nutritious and also delicious. Fungi known as yeasts are important in the making of bread and wine.

Visual Reading Tool: Read a Diagram

1. The diagram shows the the life cycle of *Rhizopus stolonifer* fungi. Shade the arrows that show sexual reproduction in one color. Shade the arrows that show asexual reproduction in another color.

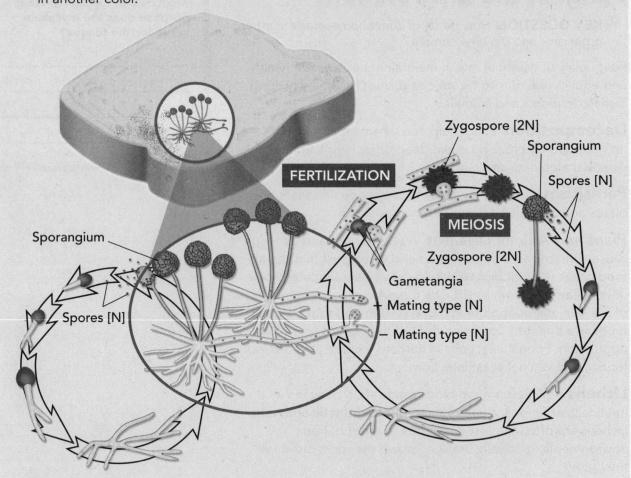

2. Using the figure shown, explain the reproduction of bread mold.

_____

_____

_____

_____

_____

Review Vocabulary

Choose the letter of the best answer.

1. capsid

    A. a dividing cell

    B. a viral protein coat

    C. a common mold

2. chitin

    A. a pathogen

    B. a decomposer

    C. the content of a fungal cell wall

Match the vocabulary term to its definition.

3. _____ mycelium

4. _____ emerging disease

5. _____ conjugation

a. an unknown disease or a well-known disease that suddenly becomes harder to control

b. a process in which two protists exchange genetic material

c. a mass of underground, branching hyphae

Review Key Questions

Provide evidence and details to support your answers.

6. Why are viruses considered to be nonliving?

_____

_____

7. What are the main roles that prokaryotes play in the environment?

_____

_____

_____

_____

8. What roles do protists play in the environment?

_____

_____

_____

_____

What Is a Plant?

READING TOOL **Connect to Visuals** As you read Lesson 1 of this chapter, complete the graphic organizer about the basic needs of plants.

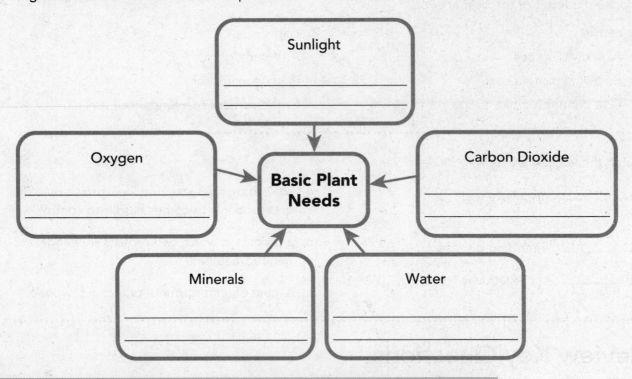

| Sunlight |
| _____ |
| _____ |

| Oxygen |
| _____ |
| _____ |

Basic Plant Needs

| Carbon Dioxide |
| _____ |
| _____ |

| Minerals |
| _____ |
| _____ |

| Water |
| _____ |
| _____ |

Lesson Summary

✎ As you read, circle the answers to each Key Question. Underline any words you do not understand.

What Do Plants Need to Survive?

✎ **KEY QUESTION** *What are the basic needs of plants?*

Plants dominate Earth and have adapted to their stationary lifestyle. In order to survive, they need sunlight, gas exchange, water, and minerals.

Sunlight Plants use the sun's energy to carry out photosynthesis. Every plant displays adaptations shaped by the need to gather sunlight.

Gas Exchange Plants require oxygen to undergo cellular respiration and carbon dioxide to carry out photosynthesis. They exchange these gases with the atmosphere.

Water and Minerals Land plants draw water from the ground, which enables them to take in essential minerals from the soil. Many plants have specialized tissues that carry water and minerals from the soil and distribute them throughout the plant.

The History and Evolution of Plants

⚲ KEY QUESTION *How did plants adapt to life on land?*

For most of Earth's history, land plants did not exist. Life was concentrated in bodies of water, including oceans, lakes, and streams. Photosynthetic prokaryotes added oxygen to the atmosphere and provided food for consumers.

Origins in the Water Ancestors of land plants lived in water, like green algae, and most were unicellular, though some were multicellular. Green algae were classified as protists, but because they have cell walls and photosynthetic pigments, they are now grouped as part of the plant kingdom.

The First Land Plants The oldest land plants appeared about 472 million years go. They lacked leaves and roots, were short, and grew close to the ground in moist environments because they faced the challenge of obtaining water. Eventually, they adapted to the land. The appearance of plants on land changed the rest of life on Earth. New ecosystems emerged, and organic matter began to form soil. One group developed into mosses; another gave rise to ferns, cone-bearing plants, and flowering plants. The demands of life on land favored the evolution of plants that were able to draw water from the soil, resist drying out, and reproduce without water.

An Overview of the Plant Kingdom All plants are eukaryotes, have cell walls containing cellulose, and undergo photosynthesis using chlorophyll a and b. They are divided into five groups based on four features: embryo formation, specialized water-conducting tissues, seeds, and flowers. The four features that define plant evolution are listed below.

➤ Embryos that develop within a plant are protected from harsh land elements.
➤ Plants with water-conducting tissue can draw water to greater heights than is allowed by simple diffusion, allowing them to grow much larger.
➤ Seeds provide food for the developing embryo and protect it from drying out. Seeds can be widely dispersed from the parent plant to grow in new locations.
➤ The successes of flowering plants are due to the reproductive advantage they receive from their flowers and from the fruits they form around their seeds.

Plant scientists classify plants into finer groups within these major branches by comparing DNA sequences of various species.

Cause and Effect After plants moved to land, it took time for them to adapt. Life on land was harsh because of the lack of water. ☑ **What three factors were favored in the evolution of plants?**

_____

_____

_____

The Plant Life Cycle

🔍 **KEY QUESTION** *What feature defines most plant life cycles?*

Plants have a distinctive sexual life cycle that sets them apart from other living organisms. The life cycle of plants has two alternating phases—a diploid (2N) phase and a haploid (N) phase. This shift between the haploid phase and the diploid phase is known as the **alternation of generations**. The multicellular diploid (2N) phase is known as the **sporophyte**, or spore-producing plant. The multicellular haploid (N) phase is known as the **gametophyte**, or gamete-producing plant. Haploid (N) organisms carry a single set of chromosomes in their cell nuclei, while diploid (2N) organisms have two sets of chromosomes.

A sporophyte produces haploid spores through meiosis. These spores grow into multicellular structures called gametophytes. Each gametophyte produces reproductive cells called gametes, also known as sperm and egg cells. During fertilization, a sperm and egg fuse with each other, producing a diploid zygote. The zygote develops into a new sporophyte, and the cycle begins again. An important trend in plant evolution is the reduction in size of the gametophyte and the increase in size of the sporophyte.

Visual Reading Tool: The Plant Life Cycle

MEIOSIS

FERTILIZATION

1. On the diagram, label each stage of the plant life cycle with the following terms: *spores, gametophyte plant, sperm, eggs, sporophyte plant.*

2. During the alternation of generations, which stage is dipoid? _____

3. How many sets of chromosomes does a plant have when it is in its diploid phase? _____

4. What happens during fertilization? _____

Compare and Contrast Compare and contrast the following plant types. List each plant's key characteristics under its specific heading, and describe their similarities in the section below.

Green Algae	Mosses and Other Bryophytes	Ferns and their Relatives	Seed Plants
Similarities			

Lesson Summary

Green Algae

🔍 **KEY QUESTION** *What are the characteristics of green algae?*

Some algae are prokaryotes, like cyanobacteria, and some are protists, like the dinoflagellates. The green algae, however, are the ones that belong to the plant kingdom.

The First Plants Fossil evidence suggests that the green algae appeared well before plants first emerged on land. Fossil formations from the Cambrian Period from more than 550 million years ago show evidence of large mats of green algae. Green algae share many characteristics with larger, more complex plants, including photosynthetic pigments and cell wall composition; however, they are mostly aquatic and can absorb moisture and nutrients directly from their surroundings. Green algae are mostly aquatic. They are found in fresh and salt water, and in some moist areas on land.

Life Cycle Many green algae have life cycles that switch back and forth between haploid and diploid phases. For example, the haploid green alga Chlamydomonas reproduces asexually by mitosis, but when environmental conditions become unfavorable, it can reproduce sexually.

🔍 As you read, circle the answers to each Key Question. Underline any words you do not understand.

BUILD Vocabulary

bryophytes (bry oh fyts) group of plants that have specialized reproductive organs but lack vascular tissue; includes mosses and their relatives

vascular tissue specialized tissue in plants that carries water and nutrients

archegonia (ahr kuh goh nee uh) structure in plants that produces eggs

antheridia (an thur id ee uh) male reproductive structure in some plants that produces sperm

sporangium (spoh ran jee um) spore capsule in which haploid spores are produced by meiosis

Multicellularity Many green algae form colonies, and they provide a hint about how the first multicellular plants may have evolved.

Mosses and Other Bryophytes

🔍 **KEY QUESTION** *What factor limits the size of bryophytes?*

Mosses have a waxy coating and rhizoids (ry zoydz) that anchor them to the soil and absorb water and nutrients. Mosses belong to the group **bryophytes** (bry oh fyts). They are small and found in damp soil because they lack **vascular tissue**, which limits their height to just a few centimeters.

Life Cycle Bryophytes display alternation of generations. The gametophyte is the dominant stage of the life cycle and carries out most of the photosynthesis. Gametes are formed in reproductive structures at the tips of the gametophytes. Eggs are produced in the **archegonia** (ahr kuh goh nee uh). Sperm are produced in **antheridia** (an thur id ee uh) and need standing water to swim to the eggs to form a diploid zygote. This zygote grows into a sporophyte, capped by a **sporangium** (spoh ran jee um). Inside the capsule, haploid spores are produced by meiosis and are scattered to begin the cycle again.

Visual Reading Tool: Moss Structures

Capsule
Stalk
Leaflike structure
Stemlike structure
Rhizoid

Use the drawing of a bryophyte to help you answer the following questions.

1. Label the two stages of the moss life cycle on the diagram: *sporophyte* and *gametophyte*.

2. What purpose do the rhizoids serve?

_____

_____

3. Explain why mosses grow low and close to the ground.

_____

_____

_____

_____

4. What is created in the capsule?

_____

_____

_____

Ferns, Their Relatives, and Seed Plants

KEY QUESTION *How is vascular tissue important?*

Fossil evidence shows that about 420 million years ago, new plants with true vascular tissue emerged. This meant they could grow high above ground.

Evolution of a Transport System Vascular plants, known as **tracheophytes** (traey kee uh fyts), are named after a specialized water-conducting cell, called a **tracheid** (tray kee id). Tracheids are hollow tubelike cells with thick cell walls strengthened by lignin. Tracheids are found in **xylem** (zy lum), a tissue that carries water upward from the roots to every part of a plant. They are long, slender cells with regions on the ends and sides known as pits. The cell walls in pit regions are extremely thin, which allows water to pass through the tracheids. Vascular plants also have a second transport tissue called **phloem** (floh um), which transports nutrients and carbohydrates produced by photosynthesis. The main cells of phloem are long and specialized to move fluids throughout the plant body. Scientists estimate that the tissues can lift water to a maximum height of about 130 meters. Vascular tissues—xylem and phloem—make it possible for vascular plants to move fluids through their bodies against the force of gravity.

Seedless Vascular Plants Although the tracheophytes include all seed-bearing plants, three groups of seedless vascular plants are alive today: club mosses, horsetails, and ferns. The most numerous seedless plants, with 11,000 species, are the ferns. Ferns have true vascular tissues, strong roots, creeping or underground stems called rhizomes (ry zohmz), and large leaves called fronds. Ferns can thrive in areas with little light. They are most abundant in wet habitats.

Life Cycle The large plants easily recognized as ferns are actually the diploid sporophyte phase of the fern life cycle. Spores produced by these plants grow into thin, heart-shaped haploid gametophytes, which live independently of the sporophyte. The sperm and eggs are produced on gametophytes in antheridia and archegonia, and fertilization requires a thin film of water, so that the sperm can swim to the eggs. The diploid zygote produced by fertilization develops into a new sporophyte plant, and the cycle begins again.

As you read, circle the answers to each Key Question. Underline any words you do not understand.

READING TOOL

Make Connections Tree sap, the sticky liquid from trees, is formed in the xylem and phloem. Tree sap from some tree species can then be concentrated into syrup. Based upon what you've learned about xylem and phloem, what do you think causes the sweet taste of maple syrup?

_____

_____

_____

BUILD Vocabulary

tracheophytes (traey kee uh fyts) vascular plants

tracheid (tray kee id) hollow plant cell in xylem with thick cell walls strengthened by lignin

xylem (zy lum) vascular tissue that carries water upward from the roots to every part of a plant

phloem (floh um) vascular tissue that transports solutions of nutrients and carbohydrates produced by photosynthesis through the plant

Related Words Tracheids in plants are small hollow cells in the xylem. In the human body, there is a hollow tube called the trachea that brings air from the nose and mouth down to the lungs. ☑ **What substance is carried through tracheids?**

_____

_____

_____

Seed Plants

🔍 **KEY QUESTION** *What adaptations allow seed plants to reproduce without standing water?*

A **seed** is a plant embryo and its food supply encased in a protective covering. Each seed contains a living plant ready to sprout in the proper conditions.

The First Seed Plants Fossils of seed-bearing plants exist from almost 360 million years ago. Gametes of seed plants do not need standing water for fertilization. Adaptations that allow seed plants to reproduce without standing water include a reproductive process that takes place in cones or flowers, the transfer of sperm by pollination, and the protection of embryos in seeds.

Cones and Flowers In seed plants, male and female gametophytes grow and mature directly within the sporophyte inside cones or flowers. **Gymnosperms** bear their seeds inside cones and include pine, spruce, and fir trees. **Angiosperms** are flowering plants and include nearly all crops grown as food.

Pollen The entire male gametophyte of a seed plant is found in a pollen grain. Pollen grains are carried to the female reproductive structure by wind or animals through **pollination**.

Seeds After fertilization, the zygote contained within a seed grows into a tiny plant. Seeds can survive long periods of bitter cold, extreme heat, or drought.

The Life Cycle of a Gymnosperm Gymnosperms produce seeds that are exposed on the scales within cones.

Pollen Cones and Seed Cones Conifers produce pollen cones or seed cones. Meiosis takes place in pollen cones, which are male. Seed cones are larger than pollen cones and produce the female gametophytes. Near the base of each scale of the seed cones are two **ovules** (ahv yoolz), where haploid cells are produced through meiosis and grow and divide to produce female gametophytes. When mature, each gametophyte contains a few large egg cells, which can be fertilized by sperm.

Pollination and Fertilization Male cones release pollen grains, some of which reach female cones. Pollen grains are caught in a sticky secretion produced by the ovules in female cones. If a pollen grain lands near an ovule, the grain splits open and begins to grow a pollen tube. Once the pollen tube reaches the female gametophyte, one sperm nucleus disintegrates; the other fertilizes the egg contained within the female gametophyte. Fertilization produces a diploid zygote, which grows into an embryo that is encased to form a seed.

Flowers, Fruits, and Seeds

Compare and Contrast Complete the chart below by listing similarities and differences between monocots and dicots using descriptions and visuals.

Monocots	Similarities	Dicots

Lesson Summary

Flowering plants are the most abundant organisms in the plant kingdom.

Angiosperms

🔑 **KEY QUESTION** *How are different Angiosperms classified?*

Angiosperms produce flowers, which contain **ovaries** that surround and protect the seeds. After fertilization, ovaries within flowers develop into **fruits**.

Angiosperm Classification Flowering plants were previously classified by the number of seed leaves, or **cotyledons** (kaht uh leed uns), in their embryos. They had one (**monocot**) or two (**dicot**). Today, monocots form a single group, but dicots fall into different categories.

Angiosperm Diversity Angiosperms vary by the number of seed leaves, the strength and composition of their stems, and the number of growing seasons they live.

Monocots and Dicots Angiosperms are called either monocots or dicots based on the number of seed leaves they produce.

🔍 As you read, circle the answers to each Key Question. Underline any words you do not understand.

BUILD Vocabulary

ovaries in plants, the structure that surrounds and protects seeds

fruits structure in angiosperms that contains one or more matured ovaries

cotyledons first leaf or first pair of leaves produced by the embryo of a seed plant

monocot angiosperm with one seed leaf in its ovary

dicot angiosperm with two seed leaves in its ovary

Woody and Herbaceous Plants Woody plants are made primarily of cells with thick cell walls that support the plant body. Herbaceous (hur bay shus) plants do not produce true wood.

Annuals, Biennials, and Perennials The life span of plants is determined by genetic and environmental factors.

Flower Structure

🔍 **KEY QUESTION** *What are flowers?*

Flowers are an evolutionary advantage to plants because they attract animals such as bees, moths, or hummingbirds. These animals—drawn by the color, scent, or even the shape of the flower—carry pollen with them as they leave. Because these animals go directly from flower to flower, they can carry pollen to the next flower they visit. This means of pollination is much more efficient than the wind pollination of most gymnosperms. Flowers are reproductive organs that have four specialized parts: sepals, petals, stamens, and carpels.

Sepals The outermost portion of a flower consists of modified leaves called sepals. They enclose the bud before it opens and protect the flower as it develops.

Petals, which are often brightly colored, are found just inside the sepals. The colors and shapes of petals help to attract insects and other pollinators to the flower. Petals generally fall off a flower within several days. Losing petals also helps the plant reproduce.

Stamens and Carpels Inside the ring of petals are organs that produce male and female gametophytes. The stamens are the male parts of the flower. Each stamen consists of a stalk called a filament with an anther at its tip. Anthers are the structures in which pollen grains—the male gametophytes—are produced. The innermost floral parts are the carpels, which produce female gametophytes and, later, seeds. The carpels are fused into a broad base, forming an ovary where the female gametophytes are produced. The diameter of the carpel narrows into a stalk called the style. At the top of the style is a sticky or feathery portion known as the stigma, which is specialized to capture pollen. Botanists sometimes call a single carpel or several fused carpels a pistil.

Variety in Flowers Flowers vary greatly in shape, color, and size. While most flowering plants produce both male and female gametophytes, in some species the male and female gametophytes are produced on different plants. In some plants, many flowers grow close together to form a composite structure that looks like a single flower. Other flowers might attract a wide variety of pollinators.

READING TOOL

Compare and Contrast Flower structure is very complex, and each part of the structure plays a specific role in plant reproduction. ☑ **What is the primary difference between a stamen and a carpel?**

_____

_____

_____

_____

_____

_____

_____

The Angiosperm Life Cycle

🔍 **KEY QUESTION** *How does fertilization in angiosperms differ from fertilization in other plants?*

Angiosperms undergo alternation of generations.

Male Gametophytes Meiosis produces four haploid spore cells. Each divides to produce a generative and a tube cell. The male gametophyte with its two cells is then surrounded by a thick wall that protects it. The entire gametophyte is a pollen grain.

Female Gametophytes A diploid cell undergoes meiosis to produce four haploid cells. One cell undergoes mitosis, producing eight nuclei. Next, cells walls form seven cells, six with one nucleus and a seventh with two. These seven cells are the female gametophyte, known as the **embryo sac**.

Pollination The transfer of pollen to the female portions of the flower is called **pollination**.

Fertilization When a pollen grain lands on the stigma, it grows a pollen tube. The "generative" cell divides and forms two sperm cells. The pollen tube grows into the style, eventually reaching the ovary and entering an ovule, resulting in **double fertilization**, where a diploid zygote and **endosperm** are produced. This is distinct in angiosperms.

Visual Reading Tool: Angiosperm Gametophytes

Label the following diagram based upon Figure 22-23 in the textbook.

The Development of Gametophytes

1. _____

2N 2. _____ N 3. _____ → Pollen grain (Male gametophyte)

4. _____

2N 5. _____ N 6. _____ → Embryo sac (Female gametophyte)

7. What are the key differences between a male and a female gametophyte?

_____

_____

Vegetative Reproduction

KEY QUESTION _What is vegetative reproduction?_

Many flowering plants can also reproduce asexually by a process known as **vegetative reproduction**. This process takes place naturally in many plants, and it can be used to produce many copies of an individual plant. It does not require gametes, flowers, or fertilization.

Because vegetative reproduction does not involve seed formation, a single plant can reproduce quickly. In addition, asexual reproduction allows a single plant to produce genetically identical offspring.

Fruits and Seeds

KEY QUESTION _How do fruits form?_

The development of the seed, which protects and nourishes the plant embryo, contributed greatly to the success of plants on land. But the angiosperm seed, protected by a fruit, was an even better adaptation.

Fruit and Seed Development Once fertilization of an angiosperm is complete, nutrients flow from the vascular system into the flower to support the growing embryo within the seed. As angiosperm seeds mature, ovary walls thicken to form a fruit that encloses the developing seeds. The ovary wall surrounding a fruit may be fleshy, as it is in grapes and tomatoes, or tough and dry, like the shell that surrounds peanuts. The peanuts themselves are seeds.

Seed Dispersal The seeds of many plants, especially those encased in sweet, fleshy fruits, are often eaten by animals. The seeds are covered with tough coatings, allowing them to pass through an animal's digestive system unharmed. The seeds then sprout in the feces eliminated from the animal and help the plant disperse its seeds. Wind and water also help to disperse seeds.

Seed Germination All seeds contain plant embryos in a state of **dormancy**, during which the embryo is alive but not growing. **Germination** takes place when growth of the embryo resumes and the seed sprouts into a plant. Dormancy can allow for long-distance seed dispersal, making it possible for seeds to germinate under more ideal conditions.

Review Vocabulary

Choose the letter of the best answer.

1. All of the following is true about angiosperms, except that

   A. they produce flowers.

   B. they live in water.

   C. they have a phloem.

   D. they have at least one seed leaf.

2. Why are green algae now classified as members of the plant kingdom?

   A. They are protists.

   B. They have cell walls.

   C. They are unicellular.

   D. They live in moist environments.

Fill in the blanks with the correct terms.

3. The product of _____ is a zygote and an endosperm.

4. _____ is the specialized structure in plants that allow them to grow large and tall.

5. The life cycle of plants is marked by two phases known as _____.

6. In _____, male and female gametophytes grow and mature directly within the sporophyte inside cones and flowers.

Review Key Questions

Provide evidence and details to support your answers.

7. You're trying to identify a plant, but have no information on its characteristics, other than the fact that it lives almost all of its life as a multicellular haploid organism. Based on this information, what can you conclude about the plant?

   _____

   _____

8. What are some advantages of flowering plants?

   _____

   _____

   _____

   _____

9. Explain whether or not seeds are the reproductive structures of plants.

   _____

   _____

   _____

Roots, Stems, and Leaves

READING TOOL **Make Connections** Explain how each of the listed systems works to make plants grow and thrive.

How Do These Systems Work to Help Plants	Explanations
Plant Tissue Systems	
Roots	
Stems	
Leaves	

Lesson Summary

Plant Tissue Systems

🔑 As you read, circle the answers to each Key Question. Underline any words you do not understand.

BUILD Vocabulary

epidermis in plants, single layer of cells that makes up dermal tissue

meristem region of unspecialized cells responsible for continuing growth throughout a plant's lifetime

🔑**KEY QUESTION** *What are the main tissue systems of plants?*

The roots, stems, and leaves of plants include specialized tissue systems that help plants to thrive and grow.

Dermal, Vascular, and Ground Tissue In plants, dermal tissue includes a single layer of cells called the **epidermis**. The outer surfaces of these cells are covered in a waxy cuticle layer, protecting them from water loss. Vascular tissues include xylem and phloem. These tissues support the plant body and transport water and nutrients throughout the plant. Ground tissue produces and stores sugars, and contributes to the physical support of plants. Edible portions of plants are mostly ground tissue.

Plant Tissues and Growth Plant growth happens in **meristems**, or regions of unspecialized cells in which mitosis produces new cells that are ready for differentiation.

Meristems and Flower Development When the pattern of gene expression transforms apical meristems into floral meristems, flower development begins. Floral meristems produce a plant's reproductive organs and colorful flowers.

Roots

KEY QUESTION *What are the different structures and functions of roots?*

When seeds begin to sprout, they put out roots to draw water and nutrients from the soil. Rapid cell growth pushes the growing root tips down into the soil, providing the plant the raw materials to feed developing stems and leaves.

Types of Root Systems Plants have taproots or fibrous root systems. Taproots are large primary roots that can stretch deep into soil. Plants like grasses have branched roots growing from the base of the plant's stem, or **fibrous roots**. These help plants anchor topsoil in place.

Structure and Function of Roots Dermal, vascular, and ground tissue are all found in roots. A mature root has an outside layer, the epidermis, and contains vascular tissue and ground tissue. Roots support a plant, anchor it, store food, and absorb water and nutrients from soil.

Uptake of Plant Nutrients From soil, plants absorb inorganic nutrients, like nitrogen, phosphorus, potassium, magnesium, and trace elements. Cell membranes on the root epidermis use proteins to transport dissolved nutrients from soil into the plant.

Water Movement and the Vascular Cylinder Cells in all three tissue systems work together to transport water into roots. The vascular cylinder is enclosed by the endodermis. Where these cells meet, cell walls form a waterproof zone called the **Casparian strip**. This structure creates a one-way-only passage of water and nutrients into the vascular cylinder.

Root Pressure Water inside the Casparian strip travels upward as root pressure forces it through the vascular cylinder and into the xylem. As more water is forced up, water in the xylem is forced into the roots.

Stems

KEY QUESTION *What are the functions of stems, and how does growth in stems occur?*

Stems produce leaves, branches, and flowers; hold leaves up to the sun; and transport substances throughout the plant. Stems vary in size, shape, and method of development.

Anatomy of a Stem Stems contain all three tissue systems and distinct **nodes**, where the leaves are attached. Tissue arrangement follows two patterns. In monocots, clusters of xylem and phloem tissue, called **vascular bundles**, are scattered through stem ground tissue. In gymnosperms and dicots, vascular bundles are arranged in a ring.

BUILD Vocabulary

taproot large primary root

fibrous roots in plants like grasses, the branched roots that grow from the base of the stem

Casparian strip waterproof strip that surrounds plant endodermal cells and is involved in the one-way passage of materials into the vascular cylinder in plant roots

node part on a growing stem where a leaf is attached

vascular bundle clusters of xylem and phloem tissue in stems

Related Words Vascular bundles contain two types of tissues, xylem and phloem, which carry different things through a plant. ☑ **What does xylem carry, and where else is xylem found in the plant?**

_____

_____

_____

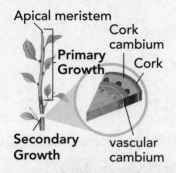

Apical meristem
Cork cambium
Primary Growth
Cork
Secondary Growth
vascular cambium

Connect to Visuals
Figure 23-9 shows primary and secondary growth in a plant.
☑ Explain how the parts of a plant function together during both primary and seconday growth.

_____

_____

_____

_____

_____

_____

_____

_____

_____

BUILD Vocabulary

primary growth pattern of growth that takes place at the tips and shoots of a plant

secondary growth type of growth in dicots in which the stems increase in thickness

mesophyll specialized ground tissue found in leaves; performs most of a plant's photosynthesis

stomata (plural of stoma) small openings in the epidermis of a plant that allow carbon dioxide, water, and oxygen to diffuse into and out of the leaf

transpiration loss of water from a plant through its leaves

Primary and Secondary Growth Plant growth is carefully controlled to produce characteristic sizes and shapes in adult plants.
➤ **Primary growth** of stems is the result of the division and elongation of cells produced in the apical meristem.
➤ **Secondary growth** occurs in meristems called the vascular cambium and cork cambium; this is when older stems and roots increase in thickness and length.

Leaves

🔍 **KEY QUESTION** *What are the different structures and functions of leaves?*

Using energy captured in their leaves, plants make sugars, starches, and oils that feed virtually all animals.

Anatomy of a Leaf The structure of leaves is optimized to absorb light and perform photosynthesis. Leaves include blades attached to stems by petioles, and they have an outer dermal covering and inner ground and vascular tissues.

Dermal Tissue Leaf epidermis is a specialized layer of tough, irregularly shaped cells with thick outer walls that resist tearing. They are covered by a waxy layer that helps reduce water evaporation.

Vascular Tissue Vascular tissues in leaves and stems are part of the plant's fluid transport system. Xylem and phloem cells are bundled in leaf veins.

Ground Tissue The area between leaf veins is filled with specialized ground tissue cells called **mesophyll**, where photosynthesis occurs.

Photosynthesis The air spaces in mesophyll layers connect to the plant's exterior through **stomata**, or small openings in the epidermis allowing carbon dioxide, water, and oxygen to diffuse into and out of leaves.

Transpiration **Transpiration** is the loss of water through leaves, which may be replaced by water drawn into the leaf through xylem in the vascular tissue. Transpiration cools leaves on hot days, but threatens leaves if water is scarce.

Gas Exchange and Homeostasis Plants exchange gases with the air. A plant's control of gas exchange is one of the most important elements of homeostasis.

Gas Exchange Leaves take in carbon dioxide and give off oxygen during photosynthesis. Plant leaves allow for gas exchange by opening stomata.

Homeostasis Plants maintain homeostasis by keeping their stomata open enough to allow photosynthesis to occur, but not so much that they lose excessive water. Guard cells are specialized cells regulating the movement of gases, like water vapor and carbon dioxide, into and out of leaves. When water is abundant, it flows into the leaf, raising water pressure in guard cells and opening stomata. When water is scarce, water pressure in guard cells decreases and stomata close, reducing water loss by limiting transpiration.

Transpiration and Wilting Osmotic pressure keeps leaves and stem rigid. High transpiration rates, or water loss, lead to wilting, or pressure loss in leaves.

Transport in Plants

🔑 **KEY QUESTION** *What are the major forces that transport water and nutrients in a plant?*

Active transport and root pressure cause water to move from soil into plant roots, then up the plant stem. Other forces are needed to lift it higher into the plant.

Transpirational Pull Force in water transport is provided by water evaporation from leaves during transpiration. As water evaporates, cell walls dry out and water is pulled from the vascular tissue.

How Cell Walls Pull Water Upward Cohesion and adhesion work together to pull water upward in plant cells. The tendency of water to rise in a thin tube is called capillary action. Water is attracted to the walls of plants' inner tubes and attracted to other water molecules. The thinner the tube, the higher the water will rise inside it.

Putting It All Together The combination of transpiration and capillary action lifts water upward through the xylem tissues of a plant.

Nutrient Transport The pressure-flow hypothesis states that sugars are transported through phloem via water pressure from osmosis to the places a plant needs it most. The pressure-flow system gives plants enormous flexibility in responding to their changing needs.

BUILD Vocabulary

guard cell specialized cell in the epidermis of plants that controls the opening and closing of stomata

capillary action tendency of water to rise in a thin tube

Multiple Meanings *Capillary* is a term from mid-17th-century French that means "hair." The smallest blood vessels in the human body are called capillaries. ☑ **What do the vascular cells of a plant and human capillaries have in common?**

_____

_____

_____

READING TOOL

Apply Prior Knowledge In earlier chapters you learned about the properties of water—specifically, cohesion and adhesion. Cohesion is the attraction between molecules of the same substance, and adhesion is the attraction between different kinds of molecules. ☑ **Explain how cohesion and adhesion work together to cause capillary action.**

_____

_____

_____

_____

_____

_____

_____

LESSON 2 Plant Hormones and Tropisms

READING TOOL **Compare and Contrast** Compare each of the items and how they work in helping plants grow and thrive.

Items	Comparisons
Auxins and Cell Elongation vs. Auxins and Branching	
Cytokinins vs. Ethylene vs. Abscisic Acid	
Phototropism vs. Thigmotropism vs. Gravitropism	
Photoperiods and Flowering vs. Photoperiods and Dormancy	

Lesson Summary

Hormones

BUILD Vocabulary

hormone chemical produced in one part of an organism that affects another part of the same organism

target cell cell that has a receptor for a particular hormone

receptor on or in a cell, a specific protein whose shape fits that of a specific hormone

auxin hormone produced in the tip of a growing plant that stimulates cell elongation and the growth of new roots

🔍 **KEY QUESTION** *What roles do plant hormones play?*

Plants respond to light, moisture, temperature, and gravity—through **hormones**, or chemical signals that affect growth, activity, and development of cells and tissues. They control development of cells, tissues, and organs, and coordinate responses to the environment. Cells affected by a particular hormone are called **target cells**. To respond to a hormone, target cells contain hormone **receptors**—usually proteins—to which hormone molecules bind.

Auxins **Auxins** stimulate cell elongation and new root growth. They are produced in the shoot apical meristem and transported to the rest of the plant.

Auxins, Cell Elongation, and Branching To elongate cells, auxins collect in shaded parts of shoots, which stimulates those cells to lengthen, bending the shoot toward the light. Apical dominance means the closer a bud is to the stem's tip, the more it is inhibited; the closer it is to the stem, the stronger it is. This is why plant bases grow faster than plant tops.

Cytokinins Cytokinins are plant hormones produced in growing roots and developing fruit and seeds. They stimulate cell division, interact with auxins to balance root and shoot growth, and stimulate regeneration of damaged tissues.

Ethylene Fruit tissues release small amounts of the hormone ethylene, which stimulates fruits to ripen. They also help plants to seal off and drop organs that are no longer needed, like petals after pollination.

Gibberellins Gibberellins are a type of hormones that produce growth in plants. *Gibberella fujikuroi* is a fungus that causes extraordinary growth by mimicking this hormone.

Abscisic Acid Gibberellins interact with another hormone, abscisic acid, in controlling seed dormancy by inhibiting cell division and halting growth. Abscisic acid puts seed embryos into dormancy until conditions are right for growth. Without the opposing effect of abscisic acid, the gibberellins can signal germination.

Tropisms and Rapid Movements

⚲ KEY QUESTION *What are examples of environmental stimuli to which plants respond?*

Plants respond to the environment, just like other living things. Some movements are very slow, while others are extremely fast.

Tropisms Plant sensors that detect environmental stimuli signal elongating organs to reorient their growth. These growth responses are called tropisms. Plants respond to environmental stimuli such as light, touch, and gravity.

Light, Touch, and Gravity The tendency of a plant to grow toward a light source is called phototropism. Changes in auxin concentration are responsible for this action, which can occur within a matter of hours in seedlings. Some plants respond to touch, a process called thigmotropism. Examples include vines and climbing plants that exhibit thigmotropism when encountering objects like trees or trellises and wrapping themselves around them. Auxins also affect gravitropism, the response of a plant to gravity. Auxins migrate to lower, or shadier, sides of horizontal roots and stems, which causes stems to bend upright, but roots to bend downward.

Rapid Movements Some plant responses to environmental factors are so quick that they cannot be called tropisms. One example is the rapid response when leaves of the *Mimosa pudica* are touched. Within seconds of touching this "sensitive plant," the two leaflets fold together completely.

BUILD Vocabulary

apical dominance phenomenon in which the closer a bud is to the stem's tip, the more its growth is inhibited

tropism movement of a plant toward or away from stimuli

phototropism tendency of a plant to grow toward a light source

thigmotropism response of a plant to touch

gravitropism response of a plant to the force of gravity

Suffixes The suffix *-ism* comes from a Greek word and is used to form action nouns from verbs.
☑ **What action is being carried out by a plant when it goes through thigmotropism?**

_____

_____

_____

READING TOOL

Apply Prior Knowledge

Venus flytraps are one of a few species of plants that are carnivorous. Their leaflets can shut quickly when an insect lands on them. The plant then dissolves the insect and uses its nitrogen and nutrients to support growth.
☑ **Why is nitrogen important to plants? What important biological macromolecules require nitrogen?**

_____

_____

_____

_____

Response to Seasons

KEY QUESTION *How to plants respond to seasonal changes?*

Year after year, some plants flower in the spring, summer, or fall. Some plants flower only when daylight is short, while some plants flower only when daylight is long.

Photoperiod and Flowering Plants flower according to their photoperiod, or the number of hours of light and darkness received. Some plants respond to changing photoperiods, called **photoperiodism**, a major factor in the timing of seasonal activities.

Winter Dormancy As cold weather approaches, many plants prepare by turning off photosynthetic pathways, transporting materials from leaves to roots, and sealing off leaves from the rest of the plant.

Leaf Loss and Changes to Meristems Some plants lose their leaves during cold months. They absorb less light as days shorten, auxin production drops, and ethylene production increases, shutting down the leaf. Hormones also produce changes in apical meristems, stopping them from producing leaves and forming a waxy layer of cold protection. Xylem and phloem tissues pump themselves full of ions and organic compounds, which act like antifreeze to prevent tree sap from freezing.

READING TOOL

Applying Prior Knowledge
Plants need sunlight as part of their nutrients to grow properly. People also need sunlight to properly grow. ☑ **If plants don't get enough sunlight, they wither and possibly die. What happens to people who don't get enough sunlight?**

_____

_____

_____

Visual Reading Tool: Photoperiod Effects on Flowering

Effect of Photoperiod on Flowering	Long Day Midnight / Noon	Short Day Midnight / Noon
Short-Day Plant		
Long-Day Plant		

1. Explain the difference between the ways a short-day plant flowers on long days and on short days.

_____

_____

_____

_____

2. Explain the difference between the ways a long-day plant flowers on long days and on short days.

_____

_____

_____

_____

LESSON 3 Plants and People

READING TOOL **Main Idea and Details** For each section within the lesson, identify the main idea and one to three supporting details. Several answers are already filled in for you.

Section	Main Ideas	Details
Agriculture	The systematic cultivation of plants began long before humans took part in it.	Ants harvest plant seeds, spread them around, and fertilize them.
Worldwide Patterns		
New Plants		
Changes in Agriculture		
Industrial Agriculture		
Fiber, Wood, and Medicine		

Lesson Summary

READING TOOL

Connect to Visuals
Plants do so much more than just feed humans. View Figure 23-26 in your textbook to read about different products that are made from plants. ☑ **Look around the room you're in right now and make a list of things that are made using plants.**

_____

_____

_____

_____

Agriculture

🔍 **KEY QUESTION** *Which crops are the major food supply for humans?*

Agriculture, or the systematic cultivation of plants for consumption—began with ants, who harvested seeds, spread them around, and fertilized them. Scientists believe ants had been "farming" several millions years before humans began growing food plants.

Worldwide Patterns The beginnings of human civilization can be traced back to the cultivation of crop plants about 10,000 to 12,000 years ago in multiple places worldwide. Once people discovered plants could be grown for food, they stopped migrating, which led to the establishment of social institutions. Today, agricultural pursuits occupy more humans than any other job. North America has some of the most productive cropland in the world. About 80% of U.S. cropland is used to grow wheat, corn, soybeans, and hay, three of which come from grasses.

New Plants The discovery and introduction of new crop plants has frequently changed regional agriculture. Continuing to introduce new plants into cultivation ensures strong genetic diversity in the food supply, and decreases chances that pests or disease could devastate farming.

Changes in Agriculture Between 1950 and 1970, a worldwide effort to combat hunger and malnutrition, called the green revolution, led to dramatic improvements in farming techniques and crop yields, greatly increasing the world's food supply. At the heart of this was the use of high-yield varieties of seed and artificial fertilizers.

Industrial Agriculture Improved farming methods made it possible to increase crop yields and produce food cheaply. However, the large-scale cultivation of a small number of crops has reduced genetic diversity and left our food supply vulnerable to insects and disease. As populations increase, it is necessary to safeguard genetic diversity in crop plants and address challenges caused by industrial farming methods.

Fiber, Wood, and Medicine

🔍 **KEY QUESTION** *What are some examples of benefits besides food that human derive from plants?*

Plants produce the raw materials for our homes and clothes, and important items like paper for printing or toilet paper. Additionally, some of our most powerful and effective medicines, like those used to fight cancer, come from plants.

Review Vocabulary

Match the vocabulary term to its definition.

1. _____ mesophyll

   a. unspecialized cells responsible for growth throughout a plant's lifetime

2. _____ meristem

   b. specialized ground tissue found in leaves that performs photosynthesis

3. _____ auxin

   c. substance that regulates plant growth by stimulating cells and roots

Fill in the blanks with the correct terms.

4. _____ is where a plant's stems increase in thickness, while _____ is where a plant's tips and shoots grow.

5. _____ is a plant's tendency to grow toward a light source, while _____ is a plant's response to touch, and _____ is a plant's response to the force of gravity.

Review Key Questions

Provide evidence and details to support your answers.

6. What are the principal organs of plants and what three types of tissue do they contain?

   Organs: _____   _____   _____

   Tissues: _____   _____   _____

7. Explain how root systems help feed plants.

   _____

   _____

   _____

8. What would happen to a low-growing fruit bush that was infected by the *Gibberella fujikuroi* fungus?

   _____

9. With our current agricultural methods, what would happen if disease or insects ravaged the food crops the United States gets from grasses?

   _____

   _____

   _____

Introduction to Animals

READING TOOL **Active Reading** As you read, keep track of the 5 things animals do to survive. Describe each of these processes in the graphic organizer below.

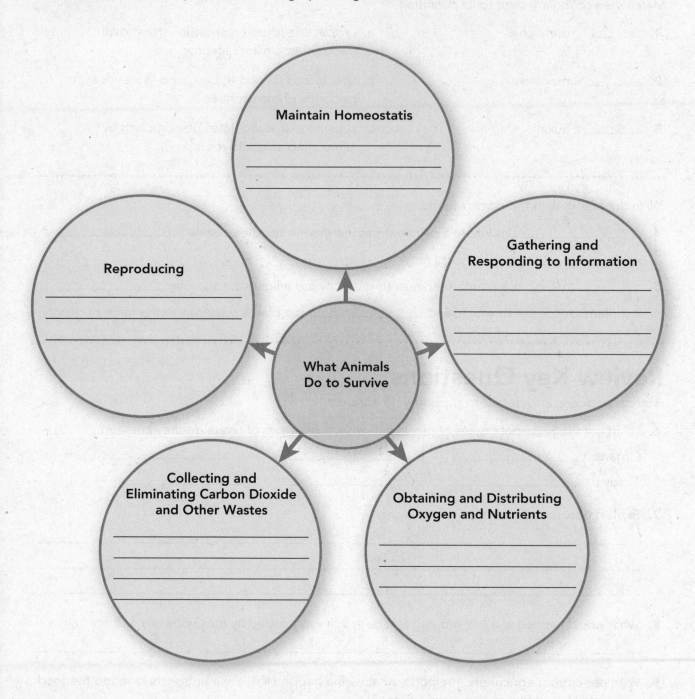

Maintain Homeostatis
_____
_____
_____

Reproducing
_____
_____
_____

Gathering and Responding to Information
_____
_____
_____
_____

What Animals Do to Survive

Collecting and Eliminating Carbon Dioxide and Other Wastes
_____
_____
_____
_____

Obtaining and Distributing Oxygen and Nutrients
_____
_____
_____

Lesson Summary

What Is an Animal?

KEY QUESTION *What characteristics do all animals share?*

Animals are multicellular, heterotrophic, eukaryotic organisms with cells that lack cell walls. Although diverse, they share some characteristics. Animals are classified into two broad categories: invertebrates and chordates.

Invertebrates Over 95 percent of animal species are informally called invertebrates. **Invertebrates** include all animals that lack a vertebral column. Because the category lumps together organisms that lack a characteristic rather than share one, they do not form a clade.

Chordates All members of the phylum Chordata are called **chordates**, and exhibit certain characteristics during at least one stage of life: a dorsal hollow nerve cord, a tail that extends beyond the anus, and pharyngeal pouches. Most chordates are **vertebrates** that develop a backbone (vertebral column), made of vertebrae (spinal bones). Nonvertebrate chordates do not have backbones.

What Animals Do to Survive

KEY QUESTION *What essential functions must animals perform to survive?*

Animals keep their internal environments stable, or maintain homeostasis. Animals maintain homeostasis by gathering and responding to information, obtaining and distributing oxygen and nutrients, and collecting and eliminating carbon dioxide and other wastes. They must also reproduce.

Maintaining Homeostasis Homeostasis in the body often works by using **feedback inhibition**, which is when a stimulus produces a response that opposes the original stimulus.

Gathering and Responding to Information The nervous system gathers information using receptors that respond to stimuli. Other nerve cells collect, process, and respond to that information.

Obtaining and Distributing Oxygen and Nutrients All animals must obtain oxygen to perform cellular respiration. Oxygen diffuses across the skin of small water animals, while larger animals have respiratory systems. Most animals eat to obtain nutrients and have digestive systems that break food down for use by the body. Acquired oxygen and nutrients must be transported throughout the body, often requiring interactions between circulatory systems and respiratory systems or digestive systems.

As you read, circle the answers to each Key Question. Underline any words you do not understand.

BUILD Vocabulary

invertebrate type of animal that lacks a backbone, or vertebral column

chordate type of animal that, at some point in its life, shows a dorsal nerve cord, a tail, and a pharyngeal pouch

vertebrate type of animal that has a backbone

feedback inhibition process in which a stimulus produces a response that opposes the original stimulus; also called negative feedback

Prefixes The prefix *in-* can mean "in, on, or not." ☑ **In the term** *invertebrate*, **which definition do you think fits the prefix** *in-* **and why?**

_____

_____

_____

_____

Collecting and Eliminating Carbon Dioxide and Other Wastes Animals' metabolic processes generate wastes needing to be eliminated. Many animals use respiratory systems to get rid of carbon dioxide. Most complex animals have excretory systems to process wastes and then expel them, or to store and expel them.

Reproducing Most animals reproduce sexually, which helps maintain genetic diversity. Many invertebrates and some vertebrates can also reproduce asexually.

Visual Reading Tool: Body Plan Trait Evolution

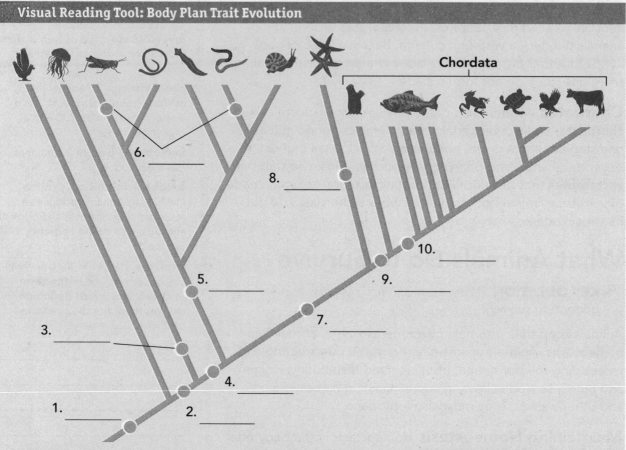

Single-celled animal ancestor

Using the figure as your guide, put each item listed below in the order in which animals developed body plan traits—from the single-celled animal ancestor to the chordates.

- **A.** Radial symmetry
- **B.** As adults, radial symmetry and no cephalization
- **C.** Mouth-first development
- **D.** Multicellularity
- **E.** Initial segmentation
- **F.** Chordate segmentation
- **G.** Tissues: 2 germ layers
- **H.** Backbone development
- **I.** Anus first development
- **J.** Organs: 3 germ layers; bilateral symmetry; cephalization

Animal Body Plans

⚲ KEY QUESTION *What are some features of animal body plans?*

Each animal clade has a unique organization of particular body structures, often called a body plan, which are part of biological classification. Features of animal body plans include levels of organization, body symmetry, formation of body cavities, patterns of embryonic development, segmentation, cephalization, and limb formation.

Levels of Organization The cells of most animals develop into specialized cells organized into tissues. Animals typically have several types of tissues, like epithelial, nervous, muscle, and connective tissues. During development, tissues combine to form organs. Organ systems work together to maintain homeostasis.

Body Symmetry Most animals exhibit body symmetry: radial or bilateral. Radial symmetry is a body plan in which any number of imaginary planes drawn through the center of the body could divide it into equal halves. Bilateral symmetry is a body plan in which a single imaginary plane can divide the body into left and right sides that are mirror images of each other.

Patterns of Embryological Development Animals reproducing sexually begin life as zygotes, or fertilized eggs. Through development, the zygote forms a hollow ball of cells, and then folds in on itself, elongating into a tube, which becomes the digestive tract. In some clades the mouth develops first; in some, the anus. Embryonic animal cells differentiate into three germ layers—endoderm, mesoderm, and ectoderm—each developing into different organs and systems. Animals with radial symmetry only have the endoderm and ectoderm. Most complex animals have a body cavity, or coelom.

Segmentation Many bilaterally symmetrical animals develop repeated parts, or segments. Segmented animals typically have some internal and external body parts repeated on each side of the body. Bilateral symmetry and segmentation are often found together.

Cephalization: Getting a Head Animals with bilateral symmetry typically exhibit cephalization, or a concentration of sense organs and nerve cells in their heads.

Limb Formation Segmented, bilaterally symmetrical animals typically have external appendages on both sides of the body.

BUILD Vocabulary

radial symmetry body plan in which any number of imaginary planes drawn through the center of the body could divide it into equal portions

bilateral symmetry body plan in which a single imaginary plane can divide the body into left and right sides that are mirror images of each other

zygote a fertilized egg

coelom (see lum) body cavity lined with mesoderm

cephalization concentration of sense organs and nerve cells at the anterior end of an animal

Using Prior Knowledge You may have heard the word *radius* in math class, which refers to the line segment from the center of a circle to its perimeter. ☑ **Look around the room. Do you see any objects that have radial symmetry? List them.**

_____

_____

_____

Animal Evolution and Diversity

Compare and Contrast Provide one similarity and one difference in the ways the identified animals evolved over time.

Animals	Similarities	Differences
Invertebrates		
Vertebrates		
Nonvertebrate Chordates		
Vertebrate Chordates		

Lesson Summary

The Cladogram of Animals

🔍 As you read, circle the answers to each Key Question. Underline any words you do not understand.

🔍 **KEY QUESTION** *How are animal clades defined?*

The features of animal body plans provide information for building the Animal Cladogram, which shows current hypotheses of relationships among clades. Animal clades are typically defined according to adult body plans and patterns of embryonic development.

Differences Between Clades Every animal clade has a unique combination of traits inherited from ancestors and new traits found only in that clade. Complex body systems are not an improvement over simpler systems. Any body system in a living animal functions well enough to enable that animal to survive and reproduce.

Evolutionary Experiments Each clade's body plan is an evolutionary experiment in which a set of body structures performs essential functions. The original versions of most major animal body plans were established hundreds of millions of years ago. As species have adapted to changing conditions, new clades are created.

Origins of the Invertebrates

KEY QUESTION *What does the cladogram of invertebrates illustrate?*

The Cambrian Explosion started about 542 million years ago and lasted 15 million years, and was when many modern phyla began appearing in the fossil record.

The Earliest Animals After the first prokaryotic cells evolved, all life remained single-celled for about 3 billion years. Research shows the first animals evolved from ancestors shared with living choanoflagellates, with the oldest evidence of multicellular life coming from 600-million-year-old microscopic fossils.

The Ediacaran Fauna Fossils from Australia's Ediacara Hills date from roughly 565 to 544 million years ago. These showed body plans different from any animals alive today, although some seem to be related to worms and jellyfishes.

The Cambrian Explosion During the Cambrian Period, animals evolved complex body plans; specialized cells, tissues, and organs; body symmetry; segmentation; front and back ends; and appendages. Some also evolved shells, skeletons, or other hard body parts.

Cladogram of Invertebrates The Invertebrate Cladogram shows current hypotheses about evolutionary relationships among major living invertebrate groups, and indicates the order in which important features evolved.

Origins of the Chordates

KEY QUESTION *What can we learn by studying the chordate cladogram?*

The most ancient chordates were related to ancestors of echinoderms. One chordate fossil of a worm from the Cambrian Period included paired muscles arranged in a series, similar to those of modern chordates. Fossil beds from the later Cambria held fossils of the earliest known vertebrate, showing muscles arranged in a series; traces of fins; sets of feathery gills; heads with paired sense organs; and skeletal structure, including a skull. These last features were likely made of **cartilage**, a strong connective tissue softer and more flexible than bone. These characteristics are shared—during some part of the life cycle—by all chordates.

Visual Reading Tool: Identifying Invertebrates

On the chart below, fill in the type of invertebrate that the row describes. Use the small icons to help you.

1.	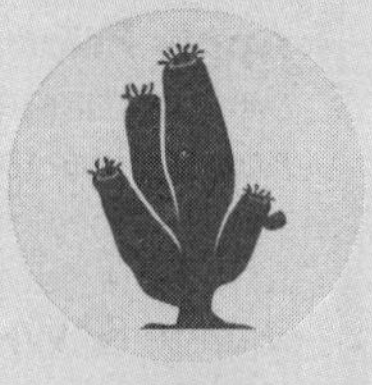	Simplest organism in clade Metazoa; they have tiny pores all over their bodies.
2.	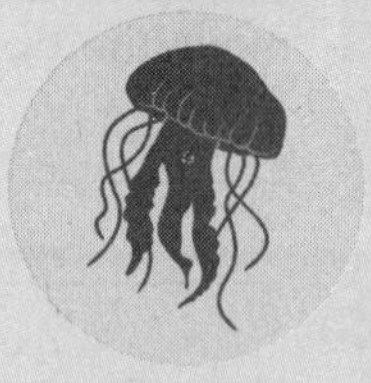	Aquatic, mostly soft-bodied, carnivorous, racially symmetrical with stinging tentacles around their mouths.
3.	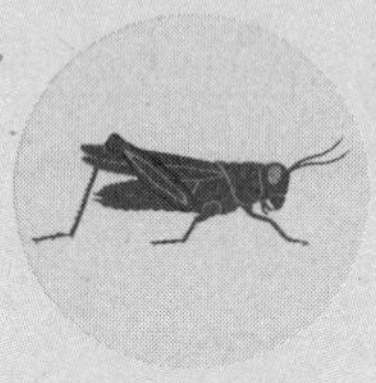	Segmented bodies, tough external skeleton, cephalization, jointed appendages.
4.	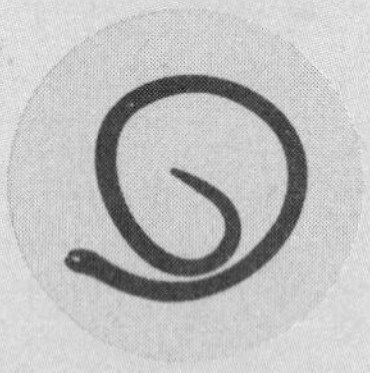	Unsegmented bodies with specialized tissues and organ system, digestive tracts with mouth and anus openings.
5.	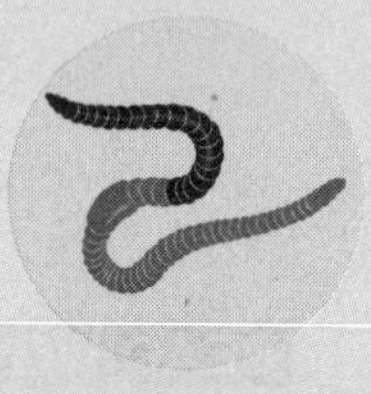	Soft, flattened, unsegmented bodies that lack a coelom and anus.
6.	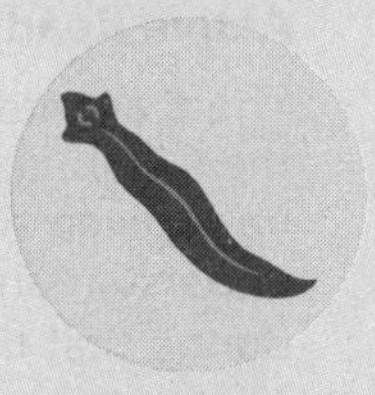	Segmented bodies with a ring-like appearance.
7.	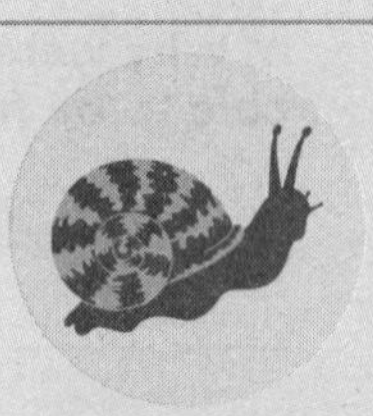	Soft-bodied animals that typically have internal or external shells and complex organ systems.
8.	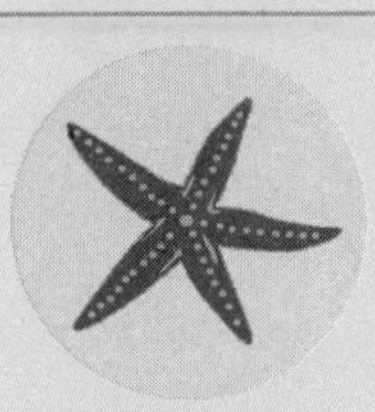	Spiny skin, five-part radial symmetry, internal plate skeleton, water vascular system.

Cladogram of Chordates
Modern chordates consist of six groups: nonvertebrate chordates and five vertebrate groups—fishes, amphibians, reptiles, birds, and mammals. Almost all living chordates are vertebrates; most of those are fishes. The Chordate Cladogram presents current hypotheses about evolutionary relationships among chordate groups. Within it are markers noting the evolutionary appearance of various characteristics that jump-started major adaptive radiations.

Nonvertebrate Chordates
Tunicates and lancelets are chordates lacking backbones. Fossil evidence shows that their ancestors diverged from vertebrate ancestors over 550 million years ago.

Jawless Fishes
The earliest fishes appeared about 510 million years ago. Fossils show they had no jaw or teeth, their skeletons were made of cartilage, and many had bony shields on their heads or other armor. Two other clades gave rise to modern lampreys and hagfishes.

Sharks and Their Relatives
Other ancient fishes evolved jaws, allowing them to bite and chew. Early fishes also evolved paired pectoral and pelvic fins attached to limb girdles. These offer greater body movement control, while tail fins and muscles allow for greater thrust. These adaptions launched the adaptive radiation of the Chondrichthyes: sharks, rays, and skates.

Bony Fishes
Another group of ancient fishes evolved skeletons of true bone, launching the radiation of bony fishes, the Osteichthyes.

Ray-Finned Fishes
Most modern bony fishes belong to the huge group called ray-finned fishes, referring to fins formed from bony rays connected by a layer of skin.

Lobe-Finned Fishes
Lobe-finned fishes evolved fleshy fins supported by larger bones. One group of ancient lobe-finned fishes evolved into the ancestors of four-limbed vertebrates, or tetrapods.

The "Fishapod"
Fossils show how lines of lobe-finned fishes evolved sturdier appendages. One of these has a mix of fish and tetrapod features and could be called a "fishapod"—part fish, part tetrapod.

Amphibians
The word *amphibian* means "double life," since most amphibians live in water as larvae and on land as adults. Most require water for reproduction, breathe with lungs as adults, have moist skin with mucous glands, and lack scales and claws. Early amphibians were ancestors of reptiles, birds, and mammals. Their adaptations to breathe air and protect themselves from drying out fueled another adaptive radiation. Only three orders of amphibians survive today.

BUILD Vocabulary

tetrapod vertebrate with four limbs

Suffixes The suffix *-pod* means "foot." It is often used in biology to describe how many limbs an animal has, but also has uses in other fields of study. In photography, a camera can sit on a tripod to be held steady. ☑ **Why do photographers refer to that piece of equipment as a tripod?**

_____

_____

_____

_____

READING TOOL
Make Connections

Now that you know what the suffix *-pod* means, let's apply other prefixes to it. ☑ **If a tetrapod has four limbs, how many limbs would a quintapod have? What about a decapod? What about a dodecapod?**

_____

_____

_____

_____

Modern birds evolved from feathered dinosaurs and are considered reptiles. In earlier chapters, you learned how climate change is affecting some birds.

☑ **Describe one way modern birds 100 years from now might evolve to combat rising global temperatures.**

_____

_____

_____

_____

Reptiles Reptiles evolved from ancient amphibians with dry, scaly skin, well-developed lungs, strong limbs, and land-developing shelled eggs. Five living reptile groups include lizards and snakes, crocodilians, turtles and tortoises, the tuatara, and birds.

Enter the Dinosaurs A great reptile adaptive radiation continued through the Triassic and Jurassic Periods. Some dinosaurs ate plants; others were carnivorous. Some lived in family groups and cared for eggs or young. Some had feathers, possibly first serving to regulate body temperature. Evolutionary lineage from feathered dinosaurs led to modern birds.

Exit the Dinosaurs The Cretaceous Period ended with a mass extinction, which included most of the dinosaurs, and many plant and animal groups. This may have been caused by a combination of natural disasters precipitated by an asteroid hitting Earth.

Birds A series of well-preserved ancient birds and feathered dinosaurs showed that modern birds had dinosaur ancestors, and so they are included in a clade containing dinosaurs. Because dinosaurs are part of a larger clade of reptiles, modern birds are also reptiles. Archaeopteryx was the first bird-like fossil discovered. From the late Jurassic Period, it was a small, running dinosaur with highly evolved feathers. Characteristics of birds include feathers; strong, lightweight bones; two scale-covered legs; and front-limb wings. Birds are endoderms; most reptiles are ectotherms.

Mammals The clade Mammalia includes about 5000 endothermic member-species sharing characteristics, including mammary glands, hair, and a four-chambered heart.

The First Mammals True mammals appeared during the late Triassic Period, and were small, resembling modern tree shrews. While dinosaurs ruled, mammals remained small and were probably more nocturnal. New evidence shows that the first members of modern mammalian groups evolved during this period. After dinosaurs became extinct, mammals underwent a long adaptive radiation. The Cenozoic Era is often called the Age of Mammals.

Modern Mammals By the beginning of the Cenozoic, three major mammal groups had evolved—monotremes, marsupials, and placentals. They differ in their means of reproduction and development.

READING TOOL **Sequence of Events** Use the following graphic organizer to identify in which order the different species of primates developed.

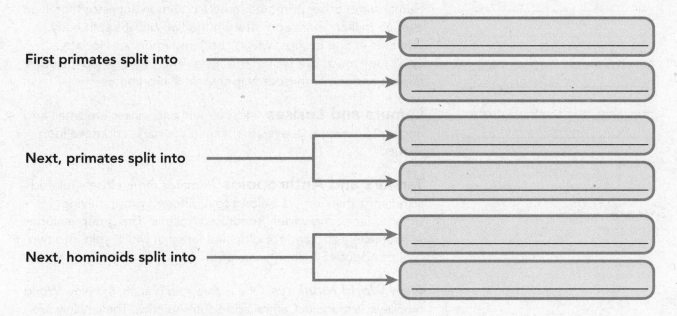

First primates split into

Next, primates split into

Next, hominoids split into

Lesson Summary

What Is a Primate?

🔑 **KEY QUESTION** *What characteristics do all primates share?*

Primates are intelligent and social creatures exhibiting complex behaviors. In general, a primate is a mammal with relatively long fingers, toes with nails instead of claws, arms that can rotate around shoulder joints, a strong clavicle, binocular vision, and a well-developed cerebrum.

Fingers, Toes, and Shoulders Primates typically have five flexible fingers and toes on each hand or foot to curl and grip objects. Most primates have thumbs and big toes, and arms well suited to climbing.

Binocular Vision Both eyes of many primates face forward, with overlapping fields of vision, depth perception, and a three-dimensional view of the world.

🔑 **As you read, circle the answers to each Key Question. Underline any words you do not understand.**

The climates in Central and South America vary greatly from the climate and habitats of Africa.

☑ **Why does it make sense that monkeys in the former areas evolved long tails, while those in the latter areas did not?**

_____
_____
_____
_____

_____
_____

_____
_____

Well-Developed Cerebrum In primates, the cerebrum (or "thinking" part of the brain) is large and intricate, enabling complex behaviors. Many primate species create elaborate social systems that include extended families, adoption of orphans, and even warfare between rival troops.

Evolution of Primates

🔑 **KEY QUESTION** *What are the major groups of primates?*

Humans and other primates share a common ancestor that lived over 65 million years ago, though the two groups split early. Primates in one groups, which contains lemurs and lorises, don't look much like typical monkeys. The other group includes tarsiers and the anthropoids, or humanlike primates.

Lemurs and Lorises Most lemurs and lorises are small and nocturnal, have large eyes that see in the dark, and have long snouts.

Tarsiers and Anthropoids Primates more closely related to humans than lemurs belong to a different group having broader faces and widely separated nostrils. The group includes Asian tarsiers and anthropoids, the latter of which split into two groups about 45 million years ago.

New World Monkeys One anthropoid branch, the New World monkeys, is found in Central and South America. They mainly live in trees, have long flexible arms, and have long prehensile tails.

Old World Monkeys and Great Apes The other anthropoid branch includes the Old World monkeys and great apes and evolved from Africa and Asia. Old World monkeys spend time in trees, but lack prehensile tails. Great apes, or **hominoids**, include gibbons, orangutans, chimpanzees, and humans.

Hominin Evolution

🔑 **KEY QUESTION** *What adaptations enable later hominin species to walk upright?*

Between 6 and 7 million years ago, hominins, the lineage that includes modern humans and closely related species, split from the lineage that led to chimpanzees. Hominins evolved **opposable thumbs** and large brains. The skull, neck, spinal column, hip bones, and leg bones of early hominin species changed shape in ways that enabled later species to walk upright. Hominins, brains are much larger than those of chimpanzees with the biggest difference being the size of the cerebrum.

Hominin Relationships The hominin fossil record includes seven species and a few subspecies. All of these are relatives of modern humans, but not all are human ancestors.

BUILD Vocabulary

hominoids group of anthropoids that includes gibbons, orangutans, gorillas, chimpanzees, and humans

opposable thumb thumb that enables grasping objects and using tools

Using Prior Knowledge Very few species on our planet have opposable thumbs. ☑ **What advantages do opposable thumbs give to animals?**

_____
_____
_____
_____

Visual Reading Tool: Comparing Primates

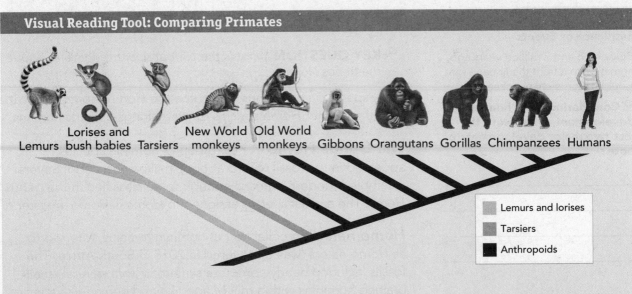

Lemurs Lorises and bush babies Tarsiers New World monkeys Old World monkeys Gibbons Orangutans Gorillas Chimpanzees Humans

Lemurs and lorises
Tarsiers
Anthropoids

Compare and contrast physical characteristics and locations of various primates. Enter your answers into the chart.

	Lemurs & Lorises	Tarsiers & New World Monkeys	Old World Monkeys & Hominoids
Physical characteristics			
Locations			

New Findings and New Questions

The study of human ancestors, which includes studying fossils and DNA, is constantly changing. Since the 1990s, fossil discoveries have more than doubled the number of known hominin species. The oldest known hominin is the *Sahelanthropus*, which is about 7 million years old, though scientists are still debating whether the creature was a true hominin, as well as how it relates to other fossil hominins and to humans.

Australopithecus

The genus *Australopithecus* lived from about 4 million to about 1.5 million years ago. They walked on two feet, or were **bipedal**. Their skeletons suggest they spent time in trees, while their tooth structure suggests they ate a lot of fruit. The best-known species is *Australopithecus afarensis*, of which the best-known specimen, called "Lucy," was discovered in 1974. In 2006, "the Dikka Baby" fossil, another *A. afarensis* specimen, was found in Africa. Leg bones confirmed that it was bipedal, and arm and shoulder bones suggest that it was a stronger climber than modern humans.

BUILD Vocabulary

bipedal having two-foot locomotion

Related Words Humans are the only purely bipedal animals on our planet. Most other animals are quadrupedal. ☑ **Based upon what you know about the word *bipedal*, and what you know about numerical prefixes, how many legs does a quadruped walk on?**

Between 6 and 7 million years ago, hominins split from the lineage that would become chimpanzees.

☑ **Considering all of hominin development, what were the last two major developments of note?**

_____

_____

_____

_____

The Road to Modern Humans

KEY QUESTION _What is the current scientific thinking about the genus Homo?_

Many species in our genus existed before _Homo sapiens_, with at least three other _Homo_ species existing alongside early humans.

The Genus Homo A new group of hominin species appeared in the fossil record about 2 million years ago. Several resembled modern humans enough to be classified in the genus _Homo_. The earliest species assigned to _Homo_ is _Homo ergaster_.

Homo naledi A collection of hominin remains, referred to as _Homo naledi_, was discovered in 2015 in South Africa. The fossils included nearly complete skeletons from several small-brained hominins with a mix of ape-like and human-like species.

Homo neanderthalensis (or H. sapiens neanderthalensis) Neanderthals flourished in Europe and Western Asia about 200,000 years ago. They made stone tools, lived in complex social groups, had controlled use of fire, were expert hunters, and buried their dead with simple rituals. Fossils showed that they survived in parts of Europe until 28,000 to 24,000 years ago.

Out of Africa—But When and Who? Researchers agree that our genus originated in Africa and migrated all over the world. Questions remain about the evolution and migration of species within our genus. Evidence suggests that some hominins left Africa long before _Homo sapiens_ evolved, and scientists believe that several species migrated in waves.

Homo erectus in Asia Some researchers suggest that groups of _Homo erectus_ left Africa and traveled to Southeast Asia, indicating that they may have wandered far from Africa.

The First Homo sapiens Paleontologists debate where and when _Home sapiens_ arose. The multiregional hypothesis suggests that modern humans evolved independently in several places, while other genetic evidence suggests that modern humans can be traced back to interbreeding ancient hominin species. The "out of Africa" theory suggests that modern humans evolved in Africa 200,000 years ago, migrated through the Middle East, and replaced earlier hominin species.

Modern Humans _Homo sapiens_ with modern skeletons arrived in the Middle East about 100,000 years ago. By about 50,000 years ago, _Homo sapiens_ were using tools made out of stone, bones, and antlers. They were also performing rituals when they buried the dead. In short, _homo sapiens started_ behaving like modern humans of today. During this time, too, Neanderthals and _Homo sapiens_ lived in the same environment for thousands of years.

Social Interactions and Group Behavior

READING TOOL **Compare and Contrast** Compare and contrast the similarities and differences among each of the identified items. List two similarities and one difference in each row.

Items	Similarities	Differences
Habituation & Insight Learning		
Classical & Operant Conditioning		
Courtship & Territoriality		
Visual, Chemical, and Sound Signals		

1. What type of conditioning, or learning, are you demonstrating by studying for a test, and why?

_____

_____

_____

_____

_____

2. Explain one similarity and one difference between human societies and bee societies.

Similarity: _____

_____

Difference: _____

_____

Lesson Summary

Behavior and Evolution

🔍 As you read, circle the answers to each Key Question. Underline any words you do not understand.

🔍 **KEY QUESTION** *How can behavior serve as an adaptation that affects reproductive success?*

Behavior is a response to a stimulus within an organism's environment. Although many behaviors are triggered by external stimuli, an individual's response to that stimulus often depends on its internal condition. Some behaviors are also influenced by inherited genes, and can therefore evolve in response to natural selection.

Learned Behavior

🔍 **KEY QUESTION** *What are the major types of learning?*

Many complex animals live in unpredictable environments where fitness depends on changing behaviors as a result of learning. Scientists have identified four major types of learning, discussed below.

Habituation The simplest type of learning is habituation, a process by which an animal decreases or stops responding to stimuli that neither reward nor harm it.

Insight Learning The most complicated form of learning is insight learning, which occurs when an animal applies something it has already learned to a new situation.

Classical Conditioning Classical conditioning is a form of learning in which a certain stimulus comes to produce a particular response, usually through association with a positive or negative experience.

Operant Conditioning Operant conditioning occurs when an animal learns to behave in a certain way to receive a reward or to avoid punishment. It was first described by B.F. Skinner, who performed tests on animals using a "Skinner Box," which had a button or lever that delivered a food reward when pressed. The animal learned through operant conditioning that pressing the lever meant it would be given food.

Behavioral Cycles

🔍 **KEY QUESTION** *How do periodic environmental changes affect behavior?*

Animals are affected by the environment, and do not behave in the same way all the time or in all places. Many animals respond to periodic environmental changes with daily behavioral cycles, called circadian rhythms, or seasonal behavioral cycles.

BUILD Vocabulary

behavior way an organism reacts to changes in its internal condition or external environment

Related Words To understand behavior, it is important to know the difference between internal and external conditions and stimuli. Internal stimuli are based on something an individual feels, like hunger, pain, or love. External stimuli are those that exist outside of the body. ☑ **What are some external stimuli that can change the behavior of an organism?**

_____

_____

READING TOOL

Cause and Effect

Domesticated animals rely on humans to take care of them.

☑ **If a cat learns that when he wakes his human up in the morning, the human provides him with food, what effects might this have on the cat's behavior? Name two.**

_____

_____

_____

_____

_____

Social Behavior

🔑 KEY QUESTION *How can social behaviors increase evolutionary fitness?*

Social behaviors, such as choosing mates, defending territories or resources, and forming social groups, can increase evolutionary fitness.

Courtship Members of sexually reproducing animal species must locate and mate with other members of the same species to reproduce. Courtship is behavior during which members of one sex advertise their willingness to mate, and members of the opposite sex choose which mate they will accept.

Territoriality and Aggression Many animals occupy and defend a specific area, or territory, that contains resources, like food, water, nesting sites, shelter, and potential mates. If a rival enters a territory, the "owner" attacks in an effort to drive the rival away.

Animal Societies A society is a group of animals of the same species that interact closely and often cooperate. Societies offer a range of advantages that can produce differential reproductive success between group members and individuals. Members of a society are often related to one another. The theory of kin selection holds that helping relatives can improve an individual's evolutionary fitness because related individuals share a large proportion of their genes. Helping relatives survive increases the chances that the shared genes will be passed to offspring.

Communication

🔑 KEY QUESTION *How do animals communicate?*

Social behavior involves more than one individual and requires communication—the passing of information from one individual to another. Animals may use a variety of signals to communicate, explained below.

Visual Signals Many animals use visual signals, and have eyes able to sense shapes and colors.

Chemical Signals Many animals have well-developed senses of smell, and they communicate with chemical signals, like pheromones.

Sound Signals Many species make and detect sounds, with some evolving elaborate sound-based communication systems.

Language The most complicated form of communication is language—a system that combines sounds, symbols, and gestures according to rules about sequence and meaning, such as grammar and syntax.

BUILD Vocabulary

society group of closely related animals of the same species that interact for the benefit of the group

kin selection theory that states that helping relatives can improve an individual's evolutionary fitness because related individuals share a large proportion of their genes

communication passing of information from organism to another

language system of communication that combines sounds, symbols, and gestures according to a set of rules about sequence and meaning, such as grammar and syntax

Multiple Meanings The word *society* is not only used to describe a group of same-species animals working together for the benefit of all. It is also used to describe people living in a more or less ordered community, as well as an organization or club formed for a particular activity or purpose.

☑ **Explain a way that being in a society benefits animals.**

_____

_____

_____

_____

Review Vocabulary

Match the vocabulary term to its definition.

1. _____ tetrapod

2. _____ bipedal

3. _____ hominoids

a. refers to two-foot locomotion

b. refers to a vertebrate with four limbs

c. group of anthropoids that includes gibbons, orangutans, chimpanzees, and humans

Fill in the blanks with the correct terms.

4. _____ is a body plan in which a single imaginary line can divide the left and right sides into mirror images of each other, while _____ is a body plan in which any number of imaginary planes drawn through the center could divide it into equal halves.

Review Key Questions

Provide evidence and details to support your answers.

5. In your own words, describe three things organisms do to maintain a state of homeostasis.

_____

_____

_____

6. Why are the cladograms continually changing?

_____

_____

7. Where did *Homo sapiens* evolve, and how did they move around Earth?

_____

_____

_____

8. Explain how visual, chemical, and sound signals coming from humans are different if they are trying to attract mates or repel rivals.

_____

_____

_____

_____

Feeding and Digestion

READING TOOL **Use Structure** As you read this lesson, complete the table below. Describe how different types of animals obtain food.

DIGESTION: How do each of the following obtain food?				
Filter Feeders	Detritivores	Herbivores	Carnivores	Nutritional Symbionts

Lesson Summary

Obtaining Food

🔑 **KEY QUESTION** *How do animals obtain food?*

All animals that obtain nutrients and energy from food are heterotrophs.

Filter Feeders Most filter feeders catch algae and small animals by using structures like modified gills as nets to filter food out of water.

Detritivores Detritus is made up of decaying plant and animal material. Detritivores feed on detritus, often obtaining extra nutrients from microorganisms that grow on and around it.

🔑 As you read, circle the answers to each Key Question. Underline any words you do not understand.

Compare and Contrast

Animals have specialized digestive tracts that digest food in stages.
☑ **How is chemical digestion different from mechanical digestion?**

_____

_____

_____

_____

_____

_____

_____

BUILD Vocabulary

digestive tract tube that begins at the mouth and ends at the anus

rumen stomach chamber in cows and related animals in which symbiotic bacteria digest cellulose

Word Origins _Digest_ comes from the Latin word _digesta_ which has its origins in the word _digerere_. _Digerere_ means "to separate, divide, or arrange," and the suffix _-gest_ means "to carry." ☑ **Based on these origins, explain the term _digest_ in your own words.**

_____

_____

_____

Herbivores Herbivores eat plants or parts of plants, like seeds and fruits, or they eat algae. Seeds and fruits are often filled with nutrients and are easy to digest.

Carnivores Carnivores eat other animals. Mammalian carnivores use teeth, claws, and speed to hunt their prey.

Nutritional Symbionts Symbiosis is a close relationship between two or more species. Symbionts are the organisms involved in a symbiosis.

Parasitic Symbiosis Parasites live within or on a host organism, where they feed on tissues or body fluids, disrupting the health of their hosts. Some parasites cause serious diseases in humans, livestock, and plants.

Mutualistic Symbiosis Mutualistic nutritional relationships benefit both participants, and often help to maintain the health of organisms.

Processing Food

🔑 **KEY QUESTION** _How does digestion occur in animals?_

After food is obtained, it must be digested and absorbed to make energy and nutrients. Many invertebrates and all vertebrates digest food as it passes through a tube called a **digestive tract**, which has two openings. Food moves in one direction, entering the body through the mouth. Wastes leave through the anus.

One-way digestive tracts often have specialized structures that perform different tasks as food passes through them. Food undergoes both chemical and mechanical digestion. The intestines absorb nutrients, and wastes are expelled.

Specializations for Different Diets

🔑 **KEY QUESTION** _How are mouthparts adapted for different diets?_

Animal mouthparts and digestive systems have evolved and adapted to the physical and chemical characteristics of different foods.

Specialized Mouthparts Carnivores and leaf-eating herbivores usually have very different mouthparts that are related to the foods they eat.

Eating Meat Carnivores typically have sharp mouthparts and structures that capture and break down food. Their sharp teeth, jaw bones, and muscles are adapted for up-and-down movements that chop meat into small pieces.

Eating Plant Leaves Herbivores have mouthparts that grind plant cell walls. Many herbivorous invertebrates have mouthparts that grind plants or algae. Herbivorous mammals like the giraffe have front teeth, muscular lips, flattened molars, and jawbones that pull and grind leaves in a side-to-side motion.

Specialized Digestive Tracts Carnivorous invertebrates and vertebrates have short digestive tracts that produce meat-digesting enzymes, but lack enzymes that break down plant cellulose. Animals called ruminants, like cattle, have a **rumen**, where symbiotic bacteria digest cellulose.

Visual Reading Tool: Carnivore or Herbivore

1. Analyze the figure shown. Determine which is a herbivore and which is a carnivore.

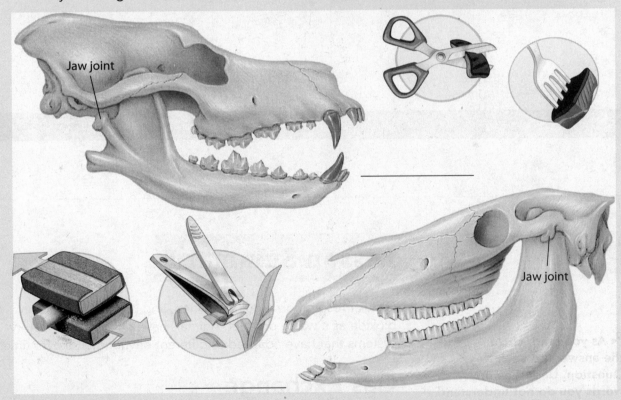

Jaw joint

Jaw joint

2. Explain how you determined your answers to complete the figure.

_____

_____

_____

LESSON 2 Respiration

READING TOOL **Compare and Contrast** Compare and contrast respiration in the following species.

Differences			
Amphibians	Reptiles	Mammals	Birds

Similarities

Lesson Summary

Cellular respiration requires oxygen, and it produces carbon dioxide as a waste product. Animals have different respiratory systems that have adapted to different environments over time.

🔍 As you read, circle the answers to each Key Question. Underline any words you do not understand.

Gas Exchange

🔍 **KEY QUESTION** *What characteristics do the respiratory structures of all animals share?*

Living cells cannot actively pump oxygen or carbon dioxide across membranes. Yet, in order to breathe, all animals must exchange oxygen and carbon dioxide with their surroundings.

Gas Diffusion and Membranes Substances diffuse from an area of higher concentration to an area of lower concentration. Gases diffuse most efficiently across a thin, moist membrane that is permeable to those gases.

Requirements for Respiration All respiratory systems share certain basic characteristics. Respiratory structures provide a large surface area of moist, selectively permeable membrane.

Respiratory Surfaces of Aquatic Animals

🔍 **KEY QUESTION** *How do aquatic animals breathe?*

Some aquatic invertebrates are small and have thin-walled bodies whose outer surfaces are always wet. They rely on diffusion of oxygen and carbon dioxide through their outer body covering. A few aquatic chordates, including lancelets, some amphibians, and some sea snakes, rely on gas exchange by diffusion across body surfaces. Large, active animals that consume larger quantities of oxygen exchange gases through gills, which are feathery structures that expose a large surface area of thin, selectively permeable membrane to water. Inside the gill membranes is a network of tiny, thin-walled blood vessels called capillaries, which help maintain differences in oxygen and carbon dioxide concentrations that promote diffusion.

Aquatic reptiles and mammals breathe with lungs and must hold their breath underwater; they come to the water's surface to breathe. Lungs are organs that exchange oxygen and carbon dioxide between blood and air.

> **BUILD Vocabulary**
>
> **gills** feathery structures specialized for the exchange of gases with water
>
> **lungs** respiratory organ in which gases are exchanged between the blood and inhaled air

---

Visual Reading Tool: Respiration through Gills

For each box shown in the figure, describe the function performed for respiration through gills.

Gill Filaments
_____
_____
_____
_____
_____

Mouth
_____
_____
_____

Gill filaments

Blood vessel

Oxygen-rich blood

Oxygen-poor blood

Operculum
_____
_____
_____

Make Connections

In earlier chapters you learned that plants need certain gases to carry out photosynthesis and cell respiration. ☑ **Describe the air that humans exhale. How is it different from respiration in plants?**

_____

_____

_____

_____

_____

_____

_____

_____

_____

_____

BUILD Vocabulary

alveoli (singular alveolus) tiny air sacs at the end of a bronchiole in the lungs that provide surface area for gas exchange to occur

Word Origins _Alveolus_ comes from the Latin word _alveus_ which means "hollow or cavity," or from _alvus_, which means "belly or beehive." ☑ **Imagine a beehive and its honeycombs. Based on the definition of _alveoli_, what do you think a beehive and alveoli have in common?**

_____

_____

_____

_____

Respiratory Surfaces of Terrestrial Animals

🔍 **KEY QUESTION** _What respiratory structures enable land animals to breathe?_

Land animals must keep their respiratory membranes moist in dry environments. They must also carry oxygen and carbon dioxide back and forth between those surfaces and the rest of their bodies.

Respiratory Surfaces in Invertebrates Respiratory structures in terrestrial invertebrates include skin, mantle cavities, book lungs, and tracheal tubes. Some land invertebrates, such as earthworms, live in moist environments and can respire across their skin if it stays moist. Other invertebrates, such as land snails, respire using a mantle cavity lined with moist tissue and blood vessels. Insects and spiders have more complex respiratory systems.

Lung Structure in Vertebrates All terrestrial vertebrates—reptiles, birds, mammals, and the land stages of most amphibians—breathe with lungs. Inhaling brings oxygen-rich air through the trachea, into the lungs. Inside the lungs, oxygen diffuses into the blood through lung capillaries, and carbon dioxide diffuses out of capillaries into the lungs to be exhaled.

**Amphibian, Reptilian, and Mammalian Lungs** A typical amphibian lung is little more than a sac with ridges. Reptilian lungs are often divided into chambers that increase the surface area for gas exchange. Mammalian lungs branch extensively, and air passages branch and rebranch, ending in bubblelike structures called **alveoli**. Alveoli provide a large surface area for gas exchange and are surrounded by a network of capillaries in which blood picks up oxygen and releases carbon dioxide. Mammalian lung structure helps take in the large amounts of oxygen required by high metabolic rates. When mammals and most other vertebrates breathe, air moves in and out through the same air passages, and some stale, oxygen-poor air remains.

**Bird Lungs** In birds, air flows mostly in only one direction. No stale air gets trapped in the system. A unique system of tubes and air sacs in birds' respiratory systems enable this one-way airflow. Thus, gas exchange surfaces are continuously in contact with fresh air. This highly efficient gas exchange helps birds obtain the oxygen they need to power their flight muscles for long periods of time.

LESSON 3 Circulation

READING TOOL **Compare and Contrast** Compare and contrast the four-chambered heart with the three-chambered heart. Describe their similarities in the middle column. Then provide three examples each of animals that have three-chambered hearts and those that have four-chambered hearts.

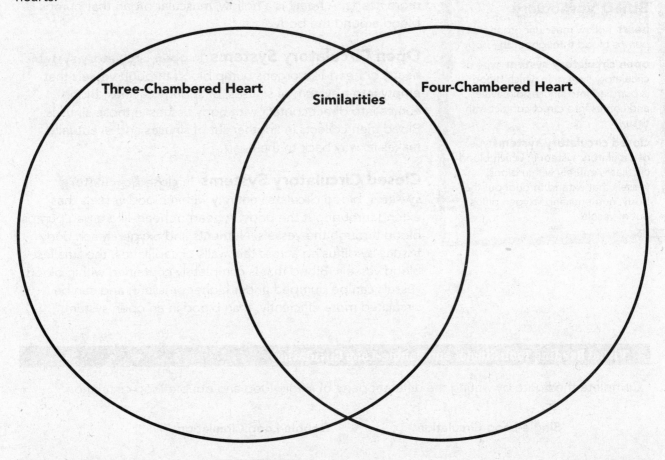

Three-Chambered Heart   Similarities   Four-Chambered Heart

EXAMPLES	
Three-Chambered Hearts	**Four-Chambered Hearts**

Lesson Summary

⚲ As you read, circle the answers to each Key Question. Underline any words you do not understand.

Open and Closed Circulatory Systems

⚲ **KEY QUESTION** *How do open and closed circulatory systems compare?*

Many animals move blood through their bodies using one or more hearts. A **heart** is a hollow, muscular organ that pumps blood around the body.

Open Circulatory Systems In **open circulatory systems**, hearts or heart-like organs pump blood through vessels that empty into a system of sinuses, or spongy cavities. Blood comes into direct contact with body tissues in those sinuses. Blood then collects in another set of sinuses and eventually makes its way back to the heart.

Closed Circulatory Systems In **closed circulatory systems**, blood circulates entirely within blood vessels that extend throughout the body. A heart or heart-like organ pumps blood through the vessels. Nutrients and oxygen reach body tissues by diffusing across thin walls of capillaries, the smallest blood vessels. Blood that is completely contained within blood vessels can be pumped under higher pressure, and can be circulated more efficiently, than blood in an open system.

BUILD Vocabulary

heart hollow muscular organ that pumps blood throughout the body

open circulatory system type of circulatory system in which blood is pumped into sinuses or cavities and comes into direct contact with tissues

closed circulatory system type of circulatory system in which blood circulates entirely within blood vessels that extend throughout the body; nutrients and oxygen diffuse out of vesels

Visual Reading Tool: Single- and Double-Loop Circulation

Complete the figure by writing the different parts of single-loop and double-loop circulation.

Single-Loop Circulation

Double-Loop Circulation

Single- and Double-Loop Circulation

✎ KEY QUESTION *How do the patterns of circulation in vertebrates compare?*

As chordates evolved, they evolved more complex organ systems and more efficient channels for internal transport.

Single-Loop Circulation Most vertebrates with gills have a single-loop circulatory system with a single pump that forces blood around the body in one direction. In fishes, for example, the heart consists of two chambers: an atrium and a ventricle. The **atrium** receives blood from the body. The **ventricle** then pumps blood out of the heart and to the gills. Oxygen-rich blood then travels from the gills to the rest of the body; oxygen-poor blood returns to the atrium.

Double-Loop Circulation As terrestrial vertebrates evolved into larger and more active forms, their capillary networks became larger. Using a single pump to force blood through the entire system would have been increasingly difficult and inefficient. Most vertebrates that breathe with lungs have evolved a double-loop, two-pump circulatory system. The first loop, powered by the right side of the heart, forces oxygen-poor blood from the heart to the lungs. After the blood picks up oxygen and drops off carbon dioxide in the lungs, it returns to the heart. Then the left side of the heart pumps the oxygen-rich blood through the second circulatory loop to the rest of the body. Oxygen-poor blood from the body returns to the heart, and the cycle begins again.

Heart-Chamber Evolution Four-chambered hearts like those in modern mammals are two separate pumps working next to one another. During chordate evolution, partitions evolved that divided the original two chambers into four. Those partitions transformed one pump into two parallel pumps. The partitions also separated oxygen-rich blood from oxygen-poor blood.

Amphibian hearts usually have three chambers: two atria and one ventricle. The right atrium receives oxygen-poor blood from the body. The left atrium receives oxygen-rich blood from the lungs. Both atria empty into the ventricle. This undivided ventricle allows blood to be moved away from the lungs when these animals dive underwater. Some mixing of oxygen-rich and oxygen-poor blood in the ventricle occurs. However, the internal structure of the ventricle directs blood flow so that most oxygen-poor blood goes to the lungs, and most oxygen-rich blood goes to the rest of the body.

READING TOOL

Make Connections
Most fish have single-loop circulatory systems, while larger terrestrial vertebrates have double-loop circulatory systems. ☑ **What caused circulatory systems to become more complex over time?**

_____

_____

_____

_____

_____

_____

BUILD Vocabulary

atrium upper chamber of the heart that receives blood from the rest of the body

ventricle lower chamber of the heart that pumps blood out of the heart to the rest of the body

Multiple Meanings Another definition for the word *atrium* is "a central glass-roofed hall that extends through several floors in a building," such as a mall or hotel. ☑ **How is this definition similar to the atrium in the heart?**

_____

_____

_____

Use Structure As you read each of the sections in the lesson, briefly describe the main ideas and key takeaways in the graphic organizer below.

Section	Description
The Ammonia Problem	
Storing Wastes that Contain Nitrogen	
Maintaining Water Balance	

Lesson Summary

The Ammonia Problem

🔑 **KEY QUESTION** *How do animals manage toxic nitrogenous waste?*

Cellular metabolism produces wastes that are released into body fluids and must be eliminated from the body. When cells break down proteins, they produce ammonia, a toxic, nitrogenous waste. Animals either eliminate ammonia from the body quickly or convert it into other compounds that are less toxic. The elimination of metabolic wastes, such as ammonia, is called **excretion**.

Storing Wastes that Contain Nitrogen

Animals that cannot dispose of ammonia as it is produced store nitrogen-containing wastes until they can be eliminated. In most cases, ammonia is too toxic to be stored in body fluids. Insects, reptiles, and birds typically covert ammonia into a sticky white compound called uric acid, which is less toxic and less water soluble. Mammals and some amphibians convert ammonia to urea, which is less toxic than ammonia, but highly soluble in water.

Maintaining Water Balance

Excretory systems interact with other systems that regulate water balance in blood and body tissues. Sometimes, excretory systems eliminate excess water along with nitrogenous wastes. Other times, excretory systems eliminate nitrogenous wastes while conserving water. Many animals use **kidneys** to separate wastes and excess water from blood in urine. Kidney cells pump ions from dissolved salts in blood in ways that create an osmotic gradient. Water then "follows" those ions passively by osmosis. This process can get rid of nitrogenous wastes and retain water, but doesn't allow the kidneys to eliminate excess salts.

Visual Reading Tool: Aquatic Animal Excretion

On the diagram below, label the direction that water and salt are flowing in or out of the fish. Also label each as either freshwater or saltwater.

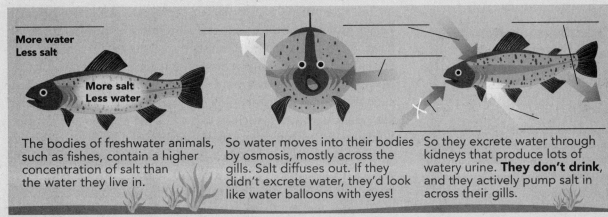

More water
Less salt

More salt
Less water

The bodies of freshwater animals, such as fishes, contain a higher concentration of salt than the water they live in.

So water moves into their bodies by osmosis, mostly across the gills. Salt diffuses out. If they didn't excrete water, they'd look like water balloons with eyes!

So they excrete water through kidneys that produce lots of watery urine. **They don't drink**, and they actively pump salt in across their gills.

Less water
More salt

More water
Less salt

The bodies of saltwater animals, such as fishes, contain a lower concentration of salt than the water they live in.

So they lose water through osmosis and salt diffuses in. If they didn't conserve water and eliminate salt, they'd shrivel up like dead leaves.

So they conserve water by producing very little urine. **They drink**, and they actively pump salt out across their gills.

Aquatic animals have to keep a certain amount of water in their cells to maintain homeostasis.

☑ **What causes water to move into invertebrates that live in freshwater?**

_____

_____

_____

_____

_____

Excretion in Aquatic Animals

⚲**KEY QUESTION** _How do aquatic animals eliminate wastes?_

Aquatic animals eliminate or conserve water depending on whether they live in fresh or salt water.

Freshwater Animals Many freshwater invertebrates lose ammonia by simple diffusion across their skin, and many freshwater fish and amphibians eliminate ammonia across gill membranes.

Saltwater Animals Marine animals release ammonia by diffusion. Many marine invertebrates have body fluids with solute concentrations similar to the seawater around them. Marine fish lose water to their surroundings because their bodies are less salty than the water around them, so they excrete salt across their gills. Their kidneys produce small quantities of urine, which conserves water.

Excretion in Terrestrial Animals

⚲**KEY QUESTION** _How do land animals remove wastes while conserving water?_

In dry environments, land animals lose large amounts of water from respiratory membranes that must be kept moist. They must also eliminate nitrogenous wastes in ways that require disposing of water even though they may not have access to water to drink.

Terrestrial Invertebrates Some terrestrial invertebrates, including annelids and mollusks, produce urine in nephridia. Nephridia are tubelike excretory structures that filter body fluid. Typically, body fluid enters nephridia and becomes more concentrated as it moves through the tubes. Urine leaves the body through excretory pores. Other terrestrial invertebrates, such as insects and arachnids, convert ammonia into uric acid. Nitrogenous wastes, such as uric acid, are absorbed from body fluids by structures called Malpighian tubules. The wastes are then added to digestive wastes traveling through the gut. The wastes lose water, and then crystallize into a thick paste. The paste leaves the body through the anus. This paste contains little water, so these adaptations minimize water loss.

BUILD Vocabulary

nephridia excretory structures of some terrestrial invertebrates that filter body fluid

Malpighian tubules structures in most terrestrial arthropods that concentrate the uric acid and add it to digestive wastes

Related Words A _nephron_ is "the filtering and excretory unit of the kidney," which is found in most terrestrial vertebrates.

☑ **Based on the definitions of _nephridia_ and _nephron_, do you think the two structures are structurally and functionally similar or different, and why?**

_____

_____

_____

_____

Terrestrial Vertebrates In terrestrial vertebrates, excretion is carried out mostly by the kidneys. Mammals and land amphibians convert ammonia into urea, which is excreted in urine. In most reptiles and birds, ammonia is converted into uric acid. Reptiles and birds pass uric acid through ducts into a cavity that also receives digestive wastes from the gut.

Adaptations to Extreme Environments Most vertebrate kidneys cannot excrete concentrated salt, thus they cannot survive by drinking seawater. Taking in extra salt would overwhelm the kidneys, and the animal would die of dehydration. Some marine reptiles and birds have evolved adaptations in the form of specialized glands in their heads that excrete very concentrated salt solutions.

Review Vocabulary

Choose the letter of the best answer.

1. Detritivores feed on which of the following?

 A. animals

 B. other detritivores

 C. microorganisms

2. Respiratory structures in terrestrial invertebrates include all of the following except:

 A. skin.

 B. gills.

 C. tracheal tubes.

Review Key Questions

Provide evidence and details to support your answers.

3. What would be a good way for a student studying dinosaurs determine whether a specific fossil is a carnivore or herbivore?

_____

_____

_____

4. What are the benefits of a closed circulatory system over an open circulatory system?

_____

_____

_____

5. Why is ammonia considered a problem that organisms need to solve?

_____

_____

_____

6. What is the relationship between surface area and diffusion?

_____

_____

_____

Response

Main Idea and Details As you read your textbook, identify the main ideas and details or evidence that support the main ideas. Use the lesson headings to organize the main ideas and details. Record your work in the table.

Heading	Main Idea	Details/Evidence
How Animals Respond		
Trends in Nervous System Evolution		
Sensory Systems		

Lesson Summary

Humans respond to stimuli by gathering information about their surroundings through senses, like vision or hearing. Then the brain decides how to respond to that information. However, the sensory world of animals is different from yours.

How Animals Respond

🔍 **As you read, circle the answers to each Key Question. Underline any words you do not understand.**

🔍 **KEY QUESTION** *How do animals respond to their environment?*

Animals sometimes need to respond to environmental conditions quickly, so they can survive. An animal's nervous system is made up of several kinds of nerve cells called **neurons**. Neurons allow information collected from the stimulus to be passed on to other cells like those in the brain.

BUILD Vocabulary

neurons nerve cell; specialized for carrying messages throughout the nervous system

Detecting Stimuli A stimulus can be light, temperature, sound, odors, vibrations, or other information in an animal's environment that causes the animal to react. Sensory neurons are specialized cells that allow the animal to notice the stimuli. Each type of sensory neuron responds to a particular stimulus such as light, heat, or a chemical. Humans and animals share similar types of sensory cells, and so animals react to stimuli that humans notice too, like light, taste, odor, temperature, sound, water, gravity, and pressure. However, many animals respond to stimuli that humans cannot detect, such as weak electric currents, because many animals have types of sensory cells that humans do not have.

Processing Information Once a stimulus is detected by the sensory neurons, they pass information about the stimulus to other nerve cells that also pass information. These are called interneurons, and they process the data to determine how the animal should respond. An animal's behavior may be more flexible and complex depending on the number of interneurons an animal has and the ways those interneurons process information. For example, worms have few interneurons and are capable of only simple responses, like swimming toward light. A more highly developed nervous system, like in a leopard, with greater numbers of interneurons, mostly in the brain, will have more complex behaviors.

Responding A response is a specific reaction to a stimulus. When an animal responds to a stimulus, body systems—including the nervous system and the muscular system—work together to generate the response. Motor neurons are nerve cells that carry directions from interneurons to muscles, which produces a response.

Trends in Nervous System Evolution

⚲ KEY QUESTION *What are some trends in nervous system evolution?*

Animal nervous systems exhibit different degrees of cephalization and specialization.

Invertebrates Invertebrates, nervous systems range from simple collections of nerve cells to complex organizations that include many interneurons.

Nerve Nets, Nerve Cords, and Ganglia A simple nervous system is called a nerve net and looks like a net. Nerve cords are interneurons grouped together. Ganglia are interneurons that are grouped together and that connect to each other.

"Heads" Cephalization is the concentration of sensory neurons into a "head." Some flatworms and roundworms show this characteristic. The nerves in a head are referred to as cerebral ganglia.

Brains When cerebral ganglia are organized into a complex structure, it is called a brain. Brains generally enable complex behavior and learning.

Chordates Cerebral ganglion are found in simple chordates. Most vertebrates show a high degree of cephalization and have highly developed nervous systems.

Parts of the Vertebrate Brain The cerebrum is part of the vertebrate brain called the "thinking" region. The cerebellum coordinates movement and controls balance.

Vertebrate Brain Evolution Brain evolution in vertebrates follows a general trend of increasing size and complexity from fishes, through amphibians and reptiles, to birds and mammals.

Sensory Systems

🔍 **KEY QUESTION** *What are some types of sensory systems in animals?*

The more complex an animal's nervous system is, the more developed its sensory systems tend to be. Sensory systems range from individual sensory neurons to sense organs that contain both sensory neurons and other cells that help gather information.

Invertebrate Sense Organs Invertebrate sense organs vary widely in complexity. Some invertebrates only sense one stimulus—like a flatworm, for example, that only detects the presence and direction of light—where others can detect several stimuli simultaneously. Invertebrates that are more cephalized have specialized sensory tissues and well-developed sense organs. Because of this complex cephalization, some cephalopods and arthropods can detect motion and color and form images through their eyes.

Other examples of different sense organs that sense the same type of stimulus are the many lenses of the eyes of an insect detecting minute changes in movement, the antennae of a midge sensing sound waves and air motion, and a garden spider detecting vibrations in its web through its legs.

Chordate Sense Organs Chordate sense organs can be simple and have few specializations. In tunicates, sensory cells in and on the siphons and other internal surfaces help control the amount of water passing through the pharynx. Lancelets have a cerebral ganglion with a pair of eyespots that detect light.

Taste, smell, and hearing are received through organs that are very sensitive to their own stimuli. Many animals can have the same parts to make up the organs, but they often have different abilities that are specialized. For example, some species, including certain fishes and the duck-billed platypuses, can detect weak electric currents in water. Some sharks use this "electric sense" to navigate by detecting electric currents in seawater caused by ocean currents moving through Earth's magnetic field. Other "electric fish" create their own electric currents and use it to communicate with one another.

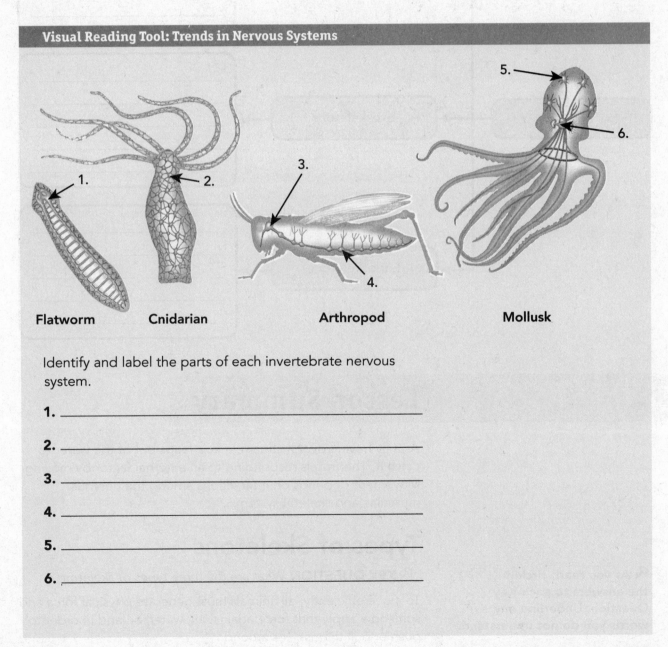

Visual Reading Tool: Trends in Nervous Systems

Flatworm   Cnidarian   Arthropod   Mollusk

Identify and label the parts of each invertebrate nervous system.

1. _____

2. _____

3. _____

4. _____

5. _____

6. _____

Movement and Support

READING TOOL **Active Reading** As you read through this lesson, take notes on the different types of skeletons that protect and support organisms. Fill in the graphic organizer below.

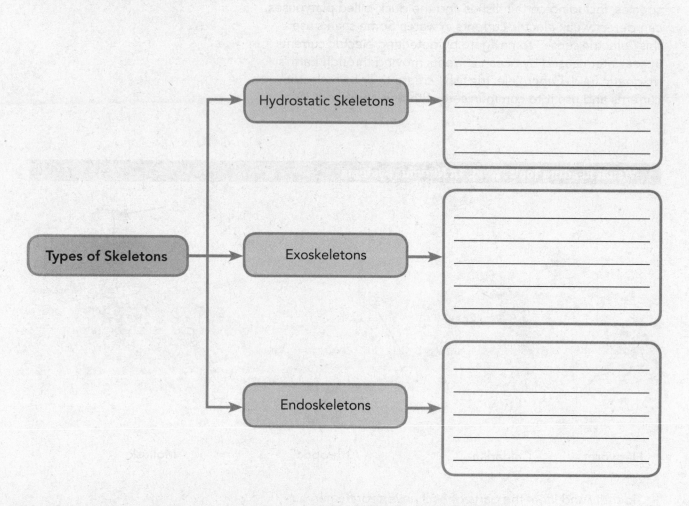

Types of Skeletons → Hydrostatic Skeletons →

Exoskeletons →

Endoskeletons →

Lesson Summary

As a fly hovers over a stream, a frog leaps out of the water to catch it. The frog is responding to an external factor by moving. Movement depends on interactions among the nervous, muscular, and skeletal systems.

Types of Skeletons

As you read, circle the answers to each Key Question. Underline any words you do not understand.

KEY QUESTION *What are the three types of skeletons?*

To move efficiently, all animals must generate physical force and somehow apply that force against air, water, or land in order to push or pull themselves around.

Skeletal Support Having a rigid body part, like a skeleton, helps animals move more efficiently by applying force generated by muscles. For example, legs push against the ground, wings push against air, fins apply force against water. Hydrostatic, exoskeletons, and endoskeletons are the main kinds of skeletal systems animals can have.

Hydrostatic Skeletons An earthworm has a hydrostatic skeleton and consists of fluids held in a body cavity, which allows the worm to change its body shape, making it shorter and/or fatter. The earthworm has longitudinal muscles that run from one end to the other, making it shorter and fatter. The earthworm can become longer and thinner by contracting circular muscles that wrap around each body segment. By alternately contracting these two sets of muscles, the earthworm is able to move.

Exoskeletons Exoskeletons are external skeletons found in arthropods and mollusks. Arthropod exoskeletons are made of complex carbohydrates called chitin. Most mollusks have hard shells made of calcium carbonate. This type of skeleton provides protection from predators and acts as a watertight covering to allow survival in dry places. One disadvantage of the exoskeleton is that it doesn't grow when the animal does. An arthropod has to break out of the exoskeleton and grow a new one in a process called molting. These skeletons are also heavy and increase in weight as the arthropod grows.

Endoskeletons A structural support system found inside the body is an endoskeleton. Endoskeletons do not protect an animal like an exoskeleton does. However, this type of skeleton can grow as the animal grows and it can grow very large because the endoskeleton is lightweight in proportion to the body it supports.

Joints Connections that divide parts of a skeleton and allow movement are known as joints. Bones are connected at joints by strong connective tissues called ligaments.

Muscles and Movements

🔍 **KEY QUESTION** *How do muscles enable movement?*

Muscles are specialized tissues that produce physical force by contracting, or shortening, when they are stimulated by the nervous system. In many animals, muscles work together in pairs or groups that are attached to different parts of a skeleton.

Movement When one muscle group contracts and the other is relaxed, it bends the joint. Muscles can only contract, so they must be stretched back into position by the opposing muscle group.

BUILD Vocabulary

hydrostatic skeleton skeleton made of fluid-filled body segments that work with muscles to allow the animal to move

exoskeleton external skeleton; tough external covering that protects and supports the body of many invertebrates

endoskeleton internal skeleton; structural support system within the body of an animal

joints place where one bone attaches to another bone

Prefixes Both *endo-* and *exo-* are prefixes with Greek origins. *Endo-* means "inside" and *exo-* means "outside." When they are put in front of the word *skeleton*, it describes the location of the structural support for that organism. ☑ **Can you name two organisms, one with an exoskeleton and one with an endoskeleton?**

_____

_____

_____

_____

_____

Vertebrate Muscular and Skeletal Systems The shapes and relative positions of bones, muscles, and joints are linked closely to the functions they perform. Paleontologists can reconstruct the habits of extinct animals by studying the joints of fossil bones and the places where tendons and ligaments once attached.

1a. — Joint flexed

1b. — Joint straight

Joint

Joint

Identify and label the two types of skeletons seen in the pictures. Draw arrows to show how each joint moves on each figure.

1. Determine the human leg extensors and flexors in the top diagram.

1a. _____

1b. _____

2. Explain how flexors and extensors work together to help a person kick a soccer ball.

_____

_____

Reproduction

READING TOOL **Compare and Contrast** As you read this lesson, keep track of the similarities and differences between sexual and asexual reproduction. Fill in the Venn diagram below.

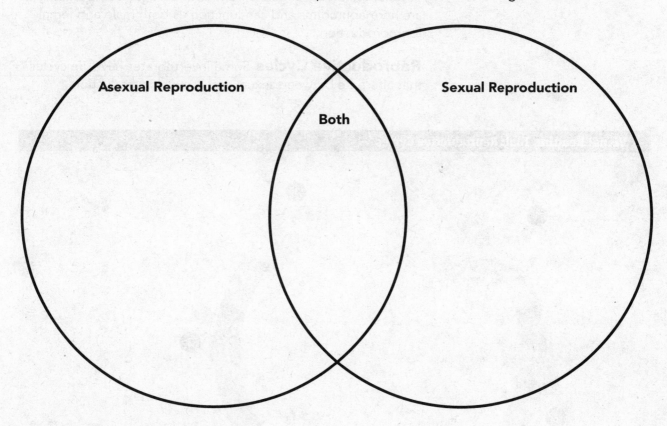

Asexual Reproduction

Both

Sexual Reproduction

Lesson Summary

Sexual reproduction can be dangerous and can require a lot of effort for the male or female. For example, a male praying mantis will be eaten by the female after they mate, and the male peacock has to grow a huge tail in order to court the female.

Asexual and Sexual Reproduction

🔑 **KEY QUESTION** *How do asexual and sexual reproduction in animals compare?*

All animals must reproduce, or their populations and species become extinct.

🔑 As you read, circle the answers to each Key Question. Underline any words you do not understand.

Asexual Reproduction Asexual reproduction requires only one parent, so individuals in favorable environmental conditions can reproduce rapidly. Offspring produced asexually carry only the single parent's DNA, so they have less genetic diversity than offspring produced sexually.

Sexual Reproduction Sexual reproduction maintains genetic diversity in a population by creating individuals with new combinations of genes from both parents. Some animals are hermaphrodites and can function as both male and female for reproduction.

Reproductive Cycles Some invertebrates have life cycles that alternate between sexual and asexual reproduction.

Visual Reading Tool: Reproductive Cycles

Provide a brief description of what happens at each of the four steps of the alternating reproductive cycle.

1. _____

2. _____
   _____

3. _____

4. _____

Internal and External Fertilization

⚷ KEY QUESTION *How do internal and external fertilization differ?*

In sexual reproduction, eggs and sperm may meet either inside or outside the body of the egg-producing individual.

Internal Fertilization During internal fertilization, eggs are fertilized inside the body of the egg-producing individual.

Invertebrates The male arthropod mates with the female and deposits sperm inside the female during fertilization. Some invertebrates, like sponges and some other aquatic animals, have eggs that are fertilized by sperm released by others of their species and taken in from the surrounding water.

Chordates In some amphibian species, males deposit "sperm packets" into their environment. Later, females will pick up these packets and put them inside their own body. Other male chordate species, like male invertebrates, mate with the female and deposit sperm inside the female.

External Fertilization Many aquatic invertebrates and vertebrates reproduce by external fertilization. In external fertilization, eggs are fertilized outside the body of the egg-producing individual.

Invertebrates Corals, worms, and mollusks release large numbers of eggs and sperm into the water. The eggs and sperm are present at the same time because gamete release is usually synchronized with tides, phases of the moon, or seasons.

Chordates In some fish species, large numbers of eggs and sperm are released into the water and the males and females spawn in schools. Other fishes and many amphibians spawn in pairs: the female releases eggs and the male deposits sperm.

Development and Growth

⚷ KEY QUESTION *Where do embryos develop?*

Mitosis, which is the cell division of the zygote, occurs after fertilization, and then the cells differentiate.

Where Embryos Develop Embryos develop either inside or outside the body of a parent in various ways. Animals may be oviparous, ovoviviparous, or viviparous.

READING TOOL

Make Connections In most species, the females choose who to mate with depending on physical characteristics and positive adaptations. This is an evolutionary mechanism to ensure that the best genes get passed down to the next generation. ☑ **In which type of fertilization is the female able to be selective about who she mates with?**

_____

_____

_____

_____

Oviparous Species Many fish, amphibians, reptiles, all birds, and few mammals are oviparous, and embryos develop in eggs outside of the parental body.

Ovoviviparous Species Guppies and some sharks are ovoviviparous. The embryos develop within the female's body, but receive no nutrients from the mother; the only nutrients they receive are in the yolk sac of their eggs.

Viviparous Species Viviparous species get nutrients from the mother's body. Some mammals nourish the young through a **placenta**, a specialized organ that enables the exchange of respiratory gases, nutrients, and wastes between the mother and the developing young.

How Young Develop Many groups of invertebrates will undergo **metamorphosis** as they develop, which is a process that involves dramatic changes in shape and form.

Visual Reading Tool: Metamorphosis

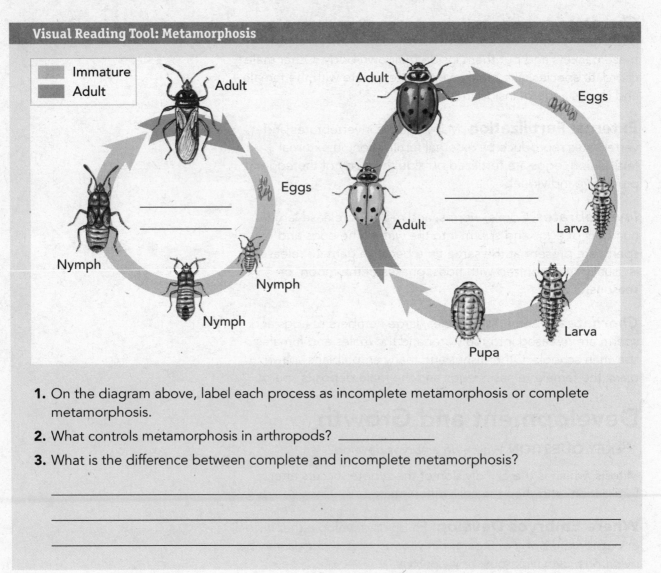

1. On the diagram above, label each process as incomplete metamorphosis or complete metamorphosis.

2. What controls metamorphosis in arthropods? _____

3. What is the difference between complete and incomplete metamorphosis?

_____

_____

_____

Aquatic Invertebrates Many aquatic invertebrates either have a single larval stage or pass through several larval stages to become an adult.

Terrestrial Invertebrates Insects may undergo gradual or incomplete metamorphosis, or complete metamorphosis. Hormones control metamorphosis in arthropods.

Amphibians Insects and most amphibians undergo metamorphosis that is controlled by hormones.

Care of Offspring Offspring either receive no care at all or are nurtured for years.

Reproductive Diversity in Chordates

🔍 **KEY QUESTION** *How are terrestrial vertebrates adapted to reproduction on land?*

Chordates first evolved in water, but some vertebrate lineages left the water to live on land. In many terrestrial chordates, reproductive strategies enable the fertilized eggs to develop somewhere other than in water.

The Amniotic Egg The amniotic egg is named after the amnion, one of four membranes that surround the developing embryo.

Mammalian Reproductive Strategies All three types of mammals nourish their young with mother's milk.

Monotremes Female monotremes secrete milk to nourish their young through mammary glands, which are pores on the surface of their abdomens. The duck-billed platypus is an example of a monotreme.

Marsupials Kangaroos are marsupials, and they crawl across their mother's fur and attach to a nipple in her pouch to drink milk when they emerge.

Placentals Placental mammals can develop the embryo for a long time inside the mother because of the placenta.

BUILD Vocabulary

amniotic egg egg composed of shell and membranes that creates a protected environment in which the embryo can develop out of water

mammary glands gland in female mammals that produces milk to nourish the young

ROOT WORDS If you break the term *metamorphosis* down into two parts—*meta* and *morph*—it may help you understand it better. From the definition, you can see that *morph* means "shape" or "form." With *meta* meaning "after," you can see the relation between the two parts of the word to mean "changing shape from a larva into an adult." ☑ **Can you name an example of an organism that goes through metamorphosis?**

_____

READING TOOL

Making Connections

In this lesson you learned about reproduction, and in the previous lesson you learned about movement and support. ☑ **Provide a brief explanation of how an endoskeleton may be related to the reproduction of ovoviviparous and viviparous species.**

_____

_____

_____

_____

_____

_____

_____

_____

_____

_____

Homeostasis

READING TOOL **Make Connections** All of the organ systems in the human body work together to maintain homeostasis. Fill in the graphic organizer below to show how they are all interconnected.

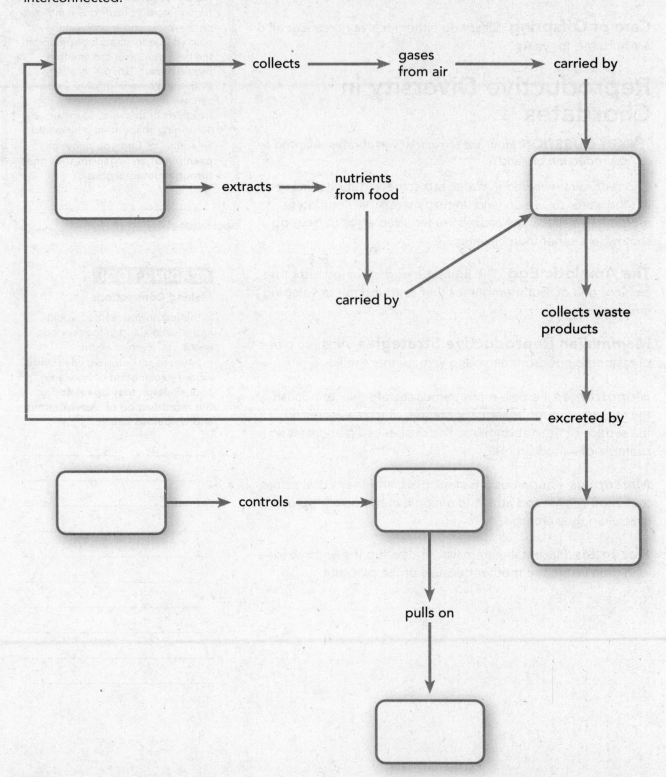

Lesson Summary

Interactions among body systems that perform the functions of regulation, nutrient absorption, reproduction, and defense from injury or illness are necessary for survival.

Interrelationship of Body Systems

🔑 **KEY QUESTION** *Why are interactions among body systems essential?*

The control of internal conditions is called homeostasis and is necessary for survival. All body systems interact to maintain homeostasis. For example, muscles would not work without a nervous system and skeletal system to direct and support them.

Fighting Disease Disease is caused when pathogens enter the body and grow, disrupting homeostasis. Most animals have an immune system that can distinguish between "self" and "others." The body works to restore homeostasis as soon as it discovers "others" in the body, by attacking the invaders.

Chemical Controls Endocrine glands are part of a chemical regulatory system. Endocrine glands interact with other body systems by releasing hormones into the blood that are carried throughout the body to regulate growth.

Body Temperature Control

🔑 **KEY QUESTION** *How do animals control their body temperature?*

Control of body temperature is essential to homeostasis and requires three components: a source of heat, a way to conserve heat, and a method of eliminating excess heat.

Ectotherms An example of an ectotherm is a lizard. Ectotherms are animals whose regulation of body temperature depends mostly on sources of heat outside its body. Most reptiles, invertebrates, fishes, and amphibians are ectotherms that regulate body temperature primarily by absorbing heat from, or losing heat to, their environment.

Endotherms An endotherm is an animal that regulates body temperature, at least in part, with the heat that its body generates. Endotherms, such as birds and mammals, have high metabolic rates that generate heat, even when they are resting. For example, birds conserve body heat when resting mostly with insulating down feathers.

BUILD Vocabulary

endocrine glands glands that releases their secretions (hormones) directly into the blood, which transports the secretions to other areas of the body to regulate growth and development

ectotherm type of animal whose body temperature is determined by the temperature of its environment

endotherm type of animal whose body temperature is regulated, at least in part, using heat generated within its body

Prefixes The word *endotherm* has two components: *Endo-* and *-therm*. *Endo-* is a prefix of Greek origin that means "within." ☑ **Based upon other words that contain the word part *therm*, what do you think it means? Think about a thermometer or thermal imaging.**

_____

_____

☑ Name two ways in which evidence suggests that endothermy has evolved among vertebrates.

_____

_____

_____

_____

_____

Comparing Ectotherms and Endotherms

Endotherms have a high metabolic rate that requires a lot of fuel. Ectothermic animals need much less food than similarly sized endotherms.

Evolution of Temperature Control Although modern reptiles are ectotherms, a great deal of evidence suggests that some dinosaurs were endotherms. Current evidence suggests that endothermy has evolved at least twice among vertebrates.

Visual Reading Tool: Endotherms and Ectotherms

	Endotherm	Ectotherm
Definition	_____ _____ _____ _____ _____ _____	_____ _____ _____ _____ _____ _____
Examples	_____ _____ _____ _____ _____ _____	_____ _____ _____ _____ _____ _____

1. In the table above, fill in the definitions and examples for endotherms and ectotherms.

2. How do endotherms regulate their body temperature if the weather outside is too hot?

_____

_____

3. How do ectotherms warm up when the weather is cold?

_____

_____

26 Chapter Review

Review Vocabulary

Match the vocabulary term to its definition.

1. _____ stimulus

2. _____ endotherm

a. an animal whose body temperature is regulated, at least in part, using heat generated within its body

b. a signal to which an organism responds

Fill in the blank with the correct term to complete the sentence.

3. The _____ is the part of the brain that coordinates movement and controls balance.

Review Key Questions

Provide evidence and details to support your answers.

4. Explain how evolution has led to increasing cephalization and specialization in animal nervous systems.

_____

_____

5. Explain how muscles, skeletons, and joints are related to movement.

_____

_____

6. Give examples and explain the difference between an insect that undergoes incomplete metamorphosis and an insect that undergoes complete metamorphosis.

_____

_____

_____

_____

7. Describe two or more body systems that work together to maintain homeostasis.

_____

_____

Organization of the Human Body

READING TOOL **Main Idea and Details** As you read your textbook, identify the main ideas and details or evidence that support the main ideas. Use the lesson headings to organize the main ideas and details. Record your work in the table. Two examples are entered for you.

Heading	Main Idea	Details/Evidence
Organization of the Human Body		
Organization of the Body. • Cells • Tissues • Organs • Organ Systems	The levels of organization in the human body are cells, tissues, organs, and organ systems.	
Homeostasis		
Feedback Inhibition • A Nonliving Example • A Living Example		Body temperature is regulated by feedback inhibition. If the body gets too hot, it will sweat to bring the temperature back down.
The Liver and Homeostasis		

Lesson Summary

Organization of the Body

🔍 As you read, circle the answers to each Key Question. Underline any words you do not understand.

🔍 **KEY QUESTION** *How is the human body organized?*

The levels of organization in the body include cells, tissues, organs, and organ systems. At each level of organization, these parts of the body work together to carry out the major body functions.

Cells A cell is the basic unit of structure and function in living things. Individual cells in multicellular organisms tend to be specialized. Specialized cells, such as bone cells, blood cells, and muscle cells, are uniquely suited to a specific function.

Tissues A group of cells that perform a single function is called a tissue. There are four basic types of tissues in the human body.

Epithelial Tissue The tissue that lines the interior and exterior body surfaces is called **epithelial tissue**. Your skin and the lining of your stomach are both examples of epithelial tissue.

Connective Tissue A type of tissue that provides support for the body and connects its parts is **connective tissue**. This type of tissue includes fat cells, bone cells, blood cells, cartilage, and ligaments.

Nervous Tissue Nerve impulses are transmitted throughout the body by **nervous tissue**. Neurons, the cells that carry these impulses, are bundled together to form a nerve.

Muscle Tissue Movements of the body are possible because of **muscle tissue**. Some muscles are responsible for the movements you control, while others are responsible for movements you cannot control.

Organs A group of different types of tissues that work together to perform a single function or several related functions is called an organ.

Organ Systems An organ system is a group of organs that perform closely related functions. For example, the brain and spinal cord are organs of the nervous system. The organ systems interact to maintain homeostasis in the body.

Homeostasis

🔍 **KEY QUESTION** *What is homeostasis?*

Your body works constantly to maintain a controlled, stable internal environment. This process is called **homeostasis**, which means "keeping things the same." Homeostasis describes the relatively constant internal conditions that organisms maintain despite changes in internal and external environments.

Feedback Inhibition The systems of the body work to keep internal conditions within a certain range. Feedback inhibition is one way the body maintains homeostasis and prevents conditions from going too far one way or the other.

A Nonliving Example One way to understand homeostasis is to look at a nonliving system that keeps conditions within a certain range, like a home heating system.
   Homeostasis is controlled by feedback inhibition. **Feedback inhibition**, or negative feedback, is the process in which a stimulus produces a response that opposes the original stimulus. Systems controlled by feedback inhibition are generally very stable.

BUILD Vocabulary

epithelial tissue type of tissue that lines the interior and exterior body surfaces

connective tissue type of tissue that provides support for the body and connects its parts

nervous tissue type of tissue that transmits nerve impulses throughout the body

muscle tissue type of tissue that makes movements of the body possible

homeostasis relatively constant internal physical and chemical conditions that organisms maintain

feedback inhibition process in which a stimulus produces a response that opposes the original stimulus; also called negative feedback

Root Words The root word *stasis* means "a state of balance or equilibrium." Organisms must maintain a state of equilibrium, or homeostasis, in order to stay alive.

☑ **Give an example of one way that the human body works to maintain homeostasis, and describe what would happen if homeostasis were not maintained.**

_____

_____

_____

_____

_____

_____

_____

_____

Make Connections The liver plays a key role in maintaining homeostasis in the human body. It maintains glucose levels when blood glucose gets too high or too low. ☑ **Describe a second way in which the liver promotes homeostasis.**

_____

_____

_____

_____

_____

A Living Example The body regulates temperature by a mechanism that is remarkably similar to that of a home heating system. A part of the brain called the hypothalamus contains nerve cells that monitor body temperature.

If the nerve cells sense that the core temperature has dropped much below 37°C, the hypothalamus produces chemicals that signal cells throughout the body to speed up their activities. Heat produced by this increase in activity causes a rise in body temperature, which is detected by nerve cells in the hypothalamus. If body temperature rises too far above 37°C, the hypothalamus slows down cellular activities to reduce heat production.

The Liver and Homeostasis The liver is one of the body's most important organs for homeostasis. When proteins are broken down for energy, ammonia, a toxic byproduct, is produced. The liver converts ammonia to urea, which is much less toxic. The liver also converts many dangerous substances, including some drugs, into compounds that can be removed from the body safely.

One of the liver's most important roles involves regulating the level of glucose. By taking glucose out of the blood, the liver keeps the level of glucose from rising too much. As the body uses glucose for energy, the liver releases stored glucose to keep the level of the sugar from dropping too low.

Visual Reading Tool: Body Temperature Control

In the human body, temperature is controlled through various feedback inhibition mechanisms. In each of the diagrams below, fill in the words START and STOP in the appropriate boxes. Then complete the sentences below so that each numbered sentence correctly describes its corresponding number in the diagram.

1.

Hypothalamus senses temperature change and sends signals that start or stop heat production.

2.

3.

Hypothalamus senses temperature change and sends signals that start or stop cooling mechanisms.

4.

1. _____ environment causes body temperature to _____.

2. Body temperature _____.

3. _____ environment and exercise cause body temperature to _____.

4. Body temperature _____.

READING TOOL **Sequence of Events** As you read your textbook, identify the sequence of events in which food is digested. Fill in the flowchart with details about the events that involve each main structure associated with digestion.

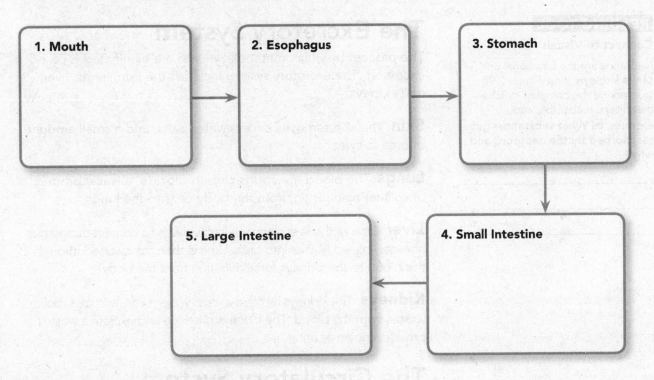

1. Mouth

2. Esophagus

3. Stomach

5. Large Intestine

4. Small Intestine

Lesson Summary

The Digestive System

KEY QUESTION *What are the structures and functions of the digestive system, excretory system, circulatory system, lymphatic system, and respiratory system?*

The digestive system converts food into small molecules that can be used by the cells of the body.

Digestion Food in the digestive system is broken down by mechanical and chemical digestion. Mechanical digestion is the physical breakdown of large pieces of food into smaller pieces by the teeth and stomach. During chemical digestion in the mouth, stomach, and small intestine, enzymes break down food into molecules that can be absorbed.

As you read, circle the answers to the Key Question. Underline any words you do not understand.

Absorption From the Small Intestine The small intestine's folded surface provides a large surface area for absorption. Its fingerlike projections, called villi, are covered with tiny projections known as microvilli, which absorb the nutrients.

Absorption and Elimination The primary function of the large intestine is to remove water from the material that is left. The concentrated waste material, called feces, forms after most of the water has been removed. Feces passes into the rectum and is eliminated from the body through the anus.

The Excretory System

The process by which metabolic wastes are eliminated is called excretion. The excretory system includes the skin, lungs, liver, and kidneys.

Skin The skin removes excess water, salts, and a small amount of urea in sweat.

Lungs The blood transports carbon dioxide, a waste product of cellular respiration, from the body cells to the lungs.

Liver One of the liver's principal activities is to convert dangerous nitrogen-based wastes into urea. Urea is then transported through the blood to the kidneys for elimination from the body.

Kidneys The kidneys remove excess water, urea, and metabolic wastes from the blood. The kidneys produce and excrete a waste product known as urine.

The Circulatory System

The circulatory system transports oxygen, nutrients, and other substances throughout the body, and it removes wastes from tissues.

Circulation Blood is pumped through the body by the heart. The right side of the heart pumps oxygen-poor blood from the heart to the lungs. Carbon dioxide diffuses from the blood, and oxygen is absorbed into the blood. Oxygen-rich blood then flows to the left side of the heart. The left side of the heart pumps oxygen-rich blood to the rest of the body. Cells absorb the oxygen that they need and load the blood with carbon dioxide by the time it returns to the heart.

Arteries Large vessels, or arteries, carry blood away from the heart to the tissues of the body.

Capillaries The smallest blood vessels are the capillaries. Their thin walls allow oxygen and nutrients to diffuse from blood into tissues and allow carbon dioxide and other waste products to move from tissues into blood.

Veins After blood passes through the capillaries, it returns to the heart through veins. Many veins contain valves, which ensure that blood flows in one direction through these vessels toward the heart.

Blood Components of blood help regulate body temperature, fight infections, and produce clots to minimize the loss of body fluids from wounds. About 55 percent of total blood volume is plasma. Plasma is made up of water, dissolved gases, salts, nutrients, enzymes, plasma proteins, cholesterol, and other compounds. Plasma proteins transport substances and are necessary for blood to clot.

The most numerous cells in blood are red blood cells. The main function of red blood cells is to transport oxygen. White blood cells guard against infection, fight parasites, and attack bacteria. Platelets and plasma proteins cause blood to clot.

The Lymphatic System

As blood circulates, some blood cells and plasma leak out through the capillary walls. Most of this fluid, known as lymph, is reabsorbed into capillaries, but the rest goes into the lymphatic system. The lymphatic system is a network of vessels, nodes, and organs that collects the lymph that leaves capillaries, "screens" it for microorganisms, and returns it to the circulatory system.

Role in Circulation Lymph collects in a system of capillaries that slowly conducts it into larger lymph vessels. These ducts return lymph to the blood through openings in veins just below the shoulders.

Role in Immunity Hundreds of small lymph nodes are scattered along lymph vessels throughout the body. Lymph nodes act as filters, trapping microorganisms, stray cancer cells, and debris. White blood cells inside lymph nodes destroy this cellular "trash."

Role in Nutrient Absorption A system of lymph vessels runs alongside the intestines. The vessels pick up fats and fat-soluble vitamins from the digestive tract and transport these nutrients into the bloodstream.

The Respiratory System

The respiratory system picks up oxygen from the air as we inhale and releases carbon dioxide as we exhale. The respiratory system consists of the nose, pharynx, larynx, trachea, bronchi, and lungs.

Make Connections In the previous lesson, you learned that all living organisms must maintain homeostasis to stay alive. As you read about the body systems, note at least one way in which each body system supports homeostasis.

☑ **What is one way the respiratory system supports homeostasis?**

_____

_____

_____

_____

_____

_____

_____

_____

_____

_____

Air Flow Air moves from the nose to the pharynx, or throat, and then into the trachea, or windpipe. Between the pharynx and the trachea is the larynx, which contains the vocal cords. From the trachea, air moves into two large tubes called bronchi leading to the lungs. These tubes divide into smaller bronchi, and then into even smaller bronchioles. The bronchioles lead to several hundred million tiny air sacs called alveoli. A delicate network of capillaries surrounds each alveolus for gas exchange.

Gas Exchange and Transport When you inhale, a muscle called the diaphragm contracts and flattens. Atmospheric pressure fills the lungs as air rushes into the breathing passages. As air enters the alveoli, oxygen diffuses across thin capillary walls into the blood. Meanwhile, carbon dioxide diffuses in the opposite direction. These processes are reversed in the lungs before the carbon dioxide is exhaled.

Breathing The force that drives air into the lungs comes from ordinary air pressure, the diaphragm, and muscles associated with the ribs and neck. Movements of the diaphragm and rib cage change air pressure in the chest cavity during inhalation and exhalation.

Breathing and Homeostasis Sensory neurons gather information about carbon dioxide levels in the body and send the information to the breathing center in the part of the brain stem called the medulla oblongata. When stimulated, the breathing center sends nerve impulses that cause the diaphragm and chest muscles to contract, bringing air into the lungs.

Visual Reading Tool: Breathing

Fill in the blanks in the diagram below to accurately describe the events of inhalation and exhalation. Draw arrows on the diagram that show the direction of movement for air, the rib cage, and the diaphragm during each process.

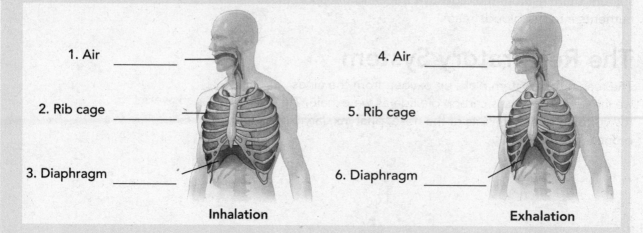

1. Air _____ _____

2. Rib cage _____

3. Diaphragm _____

Inhalation

4. Air _____ _____

5. Rib cage _____

6. Diaphragm _____

Exhalation

READING TOOL **Connect to Visuals** As you read your textbook, examine the visuals that accompany the text. For each organ system listed, select one of the visual aids and record details you learn from the visual aid in the table below. An example has been completed for you.

Body System	Visual	Details
Nervous System	The Nervous System	The nervous system is made up of the central nervous system and the peripheral nervous system.
Skeletal System		
Muscular System		
Endocrine System		
Male Reproductive System		
Female Reproductive System		

Lesson Summary

The Nervous System

🔍 **KEY QUESTION** *What are the structures and functions of the nervous system, skeletal system, muscular system, integumentary system, endocrine system, and male and female reproductive systems?*

🔍 As you read, circle the answers to the Key Question. Underline any words you do not understand.

The nervous system collects information about the internal and external environment, processes that information, and responds to it. All of these messages are carried by electrical signals, called impulses, through nerve cells called neurons.

The basic unit of the nervous system is the neuron, or nerve cell. Label the parts of a nerve cell in the diagram below.

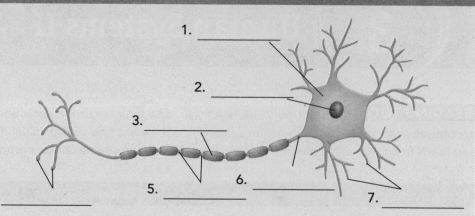

1. _____

2. _____

3. _____

4. _____

5. _____

6. _____

7. _____

Cause and Effect The peripheral nervous system sends messages in two different ways. An individual can control his or her somatic nervous system, but cannot control his or her autonomic nervous system. ☑ **Give an example of how your autonomic nervous system is working right now.**

_____

_____

_____

_____

_____

_____

Neurons Neurons can be classified into three types: sensory neurons, motor neurons, and interneurons. A neuron has a cell body, multiple dendrites, and an axon.

The Nerve Impulse Neurons carry information by creating small electrical currents. When a neuron receives a large enough stimulus, this neuron changes suddenly, producing a nerve impulse called an action potential.

The Central Nervous System The central nervous system includes the brain and spinal cord. Sensations from various body areas are "felt" by specific brain regions. Commands to muscles originate in other brain areas. The spinal cord links the brain to the rest of the body.

The Peripheral Nervous System The sensory division of the peripheral nervous system gathers information and transmits impulses from sense organs to the central nervous system. The motor division transmits impulses from the central nervous system to the muscles and glands.

Somatic Nervous System The somatic nervous system regulates activities such as the movement of skeletal muscles.

Autonomic Nervous System The autonomic nervous system regulates activities that are not under conscious control like heart rate and digestion.

The Skeletal System

The skeleton supports the body, protects internal organs, assists in movement, stores minerals, and is a site of blood cell formation.

Bones Bones are surrounded by tough connective tissue called periosteum. Beneath the periosteum is a thick layer of compact bone with nerves and blood vessels. A less dense tissue known as spongy bone may be found under the compact bone. Inside many bones are cavities containing bone marrow.

Joints A place where two or more bones meet each other is called a joint. Joints contain connective tissue that holds bones together and permits bones to move without damaging each other. Joints can be classified as immovable, slightly movable, or freely movable.

The Muscular System

There are three different types of muscle tissues that are specialized for different functions: skeletal, smooth, and cardiac muscle. Skeletal muscles are usually attached to bones. Most skeletal muscle movements are consciously controlled by the central nervous system. Smooth muscle movements are usually involuntary. Most smooth muscle cells can function without direct stimulation by the nervous system. Cardiac muscle is only found in the heart. Cardiac muscle cells can contract on their own without stimulation by the nervous system.

Muscle Contraction and Movement Muscles produce movements by shortening, or contracting. A muscle produces force by contracting in one direction. Muscles work in opposing pairs around joints. When one muscle in the pair contracts, the other muscle in the pair relaxes.

The Integumentary System

Skin and its related structures—the hair, nails, and glands—make up the integumentary system. The integumentary system serves as a barrier against infection and injury, helps to regulate body temperature, removes wastes, gathers sensory information, and produces vitamin D.

The outer layer of the skin is the epidermis. The dermis lies below the epidermis. It contains blood vessels, nerve endings, glands, sensory receptors, smooth muscles, and hair follicles. Beneath the dermis is a layer of fat and loose connective tissue that helps to insulate the body. Hair protects the skin and prevents dirt from entering the body. Nails protect fingertips and toes from damage.

The Endocrine System

The glands of the endocrine system release hormones that travel through the blood and control the actions of cells, tissues, and organs.

Hormone Action Hormones affect cells by binding to specific chemical receptors located either on cell membranes or within cells. If a cell does not have receptors for a particular hormone, the hormone has no effect on it.

Control of the Endocrine System The endocrine system is regulated by negative feedback mechanisms that function to maintain homeostasis.

READING TOOL

Apply Prior Knowledge

In the last lesson, you learned about the kidneys, which are the major organ of the excretory system. The kidneys "read" the blood that flows through them, then change their filtering and reabsorption according to the needs of the body. Hormones from the endocrine system also give the kidneys instructions. Antidiuretic hormone (ADH) causes the kidneys to reabsorb more water and return it to the blood stream. ☑ **What do you think happens to ADH levels when a person is severely dehydrated?**

_____

_____

_____

_____

_____

_____

_____

Maintaining Water Balance Water balance is one example of how the endocrine system maintains homeostasis.

Blood Glucose Regulation Glucose concentration in the bloodstream is controlled by insulin and glucagon. When blood glucose concentration rises, the pancreas releases insulin. When blood glucose concentration drops, the pancreas releases glucagon.

The Male Reproductive System

In addition to producing hormones that control the development of secondary sexual characteristics, the organs of the male reproductive system produce and deliver sperm. Sperm development begins in the testes, where specialized cells undergo meiosis to form sperm nuclei. Sperm then move into the epididymis, where they mature and are stored. Glands lining the reproductive tract produce nutrient-rich seminal fluid that nourishes the sperm. The combination of sperm and seminal fluid, known as semen, is ejected through the urethra in a process called ejaculation.

The Female Reproductive System

The primary reproductive organs of the female are the ovaries. Ovaries produce hormones that control the development of secondary sexual characteristics; produce egg cells, or ova; and prepare the body nourish a developing embryo.

READING TOOL

Make Connections

During human development, different layers of cells become different body tissues. Gastrulation creates three cell layers that make up many different organs and internal structures. ☑ **Which cell layer becomes the integumentary system?**

_____

Fertilization and Early Development Human development begins with fertilization, the fusion of sperm and egg. The fertilized egg undergoes multiple rounds of mitosis. Cells then begin to differentiate, producing different body tissues.

Gastrulation Gastrulation results in the formation of three cell layers called the ectoderm, mesoderm, and endoderm. The ectoderm develops into skin and the nervous system. Mesoderm cells develop into many of the body's internal structures. The endoderm forms the lining of some organs.

Neurulation During neurulation, tissue differentiates into structures from which the spinal cord, the brain, nerve cells, and other structures will later develop.

The Placenta The placenta forms the vital connection between mother and embryo.

Later Development Throughout the rest of the first trimester, the fetus continues to grow. During the second trimester, the tissues and organs of the fetus become more complex and begin to function. During the third trimester, the fetus doubles in mass and the central nervous system and lungs complete their development.

Heading	Nonspecific Defenses		Specific Defenses: The Immune System	
Subheading	**First Line of Defense**	**Second Line of Defense**	**Recognizing "Self" and "Nonself"**	**Fighting Infections**
Details				

Lesson Summary

Classifying Diseases

🔍 **KEY QUESTION** *What causes infectious diseases?*

A disease is an abnormal condition that harms an organism. In the mid-nineteenth century, scientists proposed the germ theory of disease, which is that **infectious diseases** occur when microorganisms disrupt normal body functions. Today, we call such microorganisms **pathogens**, meaning "sickness producers." Infectious diseases are caused by viruses, bacteria, fungi, "protists," and other pathogens.

How Infectious Disease Spreads Many bacteria and viruses are spread through coughing, sneezing, and physical contact. Other types of diseases are spread through the exchange of body fluids that occurs during sexual intercourse or through blood transfusions. Many pathogens that infect the digestive tract are spread through contaminated water.

🔍 As you read, circle the answers to the Key Question. Underline any words you do not understand.

BUILD Vocabulary

infectious disease disease caused by microorganisms that disrupt normal body function

pathogen disease-causing agent

Prefixes The prefix *patho-* comes from the Greek word *pathos*, meaning "suffering" or "disease."

☑ What are three types of pathogens that can cause infectious diseases?

_____

BUILD Vocabulary

inflammatory response
nonspecific defense reaction to
tissue damage caused by injury or
infection

Related Words The verb *inflame*
means "to make sore, red, and
swollen." During the inflammatory
response, the injured area of the
body often becomes sore, red, and
swollen due to increased blood
flow. ☑ **Why is increased blood
flow an important part of the
inflammatory response?**

_____

_____

_____

_____

_____

Disease Caused by Toxins Another important category
of diseases involves toxic chemicals that may be found in food
or drinking water. Chemicals found in water that can damage
the body include compounds of mercury, arsenic, lead, and
chromium. Some of these compounds occur naturally at low
levels in streams and groundwater. However, some are released
into the environment by mining or industrial activities.

Nonspecific Defenses

🔍 **KEY QUESTION** *What are the body's nonspecific defenses
against pathogens?*

Body defenses that act against a wide range of pathogens are
called nonspecific defenses. Nonspecific defenses include the skin,
tears and other secretions, the inflammatory response, and fever.

First Line of Defense The skin is a physical barrier that
keeps most pathogens out of the body. Saliva, mucus, and tears
contain lysozyme, an enzyme that breaks down bacterial cell walls.

Second Line of Defense If pathogens do make it into
the body, the second line of defense includes the inflammatory
response and fever. The **inflammatory response** causes
infected areas to become red and painful, or inflamed.

The immune system also releases chemicals that produce a
fever. Increased body temperature may slow down or stop the
growth of some pathogens and helps to speed up the immune
response.

Visual Reading Tool: Inflammatory Response

Add labels to the factors involved in the inflammatory response shown in the diagram below.
Then fill in the blanks in the captions to describe the main steps of the response.

1. _____

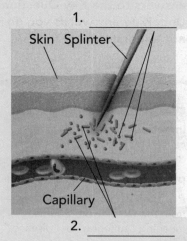 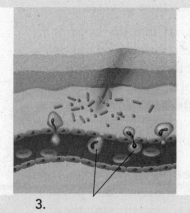 

Skin Splinter

Capillary

2. _____   3. _____

4. _____ stimulate increased blood flow to the area.

5. _____ move into the tissue.

6. White blood cells engulf and destroy _____.

Specific Defenses: The Immune System

KEY QUESTION *What is the function of the immune system's specific defenses?*

The immune system's specific defenses distinguish between "self" and "other," inactivating or killing foreign substances or cells.

Recognizing "Self" and "Nonself" The immune system recognizes cells that belong in the body and treats these as "self." When the immune system recognizes a bacterium or virus as "other," it uses cellular and chemical weapons to attack it. After encountering an invader, the immune system "remembers" it. This immune "memory" enables a more rapid and effective response if the same pathogen attacks again.

Specific immune defenses are triggered by molecules called antigens. An antigen is any foreign substance that can stimulate an immune response.

Fighting Infections The specific immune response has two main styles of action: humoral immunity and cell-mediated immunity. Humoral immunity depends on the action of B cells releasing antibodies that circulate in the blood and the lymph looking for foreign antigens. Cell-mediated immunity uses T cells to directly attack specific foreign invaders such as viruses, fungi, and abnormal cancer cells inside living cells.

Immune System Disorders

KEY QUESTION *What health problems result when the immune system does not function properly?*

Problems with immune system function can result in conditions such as allergies, asthma, autoimmune disease, and AIDS.

Allergies Antigens that cause allergic reactions are called allergens. Allergens can trigger an inflammatory response. Drugs called antihistamines help relieve allergy symptoms.

Asthma In asthma, the air passages narrow, causing wheezing and difficulty breathing.

Autoimmune Disease When the immune system attacks the body's own cells, it produces an autoimmune disease.

HIV and AIDS Acquired immunodeficiency syndrome (AIDS) is caused by the human immunodeficiency virus (HIV). HIV attacks key cells within the immune system, leaving the body with inadequate protection against pathogens. Over time, HIV cripples the ability of the immune system to fight HIV itself and other pathogens, which leads to AIDS. At present, there is neither a cure for nor a reliable vaccine against AIDS.

BUILD Vocabulary

antigen any foreign substance that triggers an immune response

humoral immunity immunity depends on the action of B cells releasing antibodies that circulate in the blood and the lymph looking for foreign antigens

cell-mediated immunity immune response that uses T cells to directly attack specific foreign invaders such as viruses, fungi, and abnormal cancer cells inside living cells

Related Words Antigens are often small molecules that are on the outer surfaces of bacteria, viruses, or parasites. Once the body recognizes an antigen, it begins to attack it. ☑ What do we call the proteins that tag antigens for destruction?

_____

READING TOOL

Active Reading HIV and AIDS are two different conditions that are often confused or grouped into one category. However, HIV occurs first, and then leads to AIDS. ☑ How does HIV lead to immunodeficiency (AIDS)?

_____

_____

_____

_____

_____

_____

Review Vocabulary

Choose the letter of the best answer.

1. Which lines interior and exterior body surfaces?

   A. muscle tissue

   B. nervous tissue

   C. epithelial tissue

2. Which refers to any foreign substance that triggers an immune response?

   A. antigen

   B. allergen

   C. antibody

Match the vocabulary term to its definition.

3. _____ relatively constant internal conditions

4. _____ when a stimulus produces an opposing response

5. _____ disease-causing agent

   a. feedback inhibition

   b. homeostasis

   c. pathogen

Review Key Questions

Provide evidence and details to support your answers.

6. Describe homeostasis.

_____

_____

7. What are the main structures and functions of the circulatory system?

_____

_____

_____

8. How does the endocrine system control the actions of specific cells?

_____

_____

_____

9. Describe a nonspecific immune defense used by the body.

_____